The rise of devils

Manchester University Press

For Ning n' Puddin'

The rise of devils

Fear and the origins of modern terrorism

James Crossland

Manchester University Press

The right of James Crossland to be identified as the author of this work has been asserted in accordance with the Copyright, Designs and Patents Act 1988.

Published by Manchester University Press
Oxford Road, Manchester M13 9PL

www.manchesteruniversitypress.co.uk

British Library Cataloguing-in-Publication Data
A catalogue record for this book is available from the British Library

ISBN 978 1 5261 6067 6 hardback

First published 2023

The publisher has no responsibility for the persistence or accuracy of URLs for any external or third-party internet websites referred to in this book, and does not guarantee that any content on such websites is, or will remain, accurate or appropriate.

Typeset in Minion Pro
by R. J. Footring Ltd, Derby
Printed in Great Britain
by Bell & Bain, Ltd, Glasgow

MIX
Paper | Supporting responsible forestry
FSC
www.fsc.org
FSC® C007785

Contents

Contents

Figures

List of figures

Dramatis personae

Alexander II (1818–1881)
Russian tsar who issued the Emancipation Manifesto in 1861. Assassinated by People's Will.

Louis Andrieux (1840–1931)
Prefect of Paris police (1879–1881). Used spies and agents provocateurs to infiltrate socialist and anarchist meetings.

Mikhail Bakunin (1814–1876)
Anarchist philosopher, rival of Karl Marx and one-time conspirator with Sergei Nechaev.

Oskar Becker (1839–1868)
German nationalist and failed assassin of King Wilhelm of Prussia.

Antoni Berezowski (1847–1916)
Polish nationalist and failed assassin of Tsar Alexander II.

Alexander Berkman (1870–1936)
Failed assassin of Henry Clay Frick and lover of Emma Goldman.

Otto von Bismarck (1815–1898)
Chancellor of Prussia and unifier of Germany. Passed anti-socialist laws in the 1870s.

Louis Auguste Blanqui (1805–1881)
Revolutionary socialist and preacher of proto-terrorist concepts.

John Brown (1800–1859)
Abolitionist militant and leader of the raid on Harper's Ferry, West Virginia, in 1859.

Nikolai Chernyshevsky (1828–1889)
Radical thinker and author of the nihilist-influencing *What Is To Be Done?*

Gustave Paul Cluseret (1823–1900)
'Professional revolutionary', Fenian, Communard and conspirator with Bakunin. Later represented Toulon in the Chamber of Deputies.

Ferdinand Cohen-Blind (1844–1866)
Failed assassin of Bismarck. Committed suicide in police custody.

Leon Czolgosz (1873–1901)
Assassin of President William McKinley and exemplar of individual ('hot-head') terrorism.

Charles-Marie Espinasse (1815–1859)
Napoleon III's anti-radical enforcer. Killed in action at the Battle of Magenta.

Patrick Ford (1837–1913)
Editor of *Irish World* and supporter of Jeremiah O'Donovan Rossa's dynamite campaign.

Emma Goldman (1869–1940)
Anarchist writer. Rival of Johann Most and lover of Alexander Berkman.

Jean Grave (1864–1939)
Editor of anarchist magazines and key defendant at the Trial of the Thirty in 1894.

Karl Heinzen (1809–1880)
German 48er, advocate of terrorism and author of *Murder and Liberty*.

Emil Hödel (1857–1878)
Exiled member of the Social Democratic Party turned failed assassin of Kaiser Wilhelm I.

Nikolai Ishutin (1840–1879)
Nihilist and leader of terrorist groups Hell and The Organisation. Sentenced to Siberian exile for involvement in a failed assassination attempt on Tsar Alexander II.

Wang Jingwei (1883–1944)
Chinese anarchist-nationalist assassin. Would later collaborate with Japan during the Second World War.

Hemchandra Kanungo (1871–1951)
Indian nationalist and bomb-maker. Given terrorist instruction by European radicals.

Dmitry Karakozov (1840–1866)
Ishutin's cousin and failed assassin of Tsar Alexander II. Provided inspiration to Sergei Nechaev.

Nikolai Kibalchich (1853–1881)
Russian rocket scientist and chief bomb-maker for the terrorist group People's Will.

Peter Kropotkin (1842–1921)
Russian noble turned revolutionary and anarchist writer. Attendee at the 1881 London Anarchist Congress.

Vivian Dering Majendie (1836–1898)
Her Majesty's chief inspector of explosives. Worked with Scotland Yard (headquarters of the London Metropolitan Police). Pioneer of bomb disposal and forensic investigation.

Errico Malatesta (1853–1932)
Insurrectionist and conspirator with Bakunin. Attendee at the 1881 London Anarchist Congress. Would later appeal for an end to hot-head terrorism.

Karl Marx (1818–1883)
Socialist philosopher and author of the *Communist Manifesto*. Suspected by police chiefs across Europe of involvement in the Paris Commune of 1871.

William Melville (1850–1918)
Scotland Yard detective tasked with investigating Irish and anarchist terrorists. Worked for British intelligence in early 1900s and, later, the Security Service (MI5).

Nikolai Mezentsov (1827–1878)
Head of Third Section (1876–1878), Imperial Russia's secret police department. Assassinated by Stepniak (Sergei Kravchinsky).

Professor Mezzeroff – a.k.a. Richard Rogers (dates unknown)
Dynamite advocate and trainer of O'Donovan Rossa's bombers. Would be accused by a former student of being a police spy.

Louise Michel (1830–1905)
Communard, anarchist and educator. Attendee at the 1881 London Anarchist Congress.

Nikolai Morozov (1854–1946)
People's Will member and author of *The Terrorist Struggle*.

Johann Most (1846–1906)
Reichstag member turned dynamite advocate. Author of *The Science of Revolutionary Warfare* and influencer of hot-head terrorism.

Napoleon III (1803–1873)
Ruler of France. Seen by radicals of the 1860s as one of Europe's greatest despots.

Sergei Nechaev (1847–1882)
Nihilist terrorist and collaborator with Bakunin. Led People's Revenge and wrote *Catechism of a Revolutionary*.

Alfred Nobel (1833–1896)
Inventor of dynamite. Later established the eponymous Peace Prize.

Karl Nobiling (1848–1878)
Failed assassin of Kaiser Wilhelm I. Shot himself shortly after the attack.

Jeremiah O'Donovan Rossa (1831–1915)
Leader of United Irishmen of America and chief perpetrator of the dynamite campaign of the 1880s.

Felice Orsini (1819–1858)
Italian nationalist revolutionary, inventor of the Orsini bomb and failed assassin of Napoleon III.

Albert Parsons (1848–1887)
Editor of *The Alarm*. Hanged for involvement in the Haymarket bombing of 1886.

Sophia Perovskaya (1853–1881)
People's Will member and leader of the team of bombers who killed Tsar Alexander II.

Joseph-Marie Piétri (1820–1902)
Prefect of Paris police (1866–1870) and younger brother of Pierre-Marie Piétri (himself prefect of Paris police 1852–1858). Pursued plots against Napoleon III during the time of civil unrest in Paris prior to the Franco-Prussian War of 1870.

Allan Pinkerton (1819–1884)
President Lincoln's security consultant and head of the Pinkerton Detective Agency, which came to specialise in strike-breaking and anti-radical policing in the United States.

Peter Rachkovsky (1853–1910)
Head of the Okhrana (successor to the Third Section), spymaster and promoter of conspiracy theories.

Ravachol – a.k.a. François Claudius Koenigstein (1859–1892)
Infamous terrorist and initiator of the cycle of attacks that included the bombings of the Chamber of Deputies, the Café Terminus and the assassination of President Sadi Carnot of France.

Élisée Reclus (1830–1905)
Geographer, Communard and anarchist collaborator with Bakunin and Kropotkin.

Peter Shuvalov (1827–1889)
Head of the Third Section (1866–1874). Orchestrator of the trial of People's Revenge and leader of the hunt for Nechaev.

August Spies (1855–1887)
Editor of *Arbeiter-Zeitung*. Hanged for involvement in the Haymarket bombing.

James Stephens (1825–1901)
Founder of the Irish Republican Brotherhood (IRB) and collaborator with Cluseret.

Stepniak – a.k.a. Sergei Kravchinsky (1851–1895)
Member of the Tchaikovsky Circle and author of key works on Russian revolutionary movements. Assassinated Mezentsov in 1878 but would later denounce hot-head terrorism.

Wilhelm Stieber (1818–1882)
Reactionary Prussian spymaster, enemy of Marx and Bakunin and supposed spoiler of radical conspiracies.

Nikolai Tchaikovsky (1850–1926)
Leader of the Tchaikovsky Circle. Advocate of non-violent revolution.

Vera Zasulich (1849–1919)
Disciple of Nechaev and would-be assassin of Fyodor Trepov.

Timeline

1848

Europe   Revolutions across Europe. *Communist Manifesto* published.

1851

Britain   Stieber's mission to uncover socialist plots in London.

1853

United States   *Murder and Liberty* published.

1857

India   Start of rebellion against British rule.

Britain   Orsini bomb invented.

1858

France   Orsini's attack on Napoleon III and Orsini's execution.

United States   Orsini commemorations held.

Ireland   Irish Republican Brotherhood (IRB) formed.

1859

Italy   Italian War of Independence. Espinasse dies.

United States   Raid on Harper's Ferry and execution of Brown.

1860

Germany   Stieber put on trial but acquitted and leaves for Russia.

1861

United States   Pinkerton foils alleged plot to assassinate Lincoln. Outbreak of American Civil War.

Russia   Emancipation Manifesto issued.

Various   Bakunin leaves Siberia and travels through Japan, the United States and Britain.

Germany   Becker fails to kill King Wilhelm.

1863

Russia   *What Is To Be Done?* published. Ishutin starts gathering followers. Polish insurgents use Orsini bomb during uprising.

Germany   Stieber 'foils' plot to assassinate Bismarck and is rehabilitated.

1864

Britain	Formation of the International Workingmen's Association (IWMA).

1865

United States	American Civil War ends. John Wilkes Booth kills President Abraham Lincoln.
Switzerland	Ishutin tries to acquire Orsini bomb.
Ireland	O'Donovan Rossa and Stephens arrested. Stephens later escapes to France.

1866

United States/ Canada	Fenian raids into Canada. Stephens meets with Cluseret but is removed from power within the IRB.
Russia	Karakozov fails to kill the tsar and is executed. Shuvalov appointed head of Third Section. Hell and The Organisation broken up and Ishutin sent to Siberia.
Germany	Cohen-Blind fails to kill Bismarck.

1867

Britain/Ireland	Fenian attacks thwarted. Shooting of Sergeant Charles Brett. Trial and execution of the Manchester Martyrs. Bombing of Clerkenwell Prison.
France	Berezowski fails to kill the tsar.
Britain/Sweden	Alfred Nobel patents dynamite.

1868

Australia	Henry O'Farrell fails to kill the Prince of Wales. Irish plot suspected.
Russia	Nechaev forms nihilist group that includes Zasulich.
Egypt	Becker dies.

1869

Switzerland	Nechaev meets with Bakunin. *Catechism of a Revolutionary* published.
Russia	Zasulich imprisoned. People's Revenge formed. Nechaev murders one of his followers and flees Russia.
France	Blanqui and other radicals return to France.

1870

France	Victor Noir riots. 'May Plot' uncovered. France goes to war with Prussia. Napoleon abdicates. Bakunin and Cluseret try to seize Lyon. Blanqui attempts coup in Paris.
Switzerland	Bakunin breaks ties with Nechaev.

Timeline

1871

France	Paris Commune's rise and fall. Development of IWMA–Communard conspiracy theory.
Germany	Bismarck proposes Alliance of Emperors.
United States	O'Donovan Rossa freed and exiled to United States.
Russia	Trial of People's Revenge.
Britain	Majendie appointed inspector of explosives.

1872

Belgium	Bakunin excommunicated from IWMA.
Switzerland	Nechaev arrested in Zurich. Reclus joins Bakunin in Geneva.

1873

Russia	Trial of Nechaev. Zasulich released from jail.
Britain	Napoleon III dies.
New Caledonia	Michel transported to New Caledonia.

1874

Russia	Stepniak and other radicals go 'To the People'.
Italy	Malatesta and Bakunin's uprising outside Bologna fails.

1875

United States	Ford appeals for 'a little band of heroes' in *Irish World*.

1876

United States	Skirmishing Fund established.
Switzerland	Bakunin dies.
Balkans	Cluseret and Stepniak join anti-Ottoman uprising.
Russia	Kropotkin escapes from prison.

1877

Russia	Trial of the 'To the People' marchers.
Italy	Malatesta and Stepniak's uprising outside Benevento fails.
United States	Great Railroad Strike.

1878

Germany/Britain	Most leaves Germany for Britain.
Germany	Hödel and Nobiling fail to kill Kaiser Wilhelm.
Italy	King Umberto survives assassination attempt.
Spain	King Alfonso XII survives assassination attempt.
Russia	Zasulich fails to kill Trepov. Stepniak assassinates Mezentsov.

1879

Britain	*Freiheit* established.
Switzerland	*Le Révolté* established.
Russia	People's Will established. Ishutin dies.

1880

France	Michel returns to France.
Russia	*The Terrorist Struggle* published. People's Will's campaign of bombings and shootings. Third Section disbanded and Okhrana established.
United States	United Irishmen of America (UIA) established. Mezzeroff starts training bombers. Heinzen dies.

1881

Russia	Tsar Alexander II assassinated by People's Will. Perovskaya, Kibalchich and three other members executed. Holy Brotherhood established.
Britain	London Anarchist Congress agrees to propaganda of the deed as revolutionary strategy. Commencement of dynamite campaign by UIA. *Freiheit* trial leads to Most's imprisonment.
France	Blanqui dies.
United States	*New York Times* calls for a 'war on terrorism'.

1882

Russia	Nechaev dies.
Germany	Stieber dies.
Ireland	Phoenix Park murders.
United States	Most commences lecture tour.

1883

Russia	People's Will infiltrated and undone.
Britain	Marx dies. Special Branch formed.
Germany	Attempt to blow up the Germania statue on the Niederwald fails.

1884

United States	Pinkerton dies.

1885

United States	*The Science of Revolutionary Warfare* published. Mezzeroff beaten by one of his students.
France	Rachkovsky takes control of Paris Okhrana office.
Britain	Irish dynamite campaign ends. Gladstone agrees to consider Irish Home Rule.

1886

United States	Haymarket affair.
France	Paris stock exchange attacked.
Britain	Stepniak warns about hot-head terrorism.

1887

United States.	Spies and Parsons executed.

1888

France	Cluseret enters Chamber of Deputies.

Timeline

1889
Russia	Chernyshevsky dies. Shuvalov dies.

1891
France	Ravachol commits grave robbery and murder. Clichy riot.

1892
France	Ravachol's attacks terrorise Paris until he is apprehended and executed. Mythologising of his death and revenge attack carried out on Café Very. Malatesta publishes article trying to quell hot-heads.
United States	Berkman fails to assassinate Henry Clay Frick. Goldman derides and publicly whips Most.
Britain	Michel's anarchist school raided. Walsall anarchists raided after infiltration by Melville's agent provocateur.

1893
France	Serbian ambassador stabbed in Paris. Chamber of Deputies bombed. Villainous Laws passed.
Spain	Liceu Theatre bombed.

1894
France	President Sadi Carnot assassinated. Café Terminus bombed. Trial of the Thirty acquits Grave.
Britain	Greenwich Observatory bombing. Anti-anarchist panic in Britain.

1895
Britain/France	Kropotkin, Grave and Reclus distance themselves from propaganda of the deed. Stepniak dies.

1897
Italy	Nobel dies.

1898
Switzerland	Empress Elizabeth of Austria assassinated.
Italy	Anti-anarchist conference in Rome agrees to international policing effort against anarchist terrorism.
Britain	Majendie dies.
Germany	Bismarck dies.

1900
Italy	King Umberto of Italy assassinated.
France	Cluseret dies.

1901
United States	Czolgosz assassinates President William McKinley. Theodore Roosevelt declares 'all mankind should band against the anarchist'.
Ireland	Stephens dies.

Timeline

1902

India	Anushilan Samiti established.
Russia	Socialist Revolutionary Combat Organization (SR) established and commences spate of high-profile assassinations.
France	Pietri dies.

1903

United States	Immigration Act passed.
Russia	Black Banner formed.

1904

Russia	Second anti-anarchist conference, in St Petersburg.

1905

Britain	Aliens Act passed.
Russia	Russo-Japanese War and revolution in St Petersburg weaken Tsar Nicholas II's regime. Motiveless terrorism rampant. Black Hundreds form.
France	Michel dies.
Belgium	Reclus dies.

1906

United States	Most dies.

1907

France	Kanungo sent to Paris to learn about bomb-making.

1908

India	Anushilan Samiti fails to assassinate a British magistrate with Russian-designed bombs.

1909

Britain	MI5 established and Melville appointed its chief detective.
Japan	Wang's assassination squad meet with Japanese anarchists and Russian revolutionaries.

1910

China	Wang's assassination of Qing regent thwarted.
Russia	Rachkovsky dies.

1913

United States	Ford dies.

1914

Bosnia and Herzegovina	Gavrilo Princip assassinates Archduke Franz Ferdinand.
Europe	First World War begins.

Preface

More than two decades lie between this book's completion and the morning of 11 September 2001, when four planes were hijacked in the skies over the United States and used as weapons by nineteen terrorists to murder 2,977 people. Since then, scholars, journalists and professionals from the political, intelligence and military sectors have laboured to answer the questions these attacks posed to a world that has grown ever anxious about terrorism in their aftermath. What drives people to become terrorists? What are their goals and why do they see violence and fear as the best ways to achieve them? How serious is the threat they pose? What is a 'war on terror' and how are you meant to fight it? Do we all, as a British government minister intoned in response to a terrorist bombing perpetrated a month after the twenty-year commemoration of the 9/11 attacks, need to 'remain alert but not alarmed'?[1]

History is a hostage to cycles of repetition. These same concerns of the post-9/11 age were voiced in the 1970s and 1980s, when communist, nationalist and ethno-sectarian terrorists hijacked and bombed planes, the Red Brigades kidnapped and murdered the Italian Prime Minister Aldo Moro, and The Troubles beset Northern Ireland. Beyond the questions asked of the cause and purpose of terrorism, the reactions of wider society to political violence have also changed little over time. In a scene that would not have been out of place in the autumn of 2001, the day after a car bomb was detonated on Wall Street in 1920, New Yorkers flocked to the blast site to sing the national anthem, demonstrating patriotic defiance in the face of an outrage perpetrated by terrorists beholden to the godless internationalist creed of anarchism. Even George W. Bush's infamous declaration of a 'war on terror' was a re-rerun. In 1881 – 120 years before Bush spoke the phrase – the *New York Times* called for a similarly ill-defined 'war on terrorism' to be waged in response to a suicide bomber murdering Tsar Alexander II of Russia. It took a further two decades of bombings and targeted killings across the transatlantic world for the newspaper's call to be heeded. This occurred in 1898, when police officials from several European states met in Rome and agreed to fight a unified war against the terrorist menace, much as Interpol, Europol and other international partnerships of police and intelligence services do today. Terrorism and its impacts, in forms recognisable to those who either remember 9/11 or grew up in its aftermath, have been with us for a long time.[2]

How long is a matter of debate, determined by the thorny issue of how you define terrorism. If 'assassination designed to intimidate' satisfies, then you could do worse than to find terrorism's starting point two millennia ago in Ancient Judea, where Jewish Sicarii assassins butchered Roman officials with the aim of forcing the legions out of their homeland. For those who reject the idea that terrorism is only for the disempowered, a flipside interpretation of that era also gives us a viable point of origin. Were not the Roman Empire's perpetrations of massacres against conquered foes, as well as the disciplinary practice of decimation – the execution of one out of every ten men – on its own troops, forms of what today would be called state-sponsored terrorism? If first usage of the term is important, then the British politician Edmund Burke deriding guillotine-happy French revolutionaries as 'hellhounds called terrorists that are let loose on the people' in the mid-1790s is also a fine moment to commence the story of terrorism.[3]

Why, then, does this book start in the 1850s? Firstly, my aim here is to understand how the type of modern terrorism that most people recognise today – violence and fear of same, carried out by non-state actors for the purposes of achieving a political or ideological goal – has developed. The sanguinary labours of ancient zealots and the brutal imposition of states upon subject peoples do not concern me, although the latter does occasionally creep into my narrative. Secondly, I have been guided to my starting point by scholars who have nominated either Tsar Alexander II's killers – a nihilist group called Narodnaya Volya (People's Will) – or violent Irish republicans for the dubious honour of 'world's first terrorists'. It was the latter who, two months before the tsar was blasted to death on the streets of St Petersburg in March 1881, detonated a bomb outside a barracks in Salford, killing a child and launching a five-year campaign of attacks across Britain. John Merriman, one of the world's foremost historians of anarchism, tacitly rejected the idea of a Russian or Irish origin, however, and argued that a rogue anarchist's dynamiting of the Café Terminus in Paris in 1894 started the modern age of terror. Challenging this claim, Carola Dietze's recent study on modern terrorism's genesis has turned the clock back three decades from the time of this explosion in Paris, identifying terrorist methods in the deeds of assassins and militants from Italy, Germany, the United States and Russia during the 1860s.[4] The sum of these histories is a chronology for the period in which modern terrorism developed, which spans the 1860s through until the 1890s. With a few tweaks to either end of this passage of time, this is the chronology that *The Rise of Devils* follows.

Context is everything in history. Therefore, beyond an established chronology, I have two further reasons for starting my story in the mid-nineteenth century. Terrorists live and die by media attention. Without publicity for their grievances and deeds, the fear terrorists need to force political changes and entice new recruits to their cause cannot be created. Unsurprisingly, the emergence of mass media across Europe and the United States and the laying of telegraph cables capable of moving news across the world at hitherto unthought of speeds in the 1850s and 1860s coincided with the emergence of a trend in which violent radicals read of each other's attacks and were inspired to emulation. The same international communications network – composed of newspapers, penny presses and partisan periodicals – that produced these copycat terrorists also generated societal anxieties over terrorism, as well as a battery of conspiracy theories to explain how and why attacks were happening. The most persistent of these theories posited that the carnage was being coordinated by an international revolutionary cabal. The fear of this phantom brotherhood of murderers, coupled with the saturation press coverage given to every explosion or shooting from Chicago to St Petersburg, did not go unnoticed by terrorists themselves, who learned how the media could be weaponised to fragment societies with panic. As this book shows, the arrival of mass media in the mid-nineteenth century, and the criminally sensationalistic coverage that came with it, was vital to the development of modern terrorism.[5]

No less than headlines and fear, terrorists are also reliant on innovative means of warfare to address the imbalance between their offensive capabilities and those of states that possess, as one terrorist theorist has lamented, 'superiority in organization, training, numbers and means of destruction'. Owing to the Industrial Revolution and the wars fought in the Crimea (1853–1856), the United States (1861–1865) and across Europe (1859–1871), the mid-nineteenth century was a crucible for weapons development. Moreover, the knowledge of these new weapons was transmitted globally via the same communications networks that reported terrorist attacks and gave the perpetrators the attention they craved. For example, an 1858 edition of *Scientific American* revealed the secret to making fulminated mercury, which was 'twenty times stronger as an explosive agent than gunpowder', to whoever happened to pick up a copy of the magazine. That same year, a newly invented bomb charged by fulminated mercury was used by terrorists to kill eight people in Paris. The following decade, the invention of dynamite by the Swedish inventor Alfred Nobel was widely reported in the press and in technical magazines. This led to the explosive – originally designed for blasting rock in mining – becoming a favoured weapon of terrorists, who extolled to each other the virtues of this 'proletariat's artillery'. Aside from new explosives, this was also the age of the first machine guns, forays into chemical warfare and the sketching out by military planners, science fiction writers and even a few terrorists themselves, of the potential for using airships to shower cities with explosives. For the violent and disempowered who dreamed of evening the odds on the battlefield their oppressors had always commanded, the 1850s through to the outbreak of the First World War was an era of unheralded potential.[6]

A final note must be made about the scope and limitations of this story. *The Rise of Devils* is my history of modern terrorism's origins – it is not *the* history. There are many attacks that I do not cover, including those committed in the colonial world which, with the exception of some material concerning the Irish struggle and the Indian Nationalist movement, I leave to historians better versed in such matters to discuss.[7] These omissions exist because to include them would distract from my focus, which is on a group of people whose thoughts and deeds created the terrorist milieu that has informed communist revolutionaries, jihadists, white supremacists and various other practitioners of political violence for the better part of the last two centuries. These progenitors of modern terrorism were an eclectic bunch – philosophers, cult-leaders, ruthless criminals, shameless charlatans and dangerous fantasists. Others were earnest revolutionaries, seduced by the idea that terrorism was a remedy for the ills of a world they resolved to heal. All were pursued by police spies, who were often far from shy in using terrorist methods themselves. What follows is the story of how these revolutionaries, thinkers, killers and spies learned a lesson as heinous as it has proved enduring, resonating with menace into our own troubled age – the means by which to bring terror to the world.

Acknowledgements

During the production of this book, I have received advice on content, archival matters, terminology and translations, as well as general encouragement and collegial support from: Christopher Vaughan, Michael Durey, Constance Bantman, Mischa Honeck, Anna Geifman, Amber Paranick, Gillian O'Brien, Tom Parker, Matthew Hill, Tom Beaumont, Chris Millington, Frank McDonough, Lukasz Grzymski, Andrew Galley, Vlad Solomon, Kim A. Wagner, Olivia Saunders, Andrea Livesey, André Keil, Nick White, Malcom Craig, Megan Armstrong, Katherine Harbord, Dean Clay, Daniel Feather, James Brocklesby and David Clampin. A thank you also to Emma Brennan and Paul Clarke at Manchester University Press for greenlighting this project and helping me usher it to its conclusion, and Ralph Footring for his copy-editing and suggestions for improving the text. My wife Sarah has, as always, tolerated the near intolerable from me throughout proceedings. You are my love – by north, south, east and west.

The prophet of terror

,

No one noticed the bespectacled, prematurely balding man as he melted into the crowd at the back of the softly lit basement. He was an unremarkable sight, possessed of a face that neither words nor thoughts would remember. Clad in crumpled layers of dark grey, wrapped in a beige overcoat, if anyone were to regard him it would be only to note the intensity with which he occasionally nodded his head in response to the 'inflammatory watchwords' expelled into the sweating air by the 'fanatical visionaries' gathered around him. That affirmative gesture, combined with his humble exterior, was all the face in the crowd needed to convince the room's occupants that he was one of them – the furious downtrodden, righteous and resolved to topple the haughty despots of Europe. What if only one of the fifty or so labourers and bohemians with whom he stood shoulder to shoulder could see beyond the man's disguise to question the sincerity of his nods? Then, those who had crammed into the pokey Parisian basement club to drink and hear talk of revolution might have discovered something of the mental report that Wilhelm Stieber – Prussian police spy and self-appointed scourge of Europe's radicals – was compiling on the 'conspirators whose heads burned and whose thoughts rumbled with new world-orders' around him.

The gathering was typical of the many that Stieber had attended unnoticed since arriving in Paris just after New Year's Day 1852. Having donned his workingman's disguise on the train from Berlin, the police spy had disembarked at the Gare du Nord and hastened through the snow-scattered streets to Belleville and Montmartre. These districts of the French capital were known to house a variety of so-called red clubs, in which socialists, Jacobins and other political dissidents gathered. Given the choice, the arch-conservative and instinctive authoritarian would have sooner burnt the red clubs to the ground than stepped into them. Duty bound Stieber, however, to mask his hatred and dive into these nests of subversion to follow a lead he had picked up in London which, he believed, held the key to unravelling a great and terrible conspiracy.

Stieber's pursuit of this plot began just before Christmas 1851, when he crossed the English Channel with a mission to gather intelligence on German socialists in London. The means by which he fulfilled his brief was typical of the daring undercover work for which the police spy had made his name in Berlin. Having purchased a wig, Stieber swapped his pince-nez for an oversized pair of thick glasses and assumed the persona of a journalist named Schmidt, by which means he bluffed his way into the Soho flat of a man he had come to fear and loathe – Karl Marx. Like many of Europe's radical thinkers, Marx had taken advantage of Britain's liberal free speech and immigration laws, fleeing police persecution on the continent in 1849, with the aim to build a new life under London's leaden skies. There, in the city's West End, amidst cafés that rang with the sounds of subversive chatter, Marx ingratiated himself with fellow émigré socialists and republicans who, Stieber suspected, were up to more than simply nodding along with the German's musings on the plight of workers.

After several days of undercover eavesdropping, Stieber became convinced that the ostensibly peaceful International Communist League of agitators that Marx led was, in fact, a 'conspiratorial and treasonous' nest of insurgents who were planning, as he overheard one of them declare, 'the violent amelioration of our corrupt world'. Alarming as this intelligence was, Stieber saw little use in sharing it with the British authorities. Earlier in 1851, he had met with Richard Mayne, the head of Scotland Yard, and shared his concerns over the potential for socialists to launch terrorist attacks on the Great Exhibition being held in Hyde Park. Although Mayne thought similarly that the great and good who toured the Crystal Palace might be possible targets for violence, Stieber pushed this budding collaboration too far by demanding of Mayne that German radicals sheltering in London be extradited back to Berlin to stand trial. This, in addition to Stieber's generally paranoid demeanour, led Mayne to keep a distance from the visiting detective. It was an episode that told Stieber all he needed to know about Britain's police – they were clearly too soft on subversives and could not be trusted to do what was necessary. As such, it was on his own that 'Schmidt' went to Marx's apartment and knocked on the door, introducing himself as a socialist journalist who was desperate for an interview with his idol. Duly led into his nemesis's inner sanctum, Stieber endured a few long minutes of polite chatter before Marx handed him a smoking gun. This was *The Programme of the Communist League* – a document that called for the 'overthrow of the tyranny of the property-owners that has reigned until now'. Although there were no specific details on how the fires of revolution would be ignited, Stieber's fertile imagination, fed by years of hatred for all things 'red', filled in the blanks.[1]

Like many conservatives of his generation, Stieber's view of reformers and liberals had been shaped by the events of 1848 – a year of riots and protests in which radicals of various stripes rose across much of Europe, erecting barricades and engaging in street battles with soldiers and police. This violent eruption had long been predicted by police spies and politicians, who saw all manner of terrorist plots, secret societies and revolutionary machinations forming in the shadows of a continent irreparably altered by the emancipatory ideas of the French Revolution and the geo-political washout of the Napoleonic Wars. This had included the 1815 Congress of Vienna, at which the victors in the war against Bonaparte mapped out Europe's new, peaceful, order. At the top of their list of priorities was a resolution to work together to contain the revolutionary forces unleashed in France, and to encourage the maintenance of a conservative political order across the continent.

When the 1848 revolutions exploded to challenge this consensus, they did so with none of the ruthless organisation and conspiratorial planning that Europe's police had anticipated. Nevertheless, the rising of the masses, plus the spasm of violence required to put them down, left a scar on Stieber's mind. This bred in him a resolve to ensure that the continent would never again have to face the menace of the mob.[2]

The problem Stieber had was that many of the '48ers' had slipped the net following their uprisings and scattered to the literary salons and red clubs of Geneva, Chicago, New York and London. There, the revolutionaries nurtured resentment, with some taking to their jobbing presses to produce thousands of cheaply printed and widely disseminated pamphlets, in which their oppressors were denounced and revenge was vowed. Neither Stieber nor many of his police comrades were disposed to draw a link between the violence they meted out on the radicals and the threats of retaliation they received. Instead, they blamed the spectre of a second revolution on the diatribes of people who seemed irrationally criminal by nature – preachers of terroristic violence who simply wanted to burn the world they despised. An exemplar of this type was Karl Heinzen, a German publisher and 48er who was praised in his lifetime by a chronicler of 'sages, thinkers and reformers' as 'an uncompromising foe to clerical frauds and fossilized errors'. Heinzen couched his mission in blunter terms, speaking of how he sought to 'annihilate tyrants' with deeds rather than simply harry them with words. His justification for violence against the powers that be was simple. Faced with governments who could call on standing armies and cannon to defend their tyranny, murder, as Heinzen wrote in his 1853 treatise *Murder and Liberty*, was a form of self-defence for the oppressed. Indeed, it was 'a duty to society, when directed against a professional murderer' such as an emperor, a general or a king. His words reading like those of a man drunk on the blood of enemies he had yet to kill, Heinzen demanded a reprise of 1848 in which 'physics and chemistry may become all the more important to the revolution than all your gallantry and military science': specifically, the chemistry of bomb construction and the physics of explosions.[3]

Heinzen's call to assemble explosives and slaughter kings was only one aspect of the danger Stieber saw looming over the post-1848 world. It was not until he stood in Marx's apartment holding the socialist majordomo's plan in his quaking hands that the bewigged spy felt that he now understood the bigger picture. The radicals of Europe, having armed themselves with bombs and poisons in the manner Heinzen instructed, would re-emerge from the fog of their failure and follow *The Programme of the Communist League* to its most violent extremes. Of further worry was the scale of the threat. According to the *Programme* and the intelligence Stieber had gathered from clubs and cafés in Soho, Marx had been despatching adherents from London across the Channel to set up revolutionary cells in Paris, Berlin, Brussels, Lyon, Rome, Cologne and Metz. The leaders of these cells had been tasked with recruiting additional agents of terror from amongst Europe's 48ers, disgruntled labourers and the disillusioned youth of university campuses, whose naïve minds were being turned to murder and mayhem through revolutionary propaganda.

Determined to defeat this plot before a second, better-organised and more terroristic version of 1848 erupted, Stieber made his apologies to Marx and left London in haste, stopping briefly in Berlin to report his findings before heading to Paris, where, he believed, the continental heart of the conspiracy lay. It took only a handful of visits to the basement clubs of Belleville and Montmartre for Stieber to confirm his fears that a seething mass of 'utopian dreamers, eccentrics and fools' were amassing in the City of Light. Worse still and to his horror, they spoke openly of their ties to conspirators across Europe and on the other side of the Atlantic – dissidents on the docks of New York and in the working-class slums of Chicago, Pittsburgh and Cincinnati. No less than the 'reds' of Paris, these undesirables were just the types, thought Stieber, both to heed Heinzen's call for terrorism and to act as the foot soldiers of Marx's plan to dismantle the order of the world.[4] Someone had to stop them.

The idea that Marx was plotting a transnational campaign of revolutionary terrorism in the winter of 1851–1852 was little short of absurd. His head still spinning from the fallout of 1848, Marx was leery of the 'alchemists of revolution' who called for either an immediate and violent renewal of street fighting, or a turn to conspiracy and the plotting of assassinations. Advocate of revolution he might have been, Marx was also no fan of the murderous terrorism championed by Heinzen, whom he dismissed as a dangerously 'ignorant lout'. There were, however, some 48ers within Marx's circle who spoke openly and enthusiastically of violence. It is likely, therefore, that Stieber's claim to have stumbled across a plot for world domination through some overheard chatter and a brief encounter with Marx was the product of one man's melodramatic interpretation of radical wishful thinking. Not all the spy's claims, however, were the stuff of paranoid fantasy. The energetically subversive flavour of Paris's red clubs was far from a figment of his imagination, and nor was Stieber mistaken in recognising Marx's ability to mould minds and acquire adherents to his revolutionary cause. However, like many a conspiracy theorist before him and since, Stieber erred in his eagerness to connect these various dots and fill the gaps between them with his own prejudices, grossly inflating the size and menace of the threat.

Stieber's distorted view of Marx's conspiracy against civilisation shaped the following story he told of its defeat. Having concluded his investigations in Montmartre and Belleville, the spy retired to a rented apartment to compile his final report. It was there that a thug named Cherval, acting on behalf of Marx, accosted him armed with a dagger. With his life about to be taken, the quick-thinking Stieber clobbered his assailant with a chair, to which he then handcuffed the failed assassin. An interrogation then took place on the floor of the apartment, by the end of which Stieber had turned one of Marx's men from the ill-fated path of violent radicalism, convincing Cherval to become a double agent. Through this informer, Stieber was able to round up the entire French chapter of Marx's conspiracy, from whom he extracted information that led to further arrests in Cologne. The outcome of the subsequent trial, held in Cologne in the autumn of 1852, was the presentation to the world of Stieber's conspiracy theory, which, the proud detective claimed to the court, featured a 'communist association that was perfectly organized in Paris, Lyon, Marseilles, Strasbourg, Valenciennes, Metz, Algiers, Dijon, London, New York, Philadelphia, Liège, Verviers, Geneva, Bern...' and on and on. This assertion was confirmed by Cherval's testimony, which secured the conviction of seven Marxists on the grounds of conspiring to launch a revolution.[5]

To the eyes of the world, Stieber had ensured that the sequel to 1848 had been cancelled. However, like his account of the infiltration mission to Soho, the story told at the Cologne trial was riddled with fallacies. Faked documents were mixed with genuine pieces of socialist propaganda, which were then presented to the court together as evidence of the truth behind Stieber's claims. The story of his showdown with an assassin sent by Marx was also a carefully concocted lie. Cherval had always been Stieber's informer and he was likely acting as an agent provocateur, urging radicals to plot bigger and deadlier schemes that would bring tangibility to his handler's theories and justify further arrests. These machinations were typical of Stieber, whose button-down drabness, a contemporary recalled, did little to hide either his 'suspicious, crabbed and malicious nature' or his near pathological fear of socialism. It was at the nexus between this fear and his desire to be the hammer that crushed all radicals that Stieber concocted a colossal and violent conspiracy that he alone could defeat.[6]

Such was the angst of the post-1848 world, however, that Stieber's assertions were not written off as those of an inveterate liar or panic merchant. Instead, having 'proved' the existence of a revolutionary conspiracy at the Cologne trial, Stieber was rewarded with an increased budget from the Prussian treasury, which he used to employ secret policing methods that were as ingenious as they were nefarious. He planted fake news stories of further conspiracies in newspapers, recruited more agents provocateurs and made use of the so-called honey trap, paying prostitutes to corral union leaders and leftist writers into compromising situations, from which they could be blackmailed into becoming informers. Stieber also trained plain clothes police in the art of deep-cover infiltration and document theft, and went to forge partnerships with other police and military leaders in St Petersburg and Paris. Through these relationships, he sought to position himself as the general of a European army of spooks that could rival the legions of radicals who, despite the success of the Cologne trial, Stieber still claimed were assembling in secret, with intent on menace. So confident was he of this assertion that in 1853 he published a warning of threats to come in *Communist Conspiracies of the*

Nineteenth Century, a two-volume treatise of paranoid proclamations that was widely read by police chiefs and politicians across Europe.[7]

Stieber's anti-radical crusade could not last. He had long been despised by Prussia's progressive politicians, who watched his relentless pursuit of socialists and republicans with baleful indignation. In December 1860, the Prussian government – having adopted a more liberal character – ordered an investigation into Stieber's practices, which led to his arrest. He was accused of everything from bending informers to his will with physical threats, to blackmail, perjury, theft and the corruption of the law, specifically by keeping suspects in prison for months on end without cause or trial. Sat in the dock on charges that, ironically, smacked of state-sponsored terrorism and criminal conspiracy on his part, Stieber's fall from grace shone a light on the unscrupulous nature of the war on radicalism he had been waging. Over the course of the trial, both Stieber and the Prussian police were found to have 'superseded the civil tribunals in matters of debt and disputed accounts, and forced the parties, debtors as well as creditors, to a settlement by menaces'. In pursuit of socialists and republicans, the police had indulged in wanton prejudice and an 'abuse of power unheard of in any country'. It was also found that Stieber had used secret funds and false stories to accrue 'almost unlimited authority' within not only Prussia's police but also certain sections of the army. Tried in the courts of both law and public opinion, the once mighty defender of Europe's peace and order was now little more than a disreputable criminal.[8]

Or was he? Despite the magnitude of the charges and vitriol from the press, Stieber was acquitted and allowed to walk free, the verdict cracking a rare smile over the face of the otherwise taciturn spymaster. Stieber knew that one thing – a powerful, pervasive thing – had spared him from having to answer for his crimes: fear. True, he had exceeded the limits of his powers and gone to extra-legal lengths to pursue revolutionaries. However, in a world where Heinzen was urging the legions of disenchanted to believe that 'if one man is permitted to murder, all must be permitted to murder' and Marx was warning of a 'spectre haunting Europe', a reactionary zealot of Stieber's calibre was too valuable an asset to put behind bars. Recent events proved as much. In 1858, in the very city where Stieber had beheld the red clubs of restless 48ers and firebrand socialists, an event took place that seemed to confirm the spymaster's prophecy – the age of terrorist revolution, and the fear of it, had arrived.[9]

Part 1

Harbingers

Chapter I

Three bombs in Paris

The evening of 14 January 1858 promised to be one of spectacle and sadness for the Parisians who had flocked to their city's Opera House. That night's show was to be the final curtain call for the beloved baritone Jean-Étienne-Auguste Massol, the star act on a bill that also included the Italian stage legend Adelaide Ristori, world-renowned for her ability to imbue an otherworldly sense of suffering into the tragic characters she played. Her performances, it was said, could bring audiences to tears. The promise of such drama greatly appealed to the Opera House's honoured guest for the evening, Emperor Napoleon III, who, accompanied by his Empress Eugénie, had been planning for weeks to grace Massol's final show with his presence. Finely moustached, pensive-faced, part cocksure powerbroker, part insecure melancholic, the emperor of France was a man of frantic contradictions, as fond of melodrama as he was of empty praise. As such, Napoleon was both excited by the prospect of seeing Massol and Ristori in action and heartened by the fact that the Opera House's manager had promoted his and Eugénie's attendance, with a mind that the presence of majesty would further enhance the great event. Napoleon's satisfaction at being the centre of attention only grew as his carriage turned onto Rue le Peletier, and he saw that the thoroughfare was lined with hundreds of Parisians, assembled in the gas-lit chill to catch a glimpse of their emperor in all his splendour.

Napoleon did not disappoint his subjects, who took in the sight of his horse-drawn carriage of dark wood and polished gold, flanked by a platoon of mounted lancers dripping in gold braid, alongside which stalked a complement of gendarmes, resplendent in their distinctive uniforms and short-brimmed hats. Majestic yet threatening, the royal retinue was designed to embody all that the emperor of the French thought himself to be. As the procession slowed to a crawl outside the Opera House, the crowd surged forward chanting 'Vive l'empereur!', whilst in vain the gendarmes and lancers pushed back, struggling to keep an appropriate distance between the subjects and their sovereigns, both of whom smiled impatiently as they waited for the appreciative tumult to subside. It was a scene of bustling energy and distracting enthusiasm, perfect for the unnoticeable to unleash the unthinkable. And so it was that as the activity around the carriage reached a fever pitch, 'a tremendous explosion was heard, so loud as to throw the whole quarter into a state of alarm', followed by two more ear-splitting eruptions within seconds of each other, the sound of which was 'comparable to cannon fire'.

And yet, there was not an artillery piece to be seen on Rue le Peletier. Rather, the source of the fire and noise was three homemade bombs, tossed from the sea of faceless onlookers 'upon the pavement within a few inches of the vehicle', whereupon they 'burst with terrible force and flung deadly projectiles in all directions', piercing the joyful buzz of the crowd with the shrillness of screams. At the sound of the first detonation, Napoleon and Eugénie had instinctively drawn themselves together on the floor of their carriage, which was 'very much battered' by the successive blasts and the white-hot shrapnel that came with them. As the smoke rose around them and they disentangled from their protective knot, the royal couple were relieved to discover that they bore only superficial injuries. The worst had been suffered by Eugénie. Her left eye had been grazed by microscopic shards of glass, and her once immaculate evening dress was now 'splattered with blood'. Napoleon, for his part, received only a few scratches to the face and a ringing in his ears, in addition to his plumed hat being 'knocked to pieces by the projectiles' that had erupted from the explosions. Aside from Eugénie's eye and Napoleon's headwear, the only other injury of note sustained within the carriage was to the emperor's aide-de-camp, who had made a gruesome contribution to the scene when he gingerly removed a shard of wood from his neck, creating the projectile splatter that ruined the empress' dress.

Outside of the relatively unscathed carriage interior, the bombs had done grim work. Beneath rows of shattered gas lamps, the street was carpeted with shard-covered civilians and gendarmes. Some were screaming in shock and pain at their wounds, some were clutching broken ears, some simply lay stunned and weeping on the flagstones. Lancers with bloodied tunics and dented helmets were strewn around the carriage, the vehicle's horses had collapsed beside each other in a heap and their driver was slumped over, his dead hands still gripped to the blood-soaked reins. Beyond the explosions' epicentre, the buildings surrounding the Opera House had been pelted with 'projectiles which left a circular opening of two centimetres in diameter' across the brickwork, scarring the facades of shops and houses. This material damage was dwarfed by the human carnage. In total, 156 people – eight of whom would die from shrapnel wounds – were left casualties of the three bombs flung at Napoleon's carriage for a simple, chilling purpose: to murder an emperor and strike fear into all.[1]

Whilst they might have failed to take Napoleon's life, scenes inside the Opera House following the explosions confirmed the success of the bombers' secondary objective. As the audience collapsed into sobbing confusion, the director rushed onto the stage and announced that the final act of *William Tell* would be cancelled, whereupon Ristori and Massol were hurried to the back. This, however, did not bring an end to the drama, for the stage was now open for Napoleon to deliver the finest performance of the night. Ignoring the pleas of his entourage to let the unhurt lancers escort them back to the Tuileries Palace, the emperor declared his intention to press on with the evening as planned – a resolve the empress affirmed with a curt nod of her head. Pausing only for Eugénie to dab the blood away from her eye with a handkerchief, the royal couple exited their once splendid vehicle arm in arm and strode into the Opera House's audience chamber, appearing as if hewn from the smoke and slaughter before the panicked mass of generals, government officials and other well-to-dos of Paris. Stoic in the face of a hundred shocked expressions, Napoleon and Eugénie continued calmly up the stairs to their private box, 'preserving their coolness' and taking their seats if it were any other night at the opera. As a court-friendly chronicler would later recall, Napoleon, having conveyed 'no anxiety except to care for those who are wounded' before entering the building, was now resolved to lead his terrified people by example. He paused briefly to adjust his bomb-ruffled tunic and then took a seat, gesturing as he did so for *William Tell* to continue. With a benevolent smile cracking across his pale lips, Napoleon took in the eruption of rapturous applause from an assembly awed by his 'calm and impassable' demeanour.[2] It was a magnificent performance at a terrible moment.

The need to appear as nothing short of totally indestructible was vital for Napoleon, whose pretensions masked much that was broken beneath. In the five years since he had become France's emperor, he had worked hard to cultivate the image of himself as a man of destiny and arbiter of great affairs – the reincarnation of his all-powerful uncle, Napoleon Bonaparte. It was an image designed to offset a deeply felt sense of insecurity. Like his forebear, the third Napoleon was a product of violence and political upheaval, specifically, the revolutions that had convulsed France in 1848, from which he had risen to take the nation's reins of power once the dust had settled over Paris's barricades. The herald of a new era, Napoleon cheered republicans and liberals by casting off the shackles of the past, and styling himself as a populist, reformist president of the Second French Republic. This charade, however, did not last long. For all his apparent liberal inclinations, Napoleon was determined to establish a thread of continuity between himself and his vaunted namesake. This led, in December 1852, to him effecting another revolution in France, by proclaiming himself ruler of the newly established Second French Empire. Initially popular with his people and comfortable on his throne, Napoleon's fear of losing power soon grew, leading to the rigging of elections and the suppression of liberal and republican criticism of his regime. This pushed Napoleon's enemies into the kind of red clubs that Stieber prowled, within the rant-laden rooms of which France's radicals grew only more extreme in their opposition to their emperor and all he stood for.

Stieber was not the only spy who monitored this undercurrent of imperial resentment. Under the direction of Pierre Marie Piétri, the Paris police prefecture kept a watchful eye on dissenters against Napoleon's regime via the Sûreté – an intelligence and policing network that the emperor came to rely on more and more as his popularity waned and his paranoia grew. The activities of Piétri's men were every bit as ruthless and crafty as those practised by Stieber. Undercover agents regularly monitored Paris's red clubs, in the alleys behind which prostitutes, labourers and newspaper reporters provided information on radical plots real and imagined in exchange for payment from the Sûreté's coffers, which Napoleon furnished generously. Elsewhere, agents provocateurs stirred up trouble on the factory floors and in workingmen's clubs, hoping to prompt acts of insurrection that could justify sweeping police clampdowns. Piétri even set up fake news outlets that distributed supposedly republican broadsheets, which were subtly infused with pro-regime stories that downplayed the scale of anti-Napoleon resentment within the capital. Few of the emperor's subjects, however, were fooled by Piétri's propaganda, distributed as it was amidst a tide of police repression that rose steadily throughout the 1850s. By the time of the Rue le Peletier bombing, Napoleon's France had become a nation of enemies, governed by a ruler who craved his people's adoration whilst fearing their whispered judgements.[3]

This was why Napoleon needed to perform as he did that night at the Opera House, when fate proffered him a chance to stride past the bodies and smoke to stand tall in defiance of those who wanted him dead. It was a moment for an emperor to awe his subjects, and extract from them the sympathy and adoration that had become necessary for the would-be strong man to function. *La Bombe infernale,* an ode to Napoleon composed shortly after the attack, perfectly articulated the emperor's designs, speaking of how the attempt to 'violently take the life out of the Chosen One of the French People' had been thwarted by God, who protected the 'firm, intrepid Emperor'. At least one of those present in the Opera

House that night, however, could see through Napoleon's veneer enough to catch a glimpse of the sweating panic beneath. Ristori, the maestra of human tragedy, recalled that at a moment in the resumed *William Tell* when the word 'assassin' was mentioned, Napoleon 'gave me a glance that I shall never forget. The all-powerful sovereign, master of France, adulated by Europe, felt that he had but one fear, the assassins'.[4]

This fear was well founded. As Napoleon sensed and Piétri soon confirmed, the bombing was no random act of malice. The architect of the attack and leader of the four-man team of bombers was an Italian named Felice Orsini – one of the many dashing revolutionaries of the age who, if terrorist profiling had existed at the time, would have lit up many a red flag long before he travelled to Rue le Peletier with explosives in hand. No red club wallflower, Orsini had shouldered arms in 1848 and, in the years that followed, involved himself in numerous subversive plots. He also pulled off a daring prison break in 1854, which involved him cutting the bars out of a window and shimmying down the side of a fortress using bed sheets – a tale that, naturally, grabbed headlines across Europe. All these activities were conducted as part of Orsini's involvement with the Carbonari, a quasi-Masonic secret society whose origins were shrouded in myths and legends that tied it to the Knights Templar, the dynasty of Alexander the Great or the Egyptian Cult of Isis. Regardless of the Carbonari's existence or lack thereof in antiquity, what mattered in the nineteenth century was that its members were pledged to the destruction of tyrants – specifically those whose rule prevented the creation of a liberal, democratic future for a unified Italy.

The Carbonari's mission was born of a bitter history. Italy had been rendered an unhappy patchwork of kingdoms by the decrees of the Congress of Vienna, from which a swathe of peace treaties and territorial agreements had been agreed by Europe's great powers, as part of their aim to reassert the authority of monarchs and clamp down hard on nationalist-liberal sentiments. As part of these agreements, northern Italy had been placed under the control of the emperor of Austria, whilst the middle of the peninsula had been handed back to the Pope to govern. Both parties, naturally, were afraid of the Carbonari and their intentions.

Although he shared their passion to unify Italy and cast off its rulers, Orsini differed from his Carbonari brethren. Disenchanted with the idea of entering a 'war for the streets' rehash of 1848, Orsini favoured using a simple act of terrorism to set Italy and, perhaps, all of Europe free from the conservative consensus forged in 1815.[5]

Orsini's plan was dramatic and ambitious, defined by the kind of fantastical dice rolling that is common to many terrorist plots. At the heart of his plan were two conclusions about Napoleon: firstly, that, as the head of what Orsini dubbed Europe's premier 'government based upon despotism and treason', the emperor of the French symbolised the tyranny of the Vienna Congress and the European order it had created; and secondly, that, as a Catholic ruler and commander of the countless bayonets of the continent's largest army, Napoleon added crucial military strength to the Pope's position in Italy. Therefore, to liberate Italy and dismantle the 1815 consensus, Orsini reasoned that Napoleon would need to be killed in a manner that would not only terrify Europe's other monarchs but also incite the defeated radicals of 1848 to rise once more. With Napoleon gone, so Orsini believed, France would collapse into panic and self-protectionism and its police and army would focus on the radical threat at home, depriving the Pope of the backup he needed to hold Rome. At this point of papal vulnerability, the Eternal City would be seized by a vast people's army of workers from the city and labourers from the Italian countryside, led by the Carbonari. With Rome taken and Paris reeling, Orsini expected a gloriously earth-shattering series of events to unfold: 'a war of independence in Italy, a revolution in Paris, a war of principles and republicanism in continental Europe'. All it would take would be the death of one man.[6]

The political outcomes of acts of terrorism are seldom so neat and discernible, the more so when they fail. Realising that Napoleon had survived the three bombs thrown at him, Orsini and his accomplices – Antonio Gomez and Carlo de Rudio – melted away from the carnage they had created, adopting the personas of fearful crowd members in search of respite. Orsini's performance as a victim of the attack was enhanced by the fact that he had been struck on the temple by shrapnel from his own infernal machine. Most likely, the injury knocked Orsini stupid. As he wandered the backstreets that ran off Rue le Peletier in search of a doctor's surgery, the supposed professional revolutionary thoughtlessly discarded his pistol and dagger in the gutter. This, together with the thin trail of blood he left with every dazed step, made Orsini both suspicious to onlookers and easy for the police to track down. Barely six hours after he botched his moment of destiny, Orsini's hotel room door was bashed open by a corps of gendarmes, who found the would-be assassin passed out in a heap with a blood-stained rag wrapped around his head.

An even easier quarry for the police was the fourth member of the team, Giovanni Pierri, whose pre-attack nerves and shifty demeanour had caught the eye of an off-duty gendarme outside the Opera House. Detained before he could detonate his bomb, Pierri was already being questioned when his comrades unleashed their payloads. Now faced with an interrogator enraged at both the attempted regicide and the harm done to his fellow gendarmes Pierri cracked, confessing to having been a part of the plot and giving his captor the address of the hotel where he and de Rudio had hired a room in which to prepare their bombs. It was there that de Rudio was later seized asleep and, much like Orsini, oblivious to the fact that the team was being rounded up one by one. The papers and equipment found in Pierri and de Rudio's hotel room led the police to the final conspirator, Gomez, who had already attracted attention shortly after the bombing by slumping tearfully into the corner of a bar across the street from the Opera House, where he repeatedly muttered 'What have I done, my master, what have I done?' as the bedlam unfolded around him.[7]

The trial that followed the quartet's arrest revealed details that had an impact beyond the fear-gripped streets of Paris. Over the course of four weeks of interrogation and investigation the police discovered that rather than emerging from the red clubs of Italy or France – as many in both the Tuileries Palace and Piétri's headquarters assumed – Orsini's plan had been put together in the idyllic surrounds of the British countryside. The choice of France's cross-Channel neighbour as a base from which 'a band of assassins' could plan a terrorist attack was by no means peculiar.

The same free press and open immigration policy that had lured Marx to London had served Orsini and his accomplices well. As the court was informed, Orsini had taken full advantage of Britain's 'generous hospitality' throughout the 1850s, crossing the Channel on multiple occasions to deliver lectures on Italian unity that were well received by a British press and public who, by and large, despised the despotism of men like Napoleon, Pope Pius IX and the Austrian emperor who ruled northern Italy, Franz Joseph.[8]

During these lecture tours, Orsini made the acquaintance of a stockbroker from Derbyshire named Thomas Allsop, who supplied the Italian with a false passport to ease his movements through a France that was crawling with Sûreté spies. Orsini also consulted a Birmingham-based metalworker named Joseph Taylor, who travelled to Allsop's rural residence in the winter of 1857 to manufacture the bombs that Orsini had designed to deliver the sensational public execution his plan demanded. As the court heard, the 'infernal machines' that Taylor constructed were as revolutionary and volatile as the men who wielded them. Roughly round in shape, the 'murderous bombs consisted of a hollow cylinder of brittle cast iron, composed of two parts bound by a screw'. The top part, weightier than the lower section, was riddled with '23 protruding capsules' which, upon contact with a hard surface, would trigger a detonation of the fulminated mercury that had been packed into the cylinder, sending hundreds of shards of metal in all directions. Percussion-detonated without the attention-grabbing problem of requiring a lit fuse, the Orsini bomb was a cheaply made and easy to assemble improvised explosive device that could unleash a blast capable of killing its target whilst leaving a terrifying scene of smoke, shrapnel and destruction. In conception and design, it was a perfect terrorist weapon.[9]

Orsini's weapons innovation and the effort that lay behind his murderous plan only added to the panic that spread through Paris in the weeks after the bombing. Eugénie's ladies in waiting spread a rumour that Orsini's original target had been a ball at the Tuileries Palace, to which he and Pierri had tried unsuccessfully to gain access the night prior to the Opera House attack. With the bombs in their pockets, they had been turned away at the gate, which led them to settling on an easier, softer target. Privy councillors were convinced that more bombers were out there. Consequently, they pushed forward plans to assure the succession should the next assassination attempt prove successful. Within a day of the Rue le Peletier attack, paperwork was signed to confirm that Eugénie would serve as regent in the event of her husband's death. Addressing both the safety of their sovereign and the wounding of their lancers, the army brass declared a state of emergency, issuing a public notice in the newspapers in which they declared it their duty to 'assume a political role in times of crisis'. This led to soldiers being reassigned to bolster the ranks of the Paris police prefecture, whose chief, Piétri, stepped down in disgrace for his failure to prevent Orsini's attack.

Not that the role of police chief mattered so much now that Paris was, seemingly, faced with dangers far greater than those posed by regular criminality. Convinced of this, Napoleon appointed a military man, General Charles-Marie Espinasse, to the post of Minister for the Interior and Public Security shortly after the bombing. It speaks to the siege mentality within the Tuileries Palace that Espinasse's prior experience of combating France's enemies involved fighting Russian soldiers in the Crimea and battling Algerian insurgents. Competent he may have been in ordering the burning of villages and the bombardment of enemy lines, there was nothing in Espinasse's skill set to suggest that he was the man needed to unravel an international terrorist plot. His appointment, combined with other generals offering soldiers to back Paris's gendarmes, meant that the counter-terrorism surge which pushed its way through Paris's factories, red clubs and cafés in the spring of 1858 was one of iron fists and zero tolerance.

Such was Espinasse's will. Having declared that 'It is time for the good to be re-assured and for the wicked to tremble!', on his first day in office he sent a circular to police chiefs across France, ordering the arbitrary arrest of a quota of radicals in their respective districts and a 'redoubled surveillance over all foreigners'. This came even before the passing of the Law of Public Safety on 1 February, which added to the already considerable powers wielded by regional chiefs to arrest suspected radicals within their bailiwicks. By the end of March 1858, the total number of radicals – suspected of crimes or not – hauled in reached nearly 2,000. As the mass arrests took place, France's *cabinet noir* was also expanded. This was a system of covert letter-opening that was generally used by the Sûreté for gathering foreign intelligence but, particularly after Orsini's attack, was turned towards the domestic surveillance of republican agitators and politicians critical of Napoleon's rule. Although no secondary plot was found in the intercepted correspondence, there was still plenty of anti-Napoleon sentiment in the letters, the content of which revealed a populace that was aghast at reports of rifle-bearing soldiers kicking down doors across Paris. In some cases, the *cabinet noir* letter-openers produced intelligence that led to the arrest of ordinary citizens who espoused both hostility towards these overzealous measures and vitriol towards Espinasse. In all, over the course of 1858 as many as 400 suspected future terrorists were found guilty of making seditious murmurings and sent to either prison camps in Algeria or Devil's Island in French Guiana – a penal colony for political dissidents which served as something akin to a nineteenth-century Guantanamo Bay.[10]

As a contemporary observer to the Orsini affair noted, it was hard to argue against the idea that 'the government used the terrorist attack of 14 January to apply harsher legislation on the press and to stretch the sinews of repression even more'. As ever in moments when a fine balance was needed between national security and personal freedom, public opinion was divided on the merits of this approach. 'While some, their impressions dominated by the peril that had threatened the emperor and the fear of plots' supported Espinasse's measures, others, 'in great number, believed that the policy of harshness and intimidation would serve no end other than to exasperate spirits, increase anxiety and weaken confidence in the state of things'. Worse than these criticisms, there was even open support expressed for Orsini by certain 'ecstatic' Parisians, who were cheered by the bombing and full of praise for the Italian's 'heroism'.[11]

When even conservative quarters of the press began to stir over the summer of 1858 in response to the police crackdowns, Espinasse was forced to defend his actions to the emperor. He did so with fear and manipulation, warning Napoleon that 'the situation of 1852 and that of 1858 have much more analogy than is supposed'. Shepherded by Orsini's bombs, a new revolutionary epoch was at hand, in which the usurper of the past would lose his throne to the dissidents of the present. Napoleon disliked the bad press that Espinasse's heavy hand had laid at the door of the Tuileries Palace. His memory of the bombing and the fear for his throne, however, led Napoleon to warm to his security chief's rationale. Stifling any debate to the contrary, in June 1858 Napoleon declared in a public speech that further acts of revolutionary terror should be expected in France, given that the Opera House attack was 'merely an episode of an incessantly renewed conspiracy' against his regime.[12]

Public opinion be damned. The repression would continue until the conspiracy was destroyed.

Orsini and Pieri had both gone to the gallows in March, whilst de Rudio and Gomez had been sentenced to rot away on Devil's Island. What, then, was this conspiracy that Napoleon so feared? Born of a toxic blend of chatter from within the Tuileries Palace and Espinasse's warnings, the commonplace assumption was that emulators of Orsini were lying in wait for the emperor, most likely in radical-infested Britain. As one of Napoleon's advisers later recalled, the royal court buzzed with a feeling that 'in London, in certain quarters the assassination of the emperor is openly recommended'. What else could be expected from a nation in which 'murderous revolutionary societies are allowed, under the very eyes of the police, to hold regular meetings, where regicide is proclaimed as a right and even as a duty, and where fanatics are provided with arms, and despatched to Paris with full directions?' As the post-bombing anxiety spread across Paris, this narrative became part of a self-feeding cycle of misinformation, exchanged between regime insiders and anti-republican newspapers. The chauvinist, court-backed *Le Moniteur universel* was the chief outlet for this view. In May 1858, it ran a story claiming that 'France is now enlightened as to the real feelings of England', a place that, having offered safe harbour to 48ers, Marx and Orsini's team of bombers, had become 'a laboratory of assassins', from which further attacks would be imminent.[13]

The British public and press responded to these accusations with outrage and mockery, deriding *Le Moniteur*'s claims and Espinasse's crackdowns as the products of the kind of irrationality and hysteria that was typical on the continent. Accounts of Espinasse's wish to be furnished 'with a list of suspected persons, so that I may deal with them militarily' were published in tones of ridicule, with *The Times* pointing out that 'it is not by alienating every educated citizen and by driving every malcontent to desperation that the emperor can overcome the difficulties which threaten his government and his dynasty'. When reports emerged that Espinasse's dragnet was being cast across the Channel, in the form of Sûreté officers hunting down Orsini's accomplices on the streets of London, the *Liverpool Mercury* described the news as 'a truth full of shame and dishonour for this country'. Countering *Le Moniteur*'s accusations that Britain was wilfully harbouring terrorists, one cheeky journalist pointed out that, in the aftermath of the 1848 revolutions, Napoleon had himself sought sanctuary in London as 'an escaped felon'. The most notable riposte to *Le Moniteur*'s accusations came not from the press but from the courts. When one of Orsini's Britain-based conspirators, Simon Bernard, was put on trial at the Old Bailey, his defence lawyer skilfully transformed proceedings into, as one observer put it, a masterclass in harnessing 'the hereditary spirit of English defiance of foreign dictation'. Referencing *Le Moniteur*'s antagonistic reportage, Bernard's defence sidestepped his client's involvement in an act of terrorism and convinced the jury that Napoleon, backed by the threat of '600,00 French bayonets', was trying to bully Britain into submitting to his will. A guilty verdict would, therefore, be unpatriotic if not traitorous. Bernard was duly acquitted despite the mountain of evidence against him.[14]

Le Moniteur's anti-British bombast aside, for most at the Tuileries Palace, the question of the dangers beyond the Channel were secondary to concerns over radicals who need not cross a body of water to wreak havoc on Paris's streets. The Carbonari was far from the only revolutionary group that detested the emperor of the French. Secret societies of nationalists, socialists and republicans had formed in the wake of both the

Congress of Vienna and the 1848 revolutions, festering in Spain, Greece, Belgium, Switzerland and the Austrian Empire with malicious intentions towards Napoleon and his brother emperors. As Stieber feared and as *Le Moniteur* opined, it seemed logical that these groups were all united in an 'internationalist conspiracy' and, moreover, that Orsini's 'premeditated deed of revolutionary cosmopolitanism' was just the first salvo to be fired in their wider campaign. The paranoid Espinasse promoted this idea. In addition to ordering governors within France to round up radicals, he sent missives advising likewise to police forces in Switzerland, Belgium, Piedmont-Sardinia and other neighbouring countries, where, it was assumed, accomplices of the Rue le Peletier bombers were poised to launch the next phase of a wider murderous plan.[15]

It was amidst this chatter over continental conspiracies and attacks to come that Napoleon made a seemingly bizarre decision – to launch the very war for Italy's freedom that Orsini had tried to engender. To many of his courtiers, this was the temperamental emperor at his erratic and inconsistent worst, bouncing from one panicked thought to the next without a clear plan or strategy. There were even whispers in the halls of the Tuileries Palace that Napoleon had been so rattled by the bombs that his wits had left him. There was, however, a fear-driven calculation to the imperial mood swing. During Orsini's trial, Napoleon had received correspondence from his would-be killer, in which the latter claimed that 'assassination, in whatever garb it may be disguised, does not exist among my principles'. However, so driven by his desire for Italian unity, Orsini had allowed himself 'to be led to the attempt of 14 January' to 'see how your imperial majesty is moved by genuine Italian feelings'. In a final letter, composed on 12 March, the day before he and Pierri were guillotined, Orsini spelled out clearly where these feelings should guide the emperor, and what the consequences would be if Napoleon's courage was found wanting in this respect. 'So long as Italy is not independent', he warned, 'the tranquillity of Europe and that of your majesty will always be vain illusions'. It fell upon Napoleon to ensure this tranquillity. For it was on his will, Orsini claimed, that 'the welfare or the misfortune of my country' depended.[16]

Admirers would later claim that Napoleon was sympathetic to the Carbonari on account of his own barricade storming in 1848 and perhaps even moved by Orsini's words to lend his support to Italy's unification. Given his character, it was more likely that the emperor, conditioned to believe that he was the reincarnation of the great Bonaparte, yet terrified of all that Espinasse had been hissing into his ear, resolved upon a war in Italy as a means of asserting his martial authority and meeting the demands of other radicals who he feared would continue what Orsini had started. As the terms of the alliance Napoleon brokered with the kingdom of Piedmont-Sardinia to join him in fighting Franz Joseph – who, as steward of northern Italy, would be the target of the French invasion – made clear, this need to prevent future terrorist attacks was an important factor in Napoleon's decision for war. The Plombières Agreement, as it became known, stipulated that upon victory over the Austrians the king of Piedmont-Sardinia, Victor Emmanuel, would agree to the territories of Italian Nice and Savoy being granted to France as buffers between Napoleon's lands and the fissile Italian states where the Carbonari held sway. Napoleon also demanded that his ally introduce laws to curtail press freedom and political agitation within Piedmont-Sardinia itself. The goals of Napoleon's war were clear – placate the Orsinis-in-waiting of Italy by freeing their nation from Franz Joseph's yoke and acquire international allies who could help guard France from future terrorist attacks.[17]

This ambitious enterprise unfolded over the summer of 1859, during which a Franco-Sardinian alliance commanding 170,000 soldiers clashed with Franz Joseph's 200,000-strong army, leaving 19,000 corpses on the battlefields of Magenta and Solferino in northern Italy. This death toll included Espinasse, who, having been reassigned to frontline duties, was torn apart by a cannonball whilst leading a cavalry charge. Napoleon may have lost his enforcer, but in the wider struggle both to impose his will and to satisfy the nationalists who threatened his life, he had gained a decisive victory, finishing off the Austrians in the space of a few weeks. With Franz Joseph bested and an armistice concluded, Napoleon's war carriage began trundling its way back through Lombardy to Paris. This opened the way for the nationalist guerrilla Giuseppe Garibaldi – a member of the Carbonari whose revolutionary reputation eclipsed even Orsini's – to continue the fight for the peninsula's future that would lead to Victor Emmanuel being pronounced king of Italy in 1861.[18]

Not only could he boast of having gracefully honoured his would-be killer's political wishes, but the total nature of Napoleon's victory also did much to further his secondary goal of enhancing his domestic popularity and reputation as Europe's strongman. When word of the armistice with the Austrians reached Besançon, 'more than 3,000 people began shouting "long live the emperor" as they pressed excitedly into the inner courtyard of the Préfecture'. In Paris, 'the Champs-Élysées was crowded and bands of young men roamed about the streets arm in arm, shouting and singing and celebrating a great victory', which, as the chest-thumping *Le Moniteur* put it, was Napoleon's alone, for it was he who was always amongst 'the hottest fire' on the battlefield, where 'the dangers that the emperor ran increased still more the enthusiasm and daring of our soldiers'. This view of the emperor as an unconquerable warlord was not confined to Paris's conservative press. Once dismissed by foreign newspapers as a bombastic buffoon, the survivor of Orsini's bombs and the leader of victorious armies was now, according to the *New York Times*, 'the great conjuror of the age', who needed only to have 'fought three battles and had an hour's conversation with vanquished Austria' to turn Europe upside down. Now, so *The Times* reported, 'Lombardy is at once ceded to France, and Italy becomes a confederation under the Honorary Presidency of the Pope. The changes are so swift that the eye is dazzled.'[19]

Those less disposed to find wonder in the emperor's triumphal blood-shed interpreted events in Italy very differently, seeing the war as a product of Napoleon's fear rather than his courage. Whether they were nationalists in Italy, socialists in Britain, or the 48ers who had since scattered across the transatlantic world, the lesson to be taken from the Orsini affair was that terror – induced through a simple act of violence – could bend the will of emperors and shape the future of nations. 'Now', wrote one of the defiant radicals swept up in Espinasse's dragnet, 'we have the teachings of Orsini to guide us'. The sum of these teachings was an alternative to mass uprisings and street battles for those who sought political change through violence. An alternative in which four men, armed with little more than homemade weapons and a sense of righteousness, could imbue themselves with the power to change the world. Transmitted through communications networks that spanned continents and oceans, this vision of revolutionary violence became emulated and feared the world over.[20]

Chapter II

'The Moloch of radicalism'

Public assemblies were not uncommon in Union Square, a nexus of broad avenues and twisting trees in the centre of Manhattan, within which a crowd of hundreds could gather comfortably under the colossal equestrian statue of George Washington that stood at its centre. As shadows cut into dusk across New York on 22 April 1858, however, the square's capacity was tested by a crowd of 3,000 Italian, Polish, Austrian, French, German and Russian immigrants, who assembled under the Founding Father's gaze in a display of what the *Richmond Daily Dispatch* described as a 'most ultra' act of 'red republican celebration'. Commencing as gaslights ignited across the city, the celebration soon morphed into a procession, carried along Fourteenth Street by a stream of marchers holding red flags and homemade banners, on which were scrawled demands for freedom, liberty and an end to tyranny. Few in the 'land of the free' could argue against these sentiments. And yet, for some New Yorkers, something sinister hung over the marchers, many of whom still nursed bitter memories of the bullets and barricades of 1848. What grabbed the attention of both the gawkers who lined the streets and the journalists who trailed the procession with notebooks in hand was the fact that the émigrés had not gathered to brood hopelessly on their failed revolution. Instead, to the shock of many a reporter, these 'red republicans of the most rabid stripe' were celebrating the bombing carried out by Orsini and his team of terrorists, whose names were emblazoned on placards held aloft by scores of black-hatted marchers wearing red armbands. If this deference to would-be regicides were not alarming enough, at the procession's end its leaders clambered onto a platform outside City Hall and denounced Napoleon to the cheering crowd as a 'despot whose tyranny extended over Italy as well as France'. This public show of support for bomb-throwers was not confined to the streets of Manhattan. A week later, another gathering was held in praise of Orsini, in Boston, complete with the requisite Napoleon bashing and eulogies from émigré community leaders, who expressed their 'sympathies and aspirations with the oppressed throughout the world'. Similar gatherings took place in the weeks that followed, in Cincinnati and Chicago, where 48ers from the German communities there came out in force to honour the men whose failure to kill Napoleon had nonetheless shed Parisians' blood on Rue le Peletier.[1]

If, as one British newspaper had it, 'Orsini worship' was a disease, then these gatherings in American cities indicated that the tale of the bomber-martyrs had become a transatlantic vector for a stark message – terrorism was worthy of celebration.[2] This lauding of political violence was particularly dangerous in the United States of 1858, a nation that was an open wound of discontent, ripe for an infection like the 'Orsini disease' to take hold. The sore point was slavery: specifically, the debate between those who supported its continuance and those who believed the practice to be antithetical to the republic's values. The ferocity of this argument had already led to violence throughout the 1850s, particularly in Kansas, where pro- and anti-abolitionist militias had burned businesses, murdered political opponents and started riots. Blood had even been spilled on the sacrosanct floor of the Capitol. In May 1856, the Republican senator Charles Sumner delivered a speech that was half abolitionist plea, half personal attack. The target of this vitriol – a pro-slavery Democrat named Preston Brooks – retaliated by cornering Sumner in the Senate chamber and beating him to within an inch of his life with a cane.[3]

In this fractious environment, pro-slavery advocates could not help but fear that 'Orsini worship' would inspire abolitionists to violence. This fear was not without merit. There were many abolitionists who, despite never experiencing the oppression of the old world, could see its brutal sinews in the fabric of the new. The abolitionist newspaper editor George Lawrence Jnr drew an explicit connection between slavery in the United States and the oppression of the Italians in whose name Orsini had sacrificed himself. Toying with the notion that the same kind of violent martyrdom that had inspired the Italian War of Independence might also trigger a struggle to free the enslaved, Lawrence opined that the abolitionists needed 'men like Orsini who will dare to go through all guards to strike at the oppressor's heart'. Although squeamish about terrorism, the arch-abolitionist William Lloyd Garrison was also moved in the wake of the failed assassin's execution to reflect 'that it was the wholesale murderer Louis Napoleon who deserved to be beheaded, rather than Orsini'. Discounting any nuance in these abolitionists' takes on Orsini and his methods, the *New York Times* dubbed him 'the Moloch of radicalism', whose sacrifice would inspire an unholy alliance of 48ers, American-born abolitionists and 'cosmopolitan sympathizers', all of whom had the potential to become 'utter savages were they not absolute simpletons'. The *New York Herald* – a newspaper whose owner, James Gordon Bennett, was a supporter of slavery, reveller in hyperbole and despiser of radical causes – took this rhetoric a step further, running a piece which declared that though 'the time had not yet come for antislavery philosophers to recommend the adoption of the practice of assassination', the nation would soon 'see a new, antislavery Orsini'.[4]

This was the state of editorial opinion on the nation-harming potential of Orsini's story when, on 16 October 1859, a group of eighteen men armed with rifles and pikes emerged from the forest of auburn-tinged elms that surrounded Harper's Ferry, a town nestled at the confluence of the Potomac and Shenandoah rivers in Virginia. Their target had not been chosen at random. Since the early 1800s, Harper's Ferry had housed a federal arsenal of weapons, gunpowder and ammunition, as well as workshops and munitions stores. It had everything needed to provision a revolution. Having mustered at a farm on the outskirts of Harper's Ferry days earlier, the attackers had cleaned their rifles, gone over their plans and shared in prayers for success, before dividing into small teams so that they could approach the town undetected. When they arrived under cover of darkness, each team set to its pre-assigned task. One team swooped on the town's guards and disarmed them, whilst another rushed to the telegraph station and cut the wires needed to raise the alarm in Washington. Another team of raiders broke open the arsenal proper and took control of its storehouses whilst the rest of their comrades corralled terrified townsfolk into an old engine house at gunpoint. With the ordnance of Harper's Ferry in their hands and hostages in their custody, the attackers settled in for the revolutionary struggle they hoped was about to unfold.

This anticipation was born of the raiders' reasons for descending on Harper's Ferry – to 'frighten Virginia and detach it from the slave interest' and 'to capture the rifles to arm the slaves'. In an echo of Orsini's domino-like strategy whereby a handful of bombs would unleash a spate of emancipatory conflicts across Europe, the attackers believed that by liberating and equipping the enslaved people of Harper's Ferry for war they could alter the course of American history. No fools when it came to the divisiveness of the slavery debate, the raiders realised that news of their attack would make them villains in the eyes of men like James Gordon Bennett and Preston Brooks. However, they reasoned that as the story of their daring raid made its way across Virginia, enslaved people from all over that state and beyond would be inspired to seize the moment, break their chains and compel their masters by force of arms to give up their ways. For it was, as one of the Harper's Ferry raiders later recalled, 'the duty of every Christian man to strike down slavery and to commit its fragments to the flames'.[5]

Behind the raid with its ambitious objective was John Brown, a hollow-eyed, thick-bearded militant who had made a name for himself in the violence that had plagued Kansas for years. After skirmishing against enslavers there to no demonstrable end, Brown resolved upon the Harper's Ferry raid as a spectacular gesture that would bring the slavery debate to a combative and absolute conclusion. In addition to his stated wish to 'secure firearms to arm the slaves and strike terror into the hearts of the slaveholders', Brown, much like Orsini, believed that this one act of violence would inspire the oppressed to claim their freedom. The scale of Brown's dream was matched by his reputation for zealotry and fierce personal charisma, which led those who joined his raid to believe unblinkingly in the righteousness of both their leader and his cause. Possessed of a near-millenarian sense of wonder, one of Brown's raiders later claimed that 'there is an unbroken chain of sentiment and purpose from Moses and the Jews to John Brown of America'. Unlike in the story of Exodus, however, many of the enlaved people at Harper's Ferry were unwilling to be set free. As the euphoria of their initial success faded, the raiders realised that those they came to liberate were generally dismissive or even openly hostile to them, refusing to commit to what seemed a doomed and dangerous gambit. This judgement proved prudent when, a day after seizing the arsenal, Brown and his men were surrounded by a pro-slavery militia and a detachment of marines under the command of the future Confederate leader Robert E. Lee. In the ensuing battle seventeen people were killed – ten raiders, a marine and several townsfolk, including some of those the attackers wished to liberate – whilst Brown himself was taken alive after being struck across the temple with a sabre.[6]

This attack by a politically aggrieved citizen and his followers on a federal arsenal was received by the press and the public as something akin to a nineteenth-century 9/11, stoking a sense of shock across a nation that was stunned by the audacity of Brown's raid, yet compelled by its drama to debate his reasons for launching it.[7] Lee was blunt in his assessment. The attack was the product of 'a conspiracy and effort at insurrection and plunder', which had been perpetrated by a 'fanatical man, stimulated to recklessness and desperation by the constant teachings and intemperate appeals of wild and treasonable enthusiasts'. Pro-slavery newspapers were similarly contemptuous, with most dismissing Brown as a lunatic or a charlatan, and one describing him as a 'Kansas desperado, who for a long-time past has led a roving and plundering life at the head of some banditti'. The *Western Democrat*, however, put its finger on the fear-inducing method beneath Brown's madness. Brown was possessed of a 'terroristic mind' and guided into 'a conspiracy whose treasonable designs are not simply the secession of a few thinly settled states, but which aim to involve the whole Union in one brutal and bloody conflict' – an outcome not unlike that which had erupted months earlier in Italy. This talk of Brown's madness and comparison of his aims to Orsini's was not confined to those who resented the anti-slavery raider's cause. In an address delivered three months after Brown was hanged on 2 December 1859, the future president Abraham Lincoln described the attack on Harper's Ferry as the sad outcome of what happens when 'an enthusiast broods over the oppression of a people till he fancies himself commissioned by Heaven to liberate them. He ventures the attempt, which ends in little else than his own execution. Orsini's attempt on Louis Napoleon and John Brown's attempt at Harper's Ferry were, in their philosophy, precisely the same'.[8]

Lincoln had a point. Although Brown had studied a range of insurrectionary campaigns – from Spartacus' revolt against Rome to the guerrilla warfare waged by the jihadist Imam Shamil against the Russian Empire during the 1840s and 1850s – he had a particular interest in the struggle for Italian independence. So enamoured was Brown of the exploits of the Carbonari, he employed a British 'self-confessed conspirator and mercenary' who had served under Garibaldi as an instructor for his raiders. Brown also confided his thoughts on Harper's Ferry to the famous abolitionist and social reformer Frederick Douglass, who would probably have told the aspirant militant of Orsini's like-minded scheme to use a spectacular act of violence to engender a wider struggle. The outcome of Orsini's strategy could have also been easily read about by Brown in any number of American newspapers that covered both the Opera House bombing and its aftermath. In the wake of Harper's Ferry, these same newspapers offered little doubt that Brown's attack was a symptom of the 'Orsini disease'. Profiling one of Brown's accomplices, Francis J. Merriam, the *Chicago Tribune* spoke of how he was 'imbued with the ideas of the modern French reformers' and how 'the career of Orsini had evidentially impressed him' and his comrades. Whilst the *Tribune*'s treatment of Orsini's influence was somewhat mournful regarding the arrival of European terrorism on American shores, the ever-provocative *New York Herald* met this idea with a taunting challenge to the abolitionists who defended Brown, asking its readers ahead of his execution, if 'our red republicans will lend them the funeral paraphernalia that they used to commemorate that other crazy champion of "human freedom", Orsini'.[9]

With his customary eloquence, the philosopher, naturalist and gentleman proponent of civil disobedience Henry David Thoreau brought these debates over Brown's motivations and influences together in his 'A plea for Captain John Brown' – a vain attempt to secure a pardon for the doomed man, which initially took the form of a lecture that Thoreau delivered in the weeks leading up to Brown's execution. Taking aim at the likes of Lee, Lincoln and the *Herald*, Thoreau bemoaned the 'cold-blooded way in which newspaper writers and men generally speak of this event' without once uttering 'a single expression of sympathy for these men' and their aims. He even criticised William Lloyd Garrison, who had praised Orsini yet denounced Brown as the fool perpetrator of 'a misguided, wild and apparently insane effort' to free the enslaved. Rejecting the insanity argument, Thoreau argued that Brown was neither unsound of mind nor the 'ordinary malefactor' that dismissive journalists claimed he was. Rather, following the very best of Orsini's example, Brown understood that the United States 'government is effactually allied with France and Austria in oppressing humankind'. His crafting of a unique plot to terrorise enslavers and incite an uprising deserved not ridicule but praise, for such a plan illustrated Brown's inherent grasp of both human dignity and the principles of freedom that were worth fighting and dying for.[10]

Others with a greater interest in the terroristic aspects of Brown's strategy found much to applaud in this apparent connection between the bombers of Rue le Peletier and the emancipatory raiders of Harper's Ferry. Having delivered *Murder and Liberty* to the world in 1853, the terrorism advocate Karl Heinzen had quit Europe to get away from the watchful eyes of Stieber and his like, settling in Kentucky. There, he founded a newspaper aimed at other German émigrés, *Der Pionier*, in which Heinzen ran articles covering everything from socialism to the abolition of slavery, to the promotion of women's suffrage – the more progressively provocative the arguments, the better. Through his work calling out the corruption of politicians, the greed of industrialists and the inequalities of the world, Heinzen carved out a reputation amongst the German diaspora's most radical fringe as an 'entirely trustworthy' journalist, unafraid to speak hard truths and respected even by papers such as the *Minnesota Staats-Zeitung*, whose reporters Heinzen attacked for their lack of integrity. To the minds of others who failed to see the 'political honesty and loyalty to principle' of the straight-talking Heinzen, he was the archetype of the 'dangerous foreigner'. The *New York Herald* described him as a 'rabid red republican, who has long disgusted the sensible portion of the German people by his fierce tirades'. These tirades included calls for 'partisans of liberty, of justice, of truth, of humanity' to 'let our study be murder, murder in all its forms'. He had also coined a phrase that was applied to Brown at the time and, like so many of Heinzen's teachings, has endured in the descriptions and self-conceptions of terrorists into the present day – *freiheitskämpfer*: freedom fighter.[11]

Orsini and Brown were promoted as such by Heinzen, who regarded the pair as belonging to the 'enlightened' segment of humankind, who understood that injustice could be destroyed only through violence. No fan of Napoleon – whom he referred to as simply as 'The Bandit' – Heinzen ran articles praising Orsini's bombing, in addition to re-issuing extracts of *Murder and Liberty* in 1858 as part of the American radicals' festival of Orsini commemoration. Amidst the national hue and cry over Harper's Ferry, Heinzen extolled the virtues of Brown in much the same way as he had Orsini, applauding the raider's efforts in *Der Pionier* and needling pro-slavery journalists such that abolitionists would later describe Heinzen as 'the bravest, truest and freest German in America and the civilized world'. Although even the champion of terrorist murder could not defend Brown's raid on a tactical level, Heinzen nonetheless cheered the spirit of the deed. Moreover, like a nineteenth-century version of an internet troll, Heinzen aped Orsini by warning his readers that the death of Brown was just the beginning. 'Hang him if you dare', Heinzen wrote a month before the authorities did just that, for 'the Mason–Dixon line no longer divides the nation. A gallows now separates North from South'. These words amounted to nothing less than Heinzen pleading with his readers to ignore Thoreau's heartfelt panegyric and Lincoln's efforts to depict Brown as a madman. Instead, Heinzen highlighted the terrorist instincts worthy of praise in Brown, presenting him as both an adherent to the message of *Murder and Liberty* and the revolutionary successor to the lauded Orsini.[12]

Testament to Orsini's influence beyond 48ers and abolitionists, Americans who would have likely spat in the faces of Thoreau and Heinzen also took inspiration from his attack. The actor and future murderer of Lincoln, John Wilkes Booth, expressed his admiration for Orsini's assassination attempt to a gathering of fellow defenders of slavery in 1858 – albeit with the boast that, had the bomb been in his hand outside the Opera House, the job would have been done properly. Others, like an Italian immigrant in Baltimore named Cipriano Ferrandini, seemed to have taken their admiration of Orsini beyond the realms of the hypothetical. In early 1861, the violently anti-Lincoln views held by Ferrandini and other pro-slavery members of a secret society in Baltimore caught the attention of a spy in the employ of Allan Pinkerton, a friend of Brown's who had become Lincoln's private security consultant after the latter's electoral victory in November 1860. The head of the burgeoning Pinkerton Detective Agency lived for such whispers of conspiracy. As a young man in 1830s Glasgow, Pinkerton had become an adherent to Chartism – a radical working-class movement that aimed to extend the voting franchise in Britain. Having emigrated to the United States in 1842, Pinkerton established a new career as a private detective in his adopted home of Chicago and became a passionate supporter of the abolitionist cause. Indeed, rumours abounded in the aftermath of Harper's Ferry that Pinkerton was planning to use heavies from his agency to bust Brown out of jail. Immersed in the same secret world that Stieber occupied, in the wake of Brown's execution Pinkerton grew ever more paranoid about the intentions of the anti-abolitionist movement. He was, therefore, receptive to his spy's report and ordered a full investigation into Ferrandini and his followers.[13]

Using his Louisiana accent to ingratiate himself with the mostly southern attendees, Pinkerton's man infiltrated an anti-abolitionist meeting chaired by Ferrandini at Barnum's Hotel in Baltimore on the evening of 8 February 1861. He arrived just in time to hear Ferrandini raise his voice above the clatter and noise, instantly killing the cacophony of Lincoln-hate that had rumbled through the meeting up until then. Ferrandini's reputation guaranteed this attention and silence. Despite occupying the lowly position of Barnum's in-house barber, he was a former soldier, who was known as both 'enthusiastic and fanatic' in his loathing of abolitionists and respected by all present as a 'military captain whose orders were to be obeyed'. Ferrandini knew this, and so clambered atop a table and delivered 'an address which, for its treasonable nature and its violent opposition to all laws, human and divine', the spy reported to Pinkerton, 'has scarcely a parallel'. The source of the spy's horror was the conclusion of Ferrandini's speech, wherein he revealed a plan to assassinate Lincoln when his train stopped at Calvert Street Station in Baltimore, en route to the inauguration ceremony in Washington.

As Ferrandini unwittingly explained to Pinkerton's spy, pro-slavery officers from the Baltimore police department were in on the plot, having agreed to create a distraction at the rear of the platform when the train pulled in. This would allow a shooter to get close enough to end Lincoln's life and, with it, the fear of his new administration outlawing slavery. Having pronounced this murderous intent with 'eyes glistening in the fires of hate', Ferrandini drew a dagger from his belt, which he raised aloft whilst declaring to riotous applause that 'this hireling Lincoln shall never, never be president. My life is of no consequence in a cause like this, and I am ready to give it for his. As Orsini gave his life for Italy, I am ready to die for the rights of the South, and to crush out the abolitionist!'[14] In an adaptation of Orsini's plan to liberate the people of Italy by killing Napoleon, Ferrandini believed that by eliminating Lincoln, he would end the prospect of America sliding into an era of emancipation for the enslaved.

To Pinkerton's frustration, Lincoln dismissed the spy's report. As the man tasked with healing the wounds of a nation that had yet to recover from the division and shock of Harper's Ferry, he was mindful that news of the president-elect having to sneak through Baltimore like a thief in the night would only emphasise to the American public how politically fissile their nation was. Pinkerton despaired at this reaction and, in the days that followed, filed further reports on secret pro-slavery groups that were plotting to end Lincoln's life. Beaten down by this barrage of unnerving intelligence, the president-elect finally agreed to change his train schedule and allow Pinkerton to position men along the route, their eyes peeled for anyone suspicious who might be lurking near the tracks. At the end of the operation, Lincoln arrived safely at his inauguration, allegedly clad in a humiliatingly unconvincing getup of soft flat hat and overcoat, which fell well short of the intent to disguise his distinctively tall, lanky frame. Once the story of these unconventional security measures got out, much of the press derided the precautions as foolhardy, with one newspaper claiming that Pinkerton's tale 'of a conspiracy to assassinate the president elect is all gammon and moonshine', much to Lincoln's chagrin.[15]

Pinkerton's operation may have been over the top, but the fallout of the so-called Baltimore plot showed that he was right to be concerned for Lincoln's life. When interviewed by a special committee convened in February 1861 to investigate the rise of political violence across the United States, Ferrandini confessed proudly that he represented a secret society of pro-slavery militiamen who had taken inspiration from the Carbonari. This clandestine group, moreover, was 'formerly a political organization' but, since Harper's Ferry, its members had become more organised and radicalised, arming themselves in anticipation of an inevitable war over the future of slavery. It is small wonder that the committee ended up posing such pointed questions to other interviewees as 'Do you know of the existence of any secret or open organization here that has for its object any violent interference with the operations of the government?' The report somehow concluded that the various pro-slavery militias and secret societies posed no imminent threat to the Union or Lincoln. However, the fact remained that an anti-abolitionist, inspired by Orsini and operating in a climate of fear in which political violence was fast becoming normalised, had openly admitted to plotting against the government and, less openly, to Pinkerton's spy, of embracing terrorist tactics to effect political change.[16]

Both Brown's raid and Ferrandini's conspiracy showed the conceptual influence Orsini's attack had on radicals – irrespective of their ideology. Moreover, even if the Baltimore plot was nothing more than the product of a paranoid spook taking a boastful firebrand at his word, the reference to Orsini in Ferrandini's speech reveals the association the bomber now had with grand acts of political violence. Beyond providing proof for the concept that terrorism could alter the trajectory of nations, there was also much awe reserved on both sides of the Atlantic for the weapon of terror that Orsini had introduced to the world. Much like his martyrdom and the war he had posthumously unleashed, interest in Orsini's bomb transcended borders and ideologies. This reputation for the Italian's grenade was made possible by global newspaper coverage of the Opera House bombing, which often included detailed dissections of the weapon's design and its components.[17]

The results of this dangerous information being disseminated worldwide were predictable. In November 1858, a Romanian governor was attacked by an unknown assailant, who used a 'fulminating bomb' packed with glass that exploded on impact in a manner not unlike Orsini's weapon. A year later, when the war broke out in Italy, Garibaldi's men stocked up on Orsini bombs, producing caches that were used in urban guerrilla fighting. The same occurred in 1863 when Polish insurgents against Russian rule developed their own version of the Italian's infernal machine. This led to an attack in which Orsini bombs were thrown from a second-floor window at the Russian viceroy of Poland as his carriage was being driven through a suburb of Warsaw. The bomb's reputation as a must-have for any radical worth their salt, and its usefulness as a tool for targeted killing, was not lost on journalists who covered the attempt on the viceroy's life. Indeed, the reporters only enhanced the bomb's image as a terrorist superweapon by noting how the shrapnel from its ignition could cut through 'the usual number of Cossacks' who guarded the viceroy's carriage, making the chances of the resulting storm of fire and metal reaching a VIP target that much greater.[18]

It was not just radicals and the press who were fascinated by what a war correspondent in Italy dubbed Orsini's 'murderous missiles'.

In the 1860s, rumours that an 'Orsini shell' was being considered by several naval chiefs as a new form of ordnance were reported in British and French newspapers. During the American Civil War that Heinzen accurately predicted would be Brown's legacy, Orsini bombs and variants, such as that patented in 1862 as the Excelsior Grenade by the Kentuckian W. W. Hanes, were used by irregular fighters on both sides. Amongst these irregulars were Irish volunteers, many of whom were militant republicans resolved to free their homeland from British rule through violence. After the war, these same veterans passed their knowledge of the bomb's potential to the so-called Scientific Department of the Irish Republican Brotherhood (IRB) in London, within the basement of which 'hand grenades and Orsini shells were manufactured by the score' in anticipation of being used in a multi-target attack on government buildings and police barracks. It was not for nothing that the Irish republican newspaper the *Freeman's Journal* came to describe hit-and-fade guerrilla attacks, terrorism and assassination as aspects of an 'Orsini mode of warfare'.[19]

The weapon's reputation not only popularised the concept of 'Orsini warfare' amongst radicals, but it also influenced media narratives that emphasised an implicit connection between acts of political violence and the presence of Orsini's bomb. When news of Ferrandini's assassination plot seeped into the newspapers, it was assumed by the journalists who had covered the Opera House bombing that the plan would involve 'an infernal machine' being 'placed under the cars or railway, like the Orsini attempt'. Even after Pinkerton supposedly foiled the Baltimore plot, rumours persisted that 'ten thousand hand grenades, similar to the Orsini Bombs' had been manufactured by other anti-abolitionist militias in Maryland. Furnished with such weapons, it was feared that these insurgents would launch 'one of the most diabolical and desperate attempts to precipitate the country into revolution that has been attempted since the attack by Orsini upon Louis Napoleon'. The usefulness of Orsini's weapon was also not lost on Brown and his men. During the planning stages for their assault on Harper's Ferry, some of the raiders discussed whether 'Orsini bombs, which can be made in N.Y., would be effective in so frightening a soldier's chivalry that our object could be accomplished during the panic' that would ensue once they descended on the town.[20]

Whether it was the idea of forcing political change through a single act of terrorism, or the range of attack possibilities his bomb proffered, Orsini cast an influential shadow over the minds of violent radicals during the 1860s. In the United States, his ideological connection to the 48ers and others who saw themselves as 'freedom fighters' – either in favour of or against slavery – provided fertile ground for this legacy to grow. Testament to the universality of the 'Orsini disease', the lesson of the Italian's sacrifice and the importance of his easy-to-detonate grenade were also recognised thousands of miles away from Brown's ambitions and Ferrandini's fury, in a place where radicals dared to dream that the death of a tsar might lead to the renewal of their long-ailing nation.

Chapter III

For those in Hell

A week after John Wilkes Booth made good on his promise to surpass Orsini in the field of assassination, 4,000 miles away from Ford's Theatre, a university student named Ivan Khudyakov was arriving at Cornavin train station in Geneva, possessed of little more than a handful of pennies and the filthy rags on his back. It had been a long journey for the nineteen-year-old, whose lack of material preparedness contrasted starkly with the importance of his mission – to acquire weapons and find allies who could hasten a revolution in Russia. It was a mission Khudyakov had been waiting much of his short life to complete. In 1860, he had enrolled at the University of Kazan, a seat of culture and learning surrounded by a city that was steadily being engulfed by the pervasive grey of Russia's nascent industrial revolution. Day after day, the impressionable Khudyakov watched from his dorm window as streams of peasants, who for generations had worked the fields through which the nearby Volga River flowed, shambled into Kazan's factories, from which belched fire, smoke and discontent, the last fuelled by long hours and dangerous working conditions.

Khudyakov's miserable impression of Russia's new industrial class was exacerbated by his loathing for the university, which he believed was controlled by a 'police organisation', specifically the 'soldiers, sub-inspectors and inspectors' who roamed the lecture theatres and dormitory halls, reporting any murmurs of radical thought to the Russian secret police – the Third Section. Although created in the 1820s in response to an attempted uprising by liberal-minded soldiers, the Third Section was the product of a centuries-old culture of autocratic control in Russia, exercised by generations of tsars over not only the peasants but, to Khudyakov's chagrin, even students who were trying to move up in the world. Frustrated by this, he transferred his studies to St Petersburg, only to discover that police snooping was just as common in the student halls and taverns of Russia's capital. Having finally abandoned his studies in protest, Khudyakov became angry and listless, wandering the city's wide cobblestoned boulevards for hours and taking in the baroque grandeur of the Winter Palace, from behind the walls of which generations of tsars had ruled absolute over millions. He reflected on his odyssey from the countryside to the metropole, feeling little but fury at the inequality and repression he had seen, and a sense of hopelessness that Russia would never move on from this state of being.

And then, in February 1861, everything looked set to change when Tsar Alexander II issued the Emancipation Manifesto. This was a bold political gambit on the part of the autocrat to drag Russia into a long overdue era of reform, prompted by years of agitation from writers, thinkers and liberal-minded politicians, many of whom bristled at how Russia's defeat in the Crimean War revealed its backwardness in comparison to other European states. The central plank of the manifesto was the tsar's call for the empire's countless peasants to be released from bondage, allowing them to own land and start businesses. Encouraging as this step seemed to reformers, by the middle of the 1860s the tsar's critics – young dissidents like Khudyakov among them – had concluded that the Emancipation Manifesto had not gone far enough to address centuries of deeply ingrained inequality. What good, thought Khudyakov, was giving peasants a crumb of freedom in a land where the gap between the downtrodden and the privileged remained an unbridgeable chasm – a land where millions still bent their knee in supplication to a man who believed himself ordained by the Almighty? What good had the reforms that accompanied the Emancipation Manifesto done for university students who still lived with the Third Section peering over their shoulders, taking notes on all they said and did? What good had the tsar's policies done for the workers of Kazan, who continued their moribund daily trudge through muddied fields into the maw of the city's poisoned factories?[1]

It was with a mind to answer these questions in the most extreme way that Khudyakov found himself in April 1865, standing in the rain on the shores of Lake Geneva, dishevelled and down to the last of his funds, yet determined to contact a group known as the European Revolutionary Committee. He believed that this was a secret union of socialists, republicans, nationalists, 48ers and other insurrectionists who, in the years since Orsini's bombing, had come together in Switzerland – a country that, like Britain, was wanting in both strict immigration and deportation laws and so played host to a number of émigrés. Perfect home though it might have been for this clandestine coalition, Switzerland did not in fact house the European Revolutionary Committee. This was because no such organisation existed. The committee was a myth born of Khudyakov's misunderstanding of the nature of Europe's secret societies, many of which had formed and fizzled out since 1848, and had been little more than a handful of dissidents and a printing press. If chasing an illusion was not bad enough, Khudyakov grew more dejected when he realised the non-existence of the European Revolutionary Committee disrupted his second purpose in Geneva. This was to obtain from the ghost army of radicals the blueprints for the infamous Orsini bomb.[2]

The attack by Polish nationalists on the tsar's viceroy in Warsaw two years earlier had demonstrated the bomb's importance to Russia's radicals, many of whom were poor and lacked resources yet were resolved to wage Orsini warfare against the tsarist regime. The man who despatched Khudyakov to Geneva – Nikolai Ishutin – was one such radical. An educated but unstable man who had failed to hold down various teaching jobs, Ishutin was bereft of any material means to combat the all-powerful tsar whom he had come to despise. And yet, the ideology to which Ishutin subscribed necessitated a reckoning with the Russian state, for Ishutin was a nihilist, of a new and violent sort. The creed of nihilism had existed in Russia since the 1840s and its adherents represented a broad church of radical interests, most of which focused on scrutinising long-accepted cultural norms and systems of power in Russia. Initially conceived of as an intellectual exercise by philosophers and academics who challenged the church, the state and other pillars of Russian society, nihilism had developed into something more violent and terroristic as the years rolled on without change, particularly after the Emancipation Manifesto turned out to be a false dawn for reform. The zealotry of the most aggrieved nihilists was intensified by their regular consumption of radical magazines like *Kolokol* which spoke openly of how 'the tsar has cheated the people'. By the mid-1860s, nihilism had become the lodestar for Russians who were tired of empty talk and instead demanded action to alter the state of their nation.[3]

Beholden to this violent strain of nihilism and intoxicated by the whiff of martyrdom that blew from the bloodstained streets of Warsaw, Ishutin dallied in revolutionary fantasies that exceeded Brown's in their ambition, and matched Heinzen's for their psychopathy. Open combat with soldiers and police had been the Poles' undoing in 1863. Of that Ishutin was certain. But what if another approach could be adopted, one that would shock the Russian state into submission by striking fear into the denizens of the Winter Palace? In search of inspiration for this strategy, Ishutin had not only Orsini's bomb-throwing example to draw on, but also the story of Brown's raid, the details of which were published in Russian newspapers and seized on with interest by nihilists, who could not help but draw parallels between the plight of America's enslaved and that of Russia's peasants. It was perhaps in emulation of Brown's example that, even before he resolved upon the need for Orsini's bomb, Ishutin gathered around him a band of followers who were radicalised both by the stagnant state of Russia and by their leader's promise that they alone could 'bring about a social revolution'.

It was in their leader's grand promises and the aim to violently alter their nation's destiny that the similarities between Ishutin's followers and Brown's raiders ended. Unlike the latter, Ishutin's nihilists knew that seizing an arsenal or attacking a government building would do little to change the state of Russia, where the Third Section prowled and the masses were held in thrall to an autocrat. Instead, something more shocking – the murder of the god-ordained tsar and the terrorising of his courtiers – was needed to shake Russia into revolution. In pursuit of this ambitious goal, however, Ishutin faced a problem that Brown had never had. The Harper's Ferry raiders had included embittered fugitives of slavery and hardened veterans of the fighting in Kansas. As Khudyakov recalled with a bizarre fondness, Ishutin's followers were mostly young students 'who had given up all the joys of life to dedicate themselves to freeing the people', despite having no skills or experience to further this end. What they lacked in knowledge of weapons and tactics, Ishutin's followers more than made up for in daydreams of murderous plots and dramatic bank robberies, which their leader ruthlessly exploited. Ishutin had read the histories of the French and American revolutions and the forlorn fighters of 1848. He yearned to carve his name into that revolutionary canon. As such, he played into the fantasies of the student nihilists who gathered around him by talking up how they would become 'the core of a vast conspiracy' that would use the kind of terrorist tactics practised by Orsini and Brown to destroy the pillars of the Russian state. It was in pursuit of this pipe dream that Khudyakov had embarked on his fool's errand to Switzerland.[4]

In keeping with Ishutin's fantastic ambitions, one of his first orders of business was to 'brand' his followers, to which end he sent a message to both Russian enemies and potential allies in Europe that they were a legitimate force to be reckoned with, and he gave his nihilist assembly a name – The Organisation. Bleakly imposing as this sounded, The Organisation was far from organised. Constantly short of money, Ishutin's followers spent more time engaged in petty theft than planning a grand terrorist offensive against the Russian state. As was their leader's will, the nihilists also focused on a twisted form of 'personal development', creating ascetic lifestyles in which they wore rags, ate little but crumbs and divorced themselves from friends, family and anything remotely joyful. These dictums of revolutionary existence were, like Ishutin's love of the Orsini bomb, inspired by a visionary other than himself. The form of self-depriving nihilism Ishutin preached to his followers had been lifted from the pages of *What Is To Be Done?*, a novel penned in 1863 by the radical writer Nikolai Chernyshevsky in which favourable allusions were made to Brown as a figure whom revolutionaries should emulate, amongst passages that depicted nihilists living communally and sleeping on beds of nails in defiance of luxury and decadence. Successfully cosplaying this fiction and blinded by their hatred of the tsar, few of Ishutin's followers recognised that they had stumbled into something that was less a professional band of freedom fighters and more one man's ugly death cult. Indeed, so dementedly loyal to the cause was one member of The Organisation, he offered to poison his father so he could gain an inheritance to fund the attacks that Ishutin claimed to be planning. This dedication was matched by other adherents, who pledged to Ishutin that if they were caught by the Third Section they would consume cyanide and, if time allowed, disfigure their faces with vials of prussic acid. In recognition of their fanaticism, Ishutin appointed these extremists within The Organisation to an unnecessary sub-group of devotees, upon whom he bestowed one of the most unsubtle names for a terrorist faction ever conceived – Hell.[5]

Despite the zealous, self-destructive character of Hell – whose total membership was probably no higher than twenty – a yawning gap existed between Ishutin's dreams and the sad reality of what his adherents were achieving. There were no firm plans to bomb the Winter Palace or murder tsarist officials, let alone draw revolutionaries from beyond Russia's borders into Hell's struggle. Still, the fictions Ishutin peddled were seductive enough to convince one of his disciples to take the initiative and bring a dose of harsh reality crashing into the nihilist's world of make-believe. As the other members of Hell sat in their black rags and talked of a revolution that would never come, Ishutin's cousin, Dmitry Karakozov, acquired a pistol with a mind to spill royal blood. Like Khudyakov, Karakozov was a university dropout who was already suffering from alcoholism and suicidal thoughts when he gravitated into Ishutin's phantasmic orbit. It is unclear if Karakozov was an actual member of Hell, or simply a troubled rogue who took on board some of his cousin's ideas. Further muddying the waters on this issue is the fact that Ishutin later testified to the police – most likely to try to save his own skin – that Karakozov was 'never a member of the circle of Hell because Hell itself did not exist', it being the product of 'nothing more than foolish talk under the influence of alcohol'.

Ishutin's claims aside, Karakozov likely never bothered to join Hell because he was already dwelling in an underworld of his own design. Sickly, depressed and convinced that things would never get better, on the morning of 4 April 1866, Karakozov positioned himself outside the gate to the Summer Garden in St Petersburg, leaning on a granite pillar with his black eyes darting to and fro. Deprived of the Orsini bomb by Khudyakov's failure in Geneva, Karakozov was left to fiddle with the double-barrelled pistol in his coat pocket, steadying his frayed nerves whilst contemplating the effectiveness of his aim. Soon, his target, Tsar Alexander II, appeared, flanked by royal guards. Neither the noble visage of the autocrat nor the threat of the Cossacks at his side could deter Karakozov, who, taking a deep breath, strode purposefully across the flagstones, took aim at his reviled oppressor and discharged his weapon. It took less than a second for this defining act of Karakozov's life to be stolen away. As his finger met the trigger, the would-be assassin's elbow was knocked away by a passerby, sending the bullet into the pavement. Snapped out of his suicidal funk by the drama of the moment, Karakozov shunned the cyanide pill in his pocket and tried to run, only to be knocked to the ground and seized by the Cossacks.[6]

The dragnet that followed was severe. Thirty-five nihilists from St Petersburg and Moscow, including Ishutin and other members of The Organisation and Hell, were collared and thrown into jail. At Karakozov's trial, his 'excessively sickly mental state' was emphasised by the defence as part of a call for clemency that fell on deaf ears, the prosecutor convincingly arguing that his purchase of a pistol and acquisition of a cyanide pill proved premeditation. Karakozov was duly found guilty not only of attempted regicide but also of 'having been affiliated with a secret revolutionary society', on which basis further trials for the members of Hell and The Organisation were convened. The failed assassin's ordeal ended on 3 September 1866, when he was publicly hanged before legions of sabre-rattling Cossacks and cheering onlookers, many of whom jeered as he kissed the cross around his neck in a final attempt at contrition. Having sniffed the odour of sad absurd-ity that hung around Ishutin, the authorities toyed with the wannabe revolutionary rather than execute him outright. After interrogation and sentencing, Ishutin's neck was laced with a slipknot and he was led up the scaffold, his fear reaching a fever pitch before the guards halted his death march and a judge appeared to commute his sentence to life in exile. Sent to a work camp in Siberia with the noose he feared still around his neck, Ishutin grew more manic as the years passed, eventually dying a quivering wretch in 1879, three years after Khudyakov perished in similar circumstances.[7]

Rather than dismiss the botched assassination attempt as the action of a mentally ill loner driven by a narcissistic fantasist and his naïve friends, the Third Section snapped to attention at the prospect that they had a Russian Orsini on their hands, and with it the promise of a plot that stretched beyond Ishutin's little circle of Hell. The paranoid mood in St Petersburg fed this fear. In 1862, the capital's streets had been gutted by fires that appeared to have been deliberately lit by dissident students in thrall to a revolutionary tract entitled *Young Russia*. This widely dissemi-nated book urged its readers 'to unfurl the great banner of the future. The red banner', to 'strike the imperial party without sparing our blows' and to unleash 'a bloody and pitiless revolution', in which 'rivers of blood will flow and perhaps, innocent victims will perish'. In response, Tsar Alexander ordered the arrest and imprisonment of *Young Russia*'s author, a nineteen-year-old nihilist who, through words alone, had taught an emperor to know fear.

By 1865, St Petersburg's blackened and scarred buildings had been repaired and the Polish uprising that had erupted a year after the fires had been suppressed. And yet, as Karakozov's attack and Ishutin's machinations demonstrated, the terrorist contagion afflicting Russia had not been contained. The fear nursed by the Third Section and the tsar was that the same radicals who had set St Petersburg alight might take inspiration from Karakozov's sacrifice and carry out further attacks. Crowning this idea that a nation of enemies lay beyond the gates of the Winter Palace was the discovery of a document that Karakozov had authored and handed out to a stranger prior to setting off with pistol in pocket to the Summer Garden. Entitled 'To My Worker Friends', the brief and desperate passages of this tract conveyed how 'saddened and burdened' Karakozov was, both with the state of his life and with his homeland, and how he was certain that 'there will be people who will take my path. If I do not succeed, they will. My death will be an example for them and inspire them.'[8]

Faced with a declaration that echoed Orsini's warning to Napoleon, Alexander reacted in a manner not unlike his fellow emperor. In this case, of course, it was not Britain that was labelled the source of the terrorist menace to a throne, but rather Poland, where the tsar's soldiers had carried out brutal repressions during the uprising in which the Orsini bomb had made its Russian debut. The assumption held by the tsar, his military advisers and the Third Section was that Karakozov was an agent of nationalist revenge who had been working with dissident Poles. To extract this by way of confession, Karakozov was 'interrogated all day and not given recreation', under the supervision of a general whom Khudyakov bitterly described as a 'descendant of Genghis Khan'. Whilst details of the methods deployed by Karakozov's ruthless interrogator remain obscure, their effectiveness cannot be disputed. Within a day, the would-be assassin broke down and confessed all he knew. Frustratingly for the tsar's men, Karakozov's testimony included a firm rejection of the idea that he was working with the Poles or, indeed, with anyone else. His interrogator remained unconvinced. Without a network of informers such as that possessed by the Polish underground, how could Karakozov have known the tsar's movements that day? How did he gain access to a gun? What of the provocations and allusions to other enemies of the tsar contained in 'To My Worker Friends'? What, indeed, of Ishutin's claims that Hell and The Organisation had ties to other terrorist groups in Europe?[9]

At the trial of the members of Hell, confessions seemingly provided some of the answers to these burning questions. His brain having been washed by Ishutin's fantasies, one of the latter's disciples testified that Hell and The Organisation had been 'formed with the aim to launch an economic revolution in the state'. To this end, Hell members had been tasked by Ishutin with 'staying in Moscow and getting acquainted with the Poles and forming relations with other societies'. As the tentacles of this terrorist network of Polish nationalists and nihilists spread, so the defendant went on, Hell established further contacts with 'the Europe Committee, whose purpose was the revolution', whilst Khudyakov worked on 'acquiring Orsini bombs to initiate the revolution and carry out regicide'. This confession, combined with circumstantial evidence of Hell members possessing copies of *Young Russia* and *What Is To Be Done?* gave the Third Section all it needed to unleash a torrent of what Khudyakov accurately described as 'patriotic rage' against all forms of anti-tsarist dissent.

Trial transcripts that presented Ishutin's delusions as fact were widely reported in court-backed newspapers, whose writers warmed to the theme by questioning how it had 'been possible that in Russia, in our midst – nay, before our very eyes – a secret society could have been founded and have existed for several years for the express purpose of murdering the Czar and subverting the established order of things?' Bereft of a clear explanation, aim was taken at the tsar's supposedly loyal subjects, and questions asked about whether the sacred bond between the sovereign and the Russian people was being catastrophically under-mined by nihilist teachings and 'socialistic propaganda' imported into the motherland from Europe. This diffusion of reformist ideas had given 'vicious and perverted minds' like those in the heads of Karakozov and Ishutin the impetus to plot with menace. As such, the only way to address the terrorist threat was to identify and nullify Russia citizens who were politically unreliable.[10]

This was the conclusion drawn by Peter Shuvalov, a Crimean War veteran who had worked for the St Petersburg police prior to being appointed head of the Third Section in the wake of Karakozov's failed attack. A man every bit as paranoid and ruthless as Stieber or Espinasse, Shuvalov fed Alexander reports that 'the spectre of revolution is about to break out in St Petersburg'. He used this fear to justify an overhaul of the Third Section, which led to smaller units of officers being assigned to constantly monitor suspects within their own districts, wherein patrons of student clubs and taverns were followed home and, sometimes, violently harassed. The connection between the members of Hell and university campuses was also addressed with blanket repression. This involved Third Section officers breaking up student reading groups at St Petersburg University, on the grounds that these assemblies fell under the illegal designation of being societies that posed a threat to state order and public security. The decree to act against such societies was enshrined in a proclamation made on 22 July 1866, which rolled back the trend of encouraging liberal ideas in the tsar's prior university reforms. As part of this roll-back, 'the rampant and malicious trend of journalism' was also targeted, to which end the fledgling liberal presses that had emerged since the Emancipation Manifesto were shut down.[11]

Beyond the specific targeting of nihilists and socialists, Shuvalov and other courtiers at the Winter Palace used Karakozov's attack as the catalyst to reaffirm traditional values, which they feared had been undermined by Alexander's reforms. Foremost amongst these was the concept of the tsar's absolute right to rule. As the US ambassador to Russia reported in the days after Karakozov's attempt, 'thousands of people at once assembled at the Winter Palace', where they 'hurrahed till his majesty showed himself again and again on the balcony'. Such outpourings of love for the tsar, combined with the guilt trip laid on reformers by court-backed newspapers, established a clear obligation for the Russian people to rally in Alexander's name or else be ostracised. This patriotic fervour was further stirred by a story that first appeared in the military newspaper *Russky Invalid*, which was picked up by the press across Europe and in diplomatic correspondence. This was the tale of how the tsar's life had been saved that fateful day outside the Summer Garden. 'Providence, taking pity on Russia', at the moment Karakozov fired 'a simple peasant' had reached out his hand, knocking the nihilist's shot wide with a gesture from his rough-hewn palm. To tie this act of godly patriotism to the idea that, despite the critics' claims, the Emancipation Manifesto had improved the lives of Russia's peasantry, the tsar's rag-clad saviour was awarded a hereditary title by his grateful sovereign and even had 'an aide de camp assigned to him to coach him in court manners'. So perfect a propaganda piece was this story, to this day some historians suspect that it was, at best, embellished and, at worst, a classic example of fake news.[12]

Russky Invalid also contributed to a narrative that tied the ramping up of patriotism to Shuvalov's suspicions of Polish involvement with Hell. As the investigation into Karakozov unfolded, the newspaper ran speculative pieces on how Polish dissidents were poised to launch further attacks in St Petersburg and Moscow. This fed into a myth that Karakozov himself had been Polish, for how could a full-blooded Russian possibly conceive of taking the Holy Tsar's life? This 'fond hope of the criminal being a Pole' – as a glib foreign correspondent from *The Times* had it – was complicated, however, by the fact that the failed assassin was Russian through and through, a native of Kostroma, north of Moscow, and the child of well-to-do parents who were privileged enough to send their boy to university. Ishutin, too, had grown up in a small town outside Moscow, living a relatively comfortable existence that guided him into a teaching career in St Petersburg. The men from Hell, therefore, should have been middle-class patriots who applauded the age of reform that their tsar had engendered. The question of why these sons of Russia stayed their applause and turned to terrorism was obscured by the narrative that the tsar's spin doctors were crafting, at the heart of which lay prejudice towards the Poles. At plays performed in the weeks following Karakozov's attack, when reference to Poland was made onstage, the crowd – often incited by Third Section plants – hissed and booed. On the streets, bullyboys in the pay of the police harassed Poles and called them traitors. Behind all this lay a conception, created in the courtroom of Karakozov's trial and spread out into the minds of Third Section officers and ordinary Russians, that all threats to the tsar ultimately stemmed from restive Poland.[13]

Conveniently for the likes of Shuvalov, as this wave of repression and patriotism washed over Russia, an incident took place in France that seemingly confirmed the Polish theory. At the International Exposition in Paris in June 1867, a Pole named Antoni Berezowski took a wayward pistol shot at Alexander's head as the latter was riding in an open-top carriage alongside the ill-fated Napoleon. As in the case of Karakozov's attempt, the attacker's pistol served him poorly. Its shoddily modified barrel all but exploded in Berezowski's hand, sending the bullet askew of its target and into the head of a horse. Unable to escape the press of the panicked crowd, Berezowski was seized by the police, arrested on charges of attempted regicide, found guilty and sent to live out the rest of his days in a French penal colony on New Caledonia. The Sûreté cabled St Petersburg a few days after Berezowski's interrogation to report that 'nothing indicates the existence of a conspiracy or the ramifications of a criminal plan' and that 'the crime is the case of one person without accomplices'. Neither a member of Ishutin's circle of nihilists nor an affiliate of the phantom European Revolutionary Committee, it seemed to the Sûreté that Berezowski was simply a disgruntled Pole turned 'misguided fanatic', who had been hanging around Paris's red clubs, taking in the speeches of socialists and republicans, hearing praise-laden tales of Orsini, and nursing thoughts of revenge for the atrocities committed against his people in 1863. This reality mattered little to the Shuvalov, for whom the true nature of Berezowski's attack was irrelevant in the face of a more sweeping assessment – the would-be assassin was a Pole, the tsar's enemies were legion and they could strike at him anywhere. The blanket repression would continue.[14]

The stoking of prejudices, the promotion of narratives of loyalty to tsar and nation and the harassment and arrests of nihilists proved as ineffectual in responding to terrorism in autocratic Russia as Lincoln's attempt to delegitimise Brown had been in democratic America. As much was noted by Konstantin Kavelin, a liberal scholar who was so distressed by the reactionary response to Karakozov's attack that he wrote directly to the Winter Palace, warning that the demonising of university students and the suppression of reform-minded newspapers would only encourage the youth of Russia to embrace nihilist violence. This sentiment was shared by the Winter Palace's official censor, who was privy to both the contents of letters exchanged between radicals that were opened during Shuvalov's crackdowns and the whispers amongst less reactionary figures at the tsar's court, many of whom doubted the wisdom of Shuvalov's hard-line measures. Referring to the inability of the Paris police prefecture to prevent Orsini's bombing, the censor rued how 'Piétri and his system have triumphed' in Russia, creating a state in which 'everyone lives in fear and there is no counting the number of spies'. To his mind, it was clear that Russia had become a place in which 'all the principles of police art are being employed to trump up conspiracies' rather than address the problem of why the tsar's life was under threat. Bluntly, the censor confided to his diary that 'our most dangerous internal enemies are not the Poles or the nihilists, but those statesmen who create nihilists by provoking indignation and aversion to the regime'.[15]

The censor's further fear was that Shuvalov had made a martyr of Karakozov, creating a home-grown terrorist hero who could provide Russia's radicals with a more relatable idol than an Italian nationalist with unobtainable bombs. This was an adroit conclusion. As a radical who was present at Karakozov's hanging recalled, it was clear to the crowds around the scaffold that the young man had been tortured by the Third Section: his 'head, hands, the whole body was loose as if there were no bones in the body, or as if his bones had all been broken. It was a terrible thing to see.' Compounding this image of the martyr was the fact that, unlike Orsini's execution, the annihilation of Hell and the hanging of Karakozov had not unleashed an emancipatory war for Russia's future. Instead, the nihilists' failed attempt to force the pace of history had engendered little more than the suppression of all dissent – proof, if any of the tsar's critics still needed it, that waiting peacefully for political change in Russia was a fool's game. For this reason, in the years after his death, Karakozov became a tragic figure in the mythos of Russia's revolutionary underground, deserving not of celebration for his sacrifice but of pledges to continue the fight he had started. What Shuvalov failed to anticipate was that the man who assumed the mantle of Karakozov's avenger would surpass Ishutin and his acolytes, both in his capacity for murderous fantasy and in his devotion to nihilist ideals. In the process, this man would forge the links with European radicals that Ishutin had craved and develop a philosophy of revolutionary violence that would influence terrorists across Russia, the continent and the wider world not only during his lifetime, but deep into the next century.[16]

Chapter IV

Breakers of worlds

The windowless wagon rattled along the moonlit thoroughfare, its driver's grip on the reins unshaken as the wheels jolted on the ice-hardened flagstones. The Third Section coachman was driving his horses to exhaustion, resolved to deliver his passenger as quickly as possible to the secure confines of the Peter and Paul Fortress. This was an island prison on the Neva River in St Petersburg, within which generations of radicals had been condemned to reflect in isolation on their failure to destroy the tsar they despised. Such was to be the fate of the armoured wagon's sole occupant. Snatched in a midnight raid on a doss house by Third Section officers, the prisoner had been struck across the temple with the hilt of a sword and bound in chains. Then, with a dozen mounted Cossacks flanking the wagon to prevent a rescue, the condemned man had been driven at pace through the freezing night to the fortress and the oblivion that lay within. As this journey reached its end and the wagon trundled into the prison courtyard, the driver and the Cossacks breathed sighs of relief. The most dangerous nihilist terrorist in Russia was now safely behind bars.

They could not know how prepared he was to escape this fate. So wanted a criminal was he, the young nihilist had taken to always concealing a lock pick on his person. Hidden inside his mouth, the prisoner smuggled the pick unnoticed into his cell – solitary, naturally, since his thoughts were too dangerous to be shared with other inmates. Once the door of iron and wood slammed shut, the prisoner spat the pick out into his hands and went to work. Within seconds he was free and massaging the cold iron burn from his pale, thin wrists. Thoughtfully pushing a mess of dark, lank hair back from his unshaven face, he walked over to where a thin pool of moonlight bathed his cell window, the grid of bars over which he examined intensely. Concluding that the pick was strong enough to handle the crumbling mortar of the window's frame, he began scraping away. By dawn, the grid of iron was loose. All that now remained was to squeeze his slender frame through the rectangular space in the wall and take a forty-foot plunge into the icy waters of the Neva below. Having accepted that his life was forfeit in the name of a higher cause, the prisoner did not hesitate. Minutes later, as a sickly red sun rose over St Petersburg, the sodden young man emerged from the ice-silver waters on the bank opposite the fortress. Unfazed by the numbing cold and unmoved by the excitement of his escape, Sergei Nechaev nursed only one feeling in that moment of triumph and freedom – to strike back a thousand-fold at those who had dared try to contain him.[1]

Mikhail Bakunin collapsed back into his chair, slapped his thick thighs and expelled a chortle of satisfaction. A fifty-four-year-old, crumple-faced bear of a man, balding yet thick of beard, Bakunin was no stranger to the kind of physical exertion and fanatical derring-do that littered Nechaev's story of escape from the notorious Peter and Paul Fortress. Indeed, it sounded like a yarn ripped from the story of his own life. Bakunin had been born to noble parents in 1814 and joined the Russian army as a teenager. Uninterested in the firing of artillery pieces and angered by Russia's treatment of the Poles, he resigned his commission in 1835 and immersed himself in the array of radical ideas that were bleeding over into Russia from literary circles in Europe. He consumed subversive literature voraciously, devouring the works of the French anarchist Pierre-Joseph Proudhon and the German philosopher Georg Wilhelm Friedrich Hegel, whilst befriending the legendary Russian socialist, Alexander Herzen. Excited by the ideas these men posited – the emancipation of the peasantry, the abolition of the nobility and the destruction of the state and the church – Bakunin became convinced that something more than simply lamenting the condition of the peasants and the workers was needed to better Russia and, indeed, the world.

His hunger for action, combined with a natural physical intensity, led to Bakunin joining the revolutions of 1848, after which he returned to Russia and continued to cause trouble with the authorities, for which he was sentenced to exile in Siberia in 1861. There, Bakunin traded on his privileged family connections to organise one of the most epic prison breaks in modern history. This involved those assigned to watch him turning a blind eye as he packed a bag and crossed thousands of miles of Siberian forests, bogs and wastes, before arriving in the small town of Olga on the Pacific coast. From Olga, he crossed the Sea of Japan to the port of Hakodate on the island of Hokkaido, spending several weeks in the Land of the Rising Sun before taking passage to San Francisco, en route to Boston and New York. He next boarded a steamer to Liverpool, where he jumped on a train down to London. It was there, two days after Christmas 1861, that Bakunin found sanctuary at his extraordinary odyssey's end in the home of his old friend Herzen, whose door he all but kicked down, offering as greeting only a table-thumping demand to know what had been happening in the world of radicalism during his time on the run.

Bakunin, of course, had his own stories to tell the astonished Herzen. Excitedly, the travel-battered insurgent revealed to the émigré socialist the world of anger that lay beyond Britain's shores. Japan, he reported, was festering with nationalist rage. A generation of dissident samurai there had been sitting under the learning tree of Yoshida Shōin – an activist who wanted to destroy the corrupt Shogunate government and repel Western incursion into his country. Three years after Shōin's execution in 1859, adherents to his cause beheaded European traders and launched attacks on foreign consulates, with the aim to unleash the same kind of internecine war in Japan that the Harper's Ferry attack had been intended to do in the United States. Curious as this political violence was, Bakunin found more of interest at his next port of call, where, like many radicals, he noted the parallels between the condition of the enslaved in the United States and the manifold oppressed of Europe. As he wrote to a friend in 1861 before he took a ship to Liverpool, the Civil War 'interests me in the highest degree' and 'my sympathies are with the North'.[2]

Informed by these experiences, as well as Herzen's accounts of Garibaldi's battles in Italy, the Polish uprising and the steady growth of socialist groups in Britain, Bakunin convinced himself that the 1860s would be a decade defined by a new global revolutionary war. The question that vexed him was how to fight it. Romantically attached as he was to street brawling and barricade storming, Bakunin's observations of the post-1848 world had convinced him that a more sophisticated strategy was needed for the forces of revolution – one based on conspiracy and the radicalising of the masses through propaganda. Once he had recovered his mind, body and finances enough to leave London, Bakunin set about constructing an international underground, criss-crossing Europe, shaking hands and pledging solidarity with almost anyone who shared his vision of a pending showdown between radicals and reactionaries. Doubtless, it was the whispers of Bakunin's conspiratorial activities that informed Khudyakov's mission to Geneva in 1865. Indeed, Khudyakov arranged a meeting with Bakunin and Herzen during his time in the city, only to come away unimpressed by the fact that both men, despite their reputations as hardened revolutionaries, seemed like learned gentlemen who enjoyed the finer things in life. Beholden as he was to Ishutin's fantasies, it is doubtful that Khudyakov would have picked up on another problem that others who encountered Bakunin often noted – his talk of a Europe-wide conspiracy was long on ambition but short on substance. During the 1860s Bakunin founded, forgot about and re-founded countless 'European Revolutionary Councils', 'Secret Societies for the Emancipation of Humanity' and 'World Alliances', many of which existed only in his head and the fevered imaginations of impressionable youth.[3]

If practical preparations for the revolutionary war to come alluded him, Bakunin, at least, had an ideological roadmap for how and why it had to occur. Having fought for the cause of pan-Slavism in 1848, Bakunin came to embrace a new ideology, one which would become synonymous with terrorism in the decades that followed – anarchism. Developed in the 1840s as an offshoot of socialism, anarchism was a philosophy that rejected the idea of overturning the powers that be within a particular state, in favour of dismantling the concept and structure of the state itself. In Bakunin's anarchist vision of the world to come, the scale of this change would have to be far reaching, with the 'centralized, bureaucratic and military organizations' of all states on earth being replaced 'by a federalist organization, based only on the absolute liberty and autonomy of regions, provinces, communes, associations and individuals'. Bakunin's means of achieving this upending of all things was no less ambitious than its end. No more would Polish nationalists fight for independence from Russian rule and Italians struggle for unity. Rather, bonded by their belief in an anarchist future, Bakunin's international network of conspirators would plot as one and 'rally not a few, but all countries into a single, coordinated plan of action, unified, furthermore, by simultaneous revolutionary uprisings in most of the rural areas and cities'. A revolution of this scale, spearheaded by what Bakunin eventually settled on calling the International Brotherhood, would be 'universal, social, philosophical and economic, so that no stone may remain unturned in all of Europe first, and then, the rest of the world'.[4]

His preaching of this world-altering vision, combined with the various phantom 'alliances' and 'committees' with which he was associated, ensured that Bakunin became the sun around which many a radical planet revolved. Having settled in Geneva far from the reach of the Third Section, Bakunin gathered around him an inner circle of adherents and happily met with brother revolutionaries like Khudyakov, whose type often came calling in search of guidance. As Herzen's daughter Natalie recalled, 'Bakunin visited us daily' at their house in Geneva where, sitting himself 'at the end of the table in the dining-cum-sitting room, he rolled himself cigarettes by the dozen'. As he smoked, read and pondered, 'often young people would arrive. Bakunin would greet them with a "hello brother, and who are you? Where are you from? Well, come sit down and tell us"'. Such a scene played out in March 1869 when Nechaev came knocking on Bakunin's door.[5]

Had Bakunin believed in God, he would have interpreted Nechaev's arrival as a gift from the heavens. He had long believed that 'the bandit is the only true revolutionary'. As such, Bakunin saw nothing but potential in the scruffily dressed, dour-faced Nechaev, the more so given that the young nihilist embodied an answer to the question of how to launch a grand revolution. Bakunin still had the hulking frame and booming voice needed to command a room, but by 1869 he was in his mid-fifties, increasingly sedentary and broken physically from his time spent on the run, during which he had lost his teeth and much of his hair and gained significant weight. His days of leading from the front were over. In Nechaev – whom he dotingly referred to as 'the boy' – Bakunin saw 'one of those young fanatics who know no doubts, who fear nothing, believers without god, heroes without rhetoric'. A younger, more physically capable version of himself, the anger-fuelled twenty-one-year-old was the hammer Bakunin needed to break the world apart.[6]

Or was he? Ostensibly, everything in Nechaev's background suggested that he was precisely what he claimed to be – a nihilist rebel and worthy successor to the martyred Karakozov. Indeed, Nechaev was obsessed with the failed assassin, referring to his attack as 'the beginning of our sacred cause'. He also spoke glowingly of terrorism as a means of engendering change, continuing Ishutin's advocacy of murdering tsarist officials and fire-bombing police stations. Nechaev's claim to carry the sacred fire of Hell was enhanced by the fact that, by the standards of radical legitimacy, he had more going for him than the ex-teacher Ishutin, the university-educated Karakozov and, especially, the noble-born Bakunin. Raised in poverty in the burgeoning industrial town of Ivanovo, Nechaev cut the mien, as a contemporary recalled, of 'a real revolutionist. A peasant who has preserved all the serfs' hatred of their masters'. He nursed this hatred throughout his adolescence, during which he strayed beyond the confines of his class to mix with the *narodniki* – the middle-class intelligentsia who gathered in literary salons and clubs in Moscow and St Petersburg to critique tsarist rule and sketch out alternative means of organising Russian society, namely around democratic, socialist or nihilist concepts. Although these reformers had been quieted by Shuvalov's crackdowns, they still assembled in secret during the latter half of the 1860s. It was at these subversive soirees that Nechaev absorbed *narodnik* ideas, revelling in the tension and fury that pulsed through the debates over what next to do in the face of the Third Section's oppression. Possessed of a dark narcissism and self-assured arrogance, Nechaev came to believe that he alone understood the way forward. His oft-stated love of Karakozov and parroting of *Young Russia*'s demands for the 'speedy and total destruction' of 'the State, or the privileged classes of so-called civilization' made him the obvious inheritor of a revolutionary tradition that had evolved from the musings of the early nihilists to Hell's talk of terrorism.[7]

Nechaev gladly embraced this destiny. In 1868, he began haunting the halls of university campuses, persuading the young, angry and easily manipulated to join him in re-forming Hell. It helped Nechaev's recruitment campaign that he was more handsome and charismatic than Ishutin, possessed of a look that one of his targets for seduction recalled as 'original, pure Russian'. His 'dark eyes, peering out every so often from behind his large, dark spectacles' were 'especially striking', so too his 'curt tone and arrogant mutterings, exactly like some kind of superior officer'. With 'his Tyrolean hat tipped to one side and an enormous scarf carelessly flung around his neck, his whole figure had the air of a bandit, and his expression was striking in its energy, malice and cruelty'. Dark and mysterious, Nechaev's personal magnetism obscured his inner unpleasantness, allowing him to seduce the disaffected of St Petersburg with an ease that put Ishutin's prior efforts to shame.[8]

An exemplar of the type whom Nechaev charmed into terrorism was Vera Zasulich. No stranger to Nechaev's ilk, Zasulich had spent time with Hell during its final months of existence, seeing through her fifteen-year-old eyes Karakozov's deterioration from hopeless alcoholic into suicidal assassin. Having graduated from school a year after the latter's failed assassination attempt, Zasulich's unfulfilling job as a desk clerk did little to quell her passion for anti-tsarist action. She was undeterred by Shuvalov's repression and attended secret nihilist meetings organised by teachers who, she recalled, 'were very young, no older than I'. It was at the conclusion of one of these meetings that Zasulich was approached by a dark-haired man with piercing eyes and a commanding presence, who offered her the chance to assist him in the rebirth of Hell.[9]

In the months that followed, Nechaev developed an abusive and controlling relationship with Zasulich, from whom he kept a cold distance whilst still intruding into her life. He would appear on her doorstep at odd hours, insisting that he was being watched by the Third Section and that only she – special as she was – could help. These attempts to seduce and flatter led Zasulich into trouble. After reluctantly agreeing to Nechaev's demand that she make her address available as a dead-letter drop for communication with others in their circle, in 1869 the police intercepted letters containing nihilist utterings and hauled in dozens of students, including Zasulich, on suspicion of being involved in plotting attacks against tsarist officials. Although she now cursed Nechaev's name, during the two years of incarceration that followed her arrest, Zasulich became inured of the terrorist mind-set he had introduced to her, fuelled as she was by a sense of injustice at her imprisonment. Naturally gifted in the art of manipulation, Nechaev understood, like all cult leaders, the significance of this process of radicalisation and so tried to emulate it. As Zasulich languished in jail, Nechaev supplied other followers with illicit books and weapons before betraying them to the police, in the hope that they would join her behind bars and become similarly hell-bent on vengeance against their captors.

Other stunts to which Nechaev was prone were more harmless, though no less telling of the lengths to which he went to warp his followers' minds. Before leaving Russia to find Bakunin, Nechaev composed a letter, which he entrusted to a confidant to circulate to St Petersburg's nihilists once he was safely across the border. In the missive, Nechaev described being captured and imprisoned in the Peter and Paul Fortress, only to have escaped in the most daring manner. Now, he needed to flee Russia until the heat was off, but he urged his followers to despair not, for he would use the opportunity to find allies abroad to further their revolutionary struggle ahead of his inevitable return. In truth, Nechaev had only been hauled in for questioning by the St Petersburg police and released without charge. Seeing in this kernel of truth the chance to grow a lie that would inflate his reputation and put a distance between himself and his detractors – many of whom within the nihilist community were starting to regard him as a troublemaker – Nechaev concocted the tall tale of the midnight carriage ride, the escape from the fortress and the vow to return.[10]

It was a version of the same lie that Nechaev told Bakunin when he arrived in Geneva a month after deceiving his followers. For all his age and experience, Bakunin was clearly regarded by the arrogant young man as being little different to the teenagers whose emotions he played like a fiddle. This reading of the ageing anarchist leader was spot on. Having dazzled with the tale of his flight from Russia, Nechaev then slipped into the old Ishutin lie, informing Bakunin that his band of fifty nihilists was the St Petersburg wing of a vast conspiracy. Nechaev further excited the old man with the promise that his disciples were so organised that they even had a date set for their day of 'world revolution' – 19 February 1870. Bakunin responded by escalating this discourse of nonsense. He rose from his chair and applauded 'the boy', before fussing around with the papers on his desk, taking up a pen and signing a small piece of card with the words 'the bearer of this is one of the accredited representatives of the Russian Section of the World Revolutionary Alliance, no. 2771' written on it. It is unclear if Nechaev swallowed Bakunin's attempt to persuade his ward-in-waiting that he had close to 3,000 card-carrying revolutionaries at his command. What is clear is that Nechaev played along, urging Bakunin to help him unite the worlds of European anarchism and Russian nihilism into an unstoppable revolutionary force.[11]

Their delusions aside, there was a thread of logic that bound Nechaev's interest in terrorist violence to Bakunin's goal of breaking and remaking the world – the former would be used to unleash the latter. Realising this, Bakunin and Nechaev quickly moved beyond the empty farce of their initial meeting to the sourcing of funds for their enterprise. They targeted Herzen, who, despite finding Nechaev obnoxious and untrustworthy, was worn down by his old comrade Bakunin's insistence that the young man represented the future of the revolutionary cause. The money Herzen gifted the pair was duly invested in a propaganda campaign, the purpose of which was to prepare Russia's radicals for their leader's return. The tone and wording of the hundreds of anti-tsarist proclamations Bakunin and Nechaev printed in Switzerland for dissemination in *narodnik* clubs and on university campuses betrayed the influence Nechaev had over his elder partner. Some of the material praised the murderous ruthlessness of Karakozov and Berezowski, demanding that the ethos of 'merciless destruction' that guided them should inspire further acts of terrorism. Other tracts were shaped by Nechaev's gift for psychological warfare. One example was a pamphlet calling for revolution, which was ostensibly written by the 'Descendants of Rurik and the Party of the Independent Nobility' – a group that was presented by Nechaev and Bakunin as being both in Russia and composed of dissident nobles who had cast off their privilege to stand shoulder to shoulder with the oppressed. This and other pamphlets sent from Geneva were deemed 'vile' by the Russian censors, who in vain tried to halt their spread by directing the police to arrest booksellers, coffee-shop proprietors and students who took receipt of them.[12]

The propaganda assault on Russia's radicals was crowned by the publishing of Nechaev's manifesto, the *Catechism of a Revolutionary*, which contained instructions for turning disaffected students into fanatical terrorists. As in the case of the pamphlets that preceded it, historians have pondered the extent to which Bakunin contributed to the *Catechism*, the violent, sociopathic content of which reads as somewhat removed from the old anarchist's penchant for 'brotherhoods' and his 1866 declaration that 'the revolution will very likely be bloody and vindictive, but this phase will not last long and will never degenerate into cold systematic terrorism'. True, Bakunin's denouncement in this context was of the guillotine-induced blood-on-the-street terror of the French Revolution but the fact remains that prior to his association with Nechaev, the elder insurgent had displayed little appetite for the kind of fatalistic violence preached in the *Catechism*. At most, it is likely that Bakunin's talk of secret societies influenced some of its details on how to organise underground terrorist groups. Beyond that, the *Catechism* reads as a manifesto drawn from the darkest corners of Nechaev's mind, woven through with Ishutin's cult-leader mentality, the murderous zealotry of Heinzen and the bloody-minded determination to do what needed to be done, as exemplified by Orsini, Brown and Karakozov – the sum of two decades' worth of terrorist practice and thought.[13]

In the tradition of Hell and The Organisation, Nechaev commanded his readers to give 'up every possession, occupation or family tie', fixate on their hatred night and day and surrender themselves completely to fatalism, with the aim of becoming as suicidally depressed as Karakozov had been. So moulded, the reader would then be ready to carry out terrorist attacks, which would spur spasms of retaliatory violence from the police. The forces of radicalism would respond to this oppression in kind until such time as the state would implode and the revolution would arrive. The fact than many a radical would perish in this cycle of repression and revenge was of little consequence to Nechaev. In fact, the bloodletting was to be welcomed. The *Catechism* openly declared that 'the revolutionary is a doomed man' whose mission was to seek a death that would 'incite the masses to revolt'. Such talk aligned with Bakunin's desire for world revolution, but where the *Catechism* strayed from the old man's dreams was in its advocacy of self-destructive terrorism to bring about this end. Echoing Heinzen, the *Catechism* declared that revolutionary terrorists did not need to think or learn about anything other than 'the science of destruction', a discipline necessary for the construction of weapons with which to wage 'a relentless and irreconcilable war to the death'. Unfeeling and unshakably committed, the terrorist would use these weapons – be they Orsini bombs, poison or the recently invented dynamite – 'to destroy himself and to destroy with his own hands everything that stands in the path of the revolution'.

Naturally, such a suicidal focus meant eschewing personal camaraderie. Terrorist cells operating independent of each other in the name of security would be formed but, in a projection of Nechaev's own sociopathic mind-set, nothing but 'revolutionary passion' would bind the members of these cells together. The murders, bombings and extortions committed by the *Catechism*'s adherents would happen without 'running to another for advice or assistance, except when these are necessary to the furtherance of the plan'. The outcome of this focused fatalism would be something more profound than the 'orderly revolt according to the classic western model' that the 48ers had pursued – it would be an annihilationist revolution, 'which destroys the entire State to the roots, exterminating all the State's traditions, institutions and classes in Russia'.[14]

Given its talk of self-destructive violence and the organisation of cells, it is small wonder that the *Catechism* has inspired the tactics and grand strategies of a variety of terrorists, from the Russian socialist revolutionaries of the early 1900s to the ISIS suicide bombers of today. Aside from its long-term impact on the development of terrorist thinking, the *Catechism* also completed the process started by Ishutin of marrying nihilism – which had originally been concerned only with critiquing tsarism and questioning Russia's social norms – to conspiratorial, revolutionary violence. Now, in a perverse extension of the nihilist's need to question the role of the church, the state and the family, the terrorists Nechaev conceived of would divorce themselves utterly from these aspects of society and seek to destroy them. Filtered through the warped minds of first Ishutin and then the *Catechism*'s author, the ideology of nihilism had become the basis for a murderous terrorist campaign.[15]

To lead this campaign, Nechaev made his triumphant return to Russia in August 1869, armed with copies of his manifesto, the blessing of Bakunin and, in a final, shameless piece of propaganda, a poem penned by one of the latter's inner circle, which praised Nechaev as a friend of Russia's youth. It was precisely this demographic that the would-be terrorist chieftain targeted for recruitment. Establishing himself in Moscow, Nechaev pronounced the formation of a group that would represent the next stage in nihilist terrorism's evolution from The Organisation and Hell – Narodnaya Rasprava (People's Revenge). Still bound to the pact of fiction he had made with Bakunin, Nechaev told prospective recruits that People's Revenge was a branch of the International Brotherhood and the bridge between Russia's nihilists and the anarchists and socialists of Europe. The reality was that People's Revenge was simply a larger, slightly better organised version of Hell, composed, at its height, in the autumn of 1869, of a few hundred students and former Ishutin followers, drawn likes moths to a flame by Nechaev's posturing as the commander of the 'Russian front' in a continent-wide revolutionary war.[16]

So ambitiously boastful was Nechaev's cosplay, however, that even those initially sucked into it began to question his 'give me revolution or give me death' demands. When one such disciple, Ivan Ivanov, dared to suggest that the Europe-wide alliance of radicals did not exist and that Nechaev's advocacy of terrorism was a step too far, the man who believed his followers to be doomed leapt on the chance to prove this point. On 21 November 1869, Nechaev lured Ivanov to the Moscow School of Agriculture. There, with the clumsy assistance of three other members of People's Revenge, Nechaev strangled Ivanov and shot him in the back of the head, though not before losing a chunk of his hand through his victim's wild attempts to bite his way out of execution. The conspirators disposed of Ivanov's body in a nearby pond which, in their haste and inexperience, they neglected to realise was too shallow and frozen to properly obscure the corpse. When the police found Ivanov's body protruding from the ice a few days later, papers in his pockets led them directly to People's Revenge. It was no spectacular act of terrorism, nor a public execution of the tsar or one of his officials. This act of premeditated murder was, however, enough for the police to put an end to Nechaev fantasies, via the arrest of over 100 suspected People's Revenge members. By the time the dragnet commenced, however, the man who had ended Ivanov's life and handed the world the poisoned chalice of the *Catechism* was long gone, seeking safe harbour once more in Bakunin's drawing room.[17]

It was an inauspicious end to the dream that Bakunin had nursed when he bade Nechaev farewell six months earlier. It was also the beginning of their parting of the ways. Already under pressure from Herzen to drop Nechaev when news of his involvement in 'brother' Ivanov's murder reached Geneva, Bakunin was also mindful that a wing of Europe's radical movement that was growing in power – the Marxists – had no time for the murderous tactics advocated in the *Catechism*. Marx's collaborator Friedrich Engels denounced Nechaev as 'either a Russian provocateur or, at least, prone to act like one', an exemplar of the 'suspicious characters' with whom Bakunin held court in his Swiss refuge. Natalie Herzen, for her part, saw right through Nechaev's tired tricks of seduction and grew to resent the troublemaker's presence in her and her father's lives. Already frustrated by his refusal to take the unsubtle hint woven into her advice that he 'go to England or America and live there until you are forgotten', she grew more exasperated as Nechaev extended his stay in Geneva into the spring of 1870. Natalie's detestation of him only grew as the fading rogue peppered her with letters declaring that he was 'head over heels' in love with her – a ploy that she knew full well was designed by Nechaev to gain further access to her father's money.[18]

Burdened by these pressures and the embarrassing realisation that Nechaev was more naughty boy than radical messiah, in June 1870 Bakunin wrote a letter of rebuke and separation from the protégé in whom he had invested so much. The key message of Bakunin's missive was that the International Brotherhood was 'wanting in quality and quantity' and 'our old relationship and our mutual obligations are at an end' – both bitter pills for the old revolutionary to swallow. Bakunin also dared to speak the unspeakable, asking Nechaev whether 'your organization [People's Revenge] ever really existed?' In posing this question, Bakunin put to paper that which his associates in Geneva had already realised. The spiel Nechaev gave about representing the Russian wing of an international conspiracy was nothing but 'fanaticism bordering on mysticism' and Bakunin was the dupe, his name used by the manipulative nihilist such that 'many people do in fact think that I stand at the head of a secret society about which, as you are aware, I know nothing'. Bluntly and with God knows what regrets, Bakunin acknowledged to his former ward that 'you deceived me'.

Such was Nechaev's magnetism, however, this denouncement of 'the boy' was followed by the pen in Bakunin's hand moving inexplicably to strike a conciliatory note. Before signing off, he assured the young murderer that 'I, and all of us, love you sincerely and have great respect for you because we have never met a man more unselfish and devoted to the cause than you'. Notably, Bakunin also pleaded with Nechaev to abandon his advocacy of terrorism, arguing that such methods would be 'fatal to the cause itself'. Bakunin understood that radicals needed legitimacy to attract followers. As such, encouraging suicidal fatalism and murdering disciples who question your wisdom was not a sure path for a revolutionary leader to follow. Much as he derided Nechaev in this respect, Bakunin could not give up the idea that a fresh conspiracy might be salvaged from the wreckage of their plot. To this end, he suggested that a new organisation, called either the People's Cause or the People's Fraternity – Bakunin seemed undecided over which name was catchier – be formed, which 'will never consist of more than fifty to seventy members', who would demonstrate 'equality' and 'frankness' towards each other, whilst rejecting spying and cultures of distrust.[19] He may have finally grasped that Nechaev was poison, but Bakunin could not quit his dream of the alluring nihilist contributing to his conspiracy to change the world.

Bakunin was not the only one unable to get over Nechaev. The fact that he was still at large after Ivanov's murder and, it was wrongly assumed, that he was plotting once more with Bakunin stirred fears in Russia that the alliance between anarchists in Geneva and nihilists in St Petersburg was an ever-pressing threat. As the British ambassador to Russia reported in 1870, it was assumed at the Winter Palace that Bakunin and Nechaev were arranging 'the wholesale murder of the higher classes of society'. Shuvalov was similarly convinced of the reality of Nechaev's fiction that he was the linchpin of a larger conspiracy, and so deployed spies to Switzerland with a brief to return the fugitive in chains before he and Bakunin could commence the next stage of their plan. These assumptions were detached from the truth, which was that by the summer of 1870 Nechaev's bonds with Bakunin were as irreparably broken as the International Brotherhood, which had been reduced by that time to no more than Bakunin's inner circle of anarchist hangers-on.[20] Their conspiracy may have died, but Bakunin and Nechaev's idea that international alliances would facilitate revolution lived on, not only in the minds of anarchists and nihilists, but also in those of people with very different plans for how to better the world. As Ishutin, Nechaev and Bakunin indulged their fantasies, an ocean away, in New York, a coalition of Irish republicans and itinerant mercenaries prepared to launch an audacious act of political violence greater than anything the Russians had envisioned – an assault that would humble the world's most powerful empire.

Chapter V

Insurgents across borders

Ireland had been beset for centuries by the often brutal indifference of its British administrators. By the late 1700s, poverty born of unequal land ownership and trade policies that saw much of the fruit of Ireland's soil exported for non-Irish profit had led to the growth of a nationalist movement, whose leaders looked to the example of the French Revolution as a means of redress for the oppressions they suffered. The failure of uprisings in Ireland in 1798 and 1803 did little to quell this spirit and the impetus for rebellion only grew when, in 1845, a blight began to take hold of Ireland's potato crops – the staple of the population's diet. As the blight ravaged farm fields and harvests failed, the government in London insisted on continuing to export much of Ireland's food, whilst providing inadequate means of relief in return. Innervated to insurrection by starvation and indifference, in July 1848 a twenty-three-year-old man from Kilkenny named James Stephens joined with the other members of the Carbonari-emulating group Young Ireland on the outskirts of the village of Ballingarry in Tipperary, with the aim to unleash yet another rebellion against British rule. Owing to a lack of arms and preparation, the fifty-odd men of Young Ireland had little effective means of fighting off police reinforcements, whose rifles and cudgels brought a swift end to their revolutionary moment. Fearing the noose or transportation, Stephens fled to Paris, where he spent the better part of the next decade mixing with the republican intelligentsia and hanging out in the city's red clubs – the same places where the likes of Orsini and Berezowski nurtured their regicidal plans and the unseen Stieber lurked. His head buzzing with the insurrectionist energy of this refuge, in 1858 Stephens travelled to New York to meet with other Young Ireland veterans and émigré adherents to the Irish republican cause – members of what was known as the Fenian movement.

Acknowledging that past methods needed to be jettisoned, Stephens insisted to his fellow Fenians that the spearhead organisation in their struggle against Britain – the Irish Republican Brotherhood (IRB) – had to become more disciplined and secretive than Young Ireland had been. For this reason, in a manner that was less sociopathic, though comparably tyrannical to the demands Nechaev would make on his followers a decade later, each member of the IRB had to swear an oath declaring 'in the presence of God' to do their 'utmost, at every risk while life lasts, to establish the independence of Ireland'. This would involve them having to 'yield implicit obedience, in all things not contrary to the law of God' to the IRB's leaders, whilst preserving 'inviolable secrecy regarding all the transactions of this secret society'. The theory of the oath as guarantor of secrecy was strong, but the practice was lacking. In 1865, informers within the IRB betrayed their leaders, including Stephens, to Dublin Castle – the headquarters from which the British had controlled Ireland for centuries. Thankfully for Stephens, the IRB had its own inside men and, at Richmond Prison in London, the Fenian chief was liberated from his cell by two guards with republican sympathies. Handed money, a revolver and advice to flee the country, Stephens took passage across the Channel, once again finding refuge in Paris.[1]

Shoved back to square one through an act of betrayal, others might have abandoned their revolutionary mission. Not Stephens, possessed as he was of a drive and ambition that a contemporary recalled could 'move and stir the Irish soul long after all the brawling windbags and leaden scribblers of the day have gone the way alike of the great and small'. Although he bitterly accepted that the secrecy oath had been a flop, Stephens nonetheless used his time in Paris to pursue what he believed was the other key to success in the IRB's war against Britain – the establishment of international alliances. Not unlike Bakunin, Stephens saw the 1860s as a decade in which a new generation of revolutionaries was emerging from the fog of 1848's failures with a shared disdain, irrespective of their political goals, for the world's powers that be. Although there is no evidence that the IRB leader paid mind to the activities of Bakunin, Ishutin or Nechaev, Stephens nevertheless shared the Russians' faith in the potential of weaponising this collective sense of injustice as a means of forming an 'international brotherhood'. The difference, of course, was that the purpose of Stephens' coalition was not to destroy tsarism or bring about the collapse of Western civilisation. Rather, he sought an alliance of republican-minded insurgents who could help the IRB liberate Ireland from British control. Beyond any romantic notions of sharing a love of freedom, for Stephens the acquisition of these allies was a matter of pragmatic necessity. Many IRB members were working class, poor and, with a few notable exceptions, lacking in military experience and access to arms. This last issue was of particular importance for Stephens, who, in a manner different to Orsini, Ishutin and Nechaev, still believed that open conflict rather than conspiratorial terrorism was the key to achieving his political goals. For it was only, as Stephens claimed, through the 'spirit and letter of the discipline of any army' that the Fenians could bring a war for Ireland's freedom to a successful conclusion.[2]

This impetus to create a rebel army led Stephens to New York in March 1866, where he had a meeting with Cesare Orsini, the younger brother of the martyred bomber of Rue le Peletier. Like the Irishman stood before him, Cesare's journey to New York was prompted by a yearning for alliances. Weeks before he shook Stephens' hand, the younger Orsini had been sitting in Marx's drawing room in London, excitedly nodding as he absorbed the words of instruction that were being hurled in his direction. Cesare welcomed this ear pounding. By 1866, Marx had become recognised as one of Europe's pre-eminent radical thinkers. Gone was the dingy Soho flat in which Stieber claimed to have foiled his plans for world domination a decade earlier. Now, Marx was a rising star of the International Workingmen's Association (IWMA) – a coalition of socialists, anarchists and assorted other radicals that had formed in London in 1864 to agitate for workers' rights – and was residing in affluent Belsize Park, penning letters to and taking meetings with a growing coterie of followers. Through these exchanges, Marx endeavoured to create networks with like-minded radicals beyond London's émigré communities. Who better to target in this respect than the brother of the man who had struck such an iconic blow against Europe's arch-tyrant, the hated Napoleon?

Having favourably taken the measure of Cesare, Marx tasked 'citizen Orsini, the brother of the immortal martyr' with travelling to New York to find more allies for the IWMA. Cesare dutifully visited the workingmen's clubs that had arisen from New York's bustling wharves and smoke-choked factories but, having recalled encountering the firebrand Stephens in Paris a year earlier, he also sought out the IRB chief. Cesare was aware that Marx had venerated the Fenians' anti-colonial struggle, opining that British rule in Ireland, no less than in India, had proven 'only that to be free at home, John Bull must enslave abroad'. Stephens was also aware of Marx's sympathy for the Fenian cause and so, having accepted Cesare's offer to join the IWMA, he dared to dream of a near future in which Fenians would march hand in glove with Britain's oppressed workers in a general rising against the imperial state.[3]

This alliance with Cesare and the socialists he represented was a bonus for Stephens, whose true purpose in New York in the spring of 1866 was to meet with a man more habituated to violence than the deep-thinking Marx – Gustave Paul Cluseret. Born in 1823 on the outskirts of Paris, Cluseret joined the army at the age of twenty, defending the interests of the French state both in the 1848 uprisings and in the Crimean War. By 1858, however, the career soldier was starting to find his 'red' streak. The sight of bomb-blasted bodies at Sevastopol and the blood of freedom-seeking citizens being shed in Paris convinced Cluseret that his martial gifts should no longer be used to empower an emperor. This led him to abandon his commission, after which he became, as a contemporary recalled, 'a Frenchman always in search of revolutions'. No less than Nechaev and his brooding brigand persona, Cluseret's look and demeanour played into his image as an eternal insurrectionist. He had a 'forceful, shrewd face, with a resolute but mostly repellent expression', framed by a well cut moustache and a high hairline, the sum of which projected both the wearied experience of a soldier and a haughty sense of self-worth. As one who fought alongside him recalled, Cluseret was prone to wearing 'all kinds of fancy uniforms' and boasting relentlessly of the feats he had performed to earn them. He was 'the vainest man I ever saw'.

As Stephens well knew, however, Cluseret had experience to back up this vanity. In 1861, the dissident Frenchman had crossed the Atlantic with thousands of other Europeans to fight for the freedom of the enslaved during the American Civil War. The reputation Cluseret earned as a fanatical republican during the conflict ensured that after its conclusion he was offered the chance to add 'propagandist' and 'spy' to his already impressive resume. This opportunity came via his employ in the service of Charles Sumner – he who was beaten on the floor of the Senate for his abolitionist sentiments in 1856. As Sumner's agent, Cluseret travelled across Europe, spreading republican ideals and firing the hearts of those opposed to Napoleon, Tsar Alexander, Franz Joseph and Queen Victoria. Naturally, Cluseret had sympathy for the Fenians, seeing their struggle as one front in an international war between the righteous and the unjust. As he later wrote, 'in the Irish cause it was not the cause of Ireland alone that I saw, but humanity itself … Austrians, Germans, Poles, Russians, or any other nationality. They are all men who, although by the chance of birth have been born in different localities, have all alike the duties and the rights of a common humanity, and whoever infringes on the rights of one man, infringes upon them all'.[4] Bakunin could not have said it better.

As one of the radical world's most notorious figures, Cluseret appeared before Stephens in 1866 as nothing less than the IRB's saviour, for that year had been an *annus horribilis* for the Fenian cause. The source of the misery was the same problem that had beset Young Ireland in 1848 – a yawning gap between the IRB's capabilities and its ambition. This manifested most humiliatingly in April 1866, in an audacious plot to use an army of Irish American Civil War veterans to invade Canada. The plan was bold if nothing else. Having assembled at muster points in Vermont, New York State and Michigan, the Fenians were to pour across the border to seize Canadian towns and forts, with the strategic aim of terrifying the British government to the negotiating table to discuss a spectacular exchange: Canada for Ireland. Its manifold logistical and conceptual problems aside, the plan was thwarted from the start by the same problem of poor security that had led to Stephens' imprisonment a year earlier. In the weeks leading up to invasion day, a network of pub landlords, telegraph operators, dockworkers and journalists on either side of the border informed the Canadian authorities of the IRB's plans, providing details on everything from attack routes to the number of guns the invaders had to hand.[5] This, combined with the fact that only a few hundred of the 30,000 battle-hardened Fenians the IRB expected showed up for the great offensive, made disaster inevitable. Those who heeded the IRB's call to arms were routed within minutes of crossing the border, except for a small group of Fenians who managed to seize the town of Ridgeway for a few hours. Even this triumph was stifled by the arrival of Canadian reinforcements, who drove the invaders out of Ridgeway and back into the United States 'half-starved and much demoralized'. Having made it back across the Niagara River, 750 of the Fenians' force of 800 were then arrested 'under the guns of a Michigan war-steamer'.[6]

The terrorist cheerleader Heinzen might have proclaimed the Fenians' invasion to be 'perhaps the finest example of revolutionary organization of all time', but few others saw their incursion into Canada as anything other than the colossal failure it clearly was. Determined to live up to their name – the word 'Fenian' was derived from the legend of the Fianna, a relentless band of warriors from Ireland's distant past – the IRB remained undeterred. Abandoning the idea of a pitched battle, a new plan was devised for a campaign in Britain and Ireland that would involve raids on armouries, the blowing up of bridges and attacks on police stations. All of this would, it was hoped, encourage the Irish people to join a general uprising. It was for the purposes of coordinating this fresh offensive that Stephens sought out Cluseret, promising the general that 'the whole of Ireland was enrolled in the organization' and ready to rise, if only the IRB could take the lead.

As brazen as it was built on hope, Stephens' plan was tailormade for Cluseret, who nodded approvingly as the details were outlined to him in an apartment – notably, one owned by an émigré socialist – in central Manhattan. Having digested the scope of the plot, the Frenchman leapt to his feet and grasped Stephens' hand along with the latter's offer, as Cluseret recalled it, to 'give me the key to his organization'. Despite his sizeable ego, even Cluseret realised that he would need help to make Stephens' dreams a reality. Moreover, like his new partner, the Frenchman was much taken by the idea of forming an international alliance of revolutionaries. And so, with Stephens' permission, Cluseret recruited a Swiss soldier named Octave Fariola – a veteran both of Garibaldi's campaigns in Italy and of the American Civil War – to assist in planning the attacks. Like Cluseret, Fariola was susceptible to the idea of attaining 'glory and fortune' and moved by the thought that the Fenians' struggle was an extension of Garibaldi's battle for Italy's independence. Doubtless, he was also encouraged by Stephens agreeing to pay him £60 per month to be the chief of staff of Cluseret's Fenian army.[7]

Swept up in Stephens' ambitions, Cluseret endeavoured to add the finishing touches to this grand alliance of rebels. Shortly after arriving in England in January 1867, he arranged a secret meeting at the White Horse pub in London with a group of Chartists – the electoral reform activists with whom Allan Pinkerton had once associated. It was at this meeting that the conspiracy's expanding bubble started to burst. Rising from his chair at the head of the table in the pub's back room, Cluseret boasted loudly to the Chartists of how he had '2,000 Fenians, armed and equipped with revolvers, with knives and baton ferres, 500 of them being also armed with carbines', all ready to attack barracks and police stations across the British Isles. Rather than stir the revolutionary spirits of those present, Cluseret's words created a murmuring ripple of anxiety and a rapidly emptied table of half-filled pint glasses. As one of the Chartists later recalled, the Frenchman's sabre-swinging talk of armed insurrection was bad enough, but what really shocked the meeting's attendees was Cluseret's bombastic obliviousness to the fact that 'the government would surely be made acquainted with our secret'. The fearful Chartist was right to think this.[8]

Unbeknownst to the indiscreet Cluseret, the conspiracy of Fenians, IWMA members and republican mercenaries to which he belonged had been infiltrated by informers. As early as the autumn of 1865, the British Home Office had begun taking note of the number of Fenians arriving in Liverpool from the United States, concluding that the trickle of new arrivals was forming a pool of recruits from which an insurrectionary force could be raised. The mayor of Liverpool's assessment was that 'a Fenian conspiracy is spreading amongst the dock labourers at this port', of whom 3,000 were reckoned to be of Irish descent and, worse still, were rumoured to have been heard taking the IRB oath.[9] The concern led to a ramping up of payments for informers within Liverpool's Irish community, from whom information was received about the IRB's plan to raid the armoury at nearby Chester Castle in February 1867. The Fenian attack was duly repulsed by 200 soldiers who had been mobilised in anticipation.

Not only was this the first sign that the Fenian plot had been infiltrated but, crucially, the raid's thwarting deprived the IRB of access to the content of Chester's armoury, which was needed to carry out further attacks. The sense that their plan was now up in the air was exacerbated by the IRB's penchant for infighting. Two months before the Chester raid, Stephens was accused of 'incompetency, insincerity and dishonesty' in his planning of the uprising, and so was forced to give up power. As was his custom, the now former IRB chief headed for France in the wake of this humiliation, leaving the alliance he had forged, to press on. Without Stephens' voice in the room to advocate the original strategy, the rest of the conspirators – holed up in London and despairing at the news from Chester – argued over how to move forward. Cluseret and Fariola favoured guerrilla tactics, whilst the Irish-born IRB leaders argued for the continuance of direct attacks, despite their lack of weapons. The outcome of this dispute was a middle-ground strategy that served no one well. When the rising began in March 1867, it comprised a series of ineffective attacks on police stations in Ardagh, Limerick and

Tallaght, a naval watchtower on the Kerry coast and a train and barracks in Ballyknockan, carried out by small clusters of men armed with pikes, muskets and the odd shotgun or pistol. It was a far cry from Cluseret's initial demand of Stephens that he be given no less than '10,000 Fenians, thoroughly equipped' to command.[10]

Intelligence provided to the British by yet another informer – this time, a senior IRB commander who had been captured, interrogated and 'turned' prior to the uprising's launch – ensured that police and soldiers were prepared to counter these attacks. 'Panic', reported the *Irish Times*, then 'seized the insurgents, and, dreading arrest, they threw away their arms' whilst, at the leadership level, the last vestiges of Stephens' international alliance crumbled. Fariola fled to Paris and was shadowed by 'a pair of respectable elderly gentlemen, gold-spectacled and decorated, who would insist on keeping me in sight' wherever he went. Fearing that the Sûreté were onto him, Fariola returned to London in early 1868 in the mistaken belief that the heat was off, only to be met by Scotland Yard detectives who, in the time-honoured fashion of dealing with Fenianism, added the Swiss mercenary to their ranks of informers. Cluseret also absented himself from his revolutionary brothers as their uprising collapsed into shambles, slipping away from London and resurfacing in France a few days later. A more audacious character than Fariola, he not only tolerated the watchful gaze of the Sûreté but mocked and defied them by meeting up with Cesare and pledging himself to Marx's IWMA. He pushed things too far by publishing an article in 1869 that criticised Napoleon's regime, for which he served two months in jail. Regardless of these travails, Cluseret evaded both Scotland Yard and the death sentence he was awarded in absentia by a British court. It would not be the last time that the Frenchman partook of a revolution only to miraculously escape the fallout of its failure.[11]

From the borders of Canada to the walls outside Chester Castle, it was now clear to many within the Fenian movement that grand uprisings of the form imagined by Stephens led only to ruin. The question facing the IRB in the late 1860s was, therefore, the same as that which plagued Bakunin's mind – how, given the failure of open rebellion, to proceed?

Despite the example proffered by Orsini, there was little appetite for targeted killing amongst the IRB, whose leaders eschewed such murderous practices in favour of presenting themselves as a legitimate army of Irish emancipation. A fateful blunder and a dose of public hysteria, however, caused a reconsideration of this ideal, setting elements of the Irish republican movement on the path from hopeless insurrectionism to strategic terrorism. This transformation began on the morning of 18 September 1867, when thirty Fenians gathered either side of Hyde Road in Manchester brandishing clubs and pistols, with which they induced the driver of a police wagon carrying two of their compatriots to stop in his tracks. What followed should have been a simple jailbreak. Instead, in the act of shooting through the heavy lock that secured the compartment that held the prisoners, one of the Fenians put a bullet through both the wagon door and the skull of Sergeant Charles Brett, a fifty-one-year-old lifer in the Manchester police, who became the first officer to lose his life in its service.

This was no deliberate act of cop-killing but, regardless, *The Times* concluded that 'the Fenians have declared war on our institutions and have carried it to the very heart of the country'. Here was a cause for concern. Whereas in the recent past, the Fenians had confined themselves to easily snuffed-out eruptions of military adventurism in Ireland and Canada they were now, seemingly, carrying out the targeted killing of police officers in a British city. This led to past assurances of Fenian ineptitude being called into question by the press, with the bombastic *Spectator* declaring that 'hatred and indignation have taken the place of contempt'. Reckoning with the reality that terrorism was no longer something that happened in a distant colony or on the streets of Paris and St Petersburg, a furious public debate about the Fenian cause arose in the wake of Brett's death, particularly as condemnation of the killing was far from universal. The *Manchester Examiner* spoke of the 'unenlightened and too imprudent patriotism' that had forced the Fenians into such extremis, showing sympathy for the idea put forward by certain Irish republicans that Brett was simply collateral damage in a war that Britain had long been waging in Ireland. Sitting like a spider at the centre of

London's radical web, Marx, for his part, noted to Engels the 'tempestuous demonstrations in favour of the Fenians' at the meetings held by 'the intelligent sections of the working class', some of whom saw Brett's death as a catalyst for an armed showdown between the British Empire and its enemies within.[12]

For those who eschewed sympathy for the Irish cause in favour of outrage at Brett's killing, avenues for expression were in no short supply. A reward of £300 was issued by the authorities for the recapture of the prisoners liberated outside Manchester, whilst the company that produced their manacles offered an additional £200 for any information that could lead to the apprehension of the shooter. Informed by eyewitness descriptions of 'strange-suspicious-looking men' loitering about Hyde Road on the day of the attack, the police conducted a search across the Greater Manchester area. They were joined in this endeavour by members of the public who, fortified by anger, volunteered to take up lanterns and cudgels to track down the Fenians. Through a combination of hysteria and overzealousness, 'by eleven o'clock twelve to fifteen arrests had been reported from different places in the neighbourhood' around the ambush site. In all, twenty-eight men – many of whom had no connection to the attack on the police wagon but spoke with Irish brogues – were rounded up on suspicion of conspiracy to commit murder.[13]

Even after the number of accused had been whittled down, five men remained to be ushered into the dock on 29 October 1867. Three of these five were hanged, the most verbose of whom was William Philip Allen, who memorably declared to the court that he was 'an Irishman sentenced to be hanged when an English dog would have got off'. Another accused echoed these sentiments by defending the morality of the cause to liberate Ireland, where 'no man, except a paid official of the British government, can say there is a shadow of liberty'. The fact that regret was expressed by some of the defendants for Brett's death meant little alongside the prevailing narrative – the Fenians were now in the heinous business of assassination. Driven by this thought and its implications, 2,500 additional troops were summoned to guard Salford Jail, outside the walls of which gallows were erected of a size large enough to provide the crowd of 8,000 onlookers a clear view of the convicted murderers swinging from their necks.[14]

After the sentence had been carried out on 23 November 1867, Marx – who had followed the trial with fascination – wrote once more to Engels, making an assessment born of a mind that understood the big picture of radicalism, public anxiety, police crackdowns and terrorist retaliations. Asserting that the 'only thing the Fenians still lacked were martyrs', Marx opined that the executions at Salford would go down as 'an act of heroism' in Fenian minds, 'such as will now be sung at the cradle of every Irish child in Ireland, England and America'. Pointedly, he concluded that the 'only time that anyone has, to my knowledge, been executed for anything similar in a civilised state was the case of John Brown at Harper's Ferry'. Given that the abolitionist's memory was enshrined in the Union's Civil War battle song 'John Brown's Body', 'the Fenians could not wish for a better precedent' to inform their struggle.[15]

A few weeks after Marx wrote this, on 13 December 1867 a group of Fenians blew up the wall of Clerkenwell Prison in London, with the aim to free comrades held within on charges of sedition. To create the necessary breach for the prisoners to flee through, a barrel of gunpowder was placed on a cart positioned at the base of the prison wall. Unexperienced in handling explosives, the Fenians who ignited the powder with a firework created an explosion more powerful than they anticipated, destroying most of the prison wall and leaving a smoke plume that could be seen across London. The blast wave from the detonation shattered the windows of buildings for several blocks around and incinerated the clothes off the back of a prison guard who – despite being forewarned by Scotland Yard that an attempt on the wall was imminent – paid no mind to the placing of the barrel, believing that the wall 'would probably be blown up from underneath and had no conception that it would be blown down in the way it really was done'. Had the Fenians tunnelled under the foundations and mined the wall as the authorities expected, the carnage might have been limited. Instead, in addition to the destruction of several houses opposite the prison, twelve people died and 120 others were injured by the blast.[16]

Despite the bombing coming on the heels of cop-killing, the police insisted that this flare-up of Irish republican violence required only minor tweaks to the security measures that had protected Britain from Fenian violence since the early 1800s. More informers were recruited, the details of known Irish troublemakers were circulated and a small secret service department was established, staffed by detectives from Dublin Castle. However, testament to the police's sanguine attitude, by April 1868 the secret service department had been mothballed on the grounds that its maintenance was not worth the effort when compared with the modest scope of the Fenian threat.[17] Already sceptical of the police's ability to protect them and energised by newspaper reportage that painted the Fenians as terrorists, some members of the British public saw things differently. In the days after the Clerkenwell bombing, the Home Office – which was generally more concerned than Scotland Yard over the potential for further attacks – issued a call for the recruitment of 'special constables' to assist the police in monitoring city streets. The request was responded to by 100,000 civilians, who flocked to police stations across the country to do their bit. So rapid was the expansion of this volunteer movement, it was not until four months after the first intake of recruits presented themselves for service that the 'specials' issue was raised in Parliament. There, it was noted that 'no mark of approbation, no symptom of acknowledgement had been informally or formally conceded to them'. Despairing at how the 'specials' movement had taken on a life of its own independent of police control, demands that 'an inquiry is made as to the nature of their services' were put forward.[18]

There were other signs that the public's response was taking on a momentum divorced from the police's muted reading of events. In January 1868, the mayor of Bath presided over an anti-Fenian rally in the town hall, which was 'filled by citizens of all classes and shades of opinion'. Despite the apparent diversity of the assembly, when the mayor described Fenianism as 'a monstrous and unmitigated evil' synonymous with violent conspiracy, the entire room burst into applause, ahead of three cheers being sung for both the speaker and the Queen. In London that same month, an anti-Fenian march was proposed by the Metropolitan Conservative Working Men's Association, only to be cancelled at the last minute once the organisers realised that 'any demonstration at the present time calculated to exacerbate public feeling would doubtless be used by Fenian prisoners' lawyers to argue prejudice in their cases'. This decision did not, however, prevent one of the Association's leaders from printing a public letter calling for 'the people of England, and especially the metropolis' to 'morally support her majesty's government and law officers by expressing with no uncertain voice their detestation of the murderous, unconstitutional means for redressing real or imaginary wrongs' that the Fenians had embraced. Much like the police and pundits of our own times who tend to call on Islamic leaders to stamp out radicalism in their own communities, an editorial in *The Times* suggested that 'at a time when public feeling is excited' against Irish republicanism, the onus was on 'Irishmen resident in England, and particularly those of the working class' to 'voluntarily make declarations of their loyalty to the Crown and their abhorrence of all treasonable crimes'.[19]

To the mind of Robert Anderson – a Dublin Castle detective assigned to the short-lived secret service department – such overblown responses were the bothersome by-product of a press that had been riling the public since Brett's shooting. The result was a state of anxiety which, far from making the country safer, had created little but headaches for the police. As he recalled of the winter of 1868, the 'panic that prevailed in London at this time was absolutely ludicrous', with government ministers receiving 'letters from panic-stricken folk or from lunatics or cranks, reporting suspicious incidents or giving warning of plots upon public or private property'. Anderson himself was dragged into the madness. Having agreed to meet an informer who claimed to possess details of a Fenian plot to attack the Bank of England, the detective found himself crossing the threshold of a shabby East End lodging house that was 'half boudoir, half bedroom'. There, he took a seat across a rickety table from a 'charmingly elderly lady' who, after an hour of meandering discussion over weak tea, revealed that her information on the impending attack had been delivered through a séance, for 'she was in the habit of receiving heavenly visions'.[20]

Encounters with eccentrics aside, Anderson's other frustration was with the fact that despite the 'wretched men who fired the fuse' at Clerkenwell being incapable of calculating the explosive power of gunpowder, a narrative emerged in the press and amongst certain politicians that a well-oiled terrorist conspiracy was afoot. At the heart of this belief was an assumption that the recruitment of trained mercenaries like Cluseret and Fariola meant that the IRB had become as vast and dangerous an organisation as Stephens once hoped it could be. Events in the wake of the Manchester Martyrs' execution hardened this view, and suggested that a new, professional form of terrorist was being nurtured within the Fenians' ranks. A few weeks before the Clerkenwell bombing, two police officers in Dublin were shot by a suspect whom the authorities 'had no doubt is a Fenian', who was also most likely 'a hired assassin, as he knew his way around a revolver'. As the post-Clerkenwell panic reached its apogee in Britain, across the Channel the Sûreté – doubtless whilst engaged in their tracking of Cluseret and Fariola – reported the uncovering of a Fenian headquarters beneath a printing office, located within the warren of red clubs that ran through Paris's Belleville district. Of further concern was the report that documents had been found there indicating that a Fenian 'plot for destroying a portion of the British Channel Fleet by fire' was being developed.[21]

In addition to this fear of the Fenians growing bolder in their embrace of explosives was a concern that the IRB's operations were expanding. In April 1868, Henry O'Farrell, a Dublin-born émigré to Australia, fired a bullet into the back of Prince Alfred, the Duke of Edinburgh, during a royal visit to Sydney. O'Farrell's connection to the IRB was dubious and at the trial he appeared more homicidal loner than member of an international terrorist organisation. Even so, the fact that he claimed to have attacked the duke in the name of the Irish republican cause was enough to provoke anti-Irish protests in the city's streets and a call in the *Sydney Morning Herald* to 'exterminate the Fenian miscreants'. Received in a climate of paranoia, the British press added fresh details to the *Herald*'s report, claiming that O'Farrell had drawn the short straw from amongst a Sydney-based cell of Fenians, which was 'ordered from this country' to assassinate the duke. It was therefore obvious that 'there is a secret organization of Fenians in London or elsewhere, which the police are unable to ferret out'. The ramifications of this failure to tackle the apparently global expanse of the IRB were spelled out in the Dublin-based newspaper *The Nation*. Even 'without ships on sea or an army in the field', through their international alliances the Fenians still had 'it in their hands to deliver a tremendous blow to England'. This could be done by using financial support from the United States to buy guns and gain instruction from European radicals in bomb design. This would lead to attacks carried out by 'a few astute and desperate men', smuggled faceless and undetected into Ireland and Britain from abroad – an invisible army of bombers and assassins whose murderous reach could extend across Britain's empire.[22]

In his assessment of Clerkenwell and its aftermath, the soon to be British prime minister Benjamin Disraeli summed up the extent to which Stephens' dreams of an international alliance had become a reality in the minds of many concerned Britons. The 'relation between the Fenians in England and the revolutionary societies abroad', Disraeli claimed, indicated the existence of 'a system of organised incendiarism' that stretched beyond Britain's shores. Disraeli's sentiments resonated in a world in which terrorism seemed to be going global. Whether it was American-backed Fenians or Russian nihilists in search of allies in Switzerland, police and politicians across the continent were now of a mind that a war was coming, in which violent radicals – linking arms across borders – would commit targeted killings and bombings on a hitherto unthinkable scale. So palpable was this fear, it opened the door for the return to prominence of a once disgraced police chief, who had long foretold of the coming catastrophe.[23]

Part 2

Conspirators?

Chapter VI

Gathering storms

Wilhelm Stieber's capacity to see enemies everywhere had not abated since his inglorious downfall. If anything, the spymaster's obsession with terrorist conspiracies and belief that he alone could combat them had only grown since his corruption trial in 1860. Having correctly deduced that his acquittal would not equate to forgiveness from either the public or the liberals in Prussia's parliament (Landtag), in the wake of the trial Stieber packed up his dossiers on French republicans and German socialists and boarded a train bound for St Petersburg. His mission was to internationalise his war on radicalism by forming a partnership with the Third Section's then chief, Vasily Dolgorukov. However, as had occurred in 1851 in Britain and more recently in Prussia, Stieber's paranoid certainties about the scope of the danger Europe faced rendered him a man adrift in the land of the tsars. His train pulled into Nikolayevsky Station in January 1861, only a few weeks before Tsar Alexander delivered his Emancipation Manifesto. Despite falling short of the expectations nursed by nihilists and *narodniki*, the Manifesto was still pregnant with the promise of a new Russia in which Stieber's hard-line hatred for reformers and progressive politics would be out of vogue.

To make matters worse, Dolgorukov was too soft for Stieber's tastes. True, the Third Section chief had pursued the notorious Ishutin-inspiring writer Chernyshevsky into Siberian exile, but not before giving him a pen and paper during his incarceration in the Peter and Paul Fortress, with which the radical penned *What Is To Be Done?* In addition to allowing Chernyshevsky to shape the minds of the Hell generation of nihilists with this text, Dolgorukov was also disposed to light-touch methods of anti-radical policing, such as issuing fines, placing dissidents under house arrest or, in serious cases, having anti-tsarist students hauled before provincial governors for a paternalistically stern telling off. It was only after the fires spread across St Petersburg in 1862 that some of Stieber's hard-line influence began to rub off on the Third Section, in the form of tighter surveillance and the establishment of a special investigative commission for combatting political criminals.[1]

By then, however, Stieber had abandoned his hopes of constructing an anti-radical alliance with Dolgorukov and was planning his return to Berlin, where the political winds had started to blow back in his favour. The force of nature behind this change was Otto von Bismarck, whom King Wilhelm of Prussia appointed chancellor in September 1862. Bismarck was an ardent monarchist and a ruthless political operator, contemptuous of those he deemed his intellectual inferiors – which was most people – and possessed of abilities that provoked awe and revulsion in equal measure. Too much like the tyrant Napoleon for some Prussians' comfort, Bismarck was, the liberal politician Ludwig Bamberger recalled, the most morally ambiguous of creatures, with plotting eyes that were either 'mistrustful/friendly, lurking/bright, cold/flashing, determined not to reveal what goes on behind them unless he intends it'. The one thing Bamberger knew for certain was that Bismarck was a 'predatory beast' who lived to dominate his enemies, particularly those of a radical disposition.[2] A stiff-backed arch-conservative, Bismarck was the political master whom Stieber had been waiting his life to serve.

In addition to sharing the chancellor's loathing of radicals, Stieber was also moved by Bismarck's political mission – to complete the unification of Germany. This idea had been potent in German politics since 1815, when the Congress of Vienna had agreed to separate the German world into thirty-nine states, which comprised a German Confederation. Now, with Austria having been humiliated in the war with Napoleon and the latter posturing as Europe's strongman, there was a renewed impetus in Prussia to take the lead in the unification project and establish itself as the military guardian of the German world. The problem was that debate on how best to do this had stalled in the Landtag, where progressives and conservatives were at odds over the issue of how much power Wilhelm would have over the army in this new political constitution. To Stieber's consternation, this political squabble had led to terrorist violence.

In the summer of 1861, a law student named Oskar Becker, who was convinced that Wilhelm was the source of the Landtag's deadlock, fired a pistol at his sovereign as the latter was strolling through a public garden in Baden Baden. Wilhelm received only a flesh wound to his neck and Becker was quickly apprehended, boasting proudly that 'I fired at the king!' as he was dragged away. Like many assassins of this era, Becker evoked Orsini's name at his trial, claiming to the jury that the Italian's nation-shaping actions had inspired him to solve Prussia's political impasse by ending the life of its king. The judge, however, was unmoved by this warped sense of patriotism and so gave Becker twenty years. This verdict dealt with the immediate danger, but Wilhelm nonetheless slumped into a state of torpid depression in the trial's aftermath, during which he mused on the Gordian knot that had been woven around his unhappy kingdom. Faced with political stalemate, the Napoleonic menace and the threat of assassination from those murderously dissatisfied with the state of things, it was small wonder that the king considered abdicating.[3]

It was from this pit of despair that Wilhelm reached out to Bismarck and tasked him with solving Prussia's problems – a mission the chancellor grasped with relish. In the Landtag, Bismarck outmanoeuvred the progressives by declaring that, in instances of political deadlock, the decision on how to move forward had to defer to the monarch. The new chancellor also unleashed a campaign against progressive and radical voices beyond the debating chamber. Using an obscure law from 1851 to pursue instances of slander, falsehood and hate-mongering, Bismarck issued an edict declaring that newspapers and magazines containing a 'general attitude' deemed offensive to the monarch or 'dangerous to the public welfare' would be banned.[4] As the chancellor continued to rattle leftist beehives with his sabre, Stieber grew concerned about retaliation. It was not simply the Becker-like rogues of the world whom he feared.

To his mind, Bismarck was not unlike Napoleon – less a man than he was a symbol of conservative power in Europe. As such, the chancellor was a prime target for the kind of radical internationalist terrorist groups whose existence Stieber had warned the world of for years.

Beyond his long-standing prejudices, Stieber had reason to believe that such a group was lurking on Prussia's doorstep. In the multi-ethnic Austrian Empire, Franz Joseph's chief of internal security, General Ludwig von Benedek, had been noting subversion amongst the Hungarian, Serbian, Czech and Polish troops of the army since the humiliating defeats they suffered in Italy in 1859. Already possessed of little affection for their German-speaking officers, these troops, Benedek feared, were being radicalised by the Viennese intelligentsia and the various French, Russian and Italian thinkers with whom they mingled in the capital's bustling coffee shops and elegant bars. Their minds poisoned by this underworld of 'international revolutionaries, lawyers and doctors without practices, ambitious money-hungry journalists and dissatisfied professors and schoolteachers', Benedek was convinced that an attack in which a radicalised soldier would go rogue and shoot up a barracks or a royal procession was inevitable. Stieber's spies in Austria confirmed this hypothesis to their master. Having infiltrated a socialist meeting, one spy reported that radical propaganda – most likely produced by Bakunin or Herzen – was finding its way into the hands of not only factory workers but also Benedek's soldiers, who were being bludgeoned with the mantra that 'the state's permanent armies are the mainstay of despotism'. To the mind of Stieber's man, only the 'summary expulsion of all foreign suspects engaged in subversive activities' in Austria could prevent disaster, for violent 'agitations are the work of foreigners who have been allowed to reside in Austria as long as they do not commit any public offence'.[5]

It was amidst these concerns over a terrorist conspiracy being hatched in Austria that a curious episode unfolded in Berlin on 6 May 1863. That morning, Stieber positioned himself on the fourth floor of a building overlooking the Wilhelmstrasse, watching through a set of eyeglasses as Bismarck's carriage wove its way through the clutter of horse traffic and handcarts, taking the same dangerously predictable route it always did when ferrying the chancellor to his office. Trapped by the bustle, the driver was forced to slow Bismarck's carriage to a crawl. In that moment, a scruffy-looking man emerged from the mass of grey and black suits on the pavement, drew a pistol and discharged a round that smashed through the carriage's side window and into the head of the figure reclining in the passenger seat. Within seconds, plain-clothes police appeared and subdued the gunman. As his colleagues wrestled the man down, a detective looked up to Stieber and received a nod of direction, in response to which he opened the carriage door. A dummy dressed in Bismarck's clothes and 'painted with the features of a distinguished gentleman' then tumbled out onto the ground, the bullet hole in its head of cloth and straw still smoking.

The man whom Stieber's men seized was an Austrian in his late twenties, who later claimed under interrogation that he knew his target was a dummy and so shot at it for fun. Stieber argued otherwise to Bismarck that the assailant was neither playful pistol-wielder nor a crazed loner in the mould of Becker. Instead, he asserted that the Austrian was one of the 'murderers for liquidation squads' that Bakunin had been despatching from Geneva with orders to kill Europe's leaders. Even by Stieber's standards, this was an absurd claim. At the time of the fracas on the Wilhelmstrasse, Bakunin was still in London recovering from his globe-spanning escape from Siberia. Barely into the early muttering stages of forming the International Brotherhood, he was at least three years away from boasting to Herzen – without evidence to support the claim – of how 'we have adherents in Sweden, Norway, Denmark, England, Belgium, France, Spain and Italy'. Moreover, Bakunin's meeting with the murderous Nechaev lay even further in the future.

Aware of Benedek's fears of subversion in Austria and doubtless informed by his friends at the Third Section of the revolutionary ideology Bakunin preached, Stieber dismissed the contextual reality and argued that Bismarck's would-be assassin was an agent of an internationalist conspiracy. That, at least, was what he told the chancellor. It is always hard to tell with Stieber where shrewd certainty and paranoid self-delusion collided, but it is notable that the Wilhelmstrasse shooter was freed without charge, his only penalty being a police escort to the Austrian border and a warning to stay out of Prussia. Whether he was another Becker whom Stieber lured into a trap or a plant paid to do for Bismarck what Pinkerton's Baltimore plot did for Lincoln, what mattered to Stieber was that his chancellor now realised the depths to which his enemies would stoop. Bismarck duly rewarded Stieber with full political rehabilitation and fresh funds from the treasury, in addition to permission to expand his system of spies and informers across the German Confederation and deeper into Russia and France with the aim to keep an eye on continent-wide anarchist and socialist conspiracies.[6]

This was a moment of vindication for the man once dismissed as an unscrupulous 'political character of some notoriety', presiding in paranoid fervour over 'the inquisitorial department of the Prussian police'. Not only had his moment of destiny arrived, but Stieber's long-held belief that a revolutionary conspiracy was at work across Europe was bolstered by the news that flew across his desk throughout the 1860s. The Polish uprising in 1863 was met with pledges of solidarity from British Chartists and support from nationalists in Italy, who were waging their own form of 'Orsini warfare' at the time under Garibaldi's leadership. In 1866, Karakozov attempted to shoot the tsar as part of a presumed Polish plot. A year later, the Fenians launched their uprising in Ireland with the help of republican insurgents from France and Switzerland whilst, at the same time in Cairo, the khedive of Egypt had two Orsini bombs thrown at him by nationalists. That same year, 1867, Bakunin wrote of the need for 'a secret organization that will rally not a few, but all countries into a single plan of action' to effect an anarchist revolution. Combined with the intelligence Stieber received from his informers on socialists plotting assassinations in Prussia and schemes to subvert soldiers in Austria, it was clear to him that various radical groups were coalescing around the practice of not only insurrection, but more blatantly terroristic methods like targeted killing and bombing. Confirming Stieber's belief in the imminence of this threat, in May 1866 Bismarck was once again – this time without question genuinely – targeted for assassination as he strolled along the Unter den Linden in central Berlin. Unhurt by the two shots fired at him, the chancellor turned on his assailant and entered a scuffle during which three additional shots were discharged, one of which grazed Bismarck's chest, presumably above the bulletproof vest that Stieber later claimed he had given his master in anticipation of such an attack.[7]

As Bismarck nursed his wounds, the arrest and processing of his attacker unfolded under Stieber's supervision at the nearest police station. There, it was ascertained that the assailant was a twenty-two-year-old law student named Ferdinand Cohen-Blind, whose 48er father had worked for Heinzen at *Der Pionier* and was a known advocate of terrorism. The son had taken his father's views to heart. Like Becker, Cohen-Blind cited Orsini as his inspiration, believing that the death of the tyrannical chancellor would lead to a new age of political freedom in Prussia. A sensational trial would have doubtless followed, with Stieber opining to the court and the press about how Cohen-Blind's plan evidenced a wider plot against the Prussian state, directed by Bakunin, Marx or some other arch-conspirator The shooter, however, had other plans. Having smuggled a penknife into the police station, Cohen-Blind managed to slit his own throat, albeit not before throwing cold water on Stieber's fever dreams by stating categorically that he had acted alone, driven by a personal mission to rid his homeland of 'the worst enemy of German liberty'.[8]

Stieber's beliefs were dealt a further blow by the truth of Berezowski's attempt on the tsar in 1867. Driven by the same concern that had gripped him at the Great Exhibition in London back in 1851, Stieber took a team of his best men to Paris for the International Exposition, certain that the crowds, the gathering of wealth and the presence of emperors would be irresistible for assassins. This was why he was beside the imperial carriage when Berezowski, having pushed through the crowd that had formed to catch a view of Napoleon and Alexander, exclaimed 'Long live Poland!' and took aim at the tsar, only for his modified pistol to explode, leading him to require a thumb amputation. Unlike Cohen-Blind, Berezowski was brought to trial, however, and to Stieber's disappointment, the Sûreté made public their conclusions that the shooter was not affiliated with any revolutionary organisation. This led to the press presenting him as little more than a 'misguided fanatic'. To Stieber's further ire, Berezowski's defence lawyer convincingly presented his client to the court as a hero who was trying to right the wrongs committed against Poland by the Russian state. This depiction was given weight by Berezowski's record in the Polish uprising, during which, according to his commander, he was 'one of the best soldiers in the regiment'. Through this testimony, Berezowski came close to being gifted the same veneer that Orsini, Brown and the IRB had coveted – that of legitimacy in their recourse to political violence. Given the choice of viewing Berezowski as a noble freedom fighter or crazed regicide, the court opted for something in between, finding him guilty but sparing him the guillotine. The one thing of which the court was certain was that Berezowski was no agent of an international revolutionary cabal.[9]

The court's decision did little to shake Stieber's opinions, which, owing to the spike in political violence across Europe during the 1860s, were now far from solely his own. In addition to Shuvalov buying into Ishutin and Nechaev's fantasies of being part of an international alliance of radicals, Joseph-Marie Piétri – the prefect of Paris police and brother of the Piétri of Orsini's time – was similarly convinced that a continent-wide conspiracy was directing acts of revolutionary terrorism. The prefect's suspicions were informed in part by one of his spies, who infiltrated the Lyon branch of Marx's IWMA and came away convinced that this workers' agitation group was scheming to spill blood. The IWMA's members had, the spy claimed, pledged to 'terrify the reactionaries whatever mask they wear, clericism or monarchism, bourgeoism or liberalism', by radicalising workers such that they would 'violently claim their rights'. The notion that the IWMA was more sinister than it seemed was also posited by spies in the pay of the Belgian government, who attended the organisation's congress in Basel in 1869 and noted both the violent undertones of the declarations made and the organisation's broad membership. Twenty-four delegates had come from France, twenty-one from Switzerland, ten from Prussia, six from Britain and five from Belgium itself, along with smaller delegations from Spain, Italy, Russia and Austria, and an apology from across the Atlantic, for the 'labour unions of New York usually send at least two delegates'. This was an international coterie of conspirators, coming together at a time when terrorist attacks were increasing across Europe – clearly, a cause for concern.[10]

It is true that there were advocates of violence – both of the street-level 48er variety and of the more blatant terroristic form – amongst the IWMA's members. Moreover, the organisation's ideological composition was very diffuse, comprising nationalist-liberals like the younger Orsini, feminists like Harriet Law and the anarchist Bakunin, who often clashed with Marx on matters personal and ideological., The spies at the Basel congress, however, chose to see the IWMA as a more uniform entity which, owing to the wild and boastful rhetoric of some of its members, was clearly united in its support of political violence. Reflecting the wider shrug of the shoulders towards the IWMA from the press, the centrist newspaper *Le Temps* presented a more nuanced view of proceedings in Basel. Its correspondent reported that the gathering 'did not reveal any new facts worthy of interest' beyond the same 'dreamers accustomed to using violent expressions without fully realizing their meaning'. The IWMA was just another group of dissidents blowing hot air into the wind. However, even journalists sceptical of the notion that the IWMA threatened something violent found themselves warming to secret police suspicions in the autumn of 1867, when another internationalist congress took place in Geneva.

Convened in the main hall of the city's Hôtel de Ville, the Congress of Peace and Freedom was attended by pacifists, socialists, republicans, anarchists, Fenians and even the Italian guerrilla legend Garibaldi. Crowning this rogue's gallery was Bakunin, who, as the foremost IWMA member involved, served as the star attraction for the legions of spies and journalists who filtered into Geneva to observe, as one German newspaper dubbed it, a 'playground of hatred, passion and bitterest excitement'. Seen as a vessel for subversively violent internationalism, this 'peculiar peace congress' was denounced in the conservative press as the opposite of what it claimed to be. No pacifistic assembly, the Congress of Peace and Freedom was clearly a talking shop for 'excitement to civil war', convened 'under the pretext of discussing peace', at which participants instead talked through 'plans directed at the Divine as well as against the worldly order of things'.[11]

Unable to help himself, Bakunin did little to correct this impression. Addressing the assembly with a leathered voice emboldened by conviction, the anarchist demanded that the founders of the League of Peace and Freedom get 'organised as much as possible, in all the countries of Europe', with the aim 'to extend it even into America'. If evoking the spirit of his International Brotherhood was not enough, Bakunin also declared that as 'Russian socialists and as slavs' we 'hate monarchies with all our hearts and wish nothing better than to see them overthrown across Europe and the world'. Garibaldi made an even more jarring contribution, taking to the lectern on day two of proceedings to deliver a fire-and-brimstone speech about how the Pope was the embodiment of tyranny, after which he led his supporters from the room, declaring that he was off to make war in Italy in the name of peace.[12]

The Congress of Peace and Freedom was a messy farce. However, convened at a time when assassins had tried to take the lives of Bismarck, King Wilhelm and Tsar Alexander, the Fenians had shot police and bombed prisons, and Bakunin was assembling his International Brotherhood, it prompted Piétri to lash out against suspected conspirators in France. Shortly after the Congress ended, several French university professors were arrested on Piétri's orders, on suspicion of organising a follow-up event in Paris which, the prefect claimed, was intended to incite 'hatred and contempt against the government'. Having grabbed headlines with their failed uprisings, the Fenians were also dragged into the maw of suspicion in France, with a contributor to the *Journal des Débats* opining that, despite its goal of Irish emancipation, the IRB was part of the 'revolutionary and openly socialist movement' that the IWMA was directing across Europe. Piétri agreed with this assessment. After the Clerkenwell bombing, he ordered his men to raid Paris's red clubs in search of evidence that tied the Fenians to French socialists. Taking up for the latter, the IWMA denounced the prefect for implying that Paris was the 'centre of the Fenian conspiracy of which the International was one of the principal organs'. This assertion may have been born of Stephens's affiliation with Cluseret and Cesare Orsini, but there were no grounds for believing that the Fenians were working hand in glove with the IWMA. Indeed, many Irish republicans – possessed of Catholic convictions – resented the godlessness of Europe's socialists and anarchists. At the very least, they saw little connective tissue between the struggle for Irish independence and the global revolutionary goals of internationalists like Marx and Bakunin.[13]

Spurious as Piétri's suspicions about the IWMA–Fenian connection were, they were an understandable product of the police chief's state of mind, which was plagued during the late 1860s with legitimate concerns over revolutionary violence in Paris. He may have been a regime loyalist, but even Piétri had to concede that Napoleon was to blame for engendering this state of national peril. At the start of the decade, the emperor had been riding high off his victory in Italy, enjoying a boost in public support and a bolstering of his own martial confidence. Fortified, he launched an invasion of Mexico in 1863 that quickly turned disastrous, depleting France's treasury and shattering the image he had earned at Solferino and Magenta as the world-beating reincarnation of his uncle. This collapse of prestige was followed by the ebbing of public support. Even government legislators could see trouble brewing, penning an aside for Napoleon's eyes in the annual budget for 1863 that declared that 'we are unanimous in recommending a term to be put on the Mexican expedition … this desire corresponds with the general feeling in the country'. Needing to win back his people's affections, Napoleon scaled back the Law of Public Safety that had been passed following Orsini's attack. This allowed socialists, republicans and other exiled dissidents to return to France, where, rather than thank Napoleon for his beneficent gesture, they re-energised the red clubs and riled up Parisians who were fast growing tired of their emperor. The result was a spate of violent protests through the summer 1869, complete with demands that Napoleon give up his throne.[14]

These long months of civil unrest came to a head in January 1870, when the radical journalist Victor Noir was slapped across the face and fatally shot in a petulant rage by Napoleon's cousin. Although he was put on trial for murder, few Parisians believed that the royal offender would face justice, especially given that, as a British journalist observed sniffily of Paris at the time, 'the American fashion of carrying firearms has become so general here that I have heard the prince defended on the grounds that, his visitors being journalists, he must have known they were armed'. When the predictable acquittal came, Napoleon ordered that his cousin be rushed back to the Tuileries Palace and placed under armed guard, whilst beyond the palace gates Noir was laid to rest amidst 'demonstrations at the funeral, followed by an infinity of riotous incidents' across Paris. Given Noir's affiliation with republican and socialist groups, it was unsurprising that police informers reported to Piétri that amidst a restive gathering of over 100,000 citizens on the Champs-Élysées, 'the ardent revolutionaries saw an opportunity for insurrection and prepared an attempt on the life of the emperor'.

The imminence of this assault on Napoleon's regime was confirmed on 28 January 1870, when a man named Verdier walked through the doors of the Paris police prefecture and reported to the duty officer that 'there was a conspiracy against the life of the emperor, in which affiliates of the conspirators were using the insurrection on the streets for a dual purpose'. Verdier claimed to be a protester outraged by the acquittal of Noir's killer but nevertheless horrified at the prospect of someone taking Napoleon's life in reprisal. Consequently, he was revealing all he knew to the police, detailing how he had attended meetings where a 'revolutionary movement was organizing itself to rise up in coordination with an attempt on the emperor'. The plot was far advanced and its details reflected an age when the time-honoured practice of street-level insurrection was being married by radicals to new terrorist tactics. Cells of insurgents had been formed and money issued to them for the purchase of weapons and 'the manufacture of bombs and other devices suitable for the commission of the crime'. Worst of all, the architects of this grand act of revolutionary violence were a group that Piétri had already identified as one of the pre-eminent terrorist threats France faced – the Blanqui Party.[15]

The mention of Louis Auguste Blanqui and his followers in connection with bombs, conspiracy and assassination was all Piétri needed to act on Verdier's information, ordering squads of gendarmes to arrest and deport from France followers of a man who embodied all that he, Stieber and Benedek had come to loathe and dread. A career insurgent of Bakunin's generation, Blanqui had participated in the overthrow of King Charles X in 1830, conspired with the Carbonari, founded the proto-communist League of the Just and spent most of his adult life in and out of prison. Unrepentant in his zeal for revolutionary violence, in 1869 Blanqui had returned to France from his latest stint in exile and gathered around him a following that numbered in the hundreds. Not only did the Blanqui Party's size dwarf that of Hell or People's Revenge but, unlike these Russian revolutionary groups, its backbone was not formed of angry, inexperienced and unskilled students. Amongst his adherents, the prison-moulded Blanqui could find savage intellectuals and skilled propagandists with a mind for subterfuge, one of whom ran counter-intelligence to sniff out police spies. The group also boasted science teachers with knowledge of explosive chemicals and radical toughs who, in August 1870, would attempt to seize arms from a barracks to engender a rising against the French state. More than a gang of student poseurs and all-talk assassins, the Blanqui Party was a sophisticated revolutionary group, whose members understood the importance of counter-intelligence, propaganda and the securing of weapons to violently pursue their cause.[16]

Blanqui's followers were also informed by a proto-terrorist philosophy that their leader had developed during his long decades of agitation. More outwardly violent than Bakunin's loose ideas of global insurrection, Blanqui's philosophy married socialism with the bloodier traditions of the Jacobins – the extremist architects of the French Revolution's Reign of Terror. Regarding organisation, Blanqui shared Nechaev's view on the importance of cells being under the command of a single leader who would report to Blanqui alone. Blanqui's thoughts on what these cells should do revealed a touch of Heinzen. He urged his followers to reflect on 1848, and 'consider the fearful catastrophe that might confront us today, should we resort again the same stupidity in the face of a ferocious military regime, that now has at its disposal the recent discoveries of sciences and the arts: the railways, the electric telegraph, rifled canons and the Chassepot rifle'. However, unlike Heinzen, Orsini and others who looked to level the technological playing field through basement chemistry and home-made weapons, Blanqui romanticised the street-fighting underdog. Deriding devices like the Orsini bomb as 'very dangerous to handle, having no range and can only be used when thrown out of windows', Blanqui advocated a more primordial form violence. He instructed his followers to use daggers, pistols, hand-to-hand combat and even paving stones as street artillery, in the absurd belief that, compared with explosives, 'they do nearly as much damage and are cheaper'.

His understanding of asymmetrical warfare may have been weaker than that of many of his contemporaries, but Blanqui's grasp of how to create violent radicals was strong. Tapping into the fears that Benedek nursed of attacks within barracks, he argued that uniformed soldiers march 'only under constraint and under the influence of brandy'. In contrast to these hollow adversaries, revolutionaries fought for ideas that mattered, 'motivated by enthusiasm, not fear'. This, Blanqui believed, was the subversive's ultimate weapon, for to turn the minds of an emperor's soldiers to radicalism was to deprive a tyrant of the rifles and bayonets that empowered him. A vocal advocate of revolutionary terrorism, cellular organisation and the subverting of soldiers and workers, Blanqui represented an amalgam of the Jacobin traditions of the French Revolution, the street-fighting of 1848 and the conspiratorial terrorism of the post-Orsini era. He also confirmed Stieber and Piétri's conspiracy theory by being a member of the IWMA, albeit one whose coarse advocacy of terroristic violence and Jacobin philosophies created division and rancour within the organisation.[17]

Verdier's information and Piétri's investigations into the Blanqui Party led to the uncovering of a plot that relied on terrorism to fulfil its revolutionary aims. The initial phase of the plan was to involve a spate of bombings across Paris, facilitated by a cache of infernal machines. Each device was built in the style of the Orsini bomb, albeit in a form that was disturbingly more rustic than the 1858 originals, suggesting that anyone with access to the most basic materials could now build this vaunted terrorist weapon. Gone were the days of careful machine-worked grenade shells. Instead, the Orsini bombs Piétri's men found in May 1870 had been assembled from sewing-machine parts and components from an electric telegraph, charged with the percussion-detonated substance potassium picrate. With these bombs detonating outside government buildings, the second half of the plan would be initiated, involving a lone assassin shooting Napoleon, the news of which would cause protesters on the streets to launch a full-blown uprising against the state. Notably, echoes of Orsini's conspiring with British radicals and the suspicions that the IWMA was backing terrorists bled into press reportage of this plot. The conspirators were alleged to have sketched out their plans from the safety of radical-friendly London, during a banquet at which 'some hundred Frenchmen' were joined by Chartists, who together toasted French republicans and the Fenians, whilst being waited on by 'buxom dames and pretty demoiselles'. Once the loutish debauchery was dispensed with, the radical coterie got down to their plotting, supplied, as one French newspaper asserted, by the IWMA with men and money.[18]

Suffice to say, these attacks did not happen and no credible evidence emerged of the London gathering of bombers, socialists, assassins and agitators for electoral reform. Blanqui fled to Brussels, escaping the police dragnet that netted over fifty other radicals. As questions over whether the plot even existed continued to swirl in the press, one journalist homed in on the IWMA aspect of the story, deriding 'those ridiculous rumours from France and the rest of the continent about English workingmen being mixed up in plots against foreign governments as mere idle nonsense, when they are not police fabrications'. Marx, for his part, acted decisively to lift the veil of suspicion from his organisation, attacking Piétri's investigation as the pursuit of a 'pretended plot' and drafting a resolution for IWMA members to publicly denounce assassination and conspiracy. This included issuing a warning to friends about Cluseret, whose allegiance to the IWMA and 'flighty, superficial, officious and boastful' personality put Marx on edge.[19] These efforts to dismantle the theory of IWMA connections to terrorist activity were forlorn. The infusing of terrorist methods into revolutionary activities during the 1860s and the efforts of the IRB, the Russian nihilists and Bakunin to create international alliances had stirred a potent fear, exemplified in the police investigation and press coverage of the so-called 'May Plot' of 1870. This was the fear that a new uprising – more conspiratorial, more terroristic than any before it – was about to occur. Fittingly, it was the city of Orsini's attack, the Blanqui Party's rise and Piétri's paranoia that would host this revolutionary conflagration.

Chapter VII

City of enemies

'The temperature of Lyon is utterly savage, and the government is weak. There is bound to be a revolution.' This was the assessment made by Roman Postnikov, a Third Section spy who, in September 1870, found himself in France digesting the most sensational of political developments – Napoleon III, the nephew of Bonaparte and the conqueror of Franz Joseph, was emperor no more. Like a shockwave, this news had emanated out from the French city of Sedan, within the walls of which Napoleon and his 130,000 strong Army of Châlons had been forced to retreat in the face of 200,000 heavily armed Prussians, accompanied by Bismarck with the ever-faithful Stieber by his side. Pummelled by the invader's formidable Krupp cannons, the French soldiers and their hapless sovereign were forced on 2 September to wave the white flag. An ignoble scene followed. The one-time strongman of Europe was forced to accept Bismarck's offer of a train crammed with ornate furnishings, fine wine and royal attendants, which spirited Napoleon away from the scene of his vanquishing to captivity in Hesse. This was followed by a brief exile in Britain, where he died in 1873, reportedly, with the catastrophe of Sedan still haunting his thoughts.

No less than his missteps in Mexico and his handling of the radical exiles who had returned to Paris, Napoleon's final calamity was born of his own poor judgement. As civil disorder flogged his capital in the early summer of 1870, the emperor engaged in an unwinnable battle of wits with Bismarck, who, informed by Stieber's spies of poor morale within the army and the emperor's preoccupation with managing public unrest, manipulated Napoleon into declaring war against Prussia as a means of reasserting his authority and bond to his people. This was a master stroke of political calculation on Bismarck's part which, he anticipated, would galvanise the German world behind Prussia and achieve the unification he had sought for nearly a decade. In the process, the Prussian invader would expose the weakness of a nation that Napoleon had mismanaged into oblivion. And so it went. In the weeks following the outbreak of fighting in mid-July 1870, battle after battle was lost by the French as the Prussians pushed deeper into the country, before the emperor and his army found themselves outnumbered, outgunned and bereft of any chance of reprieve within Sedan's walls. In mocking commemoration of the French defeat that followed, the fake news master Stieber disseminated a parable for the battle, which told of how the dishevelled and overweight Napoleon had been captured trying in vain to fire a mitrailleuse – a proto-machine gun that symbolised French military supremacy, which jammed at the moment when the emperor needed its power.

On the heels of military humiliation came political implosion. When news reached Paris of the emperor's defeat, the frayed ties that bound him to his people finally snapped. The city's Hôtel de Ville was seized by a loose alliance of republicans, liberals and socialists, amongst whom were participants in the Victor Noir riots. By 4 September, Napoleon's reign was over, and the patience of his enemies rewarded by the declaration of a new French Republic under the leadership of General Louis-Jules Trochu. This was not the assault by revolutionary terrorists that Stieber and Piétri had feared. Trochu did not reorganise his government around workers' councils or abolish the church and state. Rather, as a moderate republican who recognised the peril in which France still found itself, Trochu proclaimed a Government of National Defence, and with it a pledge to continue the fight against Prussia to the bitter end.[1]

Despite the lack of radicalism in Trochu's proclamation, the spy Postnikov believed that events in Paris heralded the start of something catastrophic and revolutionary. This assessment was born less of speculative paranoia than of his recent experience. In March 1870, Postnikov had arrived in Switzerland on the hunt for Nechaev, who, unbeknownst to the Third Section, was already on his way to London by the time their spy's train pulled into Cornavin Station. Adapting to circumstances, Postnikov posed as a nihilist and ingratiated himself with Bakunin's circle, in the hope that when Nechaev returned to the fold he could apprehend Russia's most wanted. Events in France and the temperament of Postnikov's host, however, complicated this patient operation. Upon hearing the news of Napoleon's fall, Bakunin stirred himself to action and ordered his followers to join him in crossing the Swiss border to seize Lyon's Hôtel de Ville in the name of revolution. To protect his cover, the Third Section spy went along with this plan and became part of the very conspiracy he was trying to foil.

Tellingly, this conspiracy amounted to little more than a comedy of errors. Louis Andrieux, a republican lawyer present in Lyon when Bakunin's 'army of malcontents' arrived, recalled how the anarchists took the gendarmerie by surprise and stormed the Hôtel de Ville. From the grand old building's balcony, one of Bakunin's followers – a 'dishevelled and stocky man, verbose and incoherent', as Andrieux had it – harangued the citizens below whilst his colleagues plastered the building's façade with posters declaring that 'the administrative and governmental machinery of the state, having become impotent, is abolished!' The certainty of this proclamation belied the fact that all was still to play for in the struggle between the forces of reaction and revolution in France. No sooner had Bakunin announced the arrival of anarchism in Lyon than a battalion of National Guards loyal to Trochu descended on the city and scattered the invaders with the swinging of sabres and the firing of rifles. Roughed up by the guards and briefly imprisoned, Bakunin and his followers – Postnikov in tow – beat a hasty retreat to Switzerland, their revolution cast to the winds.[2]

Amongst the crestfallen insurrectionists was someone who was unwilling to concede the revolutionary moment – General Cluseret. In a rare moment of sage judgement, Cluseret had opted to lay low in Paris during the Victor Noir riots and the 'May Plot' and so had avoided Piétri's round-ups of radicals. After Napoleon's surrender in September, however, Cluseret sensed an opportunity and re-emerged on the streets of Paris in his finest uniform to seek out Trochu and to offer his services as a general in the fight against Bismarck. Despite his military credentials, Cluseret was deemed too volatile a prospect by France's new leader, who sent the restless insurgent on his way. Undeterred and action hungry, Cluseret sniffed out the revolutionary opportunity Bakunin proffered in Lyon and, with the ease proffered by years of experience, slipped from the guise of French republican soldier into anarchist rebel. As was his want, Cluseret presented himself to Bakunin much as he had to Stephens in 1866 – the only man for the job of leading his revolutionaries to victory.[3]

Despite the prospect of that victory being shattered by the arrival of Trochu's troops in Lyon, Cluseret continued his search for a battle to fight and refused safe harbour in Switzerland. Instead, he drifted south to Marseilles, where yet another insurrection had broken out in response to Napoleon's fall, under the auspices of a wealthy American adventurer named George Francis Train, who was circumnavigating the world in his yacht at the time of the Franco-Prussian War. Train was a maverick in both politics and business who, later in life, was declared insane by a judge, barely escaping incarceration in an asylum. Hints of this destiny were apparent in Train's behaviour at Marseilles in October 1870. Shortly after docking, the American was told of Napoleon's abdication, where-upon he upturned a wooden box on the quayside and addressed the curious crowd that had assembled around him, declaring 'that France should not yield an inch of her territory to the rapacious Prussians'. He then pronounced himself 'a 'communist' and a member of their 'Red Republic', a branch of which he intended to preside over in Marseilles. Having arrived in the city to join Train's nascent revolution, Cluseret demanded that the wealthy American give him the funds to recruit 2,000 armed men – a more modest number than the 10,000 he had asked of Stephens but still an absurd demand in context. What followed was as sad as it was predictable. Not only did Cluseret's revolutionary foot soldiers fail to materialise but the citizens of Marseilles summoned National Guards to disperse Train and his small band of supporters. This led to Train barricading himself in the mayor's office, wherein he wrapped his body in flags and screamed at the troops to 'fire, fire you miserable cowards, fire upon the flags of France and America wrapped around the body of an American citizen if you have the courage!' As this bizarre coda to the Marseilles uprising unfolded, Cluseret quietly slipped away, leaving the fiasco to become another footnote in his long career of botched rebellions.[4]

Although Paris had been beset by street violence and threats of terrorism in the months leading up to the war, Bakunin, Train and Cluseret's faltering revolutionary efforts showed Trochu that, for the moment at least, France's enemies within were of less concern than the danger without. Fresh from their success at Sedan, in the autumn of 1870 Bismarck's armies began to converge on Paris, within which trees were felled in the Bois de Boulogne to create fields for livestock and flowerbeds were torn up to make way for mitrailleuse positions and tent hospitals. For some Parisians, this militarist vandalism stirred a sense of relish for the pending showdown between the children of the French Revolution and Bismarck's reactionary legions. Returning to the city after years in exile, the republican poet Victor Hugo remarked on how thankful he felt to no longer 'see the Bois de Boulogne at the time when it was all carriages, barouches and landaus. It pleases me now that it is a bog, a ruin, it is fine, and it is grand!' Elsewhere, in the district of Montmartre – both the highest point in the city and a hive of radical haunts – death engines of artillery were set up amidst wooden pickets and sandbag walls. These batteries were manned by socialists and anarchists from the district whom Trochu agreed to arm, accepting that their revolutionary spirit might instil the kind of backbone needed to see off the Prussians. Other residents of Paris saw folly in Trochu giving weapons to people who, months earlier, had been accused by Piétri of plotting to assassinate Napoleon and shower the city with Orsini bombs. As a spy in the pay of the Rothschilds wrote to his employers, some 'government circles fear that the Demagogic party (the "reds") will stir up trouble in Paris and in other cities during the siege'.[5]

The unease of this report distilled the anxiety that was rising within Paris. As the leaves drifted from the remaining unfelled trees in the Bois de Boulogne, the radicals grew ever more frustrated with Trochu's defence strategy, which was to tire the Prussians by letting them throw attack after attack against Paris's walls. The sense that Trochu was not embracing the epic stakes of the struggle was captured in a speech delivered at Club Favie in the radical bastion of Belleville. 'Paris is the centre of the civilized world', so one radical declared, 'its fall must be worthy of its renown. When Jerusalem fell the women threw themselves upon the enemy from the top of the walls. Of Palmyra, the queen of the desert, there remains only a mutilated column, and for centuries the sites of Babylon and Nineveh were unknown. And so, it is necessary for Paris to perish … would it not be better to escape this inglorious end by a supreme effort?' In the streets beyond the red clubs where such hopes for oblivion were nurtured, the Blanqui Party took to its printing presses and produced *La Patrie en danger* – a call-back to a publication that had stoked revolutionary fires in France generations earlier. Having returned to Paris during the war, Blanqui declared that 'there is only one enemy, the Prussian, and his accomplice, the partisan of the fallen dynasty who wants to bring order to Paris with Prussian bayonets'. To defeat this reactionary adversary, Blanqui pledged that he and his followers were public enemies no more and were willing to offer Trochu their 'most energetic and most absolute support, without any reservation or condition'.[6]

When Trochu refused to reciprocate this zealotry by switching to a more offensive strategy, this fragile truce crumbled. With the siege still raging, on 31 October Blanqui led an attempt to seize Paris's Hôtel de Ville, alongside radicalised National Guards and 'a vociferous and gesticulating mobocracy' of women, children and agitated workers. It was, as one citizen declared with diabolical exuberance, as if Paris was 'going to see another '93, and we are going to hang one another!' The significance of soldiers being amongst the mob was understood by the American ambassador, who, having heard the blaring of trumpets and the chanting of revolutionary slogans, abandoned his office and made for the Hôtel de Ville. Once there, he forced his way into the building's main hall and beheld Blanqui stood atop a table, stabbing his fingers into the air and barking orders. Beneath him, National Guards were donning red sashes and 'copying lists of the new government, which they called the government of the Commune', whilst Trochu and his cabinet bristled indignantly under lock and key in the adjoining chamber. This evocation of the mystical 'Commune' – another call-back to the French Revolution – was the first sign, as the Rothschild's spy put it, that Blanqui's group 'of some 12,000 vagabonds, capable of anything' was not a rabble that had dragged itself wine-sodden from the bowels of the red clubs. Rather, they were an organised and armed force 'that will become dangerous if not checked'. Thankfully for Trochu, this check came when loyal National Guards arrived. The outcome, as the American ambassador recorded with relief, was that Blanqui's 'little sideshow of the government of the Commune had a precarious existence of about twelve hours, and then vanished into thin air'.[7]

Blanqui may have been thwarted, but the concerns that drove his revolt continued to mount, the more so as the noose around Paris tightened. As winter set in, the City of Light was reduced to a grey and bitter war camp, in which zoo animals, cats, rats and dogs were consumed by a starving population, and violent protests were launched every other day against Trochu, only to be put down by equally violent acts of repression. In the skies above the streets of rage, the Krupp guns duelled with the defender's batteries, creating houses without walls, churches without roofs and mothers without their children. Under the twin pressures of violence in the streets and explosions in the skies, Trochu finally stepped down on 21 January 1871 and, shortly after, the new leader of the government, Adolphe Thiers, agreed to an armistice with the unrelenting Prussians. Frustrated by the months of stubborn resistance, Bismarck was in no mood to be benevolent. The agreement he made with Thiers called for all troops in Paris to be disarmed, a payment of five billion French francs to be made to the invaders, and the territories of Alsace and Lorraine to be ceded. This humiliation was crowned by the declaration of the German Empire on 18 January in the Hall of Mirrors at Versailles – the culmination of Bismarck's unification mission. Amidst this triumph, Bismarck demanded his enemies be subjected to a final indignity, namely, that 'the Germany Army should have the satisfaction of marching into Paris and remaining there till the ratification of the treaty'. For the radicals who had believed the war to be their revolution, Thiers' acquiescence was an unforgivable betrayal.[8]

Chief among those to feel this way was Louise Michel, the so-called 'Red Virgin' of Montmartre. Barely into her forties at the time of the siege, Michel was, a contemporary recalled, like 'a character from a popular novel', born and raised in a château in north-eastern France, albeit as the illegitimate child of a maid. This low-born status ensured that the adolescent Michel was subjected to 'the sly, scornful and vile teasing of other servants in the château'. This experience did much to mould her into an introspective and furious adult, possessed of a 'pale face with prominent cheekbones, a large mouth and dark glowing eyes' – features that at rest were baleful, and when animated trembled with 'great nervous energy', particularly when the subject of revolution was being discussed. This passion led Michel to volunteer for the Montmartre National Guard at the commencement of the siege, throughout which she donned a uniform and slung a rifle in a manner that adhered to her beliefs in both women's rights and the importance of every able bodied Parisian taking up the fight against Bismarck. She gathered around her a coterie of followers – Bakunists, Marxists and Jacobins – many of whom were women who rejected what Michel described as the 'stupid question' of whether females should have a part to play in such a crucial moment in France's history, a time when 'everything was beginning, or rather, beginning again after the long lethargy of the empire'.[9]

In pursuit of this revolutionary moment, Michel achieved that which had eluded Blanqui, Bakunin, Cluseret and Train. On the evening of 18 March 1871, she ran along the winding, cobble-stoned streets of Montmartre, hammering her bony fists onto any doors she could find and cursing loudly. Her cries awakened fellow 'reds' who, in the weeks following the armistice, had refused government demands that they return the cannon and rifles that Trochu had issued them back in September. This defiance led Thiers to a fateful decision – he would disarm the people of Montmartre by force. When news reached Michel that Theirs' troops were approaching to complete this mission, she grasped the gravity of the situation and raised the alarm, ensuring that, when Thiers' soldiers reached the summit of Montmartre, they would be met by a resistant mob. What happened next was forever etched in Michel's mind as a moment that 'could have belonged to the allies of kings' but instead heralded the arrival of a people's revolution. Rather than open fire on their fellow Parisians, the troops laid down their rifles and accepted offerings of bread and wine, as well as the suggestion that they join the people of Montmartre in rebellion against Thiers.[10]

Michel's sense that something wonderful had occurred was soon checked by a jarring spasm of violence. Georges Clemenceau, the mayor of Montmartre, recalled being accosted by one of the freshly 'turned' troops who, infused with radical fervour and, most likely, drunk, 'proclaimed that he wanted to go and get his rifle and fire on any soldiers who might attempt to remove the guns'. This call for blood led to the mob dragging two generals unwilling to join the revolutionary jamboree into the back garden of a guardhouse, where they were shoved against a wall and executed in a volley of gunfire. It was a scene that traumatised Clemenceau, to the extent that his personal secretary believed that 'no memory ever haunted him with such persistence as the memory of those terrible times'.[11] This is no mean thought, given that Clemenceau would go on to become the prime minister of France during the First World War.

Across the city that day similar instances of National Guards turning on the government occurred, such that by the afternoon Thiers conceded Paris to the revolutionaries and sought sanctuary with the Prussians still encamped at Versailles. The prize of the Hôtel de Ville having been abandoned, it was claimed by a mob who, bereft of a natural leader in Blanqui – who had been apprehended before the Montmartre uprising and taken in chains to Versailles – had to decide what the next steps in their revolution would be. This was difficult to figure out, given that Paris's new masters were a mix of Blanqui Party members, republican politicians, philosophers and career insurgents, divided roughly into three factions that held competing visions for their shared future. For some, the Bakuninist ideal of Montmartre representing the first act of a global, anarchist uprising was obvious. For others, the dream of a

Marxist utopia in which the workers would seize control of the state beckoned, whilst a third, vocal category, wished for a return of the blood-on-the-streets Jacobinism of the French Revolution, complete with the suppression of the church and the convening of tribunals for 'traitors'. One of the few issues on which all could agree was that they were conducting a bold experiment in governance, in which the city would be controlled by the people, for the people. This experiment – dubbed the Paris Commune – was officially begun on 28 March, following an election to legitimise the fall of Thiers and the rise of the 'reds' to whom he had bequeathed the City of Lights.[12]

Here was the confluence of both Stieber's nightmares and Bakunin's dreams – a coterie of radicals in command of one of Europe's great cities. The Commune, moreover, had at its head a 'red' legend in Louis Charles Delescluze, a sixty-year-old cane-brandishing Jacobin, whose years incarcerated on Devil's Island had left him with parchment-like skin and the facial features a bloodless ascetic. Beneath Delescluze, the Commune's leadership was a radical mixed bag. The Commune's chief of police, Raoul Rigault, was a ruthless Blanqui Party member whose primary interests were ransacking Paris's churches, assaulting priests and hunting down 'traitors' to the revolution. This extremism revolted the likes of the geographer and philosopher Élisée Reclus, a Bakunist Communard who saw the uprising as the first step towards building an anarchist society which, if he had his way, would be relatively peaceful. Rigault's violent zealotry also repelled Cluseret, who, determined to strike it third-time lucky in his quest for revolution, had slipped back into Paris in the wake of the Montmartre uprising. Once there, the silver-tongued soldier pulled off the greatest coup of his career, convincing the Communards to ignore his failures in Ireland, Lyon and Marseilles, and appoint him the revolution's generalissimo.[13]

Waist deep in the mire of radical ideas from which the Commune was trying to divine a new society stood Michel, who, like Cluseret, had the resumé of a revolutionary for all seasons. In 1858, she had written a letter to Napoleon pleading for Orsini's life and, a year later, had composed poems championing Brown and Garibaldi. During the 1860s she also became an advocate for women's rights. In the Commune, Michel's eclectic tastes for revolutionary action continued to shine through. She assisted Rigault in the monitoring of 'traitors' and declared her intention to sneak into Versailles and assassinate Thiers, with the aim to 'provoke such terror that the reaction against us would be stopped dead'. Flirtations with Jacobin terrorism aside, Michel was also a muse of the republican writer Victor Hugo, who rejected the Commune as a dangerous enterprise. Perhaps in an effort to prove Hugo wrong, Michel balanced her violent utterings with a devotion to furthering the Commune's peaceful agenda, succouring the poor of Montmartre and supporting the policies of two Marxist Communards, Elisabeth Dmitrieff and Leó Frankel, who spent much of their time in Paris organising pensions and improving working conditions for the city's bakers.[14] Social reformer, violent Jacobin, feminist and supporter of nationalist insurgents and terrorist assassins, Michel was the living, breathing manifestation of the Commune's identity crisis.

Bereft of an easy explanation for what the Commune represented or sought to achieve, outsiders perceived it as whatever evil they most feared. With the memory of the 'May Plot' and the Blanqui Party's insurrection attempts still fresh, reports of Orsini bomb factories in Montmartre and the rigging of hostage-containing houses with explosive booby traps appeared in the press. This connection between the Communards and terrorist tactics was strengthened by the claims of certain radicals within Paris, who boasted that they had taken 'delivery of thirty thousand Orsini Bombs to defend our institutions'. Albert Choppin, who served as the prefect of Paris police in the weeks before the uprising, backed this up by asserting that the Communards possessed vast stores of Orsini bombs, for 'since the Orsini attack, the bomb seems to have become a fixed idea for conspirators. They have attached themselves to it with ardour.' These and other allusions to the Communards' explosive capabilities undercut suggestions, such as that made by a British military observer at Versailles, that Paris's new masters were little more than 'the dregs of the gutter who are only stirred to the surface in the days of revolution'. Rather, in command of France's capital and prepared for

'Orsini warfare', the Communards appeared to some as cut from the same murderous cloth as the terrorists who had emerged across Europe in the previous decade.[15]

This notion dovetailed with an idea that taunted reactionary minds during the spring of 1870 – what if the IWMA was the invisible hand that had guided the Commune into power? The ever-blunt Rothschild's spy accepted this theory as fact, explaining succinctly to his employers that it was 'the socialist party of the Internationale that has seized power' in Paris, backed by the small-minded 'Red elements of the army, especially the infantry, who are determined to shed blood'. The Brussels police acted on this theory, requesting details from their spies in Britain on all IWMA congresses held prior to 1871, with a mind to find connections between the names of attendees, London-based adherents to Marx and those now known to be waving red flags in Paris. Doubtless informed by the worried mutterings of Stieber, who watched on in horror from nearby Versailles as the Commune arose, Thiers took this idea to the press, suggesting that 'Communists' had seized his capital. This unsubtle reference to IWMA involvement was picked up by newspapers outside France. As a correspondent from *The Times* explained, the revolutionaries were either 'Communists or Communalists', who represented a force that 'exists in England and in Germany, in Switzerland and in France, and it forms a vast association under the name of the Internationale'.[16]

Much as Reverend William Gibson, a British resident in Paris during the siege, bought into the idea that the Communards 'were getting help from other countries', including from 'Englishmen of red republican principles', his true fear was of the Commune's godlessness. With disgust he recorded that the church of Saint-Eustache had been trashed and turned into a red club by a Communard lout, who declared that 'there was no God' amidst a 'torrent of nonsense and blasphemy'. More sobering was Gibson's calculation that forty-seven priests had been arrested and twenty-six churches closed on the orders of the militant atheist Rigault. News of this clerical maltreatment prompted international outrage, with at least one holy man in Washington, DC, delivering a sermon entitled 'The French Commune as a Popular Medium of Evil', in which he dragged Marxists and Darwinists into the pits of damnation along with the Communards. Upon receiving word that the archbishop of Paris had been executed on 24 May by a Communard firing squad, it was left to Pope Pius IX to describe the relationship between the radicals and the almighty in suitably dramatic terms – from the darkened slums they had emerged into the City of Light as nothing less than 'devils risen up from hell'.[17]

A threat of such unholy magnitude demanded an equally apocalyptic response. Having removed himself to Versailles for fear of his life, the Rothschild's spy reported the deep concern amongst Bismarck's inner circle that 'if Thiers merely shoots a dozen anarchist leaders and pardons the rest, another revolution will flare up in less than a year'. To avoid this, Bismarck agreed to release thousands of French prisoners of war to bolster the ranks of Thiers's forces for an assault so colossal that it would wipe out all trace of the Communards. These soldiers were used to devastating effect. On 21 May, a 70,000-strong army from Versailles punched a hole through the city's defences, aided by a disgruntled Parisian who opened a gate to the invaders. The response from the Communards was as determined as it was panicked. Rigault issued orders for all Parisians to carry identity cards and surrender themselves to searches. This would, he believed, thwart Versailles' efforts to 'introduce its secret agents into Paris, with the purpose of making an "appeal to treason"'. Such was the scale of this spy fever that even Cluseret was caught up in it when, having returned from a failed sortie against the invaders, he was detained by Rigault's men on the contextually absurd charge of defeatism. This official line masked a deeper suspicion that the eternal rogue was working as a double agent for Theirs, plotting to 'excite some corps against the Commune' and undo it from within. At the very least, certain Communards believed that Cluseret's criticism of his ideologically overzealous but operationally useless troops made him politically unreliable, the more so when he issued counter-orders 'forbidding my forces from arbitrarily arresting priests' as Rigault had demanded.[18]

Delescluze's contribution to this moment of peril for the Commune was to assume command of Paris's defence and declare that 'staff officers and gold-embroidered uniform' were no longer required. Instead, he called on the 'bare-armed fighters!' and 'the people who know nothing of elaborate manoeuvres, but when they have a rifle in their hands and cobble-stones under their feet they have no fear for the strategists of the monarchist school'. Amidst this *Götterdämmerung*, truth became a casualty and fanaticism a final recourse. Fresh from ordering the archbishop's execution, on 24 May Rigault proclaimed to his comrades that the breaching of the city by forces from Versailles 'should not dishearten you but spur you to action!', for who were Parisians but 'the people who dethrone monarchs, who destroy Bastilles, the people of '89 and '93!' This appetite for destruction informed Rigault's defence strategy, which consisted of dynamiting bridges across the Seine and dragging furniture from homes, so that the streets of 'Paris bristle with barricades'. Channelling Blanqui, he also declared that 'all the cobble-stones in Paris be dug up' and stacked on balconies for use by the defenders – the most honest and true form of radical artillery.[19]

With their commanders urging them to hurl rocks at trained soldiers armed with Chassepot rifles and mitrailleuse, the Communards' defence swiftly collapsed. Rigault's barricades were abandoned by Parisians whose revolutionary spirit remained unstirred by Delescluze's call to arms, allowing the Versailles troops to push into the city street by street, showing little mercy as they went. When the 'red' bastion of Montmartre was recaptured, over forty of its residents were herded into the same garden where the revolution had commenced back in March with the shooting of Thiers's generals. There, they were subjected to the same murderous fate. Worst was reserved for one socialist Communard, who was 'dragged through the streets of Montmartre, his hands tied behind his back under a shower of blows and insults'. After having his head 'slashed open by sabres', he was carried near-lifeless into the garden behind Number Six Rue de Rosiers, placed in a twitching heap and shot, before his corpse was dismembered by vengeful Versailles troops. This was one of many atrocities meted out in the garden of Number Six, which was transformed during the reconquest of Paris into a den of blood-caked dirt and bullet-ridden walls. Similar charnel houses were created across the city, ensuring that by the time the Versailles troops claimed victory on 28 May, somewhere between 10,000 and 20,000 Parisians had been slaughtered, victims of what became known as the Bloody Week.

Complete as the Commune's annihilation was, several prominent radicals evaded the carnage. Blanqui remained in captivity at Versailles and so lived to agitate another day, whilst Leó Frankel made it out of the city and escaped to the sanctuary of London, where he became a key figure in the IWMA. After being wounded on the barricades, his fellow Marxist Elisabeth Dmitrieff also escaped Paris, reaching her native Russia, only eventually to be arrested by the Third Section and sent to Siberia. Having been captured in April 1871 and given a ten-year sentence, the intellectual turned anarchist foot soldier Élisée Reclus was released from prison on good behaviour after a year, whereupon he headed for Switzerland. A thoughtful soul, Reclus spent long nights in Geneva brooding with Bakunin over what had gone wrong in Paris, concluding that the Commune's failure lay in its leaders' decision to impose governmental structures. To Reclus's mind, the revolution should have been a force of nature, too furious and absolute to be bridled by the agendas of a few stubborn people. Cluseret had little time for such philosophical reflection. As Thiers's soldiers bludgeoned their way through Paris, the 'traitor' was released by his captors in the hope that he would join the forlorn defence of the city. This was a naïve gambit on the part of the Communards. Rather than take up the doomed position of commanding the Montmartre battery, Cluseret disguised himself as a priest and fled Paris, leaving his erstwhile comrades to their fate.[20]

Those bereft of Cluseret's genius for self-preservation reaped the whirlwind. Vanity consuming common sense, Rigault stayed on the barricades in his distinctive police uniform, only to be recognised by Thiers's troops. The soldiers endured a few seconds of spittle-soaked insults from the prized Communard, before shooting him 'down, like a dog on the street', after which 'his body lay for hours. Men and women went up and kicked it, and spit [sic] in the face of the dead assassin'. It was, the American ambassador crowed, 'a fitting end' for so ghoulish an 'architect of murder, pillage and incendiarism'. True to her revolutionary principles, Michel countenanced no retreat during the Bloody Week, even after she witnessed Delescluze meet his end, gunned down on the barricades whilst dressed for death in a black frock-coat, top hat and red sash that befitted his Jacobin sensibilities. It was only after she received word that the Versailles troops had taken her mother hostage that Michel finally agreed to leave the barricades and surrender.[21]

Despite her assumption that she would be guillotined, Michel was instead sentenced to exile and shipped off to New Caledonia along with thousands of other Communards, who endured years of privation, disease, torture and general maltreatment. It was an existence designed to break their revolutionary spirit and correct their godlessness. Rejecting this re-education, Michel settled to brood, like Reclus in distant Switzerland, on the Commune's collapse, refusing in her rage to believe that it had all been for nothing. At her trial she had echoed the refrain espoused by Orsini and Brown, warning the judges that 'if you permit me to live, I shall never cease to cry for vengeance'. It was a promise she made good on, supporting a revolt by the native Kanaks of New Caledonia in 1878. Her involvement in an anti-colonial uprising was the clearest indication to anyone paying attention that the Red Virgin was far from a spent force. Despite the Commune's destruction, Michel was more convinced than ever that the forces of revolution, whether scattered to Britain, Switzerland, Russia or a South Pacific prison, would stir from the ashes of the fires that consumed Paris. In a world left reeling and fearful from the drama of the Commune's violent rise and brutal fall, she was far from alone in this belief.[22]

Chapter VIII

Chasing chimeras

Britain's Houses of Parliament were not built to withstand an attack. Why would they be? Safely ensconced as they were on the bank of the Thames, the lifeblood that flowed through the heart of the world's greatest empire. And yet, on a warm June evening, that impregnable seat of global power fell like wheat under a sharpened scythe. The trouble had started in Hyde Park, where earlier in the day 70,000 angry Londoners had gathered to cries of violence and revolt. Not a soldier amongst them, the mob was formed of greengrocers, publicans, factory hands, shoemakers, barmaids, dockworkers and common thugs, some armed, albeit with little more than kitchen-made explosives, old sabres and twisted cudgels. They were a people's militia of the ruthless and the ordinary. Behind them on horse-back rode the men who had turned these regular people into agents of terror – a troika of self-appointed 'revolutionary officers' composed of a loud-mouthed lawyer, a Marxist journalist and the wayward son of a lord who had abandoned the peerage in favour of embracing anarchism. Guided by these rogues, the masses had marched on Westminster, where they felled a statue of the liberal prime minister William Gladstone in 'a vigorous attack with sledgehammers'. Next, led by a barrel-chested brute in dirt-matted coveralls, they broke into a chant of 'No queens! No kings!' and stormed Parliament, sending its members to flight.

In their search for a leader to organise the pursuit of their former mas-ters, the mob turned to a uniformed man named General Slaughter, 'an American adventurer, who, beyond having some knowledge of the art of war, had very little antecedents or his private character to recommend him'. He was seconded by Dennis O'Flaherty, one of the many Fenians who had joined the uprising alongside Russian immigrants from the East End and Communard refugees who, recently dispersed from the blackened heap of Paris, had found sanctuary in the radical hotbed of Soho. Under Slaughter's leadership, the revolutionaries fought a running battle across London with the police, destroying the once great city in the process. 'Buckingham Palace was fired', the Mansion House was laid waste with explosives, trenches were dug in Richmond Park and 'the Marble Arch was chipped and battered' by grapeshot. It was 'as if the end of the world was come, and the whole of London was toppling down in one common ruin'.

Such was the intention of the group that planned this rampage – the IWMA. With a 'headquarters that had long been fixed in free and tolerant London', Marx's agents easily infiltrated the crowd that had gathered in Hyde Park earlier in the evening, encouraging it to 'spoil, burn and slay'. In addition to this incitement, the revolutionary masses had been tempted to violence by the lack of soldiers in London to halt their advance. This impotence was owed to Britain's recent and crushing defeat at the hands of Germany, and the emergency deployment of troops to India, Ireland and Canada to combat a spate of insurgencies – military catastrophes made possible by liberals in Parliament, who had passed bills defunding the army. The government's failure to meet the twin challenges of German despotism and colonial uprisings had, so one observer believed, 'disgusted the people with its rulers', and hastened their transformation from loyal subjects into radicalised traitors, whose faith was now placed in 'insurrection, incendiarism, murder, rapine, playing at soldiering and whatever other crimes and follies go to make a Commune'. Britain, now in thrall to the 'reds', was dying on its knees.

This apocalypse was conjured into print in 1871 by Samuel Bracebridge Hemyng. An aristocratic barrister with a deep-rooted suspicion of foreigners, Hemyng's *The Commune in London* was released at the same time as George Tomkyns Chesney's more infamous work, *The Battle of Dorking*, a cautionary future-war thriller in which Britain was successfully invaded by Germany, and its empire stomped into ruin. Although the same fear of Bismarck's legions was woven through Hemyng's tale, the *Commune in London* added an extra layer of paranoia to Chesney's invasion-scare narrative, by emphasising how much Britain had to fear from its enemies within as from those without. It was also a story that, for all its melodrama and hyperbole, was shaped, like Chesney's fable, by recent troubling events. General Slaughter and his offsider O'Flaherty were likely allusions to Cluseret's alliance with the Fenians. Moreover, the self-appointed revolutionary leaders riling up Russian immigrants and the 'more violent among the lower orders' of the East End drew on a theory that had been posited to explain the Commune's origins – the great unwashed of Paris had been coaxed into insurrection by professional preachers of radical doctrines.[1]

Already circulating when the Commune still held sway in Paris, this theory was bolstered when, following the Bloody Week, Thiers's restored government launched a commission of inquiry into how the City of Light had been dragged to its nadir. The commission's findings were reached promptly and distributed widely across Europe over the summer of 1871, printed in the pages of the newspapers that the likes of Hemyng consumed at their clubs. Despite eyewitness observation – which generally held that the Communards were making up their revolution as they went along – the inquiry matter of factly concluded that 'two groups made the insurrection of 18 March by forming an army'. The rank and file of this force were the French 'working class who, wandering and aimless, can easily be won over by the dissolute ways of cities'. The generals of this 'army of disorder' were, obviously, Marx and Bakunin. They were, after all, the ideological leaders of the IWMA, which was described in the inquiry as an 'organization that is always ready, with its leaders assigned in advance' to incite violence. Furthermore, according to Louis Andrieux – the observer to Bakunin's failed uprising who would, in 1879, become prefect of the Paris police – the anarchist's attack on Lyon was part of a coordinated series of strikes across France, in which the IWMA and its agents, Cluseret amongst them, were involved.

The infusion of terrorist tactics into these coordinated uprisings was attested to by Ernest Cresson, the prefect of Paris police during the siege, who confirmed the rumours that the Communards possessed vast stores of Orsini bombs. Refuting any suggestions that this ordnance was left over from the plots that had been hatched during the Victor Noir riots, Cresson told the inquiry that he and his officers had raided a ware-house in Montmartre in September 1870 and 'snatched from the hands of the conspirators' as many as '24,000 Orsini bombs, of which 6,000 were primed'. These weapons, Cresson suggested, had been assembled by the Communards at the outset of the siege for the purpose of unleash-ing 'attacks of terror across Paris'. Even more disturbingly, the infernal machines were 'wheel-like in shape, containing white powder and a glass cylinder filled with sulphuric acid, and packed nails' – evidence of the Communards furthering the development of terrorism with a cruel and unusual variant of Orsini's original device.[2]

If, as these testimonies claimed, the IWMA had been instructing its members to build bombs for use in a campaign of terror ahead of the uprising, then the fact that so many Communards had escaped the Bloody Week became easier to explain. The conspirators must have planned both their insurrection and a means of escaping Paris if it failed. This kind of deep plotting also explained why, within days of the Commune being declared, similar revolutionary pledges were made in Marseilles, Lyon and Saint Étienne, all of which had seemingly been chosen as part of a nationwide uprising that would turn France into a base from which to unleash further revolutions. That Marx's representative, Dmitrieff, did not arrive in Paris until a week after the Communards seized power mat-tered as little as the fact that IWMA members comprised no more than a third of the Commune's leading council, where Jacobins tended to domi-nate. Such complicated realities were unpalatable to an afeared Europe when offered alongside a diabolically simple conspiracy that Marx, in a moment of mindless self-indulgence, fuelled the belief in by announcing to his followers in May 1871 that 'the Commune was to serve as a lever for uprooting the economic foundations upon which rests the existence of the classes and, therefore, of class rule'.[3] With this tacit endorsement by the communist major-domo and the French government's findings, Europe's police chiefs now had all they needed to conclude that the tragedy of Paris was the product of an IWMA–Communard conspiracy – the manifestation of the fear nursed across the continent since 1848.

It stood to reason that the only way to prevent another Commune's rise was to target the ideological rot from which this conspiracy had grown – internationalism, specifically of the socialist and anarchist variety. For too long, claimed the French government's inquiry, 'Parisians' had been 'drowned in a flood of foreigners', to the extent that 'they became foreigners themselves'. The minds of French workers having been twisted by the German Marx's socialism and the roaming Russian Bakunin's anarchism, they had resolved in their nation's darkest hour to 'destroy the old fabric of their country, with thoughts that could have been devoted to creating new centres of strength and action for the motherland'. Paris's cosmopolitanism was, the philosopher Elme Marie Caro believed, a problem that now need urgent attention. Otherwise, the city would remain 'an incredible base to hide and live in' for 'adventurers and conspirators of all countries', who would continue to foster dangerous alliances with dissident groups across Europe – 'Fenians in England. Lassallists in Germany. Nihilists in Russia. Mazzinists in Italy.' Its fate hanging in the balance, the City of Light now had to 'choose between two alternatives for its future: to become the heart of a new, terrifying revolutionary world order, or the soul of sainted France'.[4]

In the summer of 1871, Thiers's government made its choice. The military contest with Bismarck now over, the pressing issue of restoring France's 'good internal order' was at the forefront of Thiers's mind, alongside the need to 'suppress the disorder and to fight the International and the Commune'. To this end, the number of gendarmes in Paris was raised from 6,000 to 8,000, the recruits drawn primarily from those in the ranks of the National Guards who had refrained from turning 'red' during the uprising. The *cabinet noir* system was also expanded and Sûreté officers were despatched to the capitals of Europe to track the movements of IWMA members and exiled Communards. Culturally, there was also a move towards reaffirming the 'moral order' of a nation broken by the blunt force of revolution. This was exemplified by the construction of the Sacré-Cœur at Montmartre in 1875, a religious monstrosity of bleached stone and domes that both championed the nation's bond with Christianity and begged forgiveness from the almighty for Paris's manifold sins. In further pursuit of the 'moral order', the National Assembly voted in favour of allowing monarchists to return to its ranks and, in 1873, appointed an arch-conservative former general as president.[5]

This attempt to reaffirm conservative values and snuff out internationalist ideologies was projected beyond France's borders. As a lawyer back in 1858, Jules Favre had defended Orsini at his trial but now, as France's foreign minister, he was as nervous as anyone in Europe about the prospect of another Commune arising. In June 1871, Favre penned a letter to heads of state across the continent in which he called for a 'joint study to find a solution to the formidable problems that sinister events have posed'. With Stieber in his ear and the fear of Germany's leftists ever on his mind, Bismarck responded favourably to his erstwhile French enemy's call for a united front against the IWMA–Communard menace, proposing an alliance of Europe's three emperors – Wilhelm I, Franz Joseph and Tsar Alexander II. The purpose of this alliance was not only to stabilise the international situation in the aftermath of Germany's military triumph. Just as pressingly, Bismarck wanted to confirm the idea that a new war had now commenced between 'the system of order on a monarchical basis' and the vision of the 'social republic' as espoused by Europe's radicals, who, it was believed, would look to the martyrs of Montmartre for murderous inspiration to plot their revenge.[6]

Bismarck's championing of a war on Europe's radicals also had selfish aims. Seeing a chance to lance the boil of leftists in German politics, in 1872 Bismarck ordered the arrest of two socialist members of the Reichstag on charges of treason that stemmed from their support of the Commune and opposition to the war with France. What made this gesture particularly cynical was that both Bismarck and Stieber felt little genuine fear over the prospect of a revolutionary explosion in Germany. Despite the Paris police insisting to Stieber that 'Marx and Engels have agents in most European countries, particularly in Germany and Russia', the wily Prussian was confident in the ability of his spies to monitor the IWMA. Moreover, he realised that only the maddest of Communards would try to find sanctuary in a place as reactionary as the Kaiserreich. For the other states bordering France, however, the need for anti-Communard measures was more pressing. Riven with political instability and violent upheavals, Italy and Spain in particular offered opportunities for Communards who wanted to continue the struggle. Consequently, as the refugees from Paris mixed with Spanish republicans in Barcelona and Italian anarchists in Rome, the authorities in both nations complied with Favre's requests to extradite any Communards they captured back to France to stand trial.[7]

In Brussels, the government passed tighter laws requiring refugees from France to present identity papers at the border, where extra police were also placed with ears open to any subversive mutterings. Following Favre's lead, these security measures were extended beyond Belgium's borders by the prime minister, Jules d'Anethan, who sent an appeal to other heads of state for information on the scale of the 'International issue' in their countries. Joining the international effort, in 1872 Franz Joseph's government sent the Belgians details on how they had built a case against 'Hungarian workers affiliated with the International'. Vienna also compiled a dossier on IWMA members for the benefit of police forces across Europe. Informed by the uprising in Paris, the message of the dossier was that the days of one-off terrorist attacks like those perpetrated by Orsini, Cohen-Blind and Berezowski were over. The focus now for Europe's police had to be on conspiracies, even those of the most outwardly bland nature, for 'the most dangerous societies are most often constituted with a perfectly legal programme'.[8]

This fear that violent revolutionaries were hiding in plain sight led to security measures that straddled the line between vigilance and absurdity. As much is evident in the list of 'Foreigners Who Are Forbidden Entry into Belgium', compiled by d'Anethan's government with the help of the French in the summer of 1871. Some suspicious travellers were listed for justifiable reasons, such as having been an 'officer of the Commune' or a 'political agent of the Commune'. Others, like a certain J. B. Olsweski, were forbidden from entering Belgium on more spurious grounds. Olsweski had been a 48er and, as a resident in Paris during the Commune, was assumed to have been a participant. Similarly, a Pole named Rabinski was identified as a member of the IWMA, which was now akin in some police minds to being a terrorist. Another refugee, called Ramlow, was blacklisted for being a Red Cross worker – a neutral humanitarian who, it was feared, was using this status to cross borders freely and disseminate radical propaganda. Suspicion also fell on bohemians. A writer was singled out for producing a history of Paris's red clubs. A sculptor was prohibited entry on account of being commissioned to carve a statue of a Communard leader, whilst another refugee was thought to have been 'a member of the commission to develop a federation of romantic artists', and so was deemed beyond the pale for admission into Belgium.[9]

For all its overzealousness, this exercise in national quarantine could be effective only if other states also tightened their borders with France. This was why Belgium joined much of the rest of Europe in urging the Swiss and the British to acknowledge the severity of the Communard threat. To the frustration of Bismarck and Favre, the response from both states was muted. Indeed, for the British – the memory of the Orsini affair still raw – Paris's request to be more stringent with their borders came across as downright cheeky given that, in the spring of 1872, it was revealed that the French government had been paying sea captains to ferry Communards across the Channel and out of their hair. Notably, it was more the 'serious breach of international comity' inherent in this action than the dumping of Communards on British shores that irked the Foreign Office. This was because the presence of Communard refugees in the rookeries of the East End and the literary cafés of Soho and Fitzrovia was generally tolerated outside the circles in which Hemyng ran and the columns of presses like the *Daily Telegraph*, which published reports of how 'Communists pledged to Marx and inspired by the violence in Paris are festering in our city'. This scaremongering could not offset a deeper feeling in Britain that the offering of asylum to Communards continued the nation's proud tradition of harbouring Europe's oppressed.[10]

British policy towards the Communards was also informed by public and parliamentary perceptions of the Franco-Prussian War. When Bismarck's armies first stormed into France, British support for the chancellor was high – he was, after all, putting the Napoleonic upstart in his place. By the war's end, however, the past sins of the luckless French had been forgotten as British politicians and military observers tried to understand the scale of the threat now posed by the Kaiserreich monster the conflict had created. Compared to Bismarck's unconquerable legions, the presence of a few hundred failed revolutionaries in London was of little concern. It did not help that in the summer of 1871 Bismarck baselessly claimed that 8,000 British citizens had participated in the Commune. This raised hackles in Parliament and made rejecting the chancellor's demand that Britain join the crusade against the IWMA–Communard conspiracy that much easier.[11]

The Swiss government's response to Favre's demands that they extradite Communards was less bullish than Britain's, characterised by half-promises to pass on any noteworthy observations of the interactions between radical émigrés and Bakunin. In keeping with this pledge, Genevan police shared dossiers with the Belgians in which tales of midnight meetings between red sash-wearers and anarchists featured. The passing of this intelligence, however, did not offset the frosty attitude of the Swiss federal government, which, no less than Whitehall, tended to bristle when other states presumed to dictate its immigration policies. Amongst liberals in the Swiss federal government, moreover, a thought was nurtured that was near unspeakable in the panicked atmosphere of the early 1870s – what if the IWMA was not coordinating a violent internationalist army? What if the Communards, scarred into submission by their bludgeoning in Paris, were now simply looking to find respite from revolution in the crisp mountain air?[12]

Even within the Paris police prefecture, some suspected there might be truth to this mundane assessment of affairs. Ludomir Boleslas Matuszewicz, a Polish colonel turned Communard, was one source of this opinion. Having fled Paris for London in May 1871, Matuszewicz grew contemptuous of his émigré brethren, many of whom wiled away their days telling tall tales of heroism on the barricades, in between getting drunk, heated and messily sentimental at their memories of the Bloody Week. Offered 500 French francs by the prefecture to turn on his own, Matuszewicz agreed to send twice-daily reports on the Communards, under the codename Agent 4. The numerical designation was owed to Matuszewicz being one of as many as seven agents who were paid by the prefecture to uncover whatever plots the refugees were hatching. Most of the spies provided intelligence that aligned with the IWMA–Communard conspiracy theory, alleging that Marx and the émigrés were assembling caches of bombs and raising funds to hire an assassin who could put a bullet through the head of the hated Thiers.

Matuszewicz painted a more sanguine picture. He reported that there was little to no connection between the IWMA and the Communards and, rejecting the popular interpretation of the radicals as a united menace, he revealed the many philosophical arguments and petty denouncements that peppered their meetings. He also pointed out the frequency of Jacobin, rather than socialist or anarchist, theories in the pamphlets and speeches produced by his former comrades and offered a tonic to the hysteria of the other spies' reports by describing the mopey, grievance-laden evenings he spent amongst these supposedly excitable terrorists. Matusewicz's reports were not dismissed by his bosses in Paris, nor was he suspected of being a double agent. On the contrary, his information was often used to fact-check the more outlandish claims made by his fellow spies.[13]

Whilst this suggests that Matusewicz's handlers were disposed to take the IWMA–Communard conspiracy theory with a grain of salt, others within the Paris police prefecture were less inclined to dismiss the menace. This was in part because the threat was empowering. In the months after the Bloody Week – during which police stations had been torched by the vengeful Rigault – an ambitious officer named Justin Guillaume Lombard used the fear of the IWMA–Communard conspiracy to establish a Research Brigade within the re-established police department, the main purpose of which was to run spies like Matuszewicz beyond France's borders. Lombard also leveraged the fear of Germany, claiming that when Stieber returned to Berlin in 1871, he left over a hundred of his spies in Paris. Having presented the government with concerns about both the Communards and Stieber's machinations, Lombard was given money to boost recruitment into his Research Brigade, creating an enlarged intelligence and counter-espionage network that remained in place, funded by the treasury, into the twentieth century.[14] Though he may not have believed in them fully, for men like Lombard, the post-Commune panic and the conspiracy theory that emerged from it, had their uses.

This was true even in nations where neither the Communards nor the IWMA could plausibly be viewed as dangers to the peace. As Michel was manning barricades and Delescluze was perishing in a volley of gunfire on the streets of Paris, in central Russia a group of *narodniki* led by a chemist named Nikolai Tchaikovsky were meeting in secret to read subversive literature. Owing to their enthusiasm for foreign-penned books that critiqued tsarism, the members of the so-called Tchaikovsky Circle were deemed enemies of the state by the Third Section, on a par with Ishutin, Karakozov and the still-at-large Nechaev. Consequently, Tchaikovsky and his followers were harassed by the police, and some were detained on charges of possessing contraband texts varying from Marx's *Das Kapital* to Darwin's *On the Origin of Species*. It was always hard, however, to get anything to stick on them. This was because, with only a handful of exceptions, the Tchaikovsky Circle's members eschewed violence. As one of their number recalled, the Circle was a 'philosophical and literary movement', with few members inclined to the terrorism preached by Nechaev and his like.[15]

The pursuit of Tchaikovsky and his book readers would never provide the Third Section chief Shuvalov with the opportunities Lombard seized to boost his prestige and power. As such, Shuvalov leapt on the chance to stoke fears of the Communards at the Winter Palace. The problem he faced, however, was that with exception of a pro-Commune pamphleteering campaign by a mentally unstable former academic outside Moscow, there was little evidence that the Parisian pestilence had infected Russia. Regardless, attempts were made to ensure the imperial court and the public believed otherwise. A pogrom in Odessa in the summer of 1871 was described to the press by a Third Section spokesman as a necessary response to nihilist attempts to set up a 'Jewish Commune'. Not long after this, a university was shut down by the police, on the grounds that student protests there had been inspired by events in Paris. Shuvalov also made much of reports from his spies that IWMA branches were being set up in Warsaw, Odessa and Kaluga. Although he tried, Shuvalov was unable to shape these various pieces of information into a convincing narrative that a conspiracy was afoot to violently depose the tsar. It did not help his cause that Marx's agent Dmitrieff – the clearest Russian tie that bound the Commune to the IWMA – had seemingly dropped off the face of the earth, leading a Russian diplomat in Paris to question, in a panic, 'what has become of this Fury? Did they execute her summarily without establishing her identity? Did they move her to Versailles or to some seaport under some false name she dreamed up?'

With Dmitrieff's whereabouts unknown – she had, in fact, returned to Russia but the Third Section did not initially notice her – Shuvalov needed another menace to give weight to the idea that Russia was about to be the next victim of the IWMA–Communard conspiracy. This need led to eighty-seven emaciated nihilists being hauled in front of a court room in St Petersburg on 1 July 1871. The accused were Nechaev's followers, who had been languishing in prison since their leader abandoned them after murdering Ivanov. Without Nechaev to front the trial of members of People's Revenge, it was left to his terrorists-in-training to provide Shuvalov with a haunting face for the nameless threat he claimed was hanging over Russia. To drive the fear home, transcripts of the trial were published in the conservative *Russian Messenger*, complete with lurid details of how Nechaev's people had plotted to poison tsarist officials, bomb police stations and put public buildings to the torch, as well as allusions to the IWMA's influence from afar. In addition to ensuring, as a court official recalled, that 'the newspapers talk of nothing else' but Nechaev's adherents, for at least one Russian the scaremongering worked. Inspired to invective, Fyodor Dostoevsky penned his famous novel *The Possessed*, in which he condemned nihilist terrorism and the 'many young scoundrels, decadent boys that they are', who followed such doctrines, deriding them as 'scum' that needed 'to cut itself adrift from Russia'.[16]

Dostoevsky's demand that Nechaev and his kind be severed like a diseased limb to preserve the nation's body echoed the fear of foreign-born radical contagion that was doing the rounds in Paris. The talk in *The Possessed* of a 'vast, unnatural and illegal conspiracy' in St Petersburg also aligned with sentiments expressed by the prosecution at the trial of members of People's Revenge, whose corruption was not blamed on Nechaev alone but also on the so-called Geneva International Committee. This internationalist conspiracy, steered by Bakunin, was alleged at the trial to be preparing an uprising in St Petersburg comparable to that which had wrecked Paris. Given the anxiety across Europe in the summer of 1871, this pitch had the potential to give Shuvalov the outcome he wanted. However, the credibility of the conspiracy theory was shot once the court beheld the accused, who appeared as emaciated wraiths far removed from the demons of Dostoevsky's nightmares. Mumbling, nervous and prone to breaking into tears under cross-examination, the prison-starved nihilists evoked pity rather than fear. So unthreatening did these members of People's Revenge seem, their defence was able to convincingly argue that the supposed revolutionists were either naïve students who had fallen under the spell of a charismatic murderer, or the tragic outcomes of the oppressive 'conditions forced on young people' by the tsarist state. On this basis, most of them were acquitted. The few deemed dangerous were sent into exile, albeit not for conspiracy but for the less spectacular crime of complicity in Nechaev's murder of Ivanov. In response, the infuriated tsar berated both Shuvalov and the judge, condemning the latter for 'behaving too humanely and warmly towards the defendants' and failing to silence their lawyers when 'they dwelt excessively on the nature of conspiracy and secret societies and the differences between them'.[17]

Worse still for Shuvalov, his nemesis Nechaev remained at large – a pied piper of terrorism wandering free during a continent-wide panic over revolutionary conspiracies. Desperate to redeem himself and apprehend the *Catechism*'s author, Shuvalov turned to Lombard in early 1872, convincing him that Nechaev was just the sort of fellow to whom the exiled Communards would gravitate. Lombard was persuaded and agreed to work with the Third Section, promising to 'immediately dispatch two agents to Zurich, who will spend two weeks familiarizing themselves with Nechaev's outward appearance and his habits'. This proved difficult for Lombard's men. The reports they sent from Zurich came on a near-daily basis over the summer of 1872; however, owing to their lack of linguistic skills – neither spoke good German – and basic training in detective work, the intelligence the spies provided on Nechaev's movements was mostly unhelpful. So desperate were they for material to fill their reports, the spies were reduced in one instance to mocking the size of Bakunin's belly following a rare sighting of the legendary anarchist.[18]

In the end, it was left to the Third Section and the Swiss police to bring Ivanov's murderer to heel. Having slipped back into Switzerland prior to the Commune's rising, Nechaev drew the attention of the gendarmerie in Zurich, where he was observed trying to ingratiate himself with known socialists and anarchists. In vain, he was labouring to rebuild People's Revenge off the backs of those gullible enough to still be taken in by his 'dark rogue' persona. A handful of followers came and went as Nechaev's star faded until, ultimately, he was reduced to abandoning his grand revolutionary projects in favour of plotting to rob banks. He was, therefore, vulnerable to an approach from a Polish dissident who pledged loyalty to the *Catechism*'s terrorist mantra and urged Nechaev to plan a fresh attack on the tsar. This Pole was an agent provocateur with the Third Section, one skilled enough, moreover, to convince Nechaev to break his rule of never surfacing during daylight hours, so that the two could meet at the Café Muller in Zurich. It was there, on the afternoon of 14 August 1872, that Nechaev's tenure as Russia's most wanted came to an end. No sooner had the supposed terrorist mastermind taken a sip of his beer than the Third Section man gave a signal to a corps of hidden Swiss gendarmes who, swooping in with their batons raised, surrounded the table, disarmed Nechaev of a pistol and a pocketknife and demanded to see his papers. The Russian's attempt to assume the identity of an innocuous Serbian labourer was undone by a schoolboy error – his inability to speak Serbian. In fury, Nechaev was placed in chains and shuttled back to St Petersburg. The tall tales of dramatic arrest that he had used to enchant Bakunin had finally come true.

Nechaev's trial commenced in January 1873 amidst a febrile atmosphere in which, as the Winter Palace's censor put it, 'one would think Russia was inhabited only by nihilists'. Concerns over Nechaev's terrorist disciples attempting to spring him from captivity led to three police checkpoints being erected to shepherd observers to the court gallery, the seating in which was restricted to 280 spaces despite popular demand to catch a glimpse of the infamous revolutionary. Revelling in the attention, Nechaev put on a fiery performance, denouncing the proceedings as a 'show court' and yelling 'Down with despotism!' between loudly insisting that he did not recognise the authority of the judge and that, as an émigré, he was no longer a subject of the tsar. Unwilling to answer his charges, Nechaev was sentenced to twenty years' incarceration in the Peter and Paul Fortress, exile being rejected as a punishment by the sovereign himself, most likely because he feared that the wily nihilist might break the bonds of Siberia as Bakunin once had. Better, thought Alexander, to keep his enemy close and encased in stone.[19]

Shuvalov had little time to enjoy his triumph. Following Nechaev's trial, he was relieved of his command of the Third Section – the tsar had grown tired of the scheming police chief and so kicked him upstairs to a diplomatic career in Britain. Shuvalov may have gone, but his pursuit of imagined revolutionary conspiracies remained a part of the Third Section's institutional culture, even as the post-Commune mania started to wane elsewhere in Europe. When, in the summer of 1874, a group of *narodniki* left St Petersburg for the countryside to dispense revolutionary propaganda to peasants, the Third Section deployed officers to arrest them on the grounds that they were trying to incite a Commune-like uprising. It is true that some of the *narodniki* took inspiration from the Communards, but their aim was to relay the story of the martyrs of Montmartre, not to re-enact their deeds. As one of the propagandists recalled, their attempt to radicalise the peasants was more 'a strange awakening of the spirit against the monstrous conditions that exist in our administration' than an attack upon the tsarist state. The lack of guns or bombs in the marchers' hands supports this view, as does the fact that even state-backed Russian newspapers tended to condemn them as 'propagandists' rather than as 'insurrectionists' or 'terrorists' – terms that were now being used by the press across Europe to describe those affiliated, or assumed to be affiliated, with the Commune.

Regardless, the pamphlet-brandishing marchers were treated as dangerous enemies. No sooner had the *narodniki* commenced their trek to the countryside than 'arrest followed arrest, thick and fast', the urgency of shutting them down heightened by the Third Section's belief that 'thirty-seven provinces were "infected" by the Socialist contagion'. By the end of the operation, as many as 1,600 marchers had been appre-hended – students, booksellers, artisans and a number of people who had literally nothing to do with the 'To the People' campaign, as it came to be called. The treatment of the captives reflected the angst of their captors. Some of the marchers were held in the dank bowels of fortress prisons, locked in cages and deprived of food and sleep for years, before finally being brought to trial in 1877. Others were bundled off to Siberia to be worked into oblivion chopping wood and mining coal, whilst a select few were hanged after refusing to renounce their subversive behaviour.[20]

These harsh punishments were issued at the behest of Shuvalov's suc-cessor, Nikolai Mezentsov, who zealously continued to act as if Russia were under siege. Aware that Nechaev and Ishutin's prime recruiting grounds had been the universities, in 1874 Mezentsov sent instructions for professors to monitor their students' reading habits and alter the content of their lectures. Those who went 'To the People' would now have to be depicted as 'unhappy political fanatics', who had 'carried their impractical fantasies into the villages' with a mind to 'stoop to theft, robbery and murder'. This censoring of ideas on university campuses came in tandem with the mass confiscation of foreign literature that had been smuggled into Russia by the Tchaikovsky Circle. Such measures, so the tsar's minister of justice noted, were needed to undo the 'net of revolutionary cells and individual agents' that was believed to have been set up by Tchaikovsky prior to his group's dissolution.[21]

Shuvalov and Mezentsov's war on ideas, Favre's push for international cooperation, the restoration of the 'moral order' and Lombard's building of intelligence networks were all elements of a knee-jerk Europe-wide anti-radical clampdown in the wake of the Commune's fall. Sweeping and, at times, self-serving these reactions might have been, they were understandable given the shock of the revolutionary moment that had flared into life and been extinguished so brutally in Paris. In processing this trauma, political leaders and law enforcers conceived of a united revolutionary enemy, continent-wide and amorphous, that could be conquered only by blanket repression and an iron will. Strength alone would shatter their fears. Events would soon show, however, that these measures to thwart an imagined IWMA–Communard conspiracy were as misguided as they were dangerous. Focused as Europe's police were on chasing the chimera of a second Commune, they missed the fact that many radicals had learned invaluable lessons from the catastrophe of 1871 and were preparing for a new, more sophisticated phase in their war against kings and capital – a phase in which concerns over Tchaikovsky's literary circle and Hemyng's warnings of mob uprisings would be eclipsed by a spate of terrorist attacks that no police chief or spy could hope to prevent.

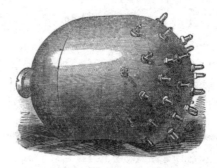

Figure 1 The first terrorist 'superweapon', the percussion-detonated Orsini bomb

Figure 2 From Hell to People's Revenge: Nikolai Ishutin (top), Dmitry Karakozov (bottom left) and Sergei Nechaev (bottom right)

Figure 3 The eternal insurgent: General Gustave Paul Cluseret

THE FENIAN GUY FAWKES.

Figure 4 *Punch* magazine's reaction to the Clerkenwell explosion – a dehumanised Fenian sitting on a barrel of gunpowder, December 1867

Figure 5 George Cruikshank's depiction of the Paris Commune – the 'blood red republic', June 1871

Part 3

Devils

Chapter IX

Murder triumphant

Seventeen years had passed since Kaiser Wilhelm survived the bullets fired at him by Oskar Becker. Back then, in 1861, Wilhelm had been the depressed steward of a divided kingdom, beset by Napoleon's empowerment and the Landtag's liberals. By 1878, the anxiety he felt in those years had been dissolved by military victories, Bismarck's suppression of the left and the unification of a nation that could boast the continent's finest army, an expanding industrial base and a rapidly growing population. The comforting triumph of this situation made it all the more surprising to Wilhelm when, in the spring of 1878, he was twice attacked with murderous intent in Germany's capital. The first attempt on his life was made by Emil Hödel, a tinsmith and consumer of Bakunin's writings, who fired a pistol high over Wilhelm's head as he took an open-top carriage ride through Berlin. In the confusion that followed, Hödel discharged two more rounds without success, before being tackled to the ground by the emperor's guards. Having barely recovered from this ordeal, the kaiser was again shot at a few weeks later, this time with more success, by a shotgun-wielding intellectual named Karl Nobiling. Once more in a roofless carriage, Wilhelm was an easy target for his assailant, who leant out of the window of an apartment on the Unter den Linden and unleashed a blast of buckshot at his sovereign. Minutes later, as the police bounded up the stairs of the building, Nobiling turned the gun on himself, only for it to misfire, causing terrible injuries that slowly killed him over the course of the following months. The kaiser survived the attack, albeit at the cost of considerable blood loss caused by thirty shot-wounds to his face, head and arms.[1]

In the weeks after the two assassination attempts, speculation abounded in the press over Nobiling and Hödel's motivations whilst, for all his reach and reputation, Stieber fumed in a similar state of bemusement. Guided by his preoccupation with the IWMA–Communard conspiracy, the spymaster's legions of informers had spent most of the 1870s infiltrating railway worker groups in Alsace-Lorraine and monitoring the distribution of socialist and anarchist pamphlets in Berlin. Little thought had been given to the idea that two gun-toting miscreants might seek revolution by simply taking the kaiser's life. The blind spot in Stieber's all-seeing eye was further apparent when investigations into Nobiling and Hödel turned up little evidence to link them to the IWMA or any other radical group. Indeed, Hödel had been deemed so dangerous by the Social Democratic Party that they kicked him out years before he turned his mind to murder. Still, the scattered applause directed at the would-be assassins by ex-Communards, Bakunin's anarchists and some IWMA members was enough for Stieber to feel confident that, despite the evidence, some form of conspiracy lay behind these seemingly unrelated acts of terrorism.[2]

Stieber's assumption exemplified a wider problem with counterterrorist thinking in the years after the Commune. What the Berlin police, the Paris police prefecture and the Third Section misunderstood was that, far from coalescing into a single conspiratorial mass that could be easily monitored, Europe's radicals spent much of the 1870s breaking apart into hard-to-trace shards. The shatter point of this fracture was an old quarrel between the two men who, adherents to the conspiracy theories believed, were directing global terrorist traffic – Marx and Bakunin. The former wrote of how the purpose of revolution was to seize the means of production and empower the workers. Bold as this idea was, Marx's vision did not go far enough for Bakunin, who held that a true revolution required the complete destruction of the state. The stubborn visionaries were further divided on the question of who the agents of change should be in either scenario. Seeing the world through the eyes of a city dweller who conjured his thoughts from London's smog, Marx identified the factory-bound wage-slave of the industrial age as his radical foot soldier, who over time would become aware of his exploitation, engendering capitalism's inevitable demise. The earth-crossing Bakunin took a view that aligned more with those who had gone 'To the People', placing his hopes in the grit of the noble peasant to force change through bold action.

Further complicating this quarrel was the revolutionary ethos presented to Europe's radicals by Nechaev. Incarcerated, the martyr's legend grew during the 1870s amongst dissident students in St Petersburg and Moscow, even as elder members of the Russian radical community denounced his violently self-destructive terrorism, seeing his ideology and tactics as a betrayal of the 'genuine nihilism' advocated by the *narodniki*. Aside from the nihilists, revolutionaries beyond Russia generally loathed the thuggish criminality of Nechaev's bloodlust and saw nothing redeemable in the *Catechism*'s teachings. These critics included the legendary socialist Herzen, who, before he died in January 1870, warned his friend Bakunin that 'the boy' would drag the names of all radicals and the ideas they espoused into the muck. Despite Herzen's denouncement and Bakunin's subsequent separation from his ward, spies at the IWMA's 1872 congress in The Hague reported that 'Bakunin and Nechaev were expected' and that 'Bakunin and Karl Marx are adopting a plan for revolution in all countries'. The reality of the radicals' schism played out dramatically once proceedings got underway. Aside from the fact that Nechaev had just been arrested, Marx knew that if Bakunin tried to leave Switzerland he would likely be apprehended by any number of police forces before he reached The Hague, joining his former protégé in chains. This gave Marx the platform to unleash a tirade to IWMA members at the congress, in which he ran down Bakunin as a fraud, a hack and, possibly, a police spy, the same accusation that Engels had previously thrown at Nechaev. To drive home the point that Bakunin – let alone his murderous former partner – were charlatans and not to be trusted, at the conclusion of the congress, Marx announced that the IWMA's headquarters would move from London to New York, putting an ocean between it and the followers of the now excommunicated 'ass' Bakunin.[3]

In addition to this rupture between the Marxists and the Bakunists in the IWMA, for police officers who chose to see it, there was ample evidence elsewhere that radicals were not only constrained by disagreements but incapable of orchestrating the much-feared Commune part *deux*. Having been sentenced to death in absentia in 1872, Cluseret fled France and bounced between the United States, Switzerland and Spain. The arrival of this one-man 'revolutionary barometer' in Madrid in 1873 led to rumours in the press that 'the Commune will be proclaimed here within ten days'. The reality of the threat Cluseret now posed was more muted, however, for, unlike Michel and Reclus, the tragedy of the Commune had done much to dampen his revolutionary spirit. In Spain, he issued a manifesto that lauded workers as the world's true revolutionaries and in 1876 he participated in an unmeaningful way in the nationalist uprisings against Ottoman rule that exploded across the Balkans. Having finally returned to France following the collapse of this last effort at insurrection, Cluseret was fined 3,000 francs in 1880 for publicly criticising a general. This, it seems, prompted the now fifty-seven-year-old former soldier to put down the red flag and sabre for good and take on a political career, which led to him becoming Toulon's representative in the Chamber of Deputies in 1888. Following a final twist in the bizarre tale of his life – in which Cluseret embraced the militarist chauvinism that swept through France in the 1890s and, with it, a belief in anti-Semitic conspiracy theories – the once notorious revolutionary died peacefully in his own bed in 1900.[4]

Even those who tried to pick up the baton of Cluseret's brand of ambitious insurrection gave the authorities little to worry about. During the 1870s, a Bakunist named Errico Malatesta led a series of uprisings in the Italian countryside that aped both Cluseret's revolutionary style and his less than spectacular track record of success. Much like the Russian peasants targeted in the 'To the People' march, the Italian farmers whom Malatesta and his followers tried to radicalise were either puzzled or incensed by the anarchist's arrival in their wheat fields and olive groves, to the extent that they summoned the police. This led to one of Malatesta's excursions ending with he and his men being chased

into a barn, whereupon they were arrested before they had had a chance
to disseminate the Bakunist literature in the knapsacks on their backs.
This fiasco was not surprising, given Malatesta's character. Far from
a conspiracy-building criminal mastermind, a friend of Malatesta's
remembered the young man as 'a pure idealist', who 'has never thought
whether he would have a piece of bread for his supper or a bed for the
night' yet was 'always renewing the struggle'. Enamoured of chasing
revolution, Malatesta was undaunted by the fact that, at the start of one
of his excursions, he managed to raise only five out of the 500-strong
force of anarchists he hoped for. It is small wonder that, when the ailing
Bakunin summoned the energy to join Malatesta on the outskirts of
Bologna in 1874 for the latter's latest insurrectionary gambit, the pair
were met immediately by soldiers, who chased them back to Switzerland.
There, in July 1876, the revolutionary juggernaut slowed to his final
crawl. Succumbing to a variety of illnesses brought on by a lifetime of
prison stints and fragile asylum, Bakunin died broken and lamenting
that, contrary to the views of both Europe's police and Malatesta, there
'was absolutely no revolutionary thought, hope or passion left amongst
the masses'.[5]

Bakunin's conclusions on the futility of inciting peasant rebellions
may have been true, but there was another party to Malatesta's follies
who saw a means of taking the revolutionary struggle in another direction – one that had more in common with Nobiling and Hödel's targeted
attacks than the uprisings favoured by Cluseret and the Communards.
Sergei Kravchinsky – known as 'Stepniak' – was a Russian artillery officer
who, having joined the Tchaikovsky Circle in 1871, immersed himself
in radical literature and revolutionary doctrines. This education led to
him joining the 'To the People' march in 1874, in the aftermath of which
he evaded the Third Section by fleeing Russia. After two years in self-
imposed exile, Stepniak wound up in the Balkans with Cluseret, where he
took up arms in what he described as a 'splendid crusade' by his brother
Slavs to cast off the shackles of Ottoman rule. When that campaign collapsed, he headed over to Italy in the spring of 1877 for a meeting with
Malatesta, who excited the Russian's imagination with his latest plans for

a sortie into the Italian countryside. Malatesta's earnest optimism must have plagued Stepniak's thoughts when, weeks later, he found himself alone in a prison cell in Benevento, the victim of a dragnet launched by a police force that was now wearily accustomed to dealing with Malatesta's schemes. To a radical as committed as Stepniak, the fiasco was no reason to give up. Instead, the frustrated Russian spent his time behind bars imagining a new way forward in the revolutionary struggle, one in which the mistakes made by Malatesta and the 'To the People' marchers would be corrected.[6]

As Stepniak was musing in his prison cell, Reclus was drawing a similar conclusion that a break with the past was needed. Having assumed a leading role amongst the anarchists of Geneva following Bakunin's death, the former Communard rejected any suggestions from his radical brethren that they should plan a second uprising. Instead, he advocated a campaign of agitation and propaganda, peppered with occasional acts of terrorism, which would be carried out over the course of many years, with the aim to gradually wear down the state to the point that it could no longer hold back the revolutionary tide. Inherent in Reclus's plan was an important realisation – the fears raised across Europe by the IWMA–Communard theory could be used to the radicals' advantage. By encouraging this fiction, new anarchists would be drawn to the cause, in the belief that they were joining a robust underground army. The same newspapers that peddled the IWMA–Communard theory would, of course, report on how the radicals' ranks were swelling, increasing both reactionary fear and revolutionary momentum. This momentum would aid the spread of anarchist ideas and, over time, encourage acts of defiance against the state, prompting panicked repression from the police. The hapless injustice of this would break citizens' faith in their rulers and weaken the credibility of state, creating the appropriate conditions for revolution. The key to this plan was patience. Reclus was, after all, a geographer, who believed that 'a secret harmony exists between the earth and the people whom it nourishes'. The firebrands who had attempted to violently force change in Paris had much to learn from the glacial way the earth beneath their feet had moved for millennia. For Reclus, time and the gradual manipulation of state and society were the way forward for radicals of the post-1871 world.[7]

Although he shared Reclus's views on the merits of manipulating enemies and converting new allies to the cause, Stepniak's recent history led him to a very different conclusion on how to achieve these ends. Peaceful propagandising had failed him in Russia, the limits of insurrection had been made glaringly apparent in the Balkans and, in the hills of central Italy, Stepniak had seen the futility of placing faith in oppressed citizens to realise their sorry lot and take back control of their lives from the state. Unlike the cerebral and patient Reclus, the Russian also was driven by the belief that he was living through an important historical moment, in which 'only a spark was wanting to change the latent aspirations' of Europe's revolutionaries into something tangible. There was no time to wait in the manner Reclus prescribed. Something urgent and violent was needed to inspire Europe's radicals and frighten their enemies. And so Stepniak conceived of 'a gloomy form, illuminated by the light of hell who, with lofty bearing and a look breathing forth hatred and defiance, made his way through the terrified crowd to enter with a firm step upon the scene of history. It was the terrorist.'[8]

Upon his release from Benevento prison in February 1878, Stepniak soon learned to that he was not alone in experiencing this epiphany. As he scanned the international section of a newspaper, his black eyes were drawn to a series of articles on Nechaev's former disciple, Vera Zasulich. Five years removed from her stint in jail for passing Nechaev's letters, Zasulich had become the living embodiment of the 'blowback' inherent in the Third Section's oppressive anti-radical policing. At the time of her incarceration, she had been a student led astray by a sociopathic narcissist. By the time Zasulich was freed in 1873, she was a committed nihilist, hardened by demonisation and maltreatment. Once at liberty, she began working for an illicit nihilist press, from which she ingested a steady diet of hate and resentment for the tsar and his court. So deep into the revolutionary rabbit hole did Zasulich burrow, when she heard that the chief of the St Petersburg police, Fyodor Trepov, had beaten and humiliated a fellow nihilist, she acquired a revolver. Then, under the guise of being a petitioner, on 24 January 1878 Zasulich marched into Trepov's office and fired at his head, her target's life spared only by her abysmal aim. Having now become the 'doomed woman' Nechaev always wished her to be, Zasulich experienced the fulfilment of a zealot. She later recalled how, despite being tied up, beaten and interrogated by Trepov's heavies, she felt overwhelmed by an 'extraordinary state of the most complete invulnerability, such as I had never before experienced. Nothing at all could confuse me, annoy me or tire me. Whatever was being thought up by these men, at that time conversing animatedly in another corner of the room, I would regard them calmly, from a distance they could not cross.' What she relished most was how, despite her failure to kill Trepov, she had terrified her oppressors. This led one of her interrogators to warn his colleagues that, even though Zasulich was bound with ropes, they had to 'be careful, or else she might stick a knife into you!'[9] Zasulich, no less than Reclus and Stepniak, had realised the utility of fear.

Stepniak was in awe of her, the more so given that she had managed to earn public plaudits rather than demonisation for her terrorist deed. As he wrote in his memoirs, in addition to filling enemies with dread, Zasulich's confident, potentially suicidal act of defiance against Trepov possessed 'the sanction of sacrifice and of public opinion'. This was clear at Zasulich's trial, during which evidence of her crime was dismissed by a court that felt little but hatred for the ruthless Trepov, concluding that it was the Third Section's brutalisation of the young woman that had turned her mind to murder. Her subsequent acquittal and canonisation by radicals served only to further innervate the forces of oppression in Russia. Following the trial, the Third Section chief, Mezentsov successfully petitioned the Winter Palace for an expanded budget of 600,000 roubles per year, much of which was to be spent on propagandising the merits of tsarist rule to the peasants. A law was also passed in March 1878 which decreed that any future assailants of public officials would be denied their day in court. Instead, Mezentsov got his wish to prosecute radicals in military tribunals, where convictions and death penalties could be assured, and the sympathies of the public could be obscured. This police repression not only stirred the desire for revenge in Stepniak but also proved to him the validity of his conclusion that the future lay in terrorists with Zasulich's daring and capacity to inspire, rather than hopeless insurrectionists like Malatesta.[10]

This belief led Stepniak to Mikhailovskaya Square in St Petersburg on the morning of 16 August 1878, the terminus of a journey he had begun shortly after reading of Zasulich's assassination attempt. As distant from the sun-drenched hills around Benevento as he was from the peasant rags he had donned during Malatesta's botched uprisings, Stepniak dressed for the occasion in a fine suit, waiting in the damp morning air for his quarry, Mezentsov. With Nechaev languishing in the Peter and Paul Fortress and Zasulich having fled to Switzerland after her acquittal, the Third Section chief thought himself safe. He rarely altered the route of his daily walk. This made it easy for Stepniak to pick his spot and await Mezentsov's arrival in the square. When he did so, bedecked in full uniform with gold braid, the Third Section chief was instantly set upon by Stepniak, who stabbed Mezentsov to death with a stiletto dagger. The assassin's accomplice, a *narodnik* from a revolutionary group called Zemlya I Volya (Land and Liberty), then added to the scene of terror by discharging his pistol into the air, scattering the crowd of shocked onlookers. Their path cleared, the terrorists hot-footed their way across the flagstones to a carriage they had prearranged for a hasty evacuation. Zasulich's example had been followed and the haughtiness of tyrants had been checked. To make this clear to his enemies, the next day Stepniak released a pamphlet entitled *A Death for a Death*, in which he claimed that Mezentsov's slaying was simply justice being served for the imprisonment and torture of the many brave souls who had dared to defy the tsar.[11]

It was no storming of the Winter Palace. Nor was it an act of haphazard street violence as preached by Blanqui, or the product of the kind of fantastic conspiracies dreamt up by Nechaev and Bakunin. Rather, Stepniak's action was a well-planned assassination with an unambiguous propaganda follow-up, designed to terrorise those of Mezentsov's ilk with the thought that they would be next – a brutally simple act of fear-inducing violence. It was, moreover, far from the only example of such terrorism to take place in the 1870s. In addition to Hödel and

Nobiling's attempts on the kaiser's life, in February 1878, in Florence, an Orsini bomb was thrown at a procession held in honour of the recently deceased King Victor Emmanuel, with the aim to disrupt this sombre exercise in monarchical worship. The same drive to strike fear into royals led an anarchist barrel-maker to fire two shots at young King Alfonso XII of Spain (both missed) as he paraded through the streets of Madrid on 24 October. A month later, Umberto I of Italy survived a knife attack by an Italian nationalist, who lunged at his prey shouting 'For Orsini!', only to be thwarted by Umberto knocking him away with his sword. All these terrorists had come to understand, independent of one another, the same truth that Zasulich, Stepniak and a perceptive German newspaper editor had – 'political murder, taught by the history of the undercurrents in other countries, from Orsini to Vera Zasulich', was now foremost on the revolutionary agenda.[12]

For many of the continent's authorities, however, the 'year of assassins' that was 1878 simply provided further evidence of the IWMA–Communard conspiracy. Following the attempted shooting of King Alfonso, the Spanish police rounded up scores of suspected accomplices and conducted six months of interrogations that yielded no evidence of the failed assassin being attached to any radical group. And yet, Shuvalov's old trick was once more attempted. The trial of the shooter in 1879 was an epic designed to capture the Spanish public's imagination, complete with a 380-page publicly disseminated indictment that included speculative evidence of international sponsorship, and suggestions that disciples of the deceased Bakunin had guided the assailant's hand from Switzerland. Even after he was publicly garrotted before a crowd of 50,000 people on the Campo de Guardias, the fear that the shooter's phantom accomplices would finish the deed led the court to rush Alfonso into a marriage with the arch-duchess of Austria to ensure a succession. Similarly, in Berlin, the Hödel and Nobiling attacks led to the passing of a fresh raft of anti-socialist laws, on the grounds that the IWMA must have had something to do with their attempts to kill the kaiser.[13]

In Russia, the emergence of this new terrorist threat led to a long-overdue questioning of the Third Section's methods. In February 1880, the tsar ordered an inquiry into his secret police force. It concluded that, for all the powers vested in it, the moribund agency was a hive of inefficiency. This was born of both complacency at having suppressed People's Revenge and the Tchaikovsky Circle, and an institutionalised inability to adapt to new challenges posed by the likes of Zasulich and Stepniak. Amongst the findings were that certain officers did not take the terrorist threat seriously and that there were plenty of instances of nihilists eluding the spies tasked with watching them. Most shockingly of all, the inquiry found that the Third Section had over a thousand unsolved cases on its books. These incomplete files lay stacked on the desks of an ill-trained coterie of detectives who were both beholden to disproven conspiracy theories and reliant on the old 'monitor the university campuses and haul them off to Siberia' model of policing, at precisely the time when the threat to the tsar and his court was evolving – in no small part as a response to these draconian blanket measures.[14]

This threat for which the Third Section was ill-prepared manifested in the form of a group composed of members of Land and Liberty and nihilists who – in a further sign of lax policing – had been communicating with Nechaev via notes passed between the bars of his cell by guards sympathetic to the plight of the charismatic terrorist. Founded in 1879 and boasting as many as 500 members, Narodnaya Volya (People's Will) was, arguably, the world's first terrorist organisation, guided by a strategy of targeted violence and propagandising that set the template for many a terrorist campaign since. This strategy was outlined by Nikolai Morozov, a nihilist who had gone 'To the People' with Stepniak, only to be convinced by the latter's killing of Mezentsov and Zasulich's attack on Trepov that more direct action against the tsarist state was needed. Morozov laid this vision out in his 1880 pamphlet *The Terrorist Struggle*. A more sophisticated work than Nechaev's *Catechism*, this tract drew on Heinzen's idea of murder being justified against repressive governments, albeit with a strategic premise so enduringly simple that it would be used over a century later by Al Qaeda's chief strategist Ayman Al Zawahiri.

Just as Al Zawahiri called for the systemic decimation of the United States through a campaign of terrorist violence and propaganda, so

Morozov conceptualised each individual act of terrorism in Russia as a single cut on the body of tsarism. Every life taken – a general here, a police chief there – would build panic and provoke greater acts of repression from the Third Section. This state-sanctioned barbarism would create 'new agents of revenge', who would bolster the ranks of People's Will and continue the cycle of violence, all the while discrediting the ability of the tsar to protect his people. So weakened, the regime's mutilated body would eventually die and, with it, tsarism. Although its premise was similar to that which underpinned Reclus's strategy, Morozov's plan was more violent. It was also more focused in terms of its purpose. Eschewing the anarchist's dream of international revolution, People's Will saw themselves as crusaders against 'the abnormalities of social relations in Russia', whose aim was to slay 'the crowned vampires' of the Winter Palace.[15] People's Will did not dream of upending the world and they did not want to raise a Commune. Their goal was more tangible – to kill the tsar and terrorise his court into submission.

Having embraced 'assassination and terroristic activity in general as the most essential point of our entire programme', People's Will made at least seven attempts on Tsar Alexander II's life. Some of these were thwarted by Cossack guards passing by at a moment when an assassin was poised to strike, whilst others were disrupted by the volatility of explosives, the incorrect connection of wires or the difficulty of shooting a moving target. One of the more spectacular failures was an attempt to blow up the tsar's train in November 1879, for which People's Will spent weeks gathering intelligence on the procedures that governed Alexander's journey from his holiday residence in the Crimea to St Petersburg. Believing that he always travelled in the rear of the train, two People's Will members buried dynamite along the tracks and waited in a nearby bush to detonate the explosives as the final carriage passed. They could not know that the tsar had decided to travel at the front of the train that day. Instead of killing the autocrat, the explosion destroyed a carriage containing oranges, creating a twisted heap of metal and marmalade.

This failure greatly disappointed People's Will's chief scientist, Nikolai Kibalchich. A university-educated expert in rocket propulsion,

Kibalchich had been arrested during the 'To the People' campaign for passing a book on republicanism to a peasant. The anger he nursed during the three-year sentence he served for this innocuous act led to Kibalchich lending his knowledge of chemicals and explosives to the tsar's more violent enemies upon his release. He also cultivated relationships with workers in chemical factories, from whom he procured a new form of dynamite more potent than that originally patented by the Swedish inventor Alfred Nobel in 1867. In February 1880, Kibalchich used this explosive to a build a time bomb which, in an audacious move that topped the efforts with the train from Crimea, was smuggled by a People's Will agent into the tsar's home, the Winter Palace. Posing as a handyman, the bomber planted the infernal machine in the recess of a dining room wall, which he then plastered over before fleeing the palace. The explosion that erupted fifteen minutes later was as destructive as Kibalchich had anticipated, but, as in the case of the train bombing, the tsar was nowhere near the detonation. This time, the losses were greater than a few crates of fruit. When the smoke cleared, eight people – most of them servants and Cossacks – lay dead, along with over fifty wounded. It is small wonder that Alexander soon came to believe that God was protecting him.[16]

Even the will of the Divine had limits. A year and half after their August 1879 declaration that the tsar was already dead, People's Will made good on this assertion. On 13 March 1881, Alexander was travelling through St Petersburg in his carriage, en route to inspect a military parade. People's Will had reconnoitred the route for weeks, taking notes on the tsar's security arrangements and liaising with Kibalchich to make sure that the right kind of bomb was available. Having identified the best place to attack, the group occupied a cheese shop that lay along the route to the parade ground, using the basement as a point from which to tunnel under the road and plant a mine that would blast upwards into the underbelly of the carriage as it passed. When the day of the planned attack came, however, the tsar's driver chose a route that took the sovereign away from the dynamite-rigged tunnel. Faced with disaster, the leader of the assassins – an aristocrat turned nihilist named Sophia

Perovskaya – thought on her feet and despatched two comrades from the cheese shop to toss dynamite-charged Orsini bombs at the autocrat's carriage. The first assailant's throw landed short of the target, erupting in a flash of white light that injured the guards but left their master unscathed. Even if the throw had been accurate, the tsar would have likely survived, for Alexander was travelling in an iron-plated carriage that Napoleon had given him following the Berezowski attack of 1867. The tsar's mistake was to leave the protection of Napoleon's gift to accost the weak-armed bomber. With Alexander now exposed in the centre of the road and his Cossacks shell-shocked, the second attacker rushed forward with a bomb clutched to his chest and detonated it within feet of the tsar. The suicide bomber did not die in vain. The storm of fire and concussion that consumed the nihilist also blasted the tsar's legs out from under him. His wounds atrocious and his femoral arteries torn, Alexander bled to death in a little under an hour.[17]

Shocking as it was, the tsar's demise seemed a sad inevitability to many of Europe's police and its press, for, by 1881, People's Will had supplanted the Communards as the new locus of fear and conspiracy. Throughout the nihilists' campaign of terror, the Sûreté monitored Russian émigrés in Paris, in the predictably misplaced belief that 'Russian nihilism is a branch of the International and both were founded by Bakunin'. Taking the conspiracy in a different direction, the prefect of Paris police, Louis Andrieux, held that the People's Will – mental deficients that they were – must have been led by a traitor of 'very high-ranking character' within the Russian government, who was using his position to shelter the terrorists from the gaze of the Third Section. The Italian police were concerned that People's Will was the spearhead of something continental, and that the nihilists would link up with Italy's anarchists and introduce dynamite terrorism into their fight against Rome. In vain, the aged and ailing Stieber issued a prescient warning to the Third Section that the Winter Palace was vulnerable to a dynamite attack, whilst in Britain a report was filed with the Birmingham police of an attempt by 'two foreigners in London – a German and a Russian' to solicit a British engineer to construct 'infernal machines intended to be used against the

Emperor of Russia'. The police tasked with monitoring Fenian activity also despaired over the prospect that Kibalchich's knowledge of explosives would somehow be acquired by the Irish. This fear was also held by a concerned member of the public, who issued an editorial plea for Scotland Yard to prepare for the inevitable alliance between People's Will and the Fenians.[18]

In Russia itself, during the months leading up to his death Alexander had urged the Third Section to beef up its oppression of nihilists, in the hope that an iron first could crush People's Will out of existence – long gone was any pretence to be Russia's reformist ruler. The tsar was, therefore, unimpressed when People's Will retaliated against this oppression by shooting Mezentsov's replacement and detonating bombs both at the Third Section's headquarters and in the Winter Palace. As one noble who survived the latter time bomb attack recalled, all Russia now felt as if it were 'living through a period of terror with the only difference being that during the French Revolution, Parisians saw their enemies'. The land of the tsars had become a state in which 'we not only do not see or know our enemies, but even have no idea how many of them there are'. This threat of terrorists being able to burst unpredictably from the shadows in violent flashes before retreating to the gloom of St Petersburg's backstreets 'produced a profound stupor in police circles', as one radical press triumphantly proclaimed, creating an environment in which 'revolution and repression appear to be competing with each other in sheer desperation of violence'. This was a Russia where Nechaev's dream of 'increasing and intensifying the evils and miseries of the people until, at last, their patience is exhausted, and they are driven to a general uprising' seemed to be coming true. It validated all that Stepniak hoped terrorism might achieve.[19]

Shocked by the tsar's brutal demise, the *New York Times* declared the need for a 'war on terrorism' in Russia. Against an enemy as faceless and relentless as People's Will, however, the questions arose of who was going to wage this 'war' and by what means. One Russian noble named Sergei Witte tried to provide answers. Having written off the secret police's counter-terrorist methods as akin to hurling 'too huge a missile at too small a target', in the wake of the tsar's murder Witte penned a letter to other concerned nobles in which he called for the formation of a 'secret organization, which would make it its business to answer each terroristic letter with a counter-blow of a similar nature'. These blows would include fake newspapers that would demonise nihilism, the raising of a volunteer force of thugs to intimidate radicals, Jews and Poles, and the recruitment of assassins who would be tasked with eliminating known nihilist leaders. This secret organisation would be known as the Holy Brotherhood.[20]

The raising of a secret organisation of patriotic zealots pledged to mimic, as Stepniak put it, 'the sanguinary traditions established by the terrorists' reflected the vengeful atmosphere that pervaded the Winter Palace in the spring of 1881. Sired by dynamite, the new tsar, Alexander III, was the source of this mood. He had received a letter from People's Will even before he could lay his father to rest; it read like a victor offering a taunting peace to the vanquished. The terrorists instructed the new tsar to 'dismiss the spies that do your government harm, disband your personal escort and burn your scaffolds', and to recognise that 'you have lost a father, but we have lost not only fathers, but brothers, wives, children, friends and property'. They also called for a general amnesty for all nihilists, and demanded that Alexander 'consider the existing social and economic conditions, and their modification in accordance with the nation's desires'. Enraged by the nerve of this ultimatum, the tsar dismissed any notion of parlaying with devils and pledged an end to any talk of liberal reform in Russia, in favour of the fanatical promotion of religious orthodoxy and nationalism. As he put it in a letter to his brother, Alexander would, unlike their father, 'never suffer autocracy to be limited'.

This reactionary riposte to People's Will was made on 21 May 1881, when 50,000 troops assembled on the Marsovo Polye in St Petersburg to receive praise from Winter Palace courtiers for their commitment to 'rooting out the horrible seditions that dishonour the land of Russia'. This was followed by pogroms, ignited by the capture of a Jewish member of People's Will and encouraged by the tsar's anti-Semitic advisers. Beneath the harassment and bombast, practical commitments to fighting the burgeoning war on terror were also made. This included the revamping of Shlisselburg Fortress – an imposing medieval edifice housed on an island in Lake Lagoda outside St Petersburg – as a secret prison for suspected terrorists, complete with forty solitary-confinement cells fitted with spy holes through which guards could keep a constant watch on the prisoners.[21]

The Holy Brotherhood also did its bit to respond to the tsar's call for vengeance, creating networks of spies within the radical Russian diasporas of Paris, London and Geneva. Beneath this practical measure, however, the Brotherhood succumbed to conspiratorial pomp. Led by a 'Council of Elders', the Brotherhood's 800 or so adherents were issued ciphers, instructed in the performance of secret handshakes and subjected to quasi-Masonic initiation rituals. Those blessed by these rites were then issued a gold medallion engraved with the dying visage of the medieval Russian hero Alexander Nevsky – as clear a sign of devotion to defending the nation and its Holy Father as could be imagined. For all this outlandish secretiveness, the operational effectiveness of the Brotherhood left much to be desired. In the summer of 1881, Witte was sent to Paris to coordinate the assassination of a People's Will fugitive named Lev Hartman. Having proceeded to the Latin Quarter, two of Witte's gunmen followed Hartman around the corner and out of their overseer's sight, only to return a few minutes later cursing in frustration. Their annoyance stemmed from the last-minute arrival of another Brotherhood member. He claimed that further authorisation was needed for the kill from a Russian diplomat who, unbeknownst to the assassins, had recently joined their secret organisation. Either that or the two men lost their nerve and simply lied to Witte. Regardless of the reason for the assassins' failure, Hartman was able to evade the Brotherhood, flee Paris and find sanctuary in the United States.

Witte's anger at this 'preposterous incident' only grew when he realised that the Brotherhood's supposedly clandestine initiation rituals had become 'the tale of the town in Russia', ensuring that 'all manner of riff-raff and ambitious climbers' were now lining up for their Nevsky medallion. Witte's disgust was justified. Five thousand miles away from St Petersburg, in Chicago, the *Tribune* published details of the organisation's membership. In Paris, Andrieux, despite being as driven to fight terrorism as any police chief of the age, believed that the Brotherhood was little more than a grift that provided salaries to the friends of Russia's well-to-do, in return for 'denouncing inoffensive people' and following 'the trail of conspiracies that, until then, had not been suspected of existing'. Within Russia itself, the Brotherhood became an object of mocking contempt, referred to by even the most reactionary of the tsar's courtiers as a 'colony of young thugs', so troublesome that 'we have to fight against it just as much as against the terrorists!'[22]

The Brotherhood was a hapless manifestation of the 'great panic' one observer described as gripping Russia in the early 1880s, and the punchline to the Brotherhood joke was that none of the money, effort or conspiratorial energy fed into it was necessary. Days after Alexander's assassination, the surviving (weak-armed) People's Will bomber was apprehended and interrogated, and gave away the names and addresses of his accomplices. This led to him, Perovskaya, Kibalchich and three others being tried in a closed tribunal, where opportunities for them to plead their case – as Zasulich had done to emancipatory effect – were near non-existent. The outcome was never in doubt. Five of the six were hanged on 16 April before 'some nine or ten thousand troops', deployed to intimidate away any hint of public support for the nihilists. A sixth defendant was spared the noose on account of being pregnant. However, she died later from an infection that set in not long after her baby was snatched from her arms by a prison warden. This pitiless triumph for the tsar and his new secret police – a better resourced and better staffed iteration of the Third Section known as the Okhrana – heralded the demise of a terrorist group that, only months earlier, had held Europe and the United States in thrall to its fear-inducing actions.[23]

As Vera Figner, one of the few senior members of People's Will to escape the dragnet, recalled, the execution of Alexander's killers ripped the heart of out the organisation, forcing it from St Petersburg, a city that had been the nihilists' heartland since the 1860s. In pieces, People's Will did manage a Parthian blow in 1883, when they convinced an Okhrana double agent to turn on his handler, who was then shot and beaten to death in his own home. This gory assassination aside, there was 'no deceiving oneself', Figner felt, for 'the main pillars of our organisation, who had established its new policy and committed revolutionary acts that had attracted the world's attention were no longer among us'. Moreover, even after pulling off the greatest act of regicide in living memory, People's Will had not been able to incite any form of anti-tsarist revolution.[24] This did not mean, however, that the nihilists' efforts were without impact. Beyond Russia, People's Will provided inspiration for radicals who had spent the decade since the Commune's fall questioning their next move. The answer was now clear – the future would belong to those who understood the value of terror. And what, as the reactions to the shocking nature of the tsar's demise showed, could be more terrifying than a 'doomed man' with an armful of dynamite?

Chapter X

The dynamite lesson

On 14 July 1881, barely two months after the tsar's murderers had swung from gallows in Semyonovsky Square, Cleveland Hall in London played host to a gathering of socialists, Communards, anarchists and Blanquists. Held in the wake of a terrorist attack that had shocked the world, this event drew the attention of reporters from the conservative *Daily Telegraph*, who raised eyebrows when speakers at this 'meeting of revolutionary delegates' professed that 'the hour has come when hopes and expectations must give place to decisive action'. The guest list for this gathering featured a who's who of Europe's radicals, all of whom had the experience and capability to make something tangible of this call to arms. With red flags mounted on the walls around them, the learned Russian subversive Tchaikovsky and the energetic insurrectionist Malatesta appeared in the hall alongside Louise Michel, who, recently returned from her prison stint in New Caledonia, was received by all as the heroic torch bearer of the Commune's sacred flame. These three were joined by another notable node in Europe's radical network, the Russian noble turned anarchist Peter Kropotkin, who had spent much of the late 1870s in Switzerland with Reclus, marshalling the remnants of Bakunin's circle. These celebrity revolutionaries had around them a hundred or so other agitators, who, the *Telegraph* ominously reported, 'appeared to belong to the working classes' – Hemyng's army of the proletariat assembled before its 'red' colonels.

Among the leaders, Kropotkin above all the grabbed the attention of the conservative press. With his schoolteacher's glasses, balding crown and chimney-broom beard, he looked every bit the philosopher-dissident he was. Following in the tradition of Bakunin, he was also a traitor to his class. As a young man of noble blood, Kropotkin had been fast-tracked to a military career, only to use his commission as a means of getting posted to Siberia, where he indulged in his passion for geography. As he mused on the timelessness of the wild landscape, he also secretly devoured anarchist literature, forming views not dis-similar to those of his future friend Reclus on the relationship between patience and revolution. Having abandoned the military to educate him-self in science and philosophy, Kropotkin joined the Tchaikovsky Circle and, after the Third Section broke it apart, served time in prison before escaping – unlike Nechaev, via a dramatic jailbreak that *actually* hap-pened – to Switzerland. There, he settled into the anarchist community that Bakunin had founded in and around Geneva and established one of the premier radical publications of the age, *Le Révolté*.

Kropotkin was a thinker rather than a fighter. As such, reporters covering the London Anarchist Congress were left stunned when he 'applauded the assassination of many Russian generals', lauded the tsar's sanguinary end and reported in *Le Révolté* of how the congress had passed 'resolutions whose avowed aim is to organise assassinations, and to overthrow the established powers by using the chemical and physical means'. This pro-terrorist sentiment was backed by Michel, who, nursing her hatreds in New Caledonia 'for ten years had dreamt of the coming storm'. Now at liberty, she urged attendees to embrace terrorism, in response to which she received 'loud shouts of "Vive la Commune!"' So alarming were the reports of these declarations, the question was asked in Britain's Parliament of 'whether the government, as defenders of law and order, are prepared to prohibit such exhibitions in future, or will extend their protection to those who attack all authority'. In response, the home secretary, William Harcourt, had to concede that, on account of Britain's 'well established and well understood' tradition of allowing free voice to radicals, no such restriction could be imposed.[1]

The ambiguities of revolutionary objectives noted at the Peace and Freedom Congress of 1867 were now seemingly a distant memory, as the 'total destruction by force of existing institutions' was discussed openly in London. According to intelligence gathered by Swiss police spies in 1880, Kropotkin and Reclus had put this idea down on paper months before the congress, drafting a plan for Europe's radicals that echoed almost verbatim Nechaev's 1869 call to 'study … mechanics, physics and chemistry'. Whether they took these words from the *Catechism* or simply aped People's Will in following Nechaev's murderous logic, it appeared that the educated anarchists of Switzerland had come to the same conclusion about the usefulness of terrorism as that reached by the Russian nihilist, the assassin Stepniak and the ex-Communard Michel. In truth, this agreement at the congress to embrace violence was neither as uniform nor as enthusiastic as reported. Kropotkin may have agreed with Reclus's strategy, but he argued for caveats to the idea of unfettered bloodshed, which included him insisting to his comrades that the word 'morality' be included somewhere in the congress's final declaration. Other attendees, however, were excited by the promise of carnage. Egged on in no small part by agent provocateurs sent from Paris by Andrieux, loose talk arose at Cleveland Hall of how, despite the need to study 'the science of chemicals … the bomb is too feeble to destroy the autocratic colossuses. Kill the property owners at the same time, prepare for peasant risings.' Somewhere between these sanguinary outbursts and Kropotkin's words of caution, the congress agreed on a revolutionary strategy that borrowed both from People's Will's violence and from Reclus's idea of using fear and manipulation to effect political change. The powers that be would be terrorised through acts of violence, engendering repression that would inspire new adherents to the revolutionary cause, furthering a desirable end in which the world would forever be changed. It was a strategy the anarchists called 'propaganda of the deed'.[2]

Unlike People's Will, the anarchist version of propaganda of the deed emphasised the importance of individual action, rather than plotting attacks in secret groups. This reflected the lack of adherence to hierarchies and structure in anarchist thinking. As such, the suggestion from one of Andrieux's agents provocateurs that the congress create a central information bureau to coordinate attacks garnered a mostly muted response. In this lay the dichotomy of the post-Commune era. Police spies, still working on the assumption that all roads led to grand conspiracies, tried to will this myth into existence by arguing for an anarchist communications hub. The true radicals had little time for this notion, and instead agreed to reject conspiratorial organisation in favour of encouraging 'lonely sentinels' to carry out 'acts of illegal protest, or revolt and of vengeance' that would infuse anarchist ideas 'into people's minds and win converts'. Implied in the many references to 'chemistry' and 'science' was the truth of how this violent educational campaign would be carried out. Admirable as Stepniak and Zasulich had been with their dagger and pistol, few at the London Anarchist Congress doubted that the true pioneers of the terrorist age were People's Will, furnished with infernal machines born from the mind of the dangerously creative Kibalchich. To replicate the conditions of fear created by the nihilists, the explosive instrument of their success needed to be embraced.[3]

Such was the pervasiveness of People's Will's dynamite lesson, its merit was understood by radicals whose aims differed greatly from the anarchists and socialists who gathered in London in July 1881. On a raining April evening three years later, a man named Richard Rogers stood behind a lectern in Kessel's Hall, Manhattan, gesticulating wildly and jabbing his finger at diagrams of dynamite cylinders and nail bombs scribbled on the blackboard behind him. Rogers addressed no more than twenty people, seated on a scattering of mismatched chairs in an echoing room designed to house ten times that number. Humble as the scene before him was, Rogers' words were incendiary enough to infuse the grandest of venues and the largest of audiences with hellfire. Replete with claims that he could transform the rag in his hand into a fuse or produce from a kitchen cupboard the ingredients needed to destroy Capitol Hill, Rogers' speech was excitedly absorbed by the trainee terrorists before him, who cheered his melodrama and asked eager questions of his science. His carefully cultivated image ensured this response.

A Scottish-born immigrant turned Chicago bartender, Rogers had spent years convincing people that he was an explosives expert with ties to People's Will, who went under the unsubtly Russian *nom de plume* of

Professor Mezzeroff. In this guise, he had penned columns on the assemblage of explosives for anarchist and Fenian periodicals and bragged to sensation-hungry journalists of how he was a 'member of two secret societies', from which he could acquire 'state secrets from Europe forty-eight hours after they have transpired'. Mezzeroff also claimed to be a Crimean War veteran who, disgusted by the 'wholesale massacre' of that imperialist squabble, had awoken to Heinzen's idea that murder was no sin, but a right to be pursued by the oppressed. Since that epiphany, he had devoted himself 'to the welfare and elevation of humanity', a cause he believed would be best served by promoting the ultimate tool of humankind's liberation – dynamite.[4]

Although he was a charlatan – his lectures cost 30 cents a piece or $30 for a monthly enrolment in his 'dynamite school' – Mezzeroff's claims that he could teach the downtrodden how to 'defend yourself against the armies of the world' were perfectly pitched to resonate with the disaffected workers and radical émigrés who mostly comprised his audience. Distant they may have been from the oppression of kaisers and tsars that had steered the London Anarchist Congress towards propaganda of the deed, the grievances felt by Mezzeroff's American audience were comparably deep-seated and dire. In 1873, the railroad-building boom that had swept the United States after the Civil War came to an abrupt halt, in tandem with the devaluing of silver. During the global economic crisis that followed, banks and railroad consortia collapsed and thousands of jobs were lost. As a witness to this first Great Depression recalled, in New York 'men who were out of employment or working at low wages' could be seen begging on every street corner; 'tens of thousands of them were very poor, and the families of many were suffering for lack of daily food'.

This misery was not accepted meekly. In 1877, cities across the Midwest and the East Coast of the United States were battered by a series of strikes and riots, in which National Guardsmen and heavies from the Pinkerton Agency – now turned from private security to strike-breaking – were deployed. Hundreds died and thousands were wounded. Such was the scale of the violence and the involvement of secret societies like the

Molly Maguires and the Knights of Labor in organising the strikes, the *Chicago Tribune* declared that the 'war in Chicago is no longer a war simply with railroad strikers but with the riff-raff, the tramps, roughs, rowdies, thieves, vagabonds'. These, 'and other elements that compose the Commune', were hell-bent, it seemed, on bringing revolution to Chicago, which was 'drifting into the condition of Paris during the reign of the Commune'. Never one to shy away from conspiracy theories, Pinkerton himself was convinced that the Molly Maguires – a secret society that had emerged from the struggle for land rights in Ireland – were the vanguard of an international revolutionary conspiracy crossing the Atlantic to bring down the coal barons of the United States.[5]

In this climate of economic depression and violent protests by those most affected, Mezzeroff's talk of arming the disempowered with the 'recipes for forty-two explosives', and his boasts of strolling down Wall Street with bombs in his pockets on the off chance he might murder a stockbroker, commanded attention. Indeed, this type of rhetoric was catnip to journalists who had followed the exploits of People's Will and reported on the resolutions of the London Anarchist Congress. Mezzeroff was regularly interviewed by the *New York Sun*, and the *Washington Post* uncritically dubbed him the 'nihilist and head chemist of the Irish dynamite party', whilst the *New York Tribune* reported that he had constructed 'a six-pound bomb that would be more destructive than a hundred-pound cannon'. This hyperbolic coverage not only sold papers but it also sold Mezzeroff, inspiring people like George Holgate, who raised eyebrows when he travelled through the Rocky Mountains in 1883 expressing 'sympathies' with 'the Black Hand movement of the Old World' and hawking homemade explosive devices. Holgate's emulation may have flattered Mezzeroff, but his intention was not to cultivate copy-cats. Rather, Mezzeroff's aim was to lure to his lectures both those left desperate and enraged by the Great Depression and, more importantly, dissident Irish republicans, whom he promised would 'study dynamite in safety in New York, and then go blow up Albion'.[6]

Mezzeroff's intent to train America's Irish in bomb-making was owed to the launching, in 1881, of a campaign of terrorist violence by a Fenian who was unbending in his determination to wage war on the British Empire – Jeremiah O'Donovan Rossa. White bearded, sharp-faced and possessed of the deep-set eyes of a zealot, O'Donovan Rossa was one of the IRB members arrested during the police operation that had collared Stephens in 1865. Although this meant he avoided the failed uprising two years later, O'Donovan Rossa languished in jail until 1871, when he was released on the condition that he exile himself from Ireland. Regarded by the British government as a gesture that would ease negotiations with Irish republican politicians, the idea of granting O'Donovan Rossa amnesty, albeit of a conditional form, came as a shock to the dissident, who had learned much about the relationship between the state and its enemies during his time behind bars.

Not unlike Zasulich, O'Donovan Rossa's resolve to combat his enemies by terrorising them was strengthened rather than broken by his years of incarceration, during which he earned a reputation for being a 'violent and outrageous' inmate, 'who produced so bad an effect on the other Fenian prisoners' that he was often placed in solitary confinement. Starved, manacled, maltreated and refused permission to exchange letters with his wife, O'Donovan Rossa dished back to his tormentors much of what he received, refusing work details, verbally abusing guards, starting fights and smashing up his cell. He even fell out with some of his fellow Fenians, who begged him to behave, lest the legitimacy of their cause be imperilled by being reduced in their captors' eyes to criminal malcontents. O'Donovan Rossa dismissed this idea, arguing that the inherent criminality of the British Empire justified all means of fighting back. He grew more emboldened, chanting 'I am a Fenian' in the face of the guards and, on one occasion, hurling a chamber pot at the prison governor.[7]

Unsurprisingly, when O'Donovan Rossa arrived in New York in 1871, he set about plotting his revenge against the British, using the bitter history of the IRB's failures and an open-minded view of scientific warfare to guide him. His drive for a fresh way of thinking about the Irish struggle resonated in the émigré communities of New York, Boston and Chicago, who for years had been subjected to the musings of a Civil War veteran turned journalist named Patrick Ford. Through his New

York newspaper, the *Irish World*, Ford had inspired readers with tales of Fenian martyrdom and his argument that anti-imperialist America, with its free speech and love of liberty, was a perfect 'base of operations' for the Irish republicans to rebuild from setbacks of the 1860s. It was this sentiment that led, on 5 December 1875, to Ford publishing an appeal in the *Irish World* for the formation of 'a little band of heroes who will initiate and keep up without intermission a guerrilla war'. Disciplined, 'unknown and unnoticed', these heroes would operate in cells, with 'each man setting about his own allotted task, and no man save the captain of the band alone knowing what any other man was to do'. They would also be armed with dynamite, for, as recent events in Europe had shown, 'anarchists and nihilists of the old world had at last in their hands an implement of destruction sufficient to destroy all the armies and navies in existence'. If these revolutionaries had taken up this 'gift of science' then why, the *Irish World* demanded, should not Irish republicans?[8] Mindful that shortly after his arrival in New York the Fenians had launched yet another doomed invasion of Canada, O'Donovan Rossa warmed to Ford's idea of jettisoning armies in favour of 'little bands' of men. The initiative, however, would require money, particularly to fulfil Ford's insistence on developing innovative weapons to arm the irregulars.

This need led, in 1876, to O'Donovan Rossa making an appeal in the *Irish World* for donations to a 'Skirmishing Fund', which would be used to provision guerrilla fighters willing to 'inflict material damage on England and give strength and prestige to the Irish cause'. Asserting that 'three men and a few pounds of dynamite are more than a match for the mightiest frigate', *Irish World* made no qualms about the need for 'Orsini warfare' to take centre stage in the Irish struggle, and with it bombings, hit-and-fade attacks, sabotage and even assassinations. No less than certain anarchists, a squeamishness towards these activities arose in the minds of some Irish republicans, particularly members of Clan na Gael, a group that had risen to prominence in the 1870s off the back of the IRB's failures. Beholden to the idea that legitimacy was vital in the war against Britain – the more so given that, at the same time O'Donovan Rossa and Ford were calling for a skirmishing campaign, republican politicians were entering into discussions with Whitehall over land reform in Ireland – many Clan members recoiled at the prospect of wanton violence, particularly if it led to civilian deaths. For O'Donovan Rossa, Ford and an Illinois-based engineer with an interest in dynamite by the name of Patrick Crowe, however, the promise of scientific warfare was too great to follow a path of restraint. In June 1880, O'Donovan Rossa established a group composed of Crowe and over a hundred other Irish republicans called the United Irishmen of America (UIA). The published minutes of the UIA's inaugural meeting in Philadelphia unabashedly signalled its terrorist strategy. The 'eternal right of the Irish people to govern themselves', the meeting declared, would be pursued by the UIA 'by every means known to the science of warfare'. As O'Donovan Rossa clarified in a follow-up statement to the *New York Sun*, 'we Irish have no artillery, no ships of war', yet they were determined to form an alliance of 'brave, death-daring men' who, 'aided by such appliances as modern science puts within easy reach', will 'harass the enemy's commerce on sea and on land, and her interests everywhere, as to make her lose more than she gains by despoiling and enslaving Ireland'.[9]

This resolve amongst Fenians to use terrorism was made a year before the Anarchist Congress endorsed propaganda of the deed. Although this indicates that the Irish were quicker to heed the dynamite lesson than the anarchists, there was still room within the Fenian cause for flights of fantasy from a bygone age. Ford had talked in the *Irish World* of acquiring Gatling guns, an American improvement on the French mitrailleuse that was capable of firing 300 rounds per minute. Yet, being a heavy, expensive and stationary weapon system, the Gatling was next to useless for the kind of guerrilla operations he and O'Donovan Rossa were calling for. The latter was also party to a scheme to use several thousand dollars from the Skirmishing Fund to construct a torpedo-armed submarine. The purpose of this innovative weapon of war was to apply terrorist tactics to the high seas, using the latest in maritime technology to create paralysis in the British Empire's trade by attacking British shipping. Trialled throughout the late 1870s, the sub – nicknamed the *Fenian Ram* – was launched in 1881, with the reported ability to remain submerged at sixty feet for a little over two hours. Promising though this seemed, the project fell apart following a dispute over money with the manufacturer. This led, in 1883, to a team of disgruntled Irish republicans raiding the warehouse where the wonder weapon was stored. They commandeered both the *Ram* and another submarine prototype, only for the latter to sink in New York's East River and the former, deemed impossible to operate without specialist instruction, to rust away in a boatshed in Connecticut.[10]

Even before the *Ram* project ground to an ignominious halt, it had become apparent to O'Donovan Rossa and Crowe that trying and failing to develop experimental weapons was no substitute for the ruthless simplicity of detonating bombs. This realisation led the pair to seek an alliance with the man whose boasts of connections to People's Will and claims of dynamite expertise made him a totem for modern terrorism – Mezzeroff. Having agreed to a salary of $483 from the UIA, Mezzeroff welcomed O'Donovan Rossa's trainee terrorists into his 'dynamite school' in Brooklyn, preparing the first class for deployment to Britain at about the same time that People's Will was gathering intelligence for its final, successful attack on the tsar. The products of this push by the UIA to reignite the Irish republican cause through terrorism were two attacks on British soil, the first of which destroyed a shed outside the walls of Salford barracks on 14 January 1881, injuring seven people and killing a child. The second attack took place on 16 March and involved O'Donovan Rossa's men sneaking through the London fog into an alleyway adjacent to the Mansion House, where they ignited a device containing fifteen pounds of gunpowder beneath a window. The explosion that should have followed was prevented by the arrival of a patrolling policeman who, drawn to the sight of the device smoking in the alleyway, rushed forward and smothered the flames with a flurry of foot stomps.[11]

As an exercise in terrorising Britain, these efforts garnered mixed results. The death of the young boy in Salford stirred talk of the 'return of outrages' to Irish affairs, but the fact that the attack on the Mansion House occurred within days of the tsar's assassination led the *Daily Telegraph* to put the UIA's efforts down to 'nihilist doings'. In Parliament, discussion of the 'abominable attempt' on the Mansion House was also voiced alongside whispers that a 'nihilistic fraternity in London' had gathered the previous evening in the city's East End to toast the tsar's demise. People's Will had stolen O'Donovan Rossa's headlines. The wider implications of the attacks were also played down in certain quarters of the press, where the Mansion House bomb was dismissed as 'less serious than it was represented' and the explosion in Salford as possibly being the work of a lone disgruntled Irishman within the barracks. Even after talk of a 'Fenian conspiracy' entered the newspapers and the authorities turned their stare across the ocean to O'Donovan Rossa, a sanguine attitude remained. According to British consular officials in New York, the Fenian was a 'political adventurer' whose 'interest in the 'liberation' of Ireland was a cynical ploy to gain prestige, money and influence within the Irish diaspora. These bombings were stunts, rather than acts of war. The memory of the IRB's past failures and the context of what had been going on in Russia did much to shape this view. The Irish, it was believed, could never be as effective in the burgeoning dark art of terrorism as the nihilists. The *Huddersfield Chronicle* spoke for the critics when it reported that, the fatality in Salford aside, Britain had little to fear from the ill-trained UIA, whose hapless attempt on the Mansion House was a world away from People's Will's 'ingenious efforts to kill the late emperor'. As such, although extra police were deployed to guard public buildings in London and Scotland Yard filed reports on 'suspicious characters' being followed near Windsor Castle, there was little sense in the spring of 1881 that Britain had to be put, as Russia recently had, on a war footing.[12]

The UIA's follow-up attacks in Liverpool and Chester in the early summer of 1881 did little to shake this view. The bombs used were small devices that killed no one and did little damage. The home secretary, Harcourt, concluded that, despite their concerning newfound taste for explosives, the Fenians had 'all of the wickedness but none of the arts or desperation of the nihilists'. Harcourt's impression that there was little infernal about Mezzeroff's machines was reinforced by the assessment of one of the world's first bomb experts – Colonel Vivian Majendie. A former soldier possessed of a fascination with scientific warfare, Majendie was appointed Her Majesty's chief inspector of explosives at

Woolwich arsenal in 1871. At the time of the UIA's campaign, he was establishing the first iteration of Scotland Yard's bomb squad. As such, Majendie forensically examined the detritus left by the Fenians' attacks, and concluded that the UIA's mostly gunpowder-charged devices were cheaply made, poorly designed and not particularly powerful.[13]

And then, in June 1881, a cache of dynamite bombs fitted with timers was discovered on board a ship in Liverpool that had crossed the Atlantic from the UIA's home territory of New York. Based on an assessment of the bombs' components, Majendie concluded that they had come from the same basement factories that had produced the previous gunpowder offerings. The press changed their tune. Fenian terrorism was now described as possessing 'many attributes in common with Russian nihilism', from the 'dangerous and diabolical' plots, to the 'meanness of the human agents' who hatched them. Testament to the fear induced by the presence of sophisticated dynamite weapons in O'Donovan Rossa's arsenal, one newspaper even resurrected a form of the IWMA–Communard theory, suggesting that the 'Fenians in England and Land Leaguism in Ireland are but different names for nihilism and socialism'. If not parties to an ideology-straddling conspiracy, it was now clear that the UIA was, at the very least, developing 'schemes of a diabolical nature that would find favour with the Russian nihilists' or had simply 'resolved on an imitation of Russian nihilists'. The *United Irishman* newspaper encouraged this idea, telling its readers to acknowledge 'the lessons to be learnt from the nihilist of Russia', 'to see what terror, nay, despair they have driven into the Winter Palace' and to dream that 'we Irishmen could make Windsor and Buckingham Palaces as miserable an abode as any other on earth' by the same means.[14]

These suggestive words were part of a canny game O'Donovan Rossa played on the question of nihilist influence, with the aim to heighten fear without compromising the legitimacy of the Fenian cause. Publicly, the UIA leader disavowed any connection between his group and the despised Russian terrorists. He even wrote letters to the State Department claiming that the story of the dynamite bombs in Liverpool was fake news concocted by the British. Beneath this façade, however, O'Donovan

Rossa, no less than Bakunin, Nechaev or Stephens before him, saw an advantage in playing up the idea that his organisation was multinational. To have his skirmishers mentioned in the same breath as those who had dynamited the tsar into oblivion would add an extra layer of menace and mystique to the UIA and, doubtless, boost enrolments in Mezzeroff's classes. To this end, O'Donovan Rossa appeared hand in glove with Mezzeroff on stage, leaning into the idea that the deadly knowledge of People's Will was being shared with the Fenians. In the pages of the *United Irishman*, the praise of nihilists intensified, with the virtues of terrorist self-sacrifice being extolled alongside a proclamation that 'a verdict of murder' had been reached in the case of the Irish v. Gladstone, and that 'four Irishmen had volunteered to carry out the verdict' – an eerily similar pronouncement to People's Will decree of 'death to the tsar' in 1879.

For his part, Crowe contributed to this fear campaign by braggadocio, insinuating that the UIA had the capability to strike the British Empire both on land and at sea. In August 1881, he gave an interview to the *Chicago Tribune* in which he made the false claim that a recent explosion on board a Royal Navy ship was the work of the UIA. Evoking the long-standing fear of internationalism, Crowe also boasted of how thousands of dynamite bombs like those discovered in Liverpool were being assembled by Fenian allies in secret factories in Canada, the United States and France. He conceded that 'some people would have to die' in the great conflagration he and O'Donovan Rossa were preparing. As justification for the carnage, Crowe argued that 'war was cruel' and Britain, having had the monopoly on violence via its ships and cannon for centuries, was overdue a lesson in that reality.[15]

These claims of sinister alliances and secret bomb factories showed that O'Donovan Rossa and Crowe understood the terrorist strategy that anarchists and nihilists had adopted, at the heart of which lay the premise that the *fear* of attack could be as potent a weapon as violence itself. Impressed by the anxiety O'Donovan Rossa's bombs and Crowe's lies created in the British press and Parliament, members of Clan na Gael, who had hitherto balked at the pair's embrace of terrorism, began to see sense in the UIA's methods. The most prominent of these pro-dynamiters was Alexander Sullivan, who tabled the issue at a Clan meeting in Chicago in August 1881, demanding that the organisation join the UIA's campaign. Sullivan's vision for participation, as recorded by a British spy who penetrated the upper echelons of the Clan, was for a corps of 'men without families' to be formed and given a 'special course of instruction in the use of explosives'. So great would the care taken in the selection of these bombers be, 'their whole career and character would be inquired into beforehand without their knowledge'. Only once this vetting process was completed satisfactorily would they be sent across the ocean to dynamite Britain. Sullivan's argument for professionalisation and, with it, enhanced secrecy eventually won over other Clan leaders, who agreed in 1883 to his suggestion that they join the campaign of 'incessant and persistent warfare' that the UIA had started.[16]

Whilst Sullivan pushed the Clan towards dynamite, other Fenians jumped on the fear bandwagon by taking a leaf out the books of the dagger-brandishing Stepniak and the assassins from People's Will. On 6 May 1882, members of a splinter group within the Fenian movement – dubbed the Invincibles – stabbed to death both the chief secretary for Ireland and the permanent under-secretary at the Irish Office in the middle of Phoenix Park in Dublin. This brazen and brutal public execution of two government officials sparked outrage across Britain, and a rumour of 'the crime being planned in Paris' by the international Fenian network that Crowe had spoken of. Much as he enjoyed spooking the press with threats to dynamite buildings, ships and ports – inanimate, symbolic objects whose destruction might incidentally cause bloodshed – Crowe distanced himself from endorsing targeted killing. He condemned the assassinations, albeit with his often-repeated caveat that 'so far as England is concerned, the assassin's knife had been her weapon for years, and in this instance, she had only been paid back in her own coin'. On the same basis that fear rather than murder was its goal, the Clan also denounced the stabbings. O'Donovan Rossa, for his part, lent into the Invincibles' deed, enjoying the assumptions made in certain quarters of the press that he had masterminded the assassinations. As in the case of the supposed Fenian–nihilist alliance, O'Donovan Rossa was waging psychological warfare. Although he publicly quashed suggestions that he was involved in the murders in Phoenix Park, he urged his supporters to refrain from condemning the Invincibles and, at a Fenian gathering at the Cooper Union in New York shortly after the assassins struck, demanded 'three cheers for the killings!'[17]

And well O'Donovan Rossa might have cheered, for the murders in Phoenix Park provided a fear force multiplier for his campaign. Six days after the stabbings, the Mansion House was again targeted by Fenians armed with a crudely made gunpowder bomb, the fuse of which petered out into a smouldering non-event before detonation could occur. Rather than melting away from the headlines amidst sniffs of mockery, mention of the failed bombing was made amidst columns on Phoenix Park, with the admission that, although the bomb's 'consequences would have been trifling', the combination of the two attacks had created 'an unpleasant effect upon the public mind' and prevented 'the public feeling calming down'. This anxiety increased when three bombs were detonated at a Glasgow gasworks in January 1883, the product of the Clan joining the fray and bringing much-needed funds and resources to the dynamite campaign. Gone were the days when *The Times* could dismiss O'Donovan Rossa as a misfit guided by the poseur Mezzeroff, who, the newspaper asserted, 'likely never made a pound of explosive in his life'.[18]

It was certainly true that the devices Sullivan's people put together were more sophisticated than anything hitherto concocted by the 'Professor'. Although they did not always explode as planned, to Majendie's mind, the tendency for timers to be used in this new generation of Irish bombs was indicative of the purely terroristic strategy the UIA and the Clan had adopted. Timers allowed for coordinated multi-bomb attacks and gave the perpetrators the opportunity to set their devices to detonate at tube stations, police barracks, on board ships and outside newspaper offices at hours of their choosing. The result was a campaign comprising no fewer than thirteen bombings, which culminated with the terrorist spectacular of 'Dynamite Saturday' in January 1885 – during which three devices detonated within minutes of each other outside Westminster Hall, in the Tower of London and in the House of Commons. Although over a hundred people were wounded during the dynamite campaign, the total number killed by the time it ceased in 1885 could be counted at less than ten.[19]

As the architects of the dynamite campaign intended, this relative lack of bloodshed did little to soothe the anxieties inflicted on Britain by four years of bombings. After two dynamite devices exploded at Paddington and Westminster tube stations in October 1883, extra police patrols were despatched to the Mansion House, the National Portrait Gallery, the Houses of Parliament and even the German embassy, which was not alone amongst political establishments in London in receiving crank letters warning of imminent attacks. The docks at Bristol and Liverpool were provisioned with extra patrolmen, with the hope of preventing 'a landing of dynamitards from abroad by keeping a strict look out for American vessels and searching passengers' luggage'. Outside Scotland Yard's headquarters, a screen of constables was placed on twenty-four-hour watch, but even this could not prevent the detonation of a bomb in a public urinal opposite the building. This grievous breach of security led to orders being issued by the Yard for 'every man on the beat, and every officer above him, in the performance of his daily duties, to acquire information as to residents, questionable characters, places used for meetings, lodging houses where Irish-Americans or men likely to be dangerous may meet'. Beset by an unseen enemy, beat-cops now had to assume the role of counter-terrorist detectives.

As had occurred in 1867, certain members of the public responded to this feeling of besiegement by enthusiastically manning Britain's ramparts. In Cardiff, a Miss Gertrude Jenner observed 'an object of suspicion' on a shop counter, which 'gave forth a smell' that she believed was that of nitro-glycerine. The police summoned by Jenner concluded that the parcel was no bomb, yet the reportage of this incident led to further scares across the city. A few days later, a man named Murphy carrying a parcel on a tram was chased away from the vehicle by frightened passengers, for, as the *Western Mail* had it, 'an Irishman with a box is about the least welcome company'. Murphy's protest that a clock was the source of the parcel's ticking was rejected by the police who detained him. After agonising for some time over the dangers of opening the Irishman's parcel, the constables reluctantly took it to a deserted park and, 'with fear and trembling', inspected its contents, only to find that it was, indeed, a timepiece bereft of any dynamite or gunpowder.[20]

Press and politicians were alive to the implications of the British public becoming afeared of suspicious packages and odd-acting Irish people. The bombers had succeeded in 'the spreading of fear and terror in England in view of extorting what is claimed by the Irish'. The disasters of Stephens' time now forgotten, the Fenians had become synonymous in the minds of many Britons with the kind of terrorist menace that had long-haunted France and Russia. As a reporter who covered a UIA meeting at the Cooper Union in 1883 surmised, 'the assassinations in Phoenix Park and the dynamite explosions had opened the press of England and the world to Ireland's grievances, and they now got columns where formerly they could not get paragraphs'. Furthermore, 'by carrying the war into the heart of England, by having recourse to the godlike means of warfare, the Irish' realised that they 'would inflict more injury upon England than Germany had upon France. Within a year, they would have England on her knees.'[21]

Here was the sum of the revolution in terrorist thinking that occurred during the 1870s and 1880s. Through the means of dynamite, the gap in violent capabilities between oppressors and oppressed once lamented by Heinzen had been narrowed. Terrorists could now appear 'godlike' in their power, inspiring fresh recruits to their campaign and causing plagues of panic so virulent that they had the potential to weaken a state to the point of concession to their political goals. Although the pursuit of this end had led People's Will to its destruction at the hands of the Okhrana, the Irish republican bombers avoided a similarly ruthless police response. A Special Branch for combatting Fenian terrorism was not created until 1883, and when it was its resources were sparse, with only a dozen detectives assigned to keep watch over London. The Branch was able to coordinate its efforts – albeit rarely and without much harmony – with anti-Fenian specialists, including Robert Anderson, who had endured the panics of 1867 and at the time of the dynamite campaign was running a spy within Clan na Gael. This led to some success in police responses to the dynamite campaign. On three occasions, suspected bombers were detained in Liverpool before they could cause any damage, an illicit explosives factory was raided in Birmingham and the extra police patrols around London led to the timely discovery of explosive devices, some of which the ever-capable Majendie was able to defuse. However, a lack of experience in counter-terrorism methods and an inability of the various departments tasked with fighting the Fenians to coordinate their efforts led to the police never getting ahead of the dynamiters. Working in small groups or sometimes even as individuals, the Irish terrorists of the 1880s were much harder to detect and foil than the IRB insurrectionists of the 1860s.[22]

In the end, it was left to the Fenians to halt the campaign and claim a form of victory. In 1885 Gladstone publicly committed his government to granting Ireland Home Rule, laying the groundwork for the first (albeit failed) attempt to pass a bill on the issue in June 1886. Satisfied that some political movement had been made, the Clan called for a suspension of the bombings and sent a circular to its members, declaring that 'the operations so far conducted have compelled the enemy to recognise the Constitutional party'. As the circular further stated, the reason for this breakthrough was obvious – 'the mystery of an unknown power striking in the dark, always able to avoid detection, is far more terrible than the damage inflicted'. Fear, it seemed, had forced Britain to acknowledge the depth of Irish grievance. So ended a terrorist campaign with a clear and discernible outcome, which, as Ford pointed out in 1886, was 'never intended for anarchical purposes' of the type advocated in London five years earlier. The campaign he and O'Donovan Rossa engendered was not a 'war against society. It was a war between the two nations of Britain and Ireland.[23] Ford had good reason to make this distinction. In the same year he penned these words, an explosion in Chicago signalled to the world that radicals with agendas more ambitious than that of those of the Fenians or the nihilists had also learned the dynamite lesson.

Chapter XI

Thoughts that light fires

Captain William Ward of the Chicago Police Department went to work on 4 May 1886 knowing it would not be an ordinary Tuesday. The prior evening, 20,000 copies of a pamphlet entitled 'Revenge! Workingmen to Arms' had been distributed across the city in response to workers being shot at the McCormick factory. The killings had been carried out by strike-breakers from the Pinkerton Detective Agency, whose founder, the former Chartist, admirer of John Brown and protector of Lincoln, Allan Pinkerton, had modified his company's *raison d'être* since the 1860s. Shocked by the Paris Commune and 'the tragic story of the sixty-seven days of its sanguinary reign', Pinkerton came to believe that striking workers and socialist writers were engineering a 'conspiracy against progress, liberty and civilization the world over'. In response to this, in the years leading up to his death in 1884, Pinkerton whittled his agency into a stick with which bosses could beat employees who stepped out of line. By the 1880s, industrialists across the United States were crying out for such a weapon, beset as they were by a dispute with their workers over the eight-hour working day. It was in the name of acquiring this basic right that the 'poor wretches' of McCormick's factory had been shot, so the 'Revenge!' pamphlet proclaimed to Chicago's workers, because 'they, like you, have the courage to disobey the supreme will of your bosses'.[1]

The same spirit of defiance hummed through the hundreds who responded to the pamphlet's call by gathering on the evening of 4 May at the corner of Des Plaines and Randolph Streets in central Chicago, at a site called the Haymarket. As leaden skies drip-fed rain onto the sea of brown and grey overcoats, the crowd absorbed the anger of the speeches delivered by editors of the anarchist magazine *The Alarm* and the *Arbeiter-Zeitung* – a newspaper that catered to the city's German community – as well as denouncements of labour exploitation from Samuel Fielden, a Yorkshire-born member of the IWMA. Cheers erupted when the speakers condemned McCormick's recourse to Pinkerton heavies armed with 'gatling guns, cannon, bayonets, patrol wagons and clubs', yet the response was a far cry from the organiser's initial call to 'reply to the white terror with the red terror'. The comparatively subdued nature of the gathering was shattered, however, when the police arrived, and Ward ordered Fielden to dismount from the horse-cart upon which he had clambered to address the crowd. Fielden had barely opened his mouth to respond when an explosion erupted behind him and Ward, followed by 'pistol firing in front and on both sides of the street'. What Ward and other officers later claimed to be an ambush by anarchists was met in kind by the police, who unloaded volleys of gunfire into the crowd, adding further chaos to the evening's mess of smoke, explosions and storm clouds. By the time the fracas subsided, four protesters and seven policemen had been killed – some of the latter by panicked friendly fire – and over a hundred had been wounded, including Fielden, who was amongst the first to take a bullet.[2]

A pall of speculation instantly fell over what came to be known as the Haymarket affair. Was it a trap laid by terrorists for the police? Did the protesters come armed? Was the bomb-thrower who ignited the chaos an anarchist or a Pinkerton agent provocateur? These and other questions abounded at the time and continue to be debated to this day.[3] The press was divided. The *New York Tribune* reported that 'the mob appeared crazed with a frantic desire for blood' even before one of their number tossed 'three bombs into the midst of a squad of officers'. The *Labor Enquirer* insisted that the 'bomb-throwing was the work of a single individual', motivated by the bitter reality that 'conservative elements have deserted the workingmen of this country'. The significance of murderous terrorism blending with the workers' struggle at the

Haymarket was recognised internationally, prompting the same politically divided responses to the bombing in Europe as there were in the United States. *Le Cri du peuple* – a paper founded by ex-Communards – put the *Tribune*'s claims that 'widespread rapine and murder' were on the protesters' minds down to a bourgeois 'obsession with conspiracy'. A socialist newspaper in Sweden waited almost a month before mentioning the Haymarket affair, convinced as its editors were that the story was reactionary fake news. Other newspapers, such as Kropotkin's *Le Révolté*, followed the *Enquirer* in arguing that a justifiably aggrieved worker had brought carnage to Chicago by tossing a 'true proletarian weapon' at Ward's men. Yes, it was a tragedy for those killed and wounded, but it was also a necessity, born of the need for America's workers to strike back against the forces of capital that oppressed them.[4]

Beneath the finger-pointing lay a fact that neither radicals nor reactionaries could dispute – the Haymarket affair and the trial that followed it brought the threat of dynamite terrorism firmly into the consciousness of the American public in a way that the recently suspended Irish bombing campaign had not. There were several reasons for this. Mezzeroff, Crowe and O'Donovan Rossa had talked up dynamite in the press, but the deeds born of their words had been perpetrated thousands of miles away, in another country. Similarly, the knee-jerk fear of terrorist attacks stirred by the arrival in New York of Lev Hartman – he who escaped the Holy Brotherhood's bungling assassins in 1881 – did not last long, once it became clear that he was seeking asylum rather than planning, as the *New York Tribune* absurdly reported, for 'he and Rossa to go to the Sandwich Islands, buy them up with the Skirmishing Fund and make them a home for dynamite Irishmen, nihilists and communists'. Beyond this scare that wasn't, the United States had avoided the worst of terrorist innovation and escalation. The potential for Brown's raid and Ferrandini's supposed plot against Lincoln to engender broader campaigns of political violence was consumed in the maelstrom of the Civil War. During the Great Railroad Strikes of 1877, violent protests took place in Chicago, Pittsburgh, New York and other cities, though the throwing of stones and the occasional discharging of firearms by striking workers were heat-of-the-moment acts, rather than the products of pre-meditated terrorist design.[5]

The only terrorist campaign worthy of the name that the post-bellum United States faced – and only then in the southern part of the country – was the one started in Tennessee by the Ku Klux Klan (KKK) in 1865. Less sophisticated than the strategic tyrannicide and bomb-driven terrorism that was emerging concurrently in Europe, the Klan's racially motivated attacks involved its members roaming the countryside beating, shooting, lynching and setting fire to private property. Focused as the KKK was on terrorising the recently emancipated rather than privileged whites, the violence its members perpetrated grabbed little attention in Washington. At the height of the Klan's campaign, the chief of the United States' Secret Service, Hiram C. Whitley, declared that the main security threats America faced were 'the internal revenue defrauders and blockade-runners'. Moreover, for all its menace, when the hammer finally dropped on the Klan via Whitley leading federal agents south of the Mason–Dixon Line in 1872, the societal fears left in the wake of the group's suppression were not comparable to those created an ocean away by the Communards. Indifference to the Klan's victims ensured that the group never became a nationally recognised menace in the same way that the nihilists of Russia or the Fenians of Britain had.[6]

The labour agitation that engendered the Haymarket affair was a different story. Here was a threat not to the lives of those emancipated from slavery in the war-ravaged South but to the capital and commerce of the nation's northern cities – the industrial engine rooms of Gilded Age America. It was a threat, moreover, that was pregnant with the fear of the foreigner that had first drawn the ire of nativists in the 1850s and stirred concerns over Orsini-emulators. This worry over a sinister strain of 'red' terrorism being transfused into the United States had not abated in the years since the Civil War, during which the country experienced a large wave of immigration from Europe. In 1883 alone, 600,000 Britons, Irish, Italians, Swedes, Poles and Germans arrived – the latter groups replete with people fleeing either the vengeance of Alexander III or the persecution of Bismarck's anti-socialist laws. The industrial strikes that were besetting the United States at the time offered opportunities for these fresh arrivals, with many being brought into railyards, steelworks, abattoirs and textile factories as strike-breaking labour. Before long, however, the more radicalised émigrés swapped sides in the labour struggle, innervated by low wages, appalling working conditions and the rotting sore of the dispute over the eight-hour working day. To this cocktail of grievances was added a final ingredient, so potent that it pushed thoughts of bomb-throwing to the picket line. That ingredient was a man who, no less than Heinzen or Mezzeroff, saw the United States' legions of disgruntled workers as empty vessels into which the murderous intent of the dynamitard could be poured – Johann Most.[7]

Born in 1846 in Bavaria, Most was a lifelong agitator who expressed his hatred of imperialist tyranny and exploitative capitalism by publishing radical newspapers and, as a member of the Reichstag, representing the German Social Democratic Workers' Party. Most's concern, however, was never solely for the plight of Germany's working class. Having followed the stories of nihilist terrorism and Fenian mutterings of skirmishers with interest, Most became convinced that bombs and daggers would hasten the revolution that Marx and his followers were resigned simply to wait for. To Most, this sluggishness from Europe's premier revolutionary was unacceptable in a world where electric-powered machines and transformative changes in steel production were altering the life of factory workers. The wage-slavery of the Second Industrial Revolution was the world's greatest evil, and the notion that backbreaking labour led to rewards its most heinous lie. Impatient to alter this status quo, Most looked less to the words of Marx and Engels and more to the deeds of People's Will and Clan na Gael for guidance. As he wrote in 1885, 'the importance of modern explosives for social revolution need hardly be stressed nowadays', nor the fact that 'the law and order rabble' who preached otherwise were 'extraordinary blackguards'. The time for talking was over. The time for dynamite – which Most dubbed the 'proletariat's artillery' – was at hand, and with it the need for downtrodden workers to follow the path blazed by the nihilists and the Fenians.[8]

Most outlined his views in an 1885 treatise entitled *The Science of Revolutionary Warfare*, in which he provided the reader with a step-by-step guide for how to become a terrorist. This included instructions on how to procure bomb ingredients – Most was working at an explosives factory at the time he put pen to paper – as well as how to assemble letter bombs, bake poison biscuits for feeding to police spies and defend oneself if faced with the 'pantomime of a court trial'. The dynamite-lauding sequel to Nechaev's more philosophically apocalyptic *Catechism*, Most's opus was the culmination of its author's transformation from Reichstag debater into violent zealot. This journey began in the mid-1870s, when Most's militancy raised the eyebrows of both his fellow socialist politicians and Stieber's spies, who paid special attention to his *Freie Presse* magazine, the circulation of which jumped from 2,000 to 18,000 in a single year. Most's reputation as one of Germany's most dangerous radicals was further enhanced when police claimed to have found a picture of his spikey haired, facially deformed visage in the pocket of the failed assassin Hödel. Unsurprisingly, Most's apartment was raided after Nobiling's attack on the kaiser. The radical-sweeping broom of Bismarck's anti-socialist laws that followed was the final straw for Most, who fled his homeland in 1878 and sought sanctuary in Britain. Such was his reputation, he was shadowed to this refuge by Belgian spies, who believed their quarry to be the latest link in a chain of terrorist prophets that stretched back from Nechaev to Heinzen. Their thoughts on what Most at liberty could achieve were stark. He would ensure that 'Germans will leave England with more fatal traces of their presence than the Italians did with Mazzini or Orsini'.[9]

Most never bombed, stabbed or shot anyone. The spies' inference that he would continue the hate-prophet's trend of inciting violence wherever he went, however, was very accurate. During his time in London, Most became a regular at the Rose Street Club in Soho – a hive of émigré activity frequented by Malatesta, Kropotkin and Tchaikovsky – in between spending long hours behind his printing press in Marylebone. Through these activities Most positioned himself as the herald of dynamite terrorism, preaching its gospel at the bar, and in his newspaper *Freiheit* (Freedom), copies of which were smuggled by his adherents into Germany, France, Poland, Italy, Belgium and the Balkans. Born of a mind that saw labour agitations, nihilist tyrannicide, Irish republicanism and anarchist calls for the dismantling of the state as elements of the same global struggle, *Freiheit* was pitched to appeal to an audience as broad as its geographical distribution. Within its pages, Most declared war on 'princes, ministers, statesmen, bishops, prelates, a good number of army officers, higher officials and various journalists and lawyers, as well as important aristocrats and the capitalists classes', for 'these are the personages on whose backs we have a stick to break'. Without basis of fact, he reported that nihilists 'were near and far' across Europe, plotting 'conspiracy and revolution'. He lauded the Fenians' newfound love of dynamite and he denounced his former colleagues in the Social Democratic Workers' Party as detestable moderates incapable of keeping up with this new, more violent and heroic breed of revolutionary.

Most also acknowledged the progenitors who had set the table for the dynamitards of the 1880s, promoting a culture of terrorist hero worship to his readers. Hödel and Nobiling were praised for their courage in facing down the kaiser, an article penned by Heinzen on early anarchist ideas was reprinted and, when Blanqui died on New Year's Day 1881, Most produced a black-bordered edition of *Freiheit* in which the legendary militant was eulogised. These reverential nods to the past were designed to create a feeling in inclusivity amongst *Freiheit* readers, making them feel as if, by picking up a copy of the newspaper, they were becoming a part of a tradition of revolutionary violence that stretched back decades. Useful as this was as a means of winning converts to his cause, Most also knew the value of sensationalising present events to boost the newspaper's circulation and enhance his own notoriety. This mind for publicity led Most to produce his most notorious provocation. Barely two months after he canonised Blanqui, he ran a joy-laden article in *Freiheit* in which the ending of the 'accursed life' of Tsar Alexander II by the 'daring young men' of People's Will was graphically detailed. 'If a single crowned wretch were disposed of every month' in the same hellish manner, Most enthused, then 'in a short time, it should afford no one gratification henceforth to still play the monarch'.[10]

Up until this point, Most had received superficial coverage in the British press, where he was generally depicted as little more than a ranting troublemaker and far from a cause for police concern. No doubt recalling Nechaev at the height of his notoriety, even Marx claimed to see nothing but 'boundless personal vanity' in Most, and 'babbling', 'illogical' and 'degenerate' inanity in *Freiheit*'s pages. Most's gloating over the tsar's demise, however, caught the attention of many in Britain, not least of whom was Queen Victoria. Already unnerved by People's Will, the re-emergent Fenians and the threat posed to her fellow monarchs by assassins and dynamitards, the queen shared her disgust over the 'revolting and bestial ferocity' of Most's words with her home secretary, William Harcourt. This royal protest contributed to an about-face in Britain's long-standing policy of offering asylum to Europe's radical fringe, which led to Most being arrested on charges of encouraging 'persons of names unknown to murder the sovereigns and rulers of Europe' in the thuggish pages of his 'violent nihilist print'. Whilst some newspapers jumped on the Most-bashing bandwagon, others showed a more sophisticated understanding of how the cycle of repression and radicalisation worked. Journalists from *The Times*, the *Liverpool Echo* and *Punch* who understood how Most was trying to recruit new adherents pointed out to their readers that the spectacle of his trial would serve only to make 'an obscure paper notorious' and give 'universal publicity to its teaching'.[11]

However logical these protests, the context in which the *Freiheit* article ran made Most appear like a threat that needed dealing with. Gone were the days when refugee Communards could recall 'in violent and bloodthirsty terms the events of the last two years', whisper talk of a second revolution and receive a £5 fine as punishment. Most's crowing came as O'Donovan Rossa's bombers were commencing their campaign and anxiety was rising across Europe over what fresh hell the triumphant People's Will would next author. It didn't help Most's cause that, when his trial commenced in the summer of 1881, he chose to be represented by an Irish republican lawyer. Guilty by association with the twin threats of Irish and nihilist terrorism, it took less than twenty minutes' deliberation for the jury to find Most guilty, for which he was sentenced to sixteen months' hard labour in Clerkenwell.[12]

As canny journalists had predicted, the spectacle of the *Freiheit* trial did much to boost the profile of the man at its centre. Sales of the offending newspaper increased and public pronouncements of support for Most came from groups such as the United Socialists of London, the Socialist Revolutionaries of Bern and the Communist Workers Educational Association. Having convened just before the trial got underway, the London Anarchist Congress passed a motion declaring that their brother-radical was the victim of an oppressive state's 'attempt still further to enslave the people'. Even with their leader incarcerated, Most's comrades at *Freiheit* continued his provocative work undaunted, running an article in praise of the Phoenix Park murderers in 1882. By the time he was released later that year, Most had achieved infamy across the transatlantic world, and was perfectly positioned to become an even greater advocate of revolutionary violence than Heinzen, Nechaev or Mezzeroff. As vain and even more ambitious than any of these prophets of terror, Most seized the moment and, having already taught the dynamite lesson to Europe, resolved to take his proselytising across the Atlantic. Aside from free-speech laws guaranteeing him a platform, this mission to the United States was vital, Most claimed, for the future of the wider revolutionary cause. He conceived of his new home as a 'nearly boundless territory' that was blessed with 'almost inexhaustible natural resources'. And yet, this nation of promise had 'been so fatally corrupted and ruined in such a short time by the capitalistic system' that its potential as a bastion of freedom was now imperilled. The United States could not be permitted to go down the same path as 'servile, rotten Europe'.[13]

This was the message Most preached during an exhaustive lecture tour that commenced in New York in December 1882, accompanied by press pronouncements that the 'king killer' had arrived to bring terror to the New World. Born of the *Freiheit* trial, this hyperbole paid dividends. On his first major outing, at the Cooper Union, Most took centre-stage at the iconic venue draped in red flags and flooded by a 'sea of black hats, which extended on all sides to the walls'. So hotly anticipated was his address, 'standing men were wedged in all the aisles', and amidst the cramped excitement and palm-smashing applause, 'copies of *Freiheit* fluttered all over the hall'. These scenes were repeated in the months that followed, during which Most appeared before thousands of angry labourers, émigré anarchists and radical intellectuals, packing working-men's clubs and theatres from Boston to San Francisco. At these lectures, Most sold copies of *The Science of Revolutionary Warfare* for ten cents a piece, as well as German translations of Nechaev's *Catechism* and copies of *Freiheit*, a new version of which he began printing in New York, taking advantage of free-speech laws to run columns that exhorted workers to kill their bosses and classified ads for bomb-making kits. In between lectures, he gave sensation-seeking reporters tours of the 'anarchist sanctum' of *Freiheit*'s headquarters, wherein Most proudly displayed 'the most extraordinary productions of fever-brained revolutionaries from all countries', emphasising the international scope of his enterprise. When not showing off to the press, he held court with his followers at Schwab's Saloon, a Manhattan red club whose proprietors had installed a loaded pistol and a picture of the notorious French revolutionary Jean-Paul Marat above the bar.[14]

Inevitably, this master of terrorist promotion was spoken of in the same breath as O'Donovan Rossa and Mezzeroff. When asked by journalists who he suspected was behind the dynamite attacks in Britain in 1883, the Irish MP John Stewart Parnell suggested that the culprits were to be found 'either among the Fenians, who are under O'Donovan Rossa's orders, or among the Socialists of the school of Most'. At the same time, the newspapers that had covered Mezzeroff and Most's lectures remarked on how the nihilist-Fenian dynamite teacher and the herald of violent revolution shared 'abnormal minds'. Mezzeroff was generally regarded as the more abnormal of the two, perhaps even by Most himself, who, despite publishing a serialised version of the former's *Dynamite Against Gladstone's Resources of Civilization* in *Freiheit*, never sought an alliance with his bomb-touting contemporary. This snub was likely because Mezzeroff was fast losing credibility in radical circles. The poor quality of his bombs and the obvious grift that lay beneath his claims led, in February 1885, to one of Mezzeroff's trainee terrorists giving him a 'thrashing', in the belief that his instructor was a police spy. Not long after this, Mezzeroff pivoted from his 'dynamite messiah' persona to opine publicly on how cholera was caused by the release of miasma from the ground following earthquakes and could be treated with special pills. This, combined with press reports that he had 'given up the manufacture of the explosive for the butter purifying business, because he thought there was more money in the latter occupation', provided a fitting snake-oil salesman's end to Mezzeroff's career, which subsided in tandem with the conclusion of the Irish dynamite campaign. The last recorded mention of him occurred in 1895, when a Puerto Rican newspaper reported a dubious sighting of the once infamous 'el terrible dinamitero'.[15]

As Mezzeroff shuffled from the stage, Most moved to its forefront, becoming, as his wife put it, the 'patriarch, the father of the anarchist movement in America'. This description sold short Most's ambition and the reality of the place he now occupied in the world of violent radicalism. Despite occasional pretensions to the contrary, he was no philosopher of anarchism, socialism or any other creed. Rather, Most was a blunt-force promoter of terrorist violence in its universal form, advocating its practice by whatever means, in the name of whatever cause, anywhere in the world where oppression was felt. His wide-ranging promotion of dynamite ensured that interest in Most from across the Atlantic did not abate after his relocation to the United States. Regularly supplied with copies of *Freiheit* sent from the British consulate in New York, Scotland Yard pored over Most's words for leads on terrorist plots or allusions to alliances with the Fenians. He was placed on a similar pedestal of menace by Bismarck's tame press, which branded him 'the representative of radical Europe' in America.[16]

As Bakunin had once been the lodestar for global insurrection, so Most was the assumed linchpin of all terrorist conspiracies. When covering a story on the invention of a new type of dynamite, a journalist in California claimed that the explosive would be 'peculiarly acceptable news to the likes of Herr Most, Louise Michelle [sic], O'Donovan Rossa, the Russian nihilists and the French anarchists' – the international alliance of dynamitards whom Most was now, seemingly, leading. Multiple newspapers reported that he had met with the nihilist Hartman and members of the IWMA in Washington, DC, in February 1883, with whom he held an 'all-night conference', which led to an enciphered order being sent to nihilists in Russia, instructing them to assassinate Tsar Alexander III at his coronation. So seriously was news of this plot taken, when the great day arrived in St Petersburg the tsar and the tsarina were shadowed by Cossack guards, whilst close to 7,000 police and Okhrana officers wandered amongst the pavilions and circus acts that had been arranged to entertain the massive crowd.

The ceremony was completed without incident, but the notion that Most had other plots brewing refused to die. In 1885, the press buzzed with news that he was planning a dynamite attack on the Swiss Federal Palace in Bern, in revenge for the arrest of two anarchists there. Back in the United States, Most also gained a reputation as the hidden hand behind labourer agitation. This led to a report of how, having departed one of Most's New York lectures brimming with animus, a gang of recently laid-off factory workers broke 'up a fancy-dress ball to be given by Mrs William H. Vanderbilt, by throwing bombs through the windows'. By the mid-1880s, therefore, Most had become the 'big evil' of revolutionary terrorism – the one-man embodiment of the violent, international conspiracy that police chiefs, spies and political leaders had long pursued.[17]

This was why, when news of the Haymarket affair broke, many an accusatory gaze turned in Most's direction. Despite not being present in Chicago on the day of the violence, he was pursued by the police, who believed he had met with the Haymarket protesters two weeks earlier, in New York, at a beer-sodden event, during which he delivered 'lurid speeches' that aroused 'all the evil passions and bloodthirsty feelings of his audience'. In truth, Most's influence on parties to the Haymarket affair pre-dated this drunken gathering. In October 1883 in Pittsburgh, he had attended a conference of socialists and anarchists, present at which was August Spies, editor of the *Arbeiter-Zeitung*, and Albert Parsons, editor of the anarchist periodical *The Alarm*. The result of their discussions with other delegates representing labour groups from as far afield as San Francisco was a declaration that cut the three men adrift from non-violent political agitators. Together, Most, Parsons and Spies called for the 'destruction of the existing ruling class by all means', and issued a warning to 'tremble, oppressors of the world', for 'not far beyond your purblind sight there dawns the scarlet and sabre lights of judgement day!' Suitably melodramatic, it was a declaration that, by Most's design, was meant to build on the call for propaganda of the deed that had been made at the London Anarchist Congress two years earlier.[18]

Most's talk of terrorism continued to rub off on Parsons, Spies and the people who read their magazines. Spies took to giving Mezzeroff-like interviews to newspapers and, in one instance, he brought a dynamite tube casing to show a reporter, along with a warning that 'we have 9,000 more like it, only loaded'. Most's political pamphlets and copies of the declaration he, Spies and Parsons made in Pittsburgh were also widely disseminated by the trio to anarchist and socialist groups, along with songs extolling the virtues of explosives, the lyrics to which were printed in *The Alarm*. Before long, readers of this and other radical magazines that ran Most's material began to muscle themselves to the forefront of the various labour agitations that were sweeping the Midwest. For this reason, when Parsons and Spies were arrested after the violence at the Haymarket, the *New York Times* asserted that 'villainous teachings' lay behind the event. Indeed, the whole bloody episode was depicted as the inevitable outcome of pro-terrorist material being distributed amongst the workers, which had led at 'least a dozen stalwart men' to 'have laid down their lives as a tribute to the doctrine of Herr Johann Most'.[19]

The need to prove the power of these 'villainous teachings' guided the prosecution's approach to the trial, which commenced on 21 June 1886 with Parson, Spies, Fielden and five others – some of whom were present at Haymarket, some of whom were not – in the dock. Most had been sought by the police and, on 12 May, was ingloriously apprehended whilst trying to hide under a bed at the house of one of his followers in

Brooklyn. The charges laid against him, however, related to an 'incendiary speech' he made on 28 April rather than specific involvement in either the protest at the Haymarket or the violence that consumed it. Given that he was not even in Chicago at the time of the fracas, it was too great a stretch to indict Most. This did not mean, however, that his shadow was lifted from the courtroom. Depicting the Haymarket affair as a crime comparable to the bombardment of Fort Sumter in April 1861 – an attack by seditious southerners that started the Civil War – the prosecutor claimed that the protesters had conceived of a 'plot to ruin our laws' with the aim 'to make anarchy rule' in the United States. All of this was driven by the murderous musings of Most and the men he had manipulated, Spies and Parsons.[20]

A copy of *The Science of Revolutionary Warfare* that had been seized from the offices of *The Alarm* was presented to the court as evidence of the bridge that Most had constructed between labour agitation and bomb-throwing. This connection was made clearer to the jurors via the reading out of extracts from an article published in *The Alarm* in 1885, in which dynamite was described as 'the good stuff', which could bring 'terror and fear to the robbers'. If this was your objective, so the article claimed, all that needed doing was to put 'several pounds of this sublime stuff into an inch pipe (gas or water pipe), plug up both ends, insert a cap with a fuse attached, place this in the immediate vicinity of a lot of rich loafers who live by the sweat of other people's brows, and light the fuse'. Then, the article concluded, 'a most cheerful and gratifying result will follow'. If this were not damning enough, excerpts of Most's writing were also shown to have been published in the *Arbeiter-Zeitung*, including a Heinzen-like letter he penned shortly before the Haymarket affair, which warned that a 'rebel who puts himself opposite the mouth of the cannons of his enemies with empty fists is a fool'. This was a clear instruction, the prosecution argued, for the Haymarket protesters to show up with dynamite and pistols in their pockets.

In vain, the defence council tried to evoke the spirit of the freedom fighter to spare his clients the noose, pleading for the jury to recognise that the violence of 'John Brown and his attack on Harper's Ferry may be compared to the socialists' attack on modern evils'. Warming to their adversary's theme and backed by copies of *The Alarm* and *Arbeiter-Zeitung*, the prosecution responded by digging deeper into America's past, suggesting that the black flag of anarchism had nothing to do with Brown's heroics on behalf of the enslaved and instead embodied a return of the piratical practices of the 1700s, when the raising of said flag meant 'for men, death; for childhood, mutilation; for women, rape'. Faced with this riposte, evidence of connections between Most and the accused, and a mountain of spurious police testimony concerning the events at the Haymarket, the judge sent Spies, Parsons and five others to the scaffold. As a British radical newspaper claimed, it had been a case of 'anarchy on trial', the outcome of which was never in doubt.[21]

The months that followed the trial were ones of fracture and soul-searching for both labour agitators and proponents of dynamite, the latter now called to task for taking Most too literally and violence too far. Amidst the predicable outcry in certain presses for a full-scale clamp-down on all 'reds', one Illinois newspaper showed nuance in arguing that there was a 'decided and discernible difference between the men who earn their bread by the sweat of their brow' and 'nihilistic blatherskites with venomous tendencies' like Most, Spies and Parsons. This argument was taken up by agitators who still demanded their eight-hour day but feared that the blood of the Haymarket had forever stained their cause. The Knights of Labor – one of the most active worker agitation groups of the era – denounced strikers who partook of violence. Radicals of a bygone age, like the 48er turned influential newspaper editor Herman Raster, tried to educate the aggrieved of the 1880s by denouncing anarchist terrorism as 'a disorganizing element of all our political and social fabric' and the likes of Spies and Parsons as 'bloody scoundrels' for succumbing to Most's rhetoric. Reflecting on the prospect of further terrorist attacks being carried out by America's restive labourers, the *National Republican* identified 'the anarchists and nihilists who have nearly taken possession of some of our leading cities' as the true culprits of the Haymarket affair. The paper even made the bold suggestion that 'the circulation of an ample volume of money among the people' was the best means of removing the grievances that had primed unhappy workers for seduction by the likes of Most.[22]

Even Mezzeroff was dragged into the Haymarket post-mortem, with the *Washington Star* arguing that the cause of terrorist violence in the United States was 'an immigration system which shuts the gates of a free country in the face of the peaceable, industrious Chinaman, and lets in a Most, a Spies, a Mezzeroff'. Depicted as the man who laid the table for Most and, through him, the bloodshed in Chicago, Mezzeroff agreed to an interview to clear his name. His tune had changed since the days when he loosely spoke of transatlantic conspiracies. Mezzeroff dismissed any suggestions that the Haymarket bombing was connected to 'the teachings of Krapotkine [*sic*] and his confederates' and rejected the idea pushed at the trial that anarchism was inherently linked to terrorism. Instead, Mezzeroff pointed out a truth that reflected his own experience of the Fenians, anarchists and nihilists who had come to his dynamite classes, stating that 'when the passions of ignorant men are aroused and there is no restraining power permitted or acknowledged, outlawry must follow'.[23] If Most was to blame for the phantom bomber at the Haymarket, or any of the other instances of violence done by radicalised workers, it was only because industrialists and politicians had made life so wretched for America's labourers that the advocate of bomb-assisted murder sounded like a man who spoke sense and offered hope.

The danger, as the Belgian police who had followed Most's journey to the United States concluded, was that he would be only the first of these heralds of terrorism to resonate in a world beset by economic downturns and labour unrest. 'The communards, the socialists and the nihilists', the spies reported, 'are far from pursuing the same ideas' and yet all now recognised that terrorist violence was the best remedy to the grievances they nurtured. Moreover, as the rise of Most to prominence demonstrated, no conspiracy would be required to organise this bloodshed. If enough lectures were delivered and books on bomb-making read, then eventually someone would take drastic action on their own initiative. The antithesis to the IWMA–Communard conspiracy, this was terrorism practised by the 'lonely sentinels' spoken of at the London Anarchist Congress. It would be a form of terrorism where bombers would no longer need People's Will or the Clan to tell them where to go and whom to attack, and could instead rely on the identification of enemies and the repeated incitement to violence in the pages of magazines like *Freiheit* and *The Alarm* to guide them – the precursor to what today is called stochastic terrorism. As Spies, languishing in jail and awaiting his execution, put it in ominous tones, 'the masses are with us' now. 'Lively times may be expected' – a statement as cruel as it was prophetic.[24]

Chapter XII

No one is safe

Léon Gambetta was one of France's most recognisable figures. Surely he would not be hard to find? If one lingered outside the Palais Bourbon – the site of the Chamber of Deputies of which Gambetta was president – then he would soon appear beneath its colonnaded facade, his stocky frame wrapped in an expensive suit, his hair pomaded just so. This assumption motivated an unemployed cotton weaver named Émile Florian to acquire a pistol and travel from Rheims to Paris in October 1881, with the aim to publicly execute Gambetta. Compared with terrorist targets of years past, the statesman was an odd choice. No tsar or kaiser, Gambetta was a republican politician who had proclaimed the end of the Second French Empire at Paris's Hôtel de Ville in September 1870. He had also questioned the reactionary 'moral order' campaign that followed the fall of the Commune. This track record meant little to Florian. Though no fan of monarchists, Gambetta had denounced the Commune as too radical, preferring reformist politics to bloody violence. To Florian, this moderate attitude made the republican as much his enemy as any cleric or king. Gambetta's death would serve as a warning to France's conceited politicians who showed indifference to the life-or-death demands of the revolutionary struggle.

After several frustrating days waiting outside the Palais Bourbon for his target to appear, Florian had a disturbing epiphany that took his reason for killing Gambetta to its logical extreme – were not the 'decorated gentlemen' of affairs who ignored him as they walked past each day all, like Gambetta, criminally aloof to his radicalism, still more to his privations? Was not each finely suited money-maker a contributor to the machinery of capital that had left him bereft of employment and crushed the spirit of thousands like him? If so, then the death of any of them by Florian's hand would make the same statement as slaying the famous politician. Guided by this revelation, Florian stalked his way to the Bois de Boulogne, where his eyes were drawn to a well dressed doctor who was leaving his practice for the day. Drawing his pistol, Florian exclaimed 'Tyrant! The justice of the people now strikes you!' and pulled the trigger. When he realised that the bullet had barely grazed his target's arm, Florian turned the weapon on himself, only to be knocked to the ground by a passer-by before he could suicide his way out of the mess he had created. Narrowly avoiding the guillotine, the would-be assassin of the haughty was sentenced to twenty years' hard labour.

The tale of Florian's hunt through Paris and his 'monomania that one could call bourgeois-phobia' would likely have faded like so much newsprint had he not during his trial exclaimed 'Long live the social revolution!' This earned Florian plaudits in *Le Révolté*, within which the demented shooter was depicted as an anarchist martyr. This followed the favourable coverage given by radical presses to another recently laid-off worker who, months before Florian's attack, had fired a round at his former boss in Lyon. No less than Florian's attack, this attempted murder demonstrated, as the anarchist writer and contributor to *Le Droit Social* Jean Grave put it, the assailant's courage to 'send packing any government that tried to impose itself the day after the revolution'. Similarly, *L'Hydre anarchiste* gave a gardener who threatened to 'set fire to the nuns who threw me out onto the pavement' after being sacked from his job at a convent the column space to promote his violent intentions and declare 'Long live anarchy and down with the bourgeoisie!'[1]

Compiling a report in 1883, the US ambassador to Germany, Aaron Sargent, perceived this praising of violence and encouragement of self-radicalisation as the pre-eminent terrorist threat Europe faced, greater than the dangers posed by either Russian assassins or Fenian bombers. Sargent drew special attention to the influence of *Freiheit*, which was being 'smuggled into the empire on as great a scale as ever', dispensing advice on 'dagger and dynamite' that was resonating in a Europe blighted by labour agitations and economic disruption. In Germany there was an additional problem. Stieber – who had died in January 1882 to jeering commemoration from radicals as the 'grand master of the German snitches' – had long laboured to protect his homeland from the 'reds'. In the process, however, the spy chief had left the Kaiserreich a tinderbox prostrate before those whom Sargent described as the match-wielding 'followers of Herr Most'. For just as Tsar Alexander II's attempts to strangle nihilism had summoned nemesis in the form of People's Will, so Stieber's machinations and Bismarck's anti-socialist laws had driven Germany's dissidents underground and now, fortified by *Freiheit*'s sentiments and explosives advice, they were ready to strike back.[2]

Evidence of this turn to terrorism in Germany emerged a few months after Sargent warned of the danger, when an associate of Most's named August Reinsdorf organised for dynamite to be planted beneath the statue of Germania – the sword-bearing personification of the Kaiserreich's unfailing strength – which had been erected on the Niederwald overlooking the Rhine. This monument to German greatness was to be officially opened by Kaiser Wilhelm on 28 September 1883, during a lavish ceremony at which high-ranking government officials and generals would be present. Their thoughts dancing with images of the powerful humbled by dynamite, Reinsdorf's associates placed sixteen pounds of the explosive beneath the giant statue the night before the kaiser's entourage arrived. Were it not for one of the bombers trying to save money by purchasing a non-waterproof fuse that became damp in an overnight downpour, the explosion would have likely wiped out much of the Reich's ruling strata and, to hammer home the propaganda of the deed, blasted fair Germania herself into dust and rubble.

The aftermath of the failed Niederwald plot confirmed Sargent's fears that terrorism was being driven by a cycle in which individuals were self-radicalising. Shortly after Reinsdorf and one of his cohorts were beheaded in February 1885, an anarchist stabbed to death the chief of police who convicted them. Whilst it is possible that Most was acquainted with the cop-killer, there is no evidence to suggest the assassination was ordered or funded from the other side of the Atlantic. The only official endorsement from Most came when, during the killer's trial, he put a call out in *Freiheit* for his readers to mount a reprisal on behalf of Reinsdorf's avenger and so continue the struggle. To the relief of the kaiser and his court, Most's appeal was not heeded. This was likely because a combination of Germany's anarchist leaders being rounded up by the police and the parallel introduction by Bismarck of new welfare provisions designed to quell radical passions led to anarchism petering out as a political force in the Reich by the mid-1880s.[3]

Outside of Germany, however, the process of self-radicalised young men dubbing themselves anarchists and carrying out terrorist attacks continued, particularly in France. There, a toxic blend of worker discontent, an increased circulation of radical magazines and a stock market crash in 1882 created perfect conditions for animus and action to come together. Charles Gallo was a product of this parlous environment. A twenty-something petty criminal, Gallo had bounced between various jobs – dyer, clerk and apprentice druggist – from which he took only dissatisfaction at the capitalist system and the bottom rung he occupied in it. Influenced by anarchist literature, in 1886 Gallo stormed onto the floor of the Paris stock exchange, armed with a revolver and a vial of prussic acid. Tossing the vitriol in the general direction of the stockbrokers, he discharged three shots into the ceiling before he was seized by security guards. Initial press reportage of the attack linked Gallo to Kropotkin and Michel, with claims that he was 'only the instrument, and that his arrest may lead to the discovery of a far-reaching anarchist conspiracy'. The reality was more mundane and unnerving. Not only was there no evidence of Gallo being tied to anyone else but, as became clear during the trial, he was a loner possessed of what the polite newspapers called 'quirks of character'. Erratic throughout proceedings, Gallo vacillated between demanding a priest to absolve him of sins and denouncing the church as a font of evil, whilst continually referring to the judge as 'Citizen President'. Having delivered a meandering lecture on anarchist theory, Gallo responded to the handing down of his twenty-year sentence by jumping around the dock, exclaiming 'Long live anarchism, death to the bourgeois judiciary, long live dynamite, bunch of idiots!'[4]

This performance played into the hands of a press that when not promoting conspiracy theories – the Anarchist International more so now than the somewhat played-out IWMA–Communard iteration – tended to depict anarchism as an ideology fit only for the mentally unsound or irredeemably sub-human. The wild-eyed Gallo was a 'young rogue, stained by unspeakable vices', so base of mind that he had been driven to violence by the mad theories proffered by the likes of Most and Kropotkin. According to *Le Petit Parisien*, the scourge of the stock exchange had a 'bilious complexion' and a 'drawn and nasal' voice, whilst *Le Figaro* described the Neanderthal malice that seeped from Gallo's every pore, possessed as he was of 'a low brow, savage jaw, beady eyes flashing with hatred' and a 'meagre beard, thin and black with a sharp point that gives him a Mephistophelean appearance'. When no evidence emerged of his attack being directed from Geneva or London, these depictions were used to dismiss Gallo and his laughably inept attack, in which despite being armed with a gun, he inflicted no fatalities. Frightening, yes, but not an undue cause for worry. He was just another sad adherent to a wicked ideology.[5]

Beneath Gallo's haplessness, however, lay something ominous. As he barged alone into a guarded building with pistol and acid in hand, Gallo displayed the same suicidal confidence that Zasulich felt when she accosted Trepov in 1878, certain that if she died, others would follow in her stead. Gallo's attack perfectly distilled the self-destructive tendencies of nihilist terrorists and the mentality of the 'lonely sentinel' that was central to anarchist propaganda of the deed. Another disturbing aspect of Gallo's plan was that the people at whom he flung the prussic acid were, no less than the unfortunate doctor whom Florian targeted, neither kings nor prime ministers but ordinary Parisians in the midst of their working day. Self-educated in anarchist ideas at a time of economic turmoil, Gallo conceived of the stockbrokers as conductors of the sinister orchestra of global finance that had wronged him, Florian and others whose travails he had read of. As such, the stockbrokers were as legitimate a target to Gallo as Napoleon's carriage or the tsar's train had been to his terrorist forebears. Three years before Gallo's attack, the perceptive Sargent had raised concerns over this fact that anarchist terrorists were 'not merely against throne and altar' but 'also against capital and industry'. These were objects of animus that were global and amorphous, and the anarchists' ambition to dismantle them with random acts of violence made the nation-shaping goals of the Fenians, People's Will and Orsini seem humble by comparison. In his self-destructive pursuit of the impossible, the self-radicalised Gallo was the archetype of the new indiscriminate and irrational breed of terrorist whom Sargent feared.[6]

Although he had no sympathy for the police tasked with thwarting these unpredictable terrorists, Stepniak – mindful that he had helped pave the way for the likes of Gallo and Florian – was concerned by their rise to prominence. Now living in London, retired from killing, running an anti-tsarist society and penning his memoirs, in 1886 the murderer of Mezentsov tried to make sense of what he called the 'new era in the revolutionary movement'. He adroitly concluded that the economic depression had created a restive generation. However, unlike the aggrieved of the past, *fin-de-siècle* radicals had access to *Freiheit*, *Le Révolté*, the *Catechism*, *The Science of Revolutionary Warfare* and decades' worth of other terrorist manuals containing the once elusive blueprints of the Orsini bomb, advice on how to modify pistols, recipes for poisons and instructions for assembling clockwork-timed dynamite devices. They had everything they needed to assail whichever enemy they thought needed killing. With the wearied scepticism of a man whose time was passing, Stepniak did not endorse the unfettered self-radicalisation this situation created. This was because, to his mind, there was an important difference between his slaying of Mezentsov and Florian's and Gallo's attacks on ordinary French citizens. Whereas the Third Section chief represented the tsarist regime, the doctor and the stockbrokers were people whose deaths would do nothing to change the social and economic conditions in France, let alone the world. Stepniak was a revolutionary assassin, a professional on a mission. Florian and Gallo were misguided 'lone wolves', easily manipulated into committing acts of pointless violence by radical magazines and saturation press coverage of attacks that inspired thoughtless emulation – self-radicalised terrorists whom Stepniak dubbed 'hot-heads'. To his dismay and the consternation of many across Europe, Florian and Gallo were not the only angry young men of the era to fit this description.[7]

Throughout the 1890s, Italy was pock-marked by a series of attacks in which self-professed anarchists detonated dynamite and tossed Orsini bombs into crowded piazzas, police barracks, town halls and even outside the offices of a socialist politician – all were now enemies. For the most part, these explosions did little more than scorch flagstones, blast chunks off stone staircases and shatter windows, leading to more arrests than they did deaths. In Spain, however, a similar wave of violence by self-professed anarchists included one of the deadliest bombings of the *fin de siècle*, in which the contemporary power of dynamite was harnessed with a nod to a fabled terrorist of the past. In November 1893, a bootlegger turned anarchist walked into the Liceu theatre in Barcelona during a performance of *William Tell* – the same play that the bomb-blasted Napoleon had stoically insisted on watching decades earlier – and dropped three dynamite-packed Orsini bombs into the orchestra pit, killing over twenty people and wounding thirty others. Whilst mainstream newspapers accused the bomber of being a murderous thug from 'the militant anarchist party who deal in bombs and dynamite', radical presses in France and Spain questioned the retaliatory rounding up of anarchists in Barcelona and defended the attack as a natural response to the 'fatal excesses of the Spanish bourgeoisie'.[8]

Such sins of decadence were not confined to Spain – nor were acts of terrorism in riposte. A month after the bombing in Barcelona, an unemployed French labourer and self-professed anarchist decided that a Parisian café that had once served cheap meals but now catered to the bourgeoisie had to learn the same lesson as the theatre-goers at the Liceu. With a sense of irony that probably escaped him, the terrorist entered the café, partook of the menu's politically objectionable fare and then stabbed a random diner. Despite claiming that he stuck his knife into 'the first well-dressed bourgeoisie I saw' without a thought given to who they were, the attacker's victim turned out to be the Serbian ambassador to France. Naturally, this fuelled press speculation that the so-called Anarchist International had manipulated this poor 'thin boy of twenty years with the face of a goat', punctured by 'small, sunken eyes that disturb you to look at', into carrying out a high-profile assassination. As in the Gallo case, this conspiracy theory did not survive the trial, during which the knifeman was found to be nothing more than the latest in a growing line of mentally unsound men who had been inspired to violence by the sentiments of anarchist magazines and newspaper reportage of like-minded terrorists.[9]

The fact that a diplomat had been attacked, however, indicated that it was not just ordinary citizens who had to fear the wrath of the hotheads, on whose hit lists there was plenty of room for the high and mighty. In 1898, an Italian anarchist possessed of a plan no more specific than to 'kill a sovereign' used a shiv to take the life of Empress Elizabeth of Austria. Two years later, the Prince and Princess of Wales narrowly escaped death in Brussels when a sixteen-year-old self-professed anarchist shot at them through the window of their train. Less fortunate was Italy's King Umberto, who, having escaped an assassin's blade in 1878, finally ran out of luck two decades later. His murderer was an Italian named Gaetano Bresci, who had immigrated to the United States and become a publisher of anarchist literature, swimming in the same circles that had radicalised Spies and Parsons. In 1898, Bresci returned to his homeland and, appalled by the state-sanctioned slaughter of eighty people in Milan who had started a riot over the cost of food, resolved to strike back against the Italian state. On 29 July 1900, Bresci tracked Umberto through the streets of Monza, picking a moment when the royal carriage came to a halt, at which point he jammed a gun through the window and shot the king repeatedly. Testament to both the power of emulation and the international scale of this terrorist epoch, Bresci's act engendered another major assassination thousands of miles away. Depressed at the state of the workers' lot and inspired by the story of the Monza attack – newspaper clippings of which he kept in his wallet – in September 1901 a Michigan steelworker named Leon Czolgosz travelled to Buffalo, New York, and attended a meet-and-greet with US President William McKinley at the Temple of Music. When it came his time to shake McKinley's hand, Czolgosz produced a revolver and shot him twice in the belly, inflicting wounds from which the president would die some days later. Like the assassin he admired, Czolgosz was not party to any conspiracy. Indeed, his detached demeanour and odd social mores led some anarchists with whom he mingled to view him as a police spy. However, such was the nature of the hot-head, it took only Czolgosz's attendance at a few anarchist lectures, and an inspiring newspaper article on regicide, for him to turn to terrorism.[10]

In keeping with the anarchist impetus to attack symbols of capital, the victims of the hot-head assassins were not solely found in palaces and parliaments. In 1892, an associate of Most's named Alexander Berkman fired two shots at the industrialist Henry Clay Frick in Pittsburgh, as an act of retaliation against the unleashing of Pinkertons on striking workers. Berkman's shots failed to hit Frick, yet the attack had a curious by-product that speaks to how Stepniak was not the only old hand who felt that the hot-heads were getting out of control. Freshly released from his latest prison stint, Most ranted to his wife about how Berkman's fool-ish deed meant that 'the capitalists will now begin anarchist-baiting and it will hinder our work'. He went a step further by denouncing Berkman's actions in *Freiheit* and, as the anarchist writer Emma Goldman recalled, made 'insinuations against Sasha's [Berkman's] motives', questioning whether someone as reckless as Berkman could truly be an anarchist. As Most had been competing unsuccessfully with Berkman for Goldman's affections at this time, sour grapes likely lay behind this animosity. Regardless, it was still a dramatic and public about-face in which 'Most, the incarnation of defiance and revolt', was now calling into question propaganda of the deed. A devout anarchist who regularly lectured on the philosophy, Goldman was so incensed that she suggested to the press that 'Herr Most is an anarchist for revenue only', tarring him with the same brush as the grifter Mezzeroff. Still not satisfied, Goldman con-fronted Most at a lecture he was set to deliver in December 1892. Rising from her chair with a horsewhip in hand, she cut him off before he could commence and 'repeatedly lashed him across the face and neck', reducing the once feared 'king killer' to a scampering wretch, whom the *New York Times* now branded 'the leader of the conservative anarchists'.[11]

Most's humiliation and deriding as a moderate had little impact, however, on the generation of terrorists he had helped to create, driven as they now were by a self-perpetuating cycle of radicalisation and revenge that was more potent than any article from *Freiheit* or lecture from its founder. The clearest evidence of this cycle in practice emerged in the same year that Most received his beating at Goldman's hands, in ever-restive France. The man who started this cycle amongst France's anarchists was a drifter from the Loire named François Claudius Koenigstein, who for a moment in the early 1890s became the world's most infamous terrorist, known by the *nom de guerre* of Ravachol. Born poor in 1859 to a broken home, Ravachol floated between several unfulfilling jobs in his twenties, before being swept up in the maelstrom of economic downturn and anarchist ideas that had consumed Florian and Gallo. Like them, he was convinced that the system of labour and capital would always be his enemy, and so resolved to become an outlaw, resorting to predatory crimes that even his later admirers found hard to defend. The first of these was grave robbery, committed in 1891 for the purposes of extracting jewels from the tomb of a noble woman in St Etienne, an excursion from which Ravachol came away with little but a handful of dead flowers and a broken crucifix. His next crime was even darker and more desperate. Long-standing rumours that a hermit living in the hills above St Etienne had amassed a small fortune led Ravachol to break into the ninety-two-year old's cabin and demand money from him. When the old man refused, Ravachol smothered him to death with a pillow and made off with several thousand francs.[12]

As he carried out these crimes, Ravachol also engaged in a process of self-radicalisation, educating himself in the violent aspects of anarchist history, the basics of explosives chemistry and the legend of the martyred Communards. Eager to join the campaign of anarchist terrorism that Gallo had begun in 1886, he also scanned the newspapers for flashpoints of unrest into which he could interject himself. Before making his murderous visit to the St Etienne hermit, Ravachol found just the cause he was looking for in a story of revolt and repression in Clichy. There, a May Day gathering had degenerated into a shoot-out between police and a group of anarchists, in the aftermath of which three of the latter were arrested and beaten. As Ravachol later put it, he had already begun to rationalise his grave-robbing, murder and burglary as the 'logical consequence of the barbaric state of a society which does nothing but increase the rigour of the laws, without going after the causes'. Poverty had driven him to savagery, just as the injustices meted out on workers had led Clichy's anarchists to take to the streets. By this rationale, the violence inflicted on those anarchists whilst in custody was cause enough for Ravachol to strike back on their behalf. Such was the logic that fuelled hot-head terrorism.

Ravachol's revenge began on 11 March 1892, when he placed an iron cooking pot packed with shrapnel and dynamite outside the home of the prosecutor in the Clichy case, the detonation of which shattered windows and destroyed a staircase, although without killing anyone. He followed this up by detonating a second bomb, this one packed with over a hundred dynamite cartridges, outside the house of the advocate-general who had dared to call for the Clichy anarchists to be guillotined. Like Ravachol's first effort, the explosion caused massive damage to the building but, miraculously, did not kill any of its occupants. Despite this lack of bloodshed, the avenger could have basked in contentment at both the fear he had created and the notoriety he had earned. Newspapers featured front-page sketches of the devastation left by his bombs, amidst ominous reports of how the notorious 'Ravachol continues his destructive work'. As a result of the 'ensuing panic', the advocate-general's house was cordoned off and assigned round-the-clock security by the Paris police prefecture.

By the early 1890s, neither explosions in Europe's cities nor security responses after the fact were anything new. Ravachol – yet another unemployed, self-radicalised anarchist – should have been unremarkable. However, arriving at the crest of the wave of violence Gallo had stirred, a brigand with an evocative nickname who, unlike most other hot-heads, managed to carry out more than one attack without being apprehended, was a prime candidate to assume the role of terrorist 'big evil' that People's Will and Most had once held. The press loved him. News of Ravachol's exploits was transmitted via telegraph across the world, prompting journalists as far away as Los Angeles to report on the 'thoroughly frightened' condition he had created in France, alongside the assertion that 'Ravachol says the anarchists have sufficient dynamite to blow up the residences of every official in Paris'. *The Times* contributed to building Ravachol's legend, dubbing him the 'head-centre of anarchism in Paris' and architect of 'the state of panic and universal suspicions' that beset France. As had occurred in the case of Most in the United States, this sensationalist press coverage elevated Ravachol in the minds of Paris's aggrieved and radical. As news of his bombs flooded the headlines and the anarchist remained at large, songs containing the lyrics 'let's blow up all the bourgeoisie' and 'long live the sound of explosions' were sung in red clubs, where the phrase 'ravacholiser' – meaning to dynamite someone – also became parlance.[13]

The means by which Ravachol's reign of terror ended contributed further to his mythos. As had happened with that other celebrity terrorist, Nechaev, a thoughtless trip to a café was his undoing. Taking coffee at the Café Very, Ravachol insisted angrily to a waiter that 'the anarchists were right to use dynamite to ensure the triumph of revolutionary doctrine!' He then urged his unnerved audience of one to read anarchist literature and barked at other customers that 'all bourgeoisie are buggers'. Linking this haranguing to the visage of a man who fit the description in the newspapers, the waiter tipped off the police before Ravachol's next visit. What followed on 30 March 1892 was a scene immortalised on the cover of *La Petit Journal* – the wild-eyed, pistol-brandishing terrorist with the unkempt moustache being dragged to the pavement by a score of gendarmes next to a toppled table whilst a well dressed detective points a gun in his seething face: the scourge of Paris reduced to a caricature of impotent rage.[14]

After two trials in which the judges and juries were assigned armed guards and Ravachol protested that his actions were a justified response to a world of state-sponsored rapine, he was sentenced to death. In a further parallel with Nechaev, the supposed terrorist mastermind was given the guillotine not for his non-fatal bombings, but for his cold-blooded murder of the aged hermit. Ravachol, at least, was allowed to embrace martyrdom in a manner that had been denied Nechaev, who, in 1882, had perished with little fanfare in the bowels of the Peter and Paul Fortress from a combination of scurvy and oedema, whilst forlornly waiting for the shattered remnants of People's Will to mount a prison break. In contrast, such was Ravachol's celebrity, from New Zealand to California newspapers reported how 'the Great Anarchist' had 'left a letter behind urging anarchists to revenge his death', before laughing his way to the gallows. There, he 'danced and spent his last moments singing' until, finally, the guillotine fell with such impatient force that it severed his attempt to cry 'Vive la révolution!' with the last of his breath.[15]

A star such as Ravachol could not implode without leaving cosmic fallout. Days after his arrest, the owners of Café Very tried to cash in by installing a commemorative plaque on the table where Ravachol had been sitting when the gendarmes pounced. This shrewd marketing move may have placed the café at the top of Paris's dark tourism list for years to come, were it not for the fact that shortly after the plaque was installed the café was destroyed by a bomb that took at least two lives. The fear of more Ravachol avengers was potent, the more so given that death had not killed his celebrity. For months after the execution, stories of the terrorist mocking his judges did the rounds amongst anarchists, placing Ravachol in the same self-righteous sphere that Orsini and Zasulich occupied in revolutionary folklore. Reports of the 'jeering blasphemy' he displayed in his final moments were relayed with relish, alongside accounts from people who claimed to have been there at the end to see Ravachol's defiant smirk become 'unalterably frozen in the rictus of death'. The radical periodical *Le Père peinard* tapped into this story, publishing a lurid account of how, when Ravachol's decapitated head rolled towards his executioners' feet, they shook with dread at the thought that the terrorist might have somehow primed his grinning mouth with dynamite.[16]

As these stories spread through polite and impolite society alike, letters scrawled with vows of vengeance and sketches of exploding bombs flooded into government offices and the Paris police prefecture during the spring of 1892. Some issued specific warnings of an attack on 1 May – the anniversary of the Clichy shootout and also the international day of agitation for worker's rights – whilst others pronounced sentences of death on politicians or spoke of how the anarchists would form a dynamite-detonating alliance with the Fenians. Testament to how the Anarchist International theory was exploited by sincere radicals and pranksters alike, many of these missives were alleged to have come from the 'Le Comite de la Dynamite', 'les Anarchist International Comité', 'les Société des Anarchists' and the 'Ravachol Vanguard', all signed off with declarations of 'Vive la anarchy!' and 'A bas la bourgeoisie!' Meanwhile, the press hummed with rumours of how the terrorised prefecture was 'overwhelmed by a mass of people seeking protection' from Ravachol's disciples.[17]

The trend of self-radicalisation ensured that these nightmare predictions of revenge became a reality. In addition to the attack on the Café Very, in December 1893 a sickly man named Auguste Vaillant, driven to suicidal depression by his lack of income and prospects, tossed a bomb packed with nails into the Chamber of Deputies, with the aim to avenge Ravachol and other 'brother' anarchists. The bomb was poorly made, and its explosion of shrapnel caused little damage beyond a loud bang and broken glass, leading the Chamber's president, after gathering himself amidst the smoke, to quip, 'The meeting shall continue'. This phlegmatic response aside, the angst over terrorism in Paris meant that Vaillant followed Ravachol to the guillotine. On the heels of this execution another avenger emerged, in the form of a Spanish-born son of a former Communard, named Émile Henry. On 12 February 1894, this avid reader of and sometimes contributor to *La Révolte* walked into the Café Terminus in central Paris, where he sat down to enjoy a beer and a cigar amongst the carefree bourgeoisie diners he despised. Then, he threw a bomb into their midst, for which he was beheaded on 21 May. A few weeks later, the final link in this chain of hot-head terrorism stretching back to Ravachol was forged when an Italian anarchist stabbed the French President Marie François Sadi Carnot to death. The assassin's rationale was simple – Carnot's government had presided over the executions of Ravachol, Vaillant and Henry, inviting anarchist vengeance.[18]

If regarded as a coherent campaign of propaganda of the deed, the Ravachol cycle of violence was an astonishing success. The legend of Ravachol, crafted by a recklessly hyperbolic press, gave the disaffected of Europe a hero to emulate once the guillotine took him. Through their attacks, these vengeful terrorists built on the state of anxiety Ravachol's bombs had created, forcing the panicked authorities to dish out harsh reprisals that in turn guaranteed increasingly brutal ripostes from the 'lonely sentinels' of anarchism. There was, however, one problem that made claiming victory problematic – neither Ravachol and his avengers, nor any of the other hot-heads of this era, had brought an end to capital, monarchy, the church or any other loathed institution. Furthermore, as one of the prominent anarchist publishers of the 1890s, Jean Grave, noted in barely concealed tones of irritation, 'since the bourgeois press has persistently presented the anarchists as criminals and maniacs, many criminals and maniacs have come to believe that we are their party'. Far from furthering the cause of anarchism, the hot-heads had brought the ideology into the deepest pits of disrepute.[19]

This fact led to a bitter debate over Ravachol amongst the anarchist community. To some, he was a messiah born of the era's inequalities – a dynamite-brandishing Robin Hood who had terrorised the 'well-fed bourgeois' and left a legacy to inspire the 'desperate ones with hollow stomachs'. As a holder of this view put it, 'we live in ugly times', and French 'society has no right to complain, for it has given birth to Ravachol – it sowed misery and reaped revolution'. So necessary a revolutionary force was Ravachol, the radical poet Laurent Tailhade continued to praise him, even after he lost an eye in a restaurant bombing of 1894, which was carried out by one of the celebrity dynamitard's adherents. Other admirers took the messiah concept to extraordinary lengths, seeing Ravachol as a modern version of that original dissident – Jesus Christ – who made a 'sacrifice and offering' of his body to redeem the world of its sins. The artist Charles Maurin captured this saintly portrayal via a woodcut of a bare-chested Ravachol standing in front of a gallows, defiantly resigned, like the Redeemer himself, to give his life for something greater.[20] Doubtless, Nechaev was spinning jealously in his grave.

Whilst some were clearly besotted by Ravachol's myth and the ways it could be deployed to inspire a new generation of violent revolutionaries, other radicals were concerned by the implications of clutching the dynamiter to anarchism's breast. Over a decade on from the London Anarchist Congress, attendees who had hoped that scientific warfare and propaganda of the deed might change the world were now starting to wonder whether their strategy was the presage to revolution, or a path to self-destruction. In 1892, a forlorn Malatesta penned an essay directed at the self-proclaimed anarchist hot-heads in which he acknowledged 'the terrible material and moral conditions in which the working-class lives' but rebuked them for using this situation as an excuse to commit murders and other senseless acts of violence. The problem, as Malatesta saw it, was that Ravachol and his like saw 'violence as an end in itself, and let themselves be swept along by savage excesses', undermining anarchism's true purpose – to better humankind. As if to prove Malatesta's point, Henry responded to this telling-off from his elder by publishing a mocking reply in the radical newspaper *L'En-Dehors*, before going off to kill innocent people at the Café Terminus.[21]

Likewise, Stepniak despaired at how 'dynamite has become the accredited symbol of anarchy' and concluded that Ravachol and Henry were less products of their unjust world and more part of 'a dark psychological phenomenon which sprung from the confusion of the ideas and recollections of political revolutions' – misguided miscreants who had sat uncritically under the learning tree of Most and other dynamite preachers. The involvement in the anarchist movement of 'an escaped common convict like Ravachol' and the other 'poor snivelling wretches' who dynamited Paris indicated to Stepniak that the revolution had taken a wrong turn and now needed to correct course. Others of his generation feared that a Rubicon had been crossed. To accommodate what Stepniak dubbed the 'dynamite anarchy' within his revolutionary theories, Kropotkin argued for a distinction between Ravachol's disreputable crimes of grave robbing and murder and his more noble efforts to carry out propaganda of the deed. Whilst in his heart Kropotkin was uncomfortable with terrorism, he was unable to shake his sympathy for the idea that the Gallos, Vaillants and Ravachols of the world were products of a brutal political and economic system, against which they had no choice but to fight back by whatever means necessary. His true lament was for the futility of it all. Writing to a friend in 1898, Kropotkin opined that as long as anarchists felt it 'was good to kill for what one believes' the bodies would keep piling up, with the powers that be sending to 'the guillotine all those who take sides with the poor'. This would prompt more retaliation and more bloodshed – a death dance without end.

Patient of mind and accepting that the revolutionary struggle would outlive Kropotkin, Malatesta and himself, Reclus was willing to tolerate the sanguinary attrition that gave his friend pause and so praised Ravachol's crimes, stating that 'I regard every revolt against oppression as a just and good act'. Living in London and still clad in mourning black for those lost in the Bloody Week, Michel was as keen on the bomb-throwers as she had been on the insurgents of Montmartre. When pressed by a journalist to comment on Ravachol, Michel conceded that she knew little about him, but argued all the same that his terrorism was a justifiable 'response to the actions of the government and the police'. When her other theory – that Ravachol was an agent provocateur employed by the prefecture to stir up anti-anarchist sentiment – was kyboshed by his beheading, Michel doubled down on her approval, pronouncing Ravachol a 'hero and a modern legend'. Viewing the carnage from afar, Goldman echoed Michel's sentiments, declaring that Ravachol and the terrorists whose deeds he inspired were all 'finely attuned to the injustice of the world'.[22]

It speaks to Henry's mental volatility that he initially condemned Ravachol, speaking of how 'robbers are too cowardly to ever become revolutionaries' and denouncing his bombing of 'houses where there are women, children, workmen and domestic servants'. Henry's rage at the harshness of a justice system that sent anarchists to the gallows, however, brought him around to Ravachol's way of thinking. Faced with a courtroom that demanded an explanation for the scourging of Paris with dynamite, Henry stated that he and the other bombers were cogs in an unbreakable revolutionary machine. When Vaillant threw his device into the Chamber of Deputies, Henry explained, 'nine-tenths of the comrades did not even know him'. And yet, in the spirit of propaganda of the deed, avengers emerged like a force of nature to strike back indiscriminately, as they had also done in the name of Ravachol. This was why, when Henry was marched to the guillotine, he was certain of what would follow. Revenge attacks would smite the pampered and privileged, who would come to 'understand that those who have suffered are tired at last of their sufferings, they are showing their teeth and they strike all the more brutally if you are brutal with them'. The police who defended the feckless bourgeoisie would also suffer. 'You have hanged us in Chicago, decapitated us in Germany, garrotted us in Barcelona, guillotined us in Montbrison and Paris', Henry proclaimed, 'but you will never destroy anarchy. Its roots are too deep. It is born in the heart of a society that is rotting and falling apart. It is the violent reaction against the established order … it is everywhere, which makes it impossible to contain. It will end by killing you.'[23] Faced with a proclamation so brutal and absolute, the world that Henry addressed was forced to consider a question with no clear answer – how could the cycle of self-radicalised terrorism be broken?

Chapter XIII

Of fright and fantasy

'It is possible', wrote *Le Figaro*'s correspondent at the court of assizes, 'that the words "criminal association" do not apply with perfect precision to the characters whose criminal trial begins today, and that they are simply attached to each other by common theories and ideas'. However, borrowing from a saying that had become common during Ravachol's rise to infamy, the reporter reminded his readers that 'every anarchist is not a thief, but certainly in every thief there are anarchist instincts'. It was this logic that led, on 6 August 1894, to the commencement of a trial in which publishers like Grave were crammed into the dock alongside artists who had painted admiring portraits of Ravachol, writers who had said nice things about Henry, and thieves with a vague allegiance to anarchism – all equally complicit, so the court was told, in conjuring the pall of terror that hung over Paris. Unsurprisingly, the radical *L'Intransigeant* wrote off proceedings as a farce in which 'the criminals and their associates are on magistrates' chairs, not on the bench'. The suggestion that *La Révolté* – its name had been changed from *Le Révolté* in 1885 and Grave had taken over from Kropotkin as editor – had encouraged violence, thefts and disturbances by self-proclaimed anarchists could not be so easily dismissed. By the 1890s, Grave had become a key figure in the anarchist movement and his stewardship of *La Révolté* had turned it into the most widely read radical publication in Europe. The question put to the court was how he and other producers of revolutionary literature had wielded this power. It was a question the man himself struggled to answer.

A year before the commencement of what the press dubbed the Trial of the Thirty, Grave spoke on behalf of his fellow anarchist publishers when he claimed that 'we are not of those who preach acts of violence, nor those who want to devour the employer and the capitalist, as these formerly devoured the priest, nor of those who incite people to do this and that or accomplish such and such an act'. Rather, 'actions are taught by example and not by writing or counsel' and 'people do not do anything but what they themselves have decided to do'. Grave's argument that terrorists were aping each other rather than being moulded by his and other's words had some credibility, as Henry's proclamations from the dock demonstrated. However, no less a hostage to the philosophical tensions that tied Kropotkin in knots, Grave also conceded that anarchist literature, 'when well understood, must in the ascendency multiply acts of violence'. Moreover, to his mind this was not necessarily a bad thing, as 'every act of individual revolt is an anti-stroke against the props of the social edifice which is crushing us'. The revolution would happen, its initiators would use violence and, as this aligned with what they had read in *La Révolté* and *Freiheit*, Grave would approve. Just don't point the finger of blame at him.[1]

Such refusals from anarchist thinkers to unconditionally condemn the hot-heads gave the authorities the justification they needed to pass in December 1893 the first raft of what became known as the Villainous Laws. This sweeping legislation decreed that anyone remotely involved in propaganda of the deed – including advocating violence in the written or spoken word – could be prosecuted. A throw-back to the blanket anti-radical measures adopted at various times in Russia, this was the French state giving up on trying to locate specific terrorists, in favour of assuming that they were everywhere. Gifted these draconian powers, on New Year's Day 1894, the police launched a six-month campaign of shakedowns and arrests in Paris, targeting artists, lecturers and anyone else who had contributed to anarchist publications, in addition to suspected bomb-makers and known thieves.

This attempt to wipe out the brains and brawn of the French anarchist movement culminated in the Trial of the Thirty, which some journalists accurately described as a cynical attempt to indict 'theorists', thugs and 'a few decadents curious about the "nice gestures" of Emile Henry and Vaillant' in a 'vast criminal conspiracy'. The desperation felt by the police at their inability to handle unpredictable and invisible enemies underpinned proceedings. There was, a correspondent from London concluded, 'no fresh information, no explosive, nor proof of any kind of anarchist conspiracy, or even isolated schemes of destruction' to justify the trial. The court felt likewise. The suggestion that painters, inventors and a War Ministry clerk who contributed thought pieces to anarchist journals in his spare time were the engineers of the recent terrorist attacks was too long a bow to draw. In the end, only those who had committed actual crimes were found guilty, while the anarchist thinkers and publishers were allowed to walk free. Like Mezentsov's efforts to present the 'To the People' propagandists as violent revolutionaries two decades earlier, the Trial of the Thirty collapsed under the weight of its conspiratorial premise.[2]

Although it offered some vindication for the anarchist thinkers, the outcome of the trial was less a cause for celebration than the herald of an ideological retreat. Under increasing pressure from the authorities, in 1895 Grave discontinued *La Révolté* and established a new organ for his views, *Les Temps nouveaux*, which promoted anarchist ideals and collective action, rather than discussing individual acts of revolutionary violence. Reclus put up money to fund the newspaper's production, seeing all means of propagandising as contributing to the goal of gradually educating the masses in anarchism's merits, ahead of the inevitable revolution. As part of his commitment to this long-term strategy, Reclus eventually went back on his initial endorsement of Ravachol and turned to thoughts not unlike those of Kropotkin and Malatesta, seeing terrorism as a diversion on the road to anarchist utopia. As Reclus told Grave in 1895, Ravachol and Henry were gone, the hot-heads had proved dangerous to the cause and 'times had changed'. Hit by a train whilst walking over a level crossing in London not long after *Les Temps nouveaux* was founded, Stepniak doubtless died with some measure of comfort at the thought that fellow radicals had warmed to his view.

Despite her impulsive show of support for Ravachol, Michel shared Reclus's and Grave's faith in education as a more potent force for change than random acts of terrorism. Years before the Trial of the Thirty, she had established a school in London where anarchist theories and scientific reasoning were taught as a means of moulding a new generation, uninfluenced by nationalistic and conservative state education. The school was closed in 1892 when a police raid discovered explosives in its basement – evidence of Michel's complicity in the dynamite outrages that was almost certainly planted by an agent provocateur from Scotland Yard. Unlike the Vaillants and Henrys of the movement, who would have struck back by blowing up a police station, Michel took this harassment on the chin and doubled down on her efforts to construct an enlightened anarchist community. She continued to lecture, agitate and offer aid to émigrés who washed up on Britain's shores throughout the 1890s, in addition to sporadically returning to her homeland, to forge radical bonds across the Channel.

Although Sûreté spies continued to follow her as she moved between lecture halls and workingmen's clubs, it was clear to the French press that the Red Virgin – now in her sixties – was no longer the one-woman army she had once seemed to be. The bourgeois *Le Journal* went so far as to praise her transformation into an activist matriarch, whose 'humanity shines through all the old clichés' of Communard menace. It was as an anarchist educator rather than as a violent revolutionist, therefore, that Michel died in 1905, having played no role in planning the terrorist attacks that blighted the *fin de siècle*. Kropotkin and Malatesta, for their parts, contributed financially and intellectually to Michel's school until its closure, stirred by the same belief that if they could 'change opinion, convince the public that government is not only unnecessary but extremely hurtful', then the word 'anarchy' would no longer be bloodstained with dynamite and fear. Through the actions of these worthies, so a hopeful journalist put it, 'anarchism renounced its terrible exploits', reducing the call for violence at the London Anarchist Congress to a moment of madness. For the old guard, terrorism had become a dead end.[3]

As one of their critics pointed out, however, the 1881 clique's change of attitude did little to 'put a stop to the activity of the terrorists' or kill faith in propaganda of the deed. Writing in the mid-1890s, the poet Camille Mauclair put it best when he described terrorism as having become 'an unseizable divinity, illogical, terrible and imbecilic, a force of nature against which reasonings and habitual justifications served nothing'. The cycles of police retaliation and radical vengeance had made terrorism inexorable. Moreover, the menace was spreading, and the hot-head was now appearing in places that had hitherto avoided the anarchist-terrorist plague. Three days after Henry's attack on the Café Terminus, a French anarchist named Martial Bourdin filled the inside pocket of his trench coat with a bomb and journeyed from the émigré-laden hub of Fitzrovia across London and down the Thames to Greenwich. As dusk set over the city, Bourdin ascended the grassy hill leading up to Greenwich Observatory, his purposeful stride conspicuous amongst those who strolled carefree and casual around him through the leafy park. Such was the intensity of Bourdin's gait, he either failed to notice a raised tree root on the path or tripped over his furious feet, creating a stumble in which the infernal machine in his pocket combusted. The blast shattered the tranquillity, raised a plume of smoke that was visible for miles, and wounded Bourdin so badly that he died within thirty minutes of his maimed body being found.[4]

The sense of safety Britain had felt from the anarchist terrorism across the Channel was such that the idea that Bourdin had tried to blow up the Observatory was initially doubted. Instead, a theory arose that he was either testing a new bomb in the park for use in France or simply handing the weapon over to a foreign agent of the phantasmal Anarchist International. Bourdin being little more than an errand boy for a continental conspiracy made sense for, as the *Liverpool Mercury* put it, anarchist immigrants had 'resolved amongst themselves to abstain from any outrages in the English metropolis, which had afforded their followers an asylum and refuge denied to them in other countries'. His shoes crunching the blood-splattered gravel and his eyes taking in the sight of the charred grass and twisted metal railings that lined the path to the Observatory, Colonel Majendie concluded otherwise. His years of inspecting and defusing Fenian bombs, in addition to examining the sites of their ignition, had given the head of Scotland Yard's nascent bomb squad the skills his fellow police officers, let alone the press, lacked to objectively assess the scene of Bourdin's demise. As Majendie reported to the Home Office, there was no doubt in his forensically wired mind that the bomber had intended to blow up the 'observatory, its contents or its inmates' – a symbolic strike, perhaps, against arrogant scientists who had presumed to control past and future by establishing Greenwich Mean Time there decades earlier.[5]

Majendie's conclusion that an anarchist bombing had been attempted in London engendered a public panic at the thought that the same 'infernal band of conspirators' that had terrorised the continent was now at work in Britain. Days after Bourdin's death, the sight of an empty mustard tin on a window ledge at the South Kensington Museum and a cigar box 'containing a clock-like arrangement' in Nottingham led to the closure of public buildings and the despatching of Majendie's trainee bomb defusers to investigate. On the heels of knee-jerk fear came irrational anger. Driven by what one newspaper dubbed 'an almost hysterical wave of vengeance against those who are plotting against the lives of their fellow creatures', residents of Soho and Fitzrovia turned out in droves to jeer and throw garbage at Bourdin's coffin as it was paraded through the streets by his fellow émigrés. The hurling of insults soon descended into the swinging of fists. In response, the police guarding the procession took their truncheons to anarchist pallbearers and anti-anarchist protesters alike, whilst extreme elements of the latter group tried to drag the 'mangled martyr's' body from the carriage for purposes unknown – though doubtless unsavoury. Even local scamps contributed to the anti-anarchist frenzy by pitching rocks through the windows of the Autonomie Club, a notorious radical haunt off Tottenham Court Road.

Bristling at the public's venom, the anarchist periodical *Liberty* flung Majendie's opinion back in his face, arguing that it was absurd to suggest that Bourdin had intended to destroy the Observatory. More likely, Majendie's assertions were part of a nefarious government initiative to stir 'prejudice against anarchism' amongst the populace. These claims of a government conspiracy were dissolved by reality. Investigations concluded that 'Bourdin was a member of an anarchist body', and that he had journeyed to the United States and France to acquire bomb-making knowledge – evidently, however, little instruction in bomb-handling – for the purposes of carrying out an attack in Britain. The question was not whether he intended to do harm at the Observatory but why, as *The Times* put it, the 'short-sighted' and 'inconceivably stupid' police had allowed him to trek across London to his target carrying a bomb in his coat. The explanation seemed depressingly simple – Scotland Yard 'really knew very little about the Anarchical movement in England'. This was not entirely true. Bourdin had been under surveillance; however, beholden as any Briton to the comforting thought that violent anarchists were a continental problem, the detectives who trailed him had been lax in their vigilance, and the bomber's movements in the hours before his death had drawn little attention. Critical though Scotland Yard had been of initiatives like the Villainous Laws dragnet in France, its 'wait and observe' approach had also failed to prevent the arrival of anarchist terrorism in Britain.[6]

Incensed by the criticism, Detective William Melville leapt into action. Initially recruited into Special Branch during the Irish dynamite campaign, by the 1890s Melville had become an anti-radical crusader and somewhat of a glory-hound, prone to bragging to journalists about how crucial his efforts were for keeping Britain safe from bombers. He shared Majendie's view that Bourdin was a man with diabolical designs undone by catastrophically poor footwork; he delighted in the public's anarchy-bashing response to his death, and crowed to a French reporter about how it was the terrorists who now had to fear their clubs being burnt to the ground by patriotic citizens. To encourage this mood and demonstrate to Londoners that he was riding to their rescue, in the days after Bourdin's demise Melville raided the Autonomie Club and interrogated its occupants, sparking press excitement over what might be uncovered in this 'notorious rendezvous of West End anarchists', where 'all the conspiracies meant to explode on the Continent were plotted'. The outcome of Melville's raid fell short of the hyperbole. Having rifled through the sideboards and inspected cigarette-butt-scattered tables, the police found 'no explosives or apparatus or ingredients for manufacturing them' and nothing else of note beyond 'a somewhat extensive assortment of anarchist literature of the usual character'. The most heinous object seized was a faded anarchist pamphlet that declared 'Death to Carnot' in blood-red letters. Disturbing, yes, but hardly a sign that the Autonomie Club was a base of operations for the supposed Anarchist International.[7]

Dramatic police raids, graphic reportage of how Bourdin's 'flesh, tendons and bones' had been strewn across Greenwich Park, Londoners attacking funeral processions and a press buzzing with whispers of anarchist conspiracy, Bourdin's bombing and its fallout epitomised the terrorist mania of the *fin de siècle*. This fear of the bombers and fascination with their deeds manifested in attempts beyond police action to fight back. A month after Bourdin's self-immolation, a Belgian acquaintance of Ravachol's entered the vestibule of the Madeleine Church in Paris carrying a bomb, which his sweating hands fumbled onto the hard stone floor, initiating an explosion that instantly killed him whilst doing little injury to anyone else or to the house of God he wished to destroy. *Le Temps* – one of France's more strait-laced newspapers – responded by calling for a national effort to prevent the anarchist's death engendering another Ravachol cycle of attacks, and it urged 'the whole public to take a part in surveillance'. This would, the journalist claimed, create a state of anxiety amongst anarchists, such that they would feel overwhelmed and abandon their 'war against society'. In a world turned upside down, the radical paper *L'Intransigeant* offered a more measured assessment, in the vein of Grave and Stepniak, noting drily of the fumbling bomber's demise that if terrorists 'took stock of dynamite they would easily see that it had killed twenty times more anarchists than bourgeoisie'.[8]

Beyond mob attacks on Bourdin's pallbearers, citizen participation in the burgeoning war on terror was also a phenomenon in Britain, albeit for reasons that were not always civic-minded. Since O'Donovan Rossa's attacks in the 1880s, Scotland Yard had regularly received requests from the public for financial rewards in exchange for information on suspected terrorists. On several occasions, this led to British citizens with Irish brogues or Russian refugees from the tsar's pogroms being reported for scheming with bombers who did not exist, as part of plots that were fabricated. For others less concerned with profiting off panic, terrorism mania provided excellent cover for the grinding of axes. An arch-conservative French priest used the arrival of an age in which 'orders for infernal machines are daily getting greater' to argue that anyone voting for socialist politicians was encouraging radicalism and, therefore, was a supporter of terrorism. Others blamed themselves rather than their political enemies for the scourge of dynamite. It was no coincidence that shortly after the Ravachol cycle of attacks ended, Alfred Nobel – he who had invented dynamite in the 1860s – contacted the foremost peace activist of the age, Bertha von Suttner, with the aim to atone for his sins and improve his image by establishing an international peace prize. These idiosyncratic responses to terrorism were elements of a global preoccupation that the Spanish polymath and future winner of the literary version of Nobel's Prize, José Echegaray, summed up in 1894, when he wrote of how 'explosives are the order of the day in the Chambers of Parliament, and the disorder of the night in theatres'. In a world where 'the lowliest wretch in the worst social rubbish heap holds a threat over all society', there was 'no person who does not worry about dynamite'.[9]

Like all good artists, Europe's writers and poets fed off this zeitgeist, responding to the dynamite attacks and police attempts to thwart them with stories that were as creatively breath-taking as they were unnervingly grounded in recent history. An exemplar of this genre was Joseph Conrad's *Secret Agent*, published in 1907 and inspired by Bourdin's calamity at the Greenwich Observatory. In addition to one of its characters being a Bourdin proxy, Conrad's tale also featured a 'Professor' who carried quick-trigger explosives on his person – evidence of the dynamite-grifting Mezzeroff's resonance nearly twenty years after he had faded into obscurity. Whilst Conrad explored the world of agents provocateurs and anarchist conspiracies with a sense of gallows satire, other authors sketched out darker dreams from their knowledge of terrorist weapons innovation and the fears, commonplace throughout the *fin de siècle*, of what warfare in the century to come would look like. Three years after the Irish dynamite campaign concluded, a Canadian ship-builder named Donald McKay penned a novel called *The Dynamite Ship*, in which the terrorists returned to London with their ill-fated *Fenian Ram* now fully operational and armed with dynamite-firing cannons. Evoking the fear of the terrorist who, 'like a spectre from the shades of darkness', had shaken cities across Europe, McKay wrote of how the advanced weapon snaked its way up the black waters of the Thames like a monster from the deep. Undetected, the submarine then unleashed its explosive payload on an unsuspecting London, causing a panic greater than anything created by Irish dissidents in the 1860s or 1880s.[10]

McKay's musings on where the terrorists' pursuit of scientific warfare might lead were taken to greater and more alarming places in 1893 by Edward Douglas Fawcett, an adventurous occultist and science fiction writer whose *Hartmann the Anarchist* used slices of recent terrorist history to tell a tale of anarchist-engineered apocalypse. In the story, a naïve journalist possessed of 'advanced revolutionary opinions' seeks out Rudolph Hartmann – a terrorist whose name was most likely inspired by the roaming People's Will member Lev Hartman. Hartmann is presumed dead by the British government but, like his real-life equivalents O'Donovan Rossa and Most, looms large as a 'big evil' in the nation's psyche. As the story progresses, it is revealed that Hartmann is alive and well and living in Switzerland, the time-honoured sanctuary of Europe's radicals and, in Fawcett's imagination, headquarters of the fabled Anarchist International. Brought to Hartmann's lair in the snow-capped mountains, the protagonist beholds twenty-five hardened revolutionists at their leader's beck and call. 'Eight are German, six Englishmen, four French, two Russians, one an Italian and the other Swiss', along with '12,000 adherents in London, many more in Paris, Berlin and elsewhere', fanatical and prepared to unleash mob violence on a Europe-wide scale.

For all his hat-tipping to past fears of insurgency nurtured by Hemyng and others in the wake of the Commune, Fawcett's focus was on giving his readers a snapshot of the horror terrorists might unleash in the not-too-distant future. Fawcett described how the journalist investigating

Hartmann finds a lightweight yet very sturdy 'silver-grey metal' substance in the anarchist's base. This mysterious material is a key component of Hartmann's airship, the *Attila*, a technological marvel designed to 'wreck civilization and hurl tyrannies into nothingness'. As the flagship of the Anarchist International, the *Attila* boasts 'three or four cannon of the quick-firing sort', machine guns, hoses capable of raining down 'streams of burning petroleum', as well as vast stores of 'dynamite and forcite bombs'. Once the ship is steered into the skies over London, its international crew of anarchists unleash their advanced arsenal, destroying warships in the Thames, burning fleeing civilians and shattering iconic monuments. This onslaught from above creates a firestorm that collapses the Houses of Parliament's clock tower, scattering rubble that pulverises 'into jelly a legion of buried wretches' and smashes 'into ruins the whole mass of buildings opposite'. Absurdist nightmare it might have been, *Hartmann the Anarchist* was, like almost all terrorist fiction of the time, built from fears of the terrorist's capacity – witnessed since Orsini first conceived of his bombs – to develop new and diabolical means of waging war on civilisation. Indeed, Fawcett's talk of anarchist airships was not entirely a product of his own imagination, for Most had discussed the possibility of bombing cities from the skies back in 1883.[11]

As alluded to by Fawcett, Conrad and other writers inured to terrorist mania, despite years of empty rumours and multiple failed attempts in court to prove its existence, the idea of an Anarchist International was as alluring as ever to those desperate to understand how and why terrorist attacks kept happening. In tones that would have brought a knowing smile to Stieber's face, the protagonist of Henry James's 1887 work *The Princess Casamassima* spoke of the 'immense underworld peopled with a thousand forms of revolutionary devotion' that lay beneath the wealthy and high society of Victorian London. Combining these conspiratorial utterings with Fawcett's future war fantasies, George Griffith's 1894 work *The Angel of the Revolution* explored the machinations of the unsubtly named 'Inner Circle of the Terrorists', who plan to spark a global revolution by attacking capital cities with airships armed with 'dynamite, melanite, fire-shells and cyanogen poison grenades'. Notably,

the revolution Griffith envisioned had no real purpose beyond inflicting mindless violence and societal turmoil. As the book's protagonist is
informed by the members of the Inner Circle – clad, of course, in dark
cowls – 'terror is an international secret society, underlying and directing the various bodies known as nihilists, anarchists, socialists'. The
Inner Circle had no ideology beyond murder and the pursuit of pointless chaos. Against such damning broad-stroke depictions of terrorism
and its adherents, it was small wonder that Grave's and Kropotkin's
efforts to draw distinctions between anarchist pontificators in search of
a better world and bomb-throwing miscreants hell bent on destruction
fell on deaf ears.[12]

As writers depicted terrorism's future, those concerned with preventing attacks in the present also reached deep into their imaginations. The
father of criminology, Cesare Lombroso, had long mused on the idea
that criminals possessed certain unpleasant physical traits – a belief the
French press had shared in its dehumanising portrayal of Gallo. To get
inside the heads of the unseen enemy through 'scientific' means, in 1891
Lombroso studied 'three hundred and twenty-one of our Italian revolutionists', as well as bombers from across Europe. He compiled a list
of their crimes alongside descriptions of their facial features, head size
and eye colour, creating a data set that he used to divide the subjects into
tyrannicides, Communards, anarchists and nihilists. Based on an analysis of the data, Lombroso drew conclusions about each group's criminal
instincts and level of psychopathy. This information, he argued, would
give the police what they needed to identify suspected radicals at a young
age and prevent their heinous crimes before they occurred.[13]

Toiling away at Scotland Yard and earning an international reputation as the 'chief of explosives in London', Majendie pursued a more
grounded approach to counter-terrorism. Even before he became the
Yard's go-to in all matters concerning bombs, Majendie had developed
a theory that 'dynamite rascals' had risen to prominence only because
they had access to explosive material. Take away the nitro-glycerine and
the gunpowder, he posited, and the threat would soon fade. As far back
as the 1870s, he had warned the government of how disgruntled miners

in England's north could pilfer dynamite cartridges for the purposes of violently venting their frustrations at their working conditions, and so drafted new laws for the storage and production of anything that went boom. Accepting, as the Greenwich bombing showed, that these preventative measures were somewhat forlorn, Majendie nevertheless threw himself into devising means of mitigating the damage that terrorists could cause. Throughout the 1880s, he peppered his government with elaborate plans for guarding the Tower of London and other public places with checkpoints and iron screens. He also reached out to explosives experts in France and Germany, developing new methods of bomb detection and defusion, and organising for a dedicated bomb-testing range to be built outside Paris. By the time he died of a heart attack in 1898 – one wonders the extent to which its cause was overwork and stress – Majendie had pioneering forensic techniques for examining terrorist attack sites and procedures for detecting and handling explosives that continue to inform police practices to this day.[14]

Others less concerned with experimental criminology and forensics adopted counter-terrorist methods that continued the dubious traditions established by Stieber. The Okhrana chief Peter Rachkovsky – a former radical and one-time member of the Holy Brotherhood – arrived in Paris in 1885 to internationalise Russia's war on terrorism, bringing with him the energy of personal ambition and more than a whiff of the sinister. As a subordinate recalled, the team of Okhrana officers Rachkovsky assembled in Paris comprised 'obscurantists, suppressors of truth, hangmen, pagans, and agents provocateurs'. Acknowledging the near-undetectable nature of the self-radicalised hot-head, Rachkovsky resolved to join his enemies in the shadows, eschewing Melville's use of photographs and media coverage to promote himself and his crusade. Instead, the faceless Rachkovsky operated an as an *éminence grise* in Europe's halls of power, meeting clandestinely with other spymasters, politicians, emperors and even, reputedly, the Pope. In addition to being a political animal, Rachkovsky was a ruthless and cynical operator who, as Lombard had during the post-Commune panic, manipulated societal fears of terrorism to construct a personal empire of spies, which a contemporary characterised as a 'fairy-tale dragon that penetrated every stratum of the population'.

By design, Rachkovsky's monster was hydra-headed, such that if one spy was uncovered or, worse still, turned to the revolutionary cause, a new devotee of the fight against radicalism would appear in their place. Established in the basement of the Russian embassy in Paris, this invisible empire of spooks was initially concerned with stomping out the remnants of People's Will and the League of French Nihilists, a group suspected of plotting to assassinate Tsar Alexander III. The fact that many of Europe's police chiefs believed in the existence of the Anarchist International, however, gifted Rachkovsky the opportunity to expand his reach beyond this initial brief. In 1891, he sent officers to London, who planted forgery equipment in Michel's school with the aim of entrapping her alongside nihilist counterfeiters whom Rachkovsky suspected of operating in the city. In 1894, one of his agents provocateurs engineered the bombing of a church in Liège, leaving behind documents suggesting that the Anarchist International was to blame. Having a personal grudge against Stepniak – the killer of one of his predecessors – Rachkovsky ran fake news articles to try to convince London's émigré community that the legendary revolutionary was a stooge in the pay of Scotland Yard.[15]

These and other schemes exemplified Rachkovsky's cunning sophistication and cerebral approach to counter-terrorism. Refusing to succumb to the sledgehammer practices of previous Russian spy chiefs, he favoured ordering his spies to infiltrate and, in some instances, start radical groups, playing a long game. Once amongst anarchists and nihilists, Rachkovsky's men were told to 'demoralise them politically' and 'inject discord among the revolutionary forces, to weaken them and at the same time to suppress every revolutionary act in its origins'. By trying to subvert radical groups and break them apart from within, Rachkovsky developed a sophisticated response to the age of the unseen bomber, whose oxygen of encouragement from like-minded souls he sought to cut off. Like Stieber's, however, Rachkovsky's methods were often legally and morally questionable, and he was sometimes less motivated by enforcement of the law than by using the state of panic across

Europe to indulge his prejudices. By the mid-1890s, he was dismissing anarchist terrorism as a threat of minor significance and becoming less concerned with what he dubbed the 'pest of dynamite' than with the idea that radicalism writ large was a disease married to a certain form of biology. This assumption led to conclusions darker than Lombroso's experiments. Raised on the same diet of anti-Semitism that had fed the pogroms of the 1880s, Rachkovsky believed that 'the subversive organisations are recruiting the majority of their members from among the Jews, the Ukrainians, Poles and other inhabitants of Russian lands'. In a tract entitled *Nihilists in General*, he argued that terrorists could be identified by 'a strange walk of the Jewish type'. Seduced by a conspiracy theory more sinister than that which lumped Communards with the IWMA or common criminals with anarchist thinkers, it is small wonder that Rachkovsky would be accused of concocting the most notorious fake document to have emerged from the paranoid maelstrom of the *fin de siècle*, the *Protocols of the Elders of Zion*.[16]

Though Rachkovsky might have been an unsavoury character, his omnipresence in the war on terror led to his methods being adopted by other police chiefs. Having worked with his Okhrana counterpart on the surveillance of Stepniak, Melville came to occupy the same space between fantasy, reality and illegality that Rachkovsky had made his bailiwick. In addition to being involved in framing Michel and having her school shut down, in 1892 Melville used an agent provocateur to entrap a group of anarchists, whose Walsall-based 'cell' he raided, undoing what the press reported to be a 'conspiracy of the most determined and dangerous character'. As was Melville's want, he notified his contacts at *The Times* ahead of the raid and ensured that he and his men were accompanied by reporters hungry for dramatic tales of spies and skulduggery. It was not for nothing that Conrad, when penning his fictionalised version of the Greenwich bombing, emphasised the disreputable nature of secret police work, going so far as to suggest that the terrorist menace was mostly a construct of paranoid detectives and corrupt informers.[17]

This assertion was incorrect. Melville's and Rachkovsky's machinations and the exhaustive press reportage of the war on terror inflated and distorted, rather than concocted, a threat that could and did target everyone from café owners to kings. Compounding the 'soft target' bombings that made victims of the general populace, the late 1890s and early 1900s was also a time when political leaders and monarchs were assassinated at a frequency unseen in modern history. In addition to Sadi Carnot, King Umberto, Empress Elizabeth and President McKinley, the prime minister of Spain and King Carlos of Portugal were also killed, whilst King Alfonso of Spain and his Queen Victoria narrowly escaped with their lives when a bouquet of flowers containing a bomb was tossed towards them by an anarchist at their wedding. As was the case with the random bombings of theatres, city parks and high streets, the police assumed that these targeted killings in multiple nations were the product of a 'vast anarchist conspiracy' that was steering a campaign to 'take the lives of the heads of the various European countries'.

First muttered following the stabbing of the Serbian ambassador in Paris in 1893, this theory led to extra police being deployed around Ehrenburg Palace for the wedding of Princess Victoria-Melita and Grand Duke Ernest Louis in 1894, a gala event attended by Queen Victoria, Kaiser Wilhelm II and Edward, Prince of Wales. The critical mass of targets and the promise that the imagined league of anarchist assassins could knock multiple names of their hit lists in one fell swoop led to this security response. Such consideration for safeguarding monarchs and politicians during this era was, however, the exception rather than the rule, as the police continued to struggle with how best to track suspected terrorists and prevent their attacks. The prefecture of the Paris police devoted time and resources to compiling a database of anarchists and developing new photographic means of cataloguing them, yet was habitually lax in issuing security details to dignitaries – an oversight that undoubtedly contributed to the ease with which Bresci took Sadi Carnot's life. Likewise, the American Secret Service was more concerned with counter-espionage in this age than with the presidential security for which it is now known. This meant that although agents were near McKinley when Czolgosz shot him, they were not anticipating a lone assassin, let alone trained in how to detect and subdue one.[18]

The stabbing of the internationally beloved Empress Elizabeth of Austria whilst she strolled carefree along the shores of Lake Geneva in September 1898 was the deed that shook Europe's police out of their state of hubris. The fair Elizabeth's murder was not only regarded as the 'most vile and wicked of anarchist crimes' by the press and world leaders but, as it involved an Italian anarchist carrying out an assassination of an Austrian monarch on Swiss soil, it was unambiguously an act of international terrorism. This led to the convening of an international anti-anarchist conference in Rome on 24 November 1898. No grassroots initiative for the fanatic and panicked, the conference was attended by statesmen and police officers from across the continent, including the Italian admiral Felix Canevaro and the French negotiator of many an international treaty Camille Barrère. With the encouragement of the assassination-fearing Queen Victoria, even the typically aloof British agreed to participate in this exercise in continental collaboration.

Furnished with a briefing from Majendie, the ambassador to Italy, Sir Philip Currie, and the veteran of the Jack the Ripper investigation, Sir Godfrey Lushington, attended the conference, albeit not without registering complaints over 'the suggested restrictions on the press' put forward by other delegates, and the idea that deporting émigrés might stem the terrorist tide. Both measures were deemed 'quite inadmissible' in a Britain where, the messy business of Bourdin aside, the authorities were confident that their counter-terrorist policing could handle any threat quietly and efficiently. Speaking as someone who had experienced the questionable side of this policing ethos, Michel condemned British participation and hissed from her London sanctuary of how the gathering in Rome was little more than a 'congress of spectres'. The suspiciousness and 'profound secrecy' to which Michel referred were not enough to prevent *The Times*'s Rome correspondent from claiming to have the inside scoop on proceedings. Based on the whispers he had heard from behind the conference chamber's doors, he assured readers that the delegates had not engaged in a 'useless exchange of abstract ideas and a waste of patience and time'. Rather, they had spent their month of secret deliberation working in perfect harmony, in recognition of the scale of the global threat they faced.[19]

This optimistic take on proceedings was half true. When they emerged from the baroque confines of the Palazzo Corsini four days before Christmas 1898, the delegates did so with a series of protocols in hand that seemingly addressed the concerns over terrorism that had unleashed societal panics, conspiracy theories and dire fictions on Europe. A system for exchanging information on anarchists and an acceptance that French methods of photographing suspects from various angles – the mugshot – were agreed measures. So too was a rejection of the idea that terrorism was defensible on the grounds of it being motivated by political injustice and social inequalities. Kropotkin's reasoning be damned. Acknowledging the fear of cosmopolitanism and internationalism that had permeated police thoughts since the Commune, a commitment to monitor émigré communities more thoroughly was also nodded through, albeit not without causing a split between the two countries to which this protocol implicitly referred. Whilst the Swiss representatives acceded, the British refused to agree to a 'settled programme of combined action' with other states on matters of censorship and deportations. As the foreign secretary, Lord Salisbury, put it, 'improved policing arrangements hardly require the deliberations of a congress to sanction them'.

Possessed of the visionary Majendie, the crusading Melville and an inherent belief that their counter-terrorism methods – even if occasionally straying into illegality – were superior to those practised on the continent, the British were loath to change their ways.[20]

Aside from standoffishness from Queen Victoria's representatives, the Monaco delegate, Baron de Rolland, made the most significant contribution to proceedings, proffering a solution to the problem that had underpinned the Trial of the Thirty's faulty logic and decades of confused press reportage on the nihilist-anarchist-socialist menace. Rolland's proposal was for an agreed definition of what constituted an anarchist act, namely anything 'having as its aim the destruction through violent means of all social organizations'. This definition targeted the Bourdins of the movement more than the Kropotkins and the Graves but, regardless, it signalled the final defeat of the thinker's attempts to uncouple their ideology from the murderousness of bombers and assassins. To be an anarchist was now to be a terrorist.[21] Through this neat formula, Europe's police believed they had devised a means of defeating terrorism by redefining the ideology that seemed to drive it. This was a comforting belief, which, as a strategy for success in the war on terror, was as mired in fantasy as any of Conrad's or Fawcett's tales.

Figure 6 Two depictions of Tsar Alexander's 1881 assassination – both convey the chaos, bloodshed and confusion of Narodnaya Volya's dynamite attack

AN ADVOCATE OF DYNAMITE.

OUTLINES OF A PAMPHLET ISSUED BY PROF. MEZZEROFF.

"Dynamite and Other Recourses of Civilization" is the title of a 23-page pamphlet written by the dynamite chemist,. Mezzeroff, in support of the explosive style of warfare, which will be delivered broadcast in the Philadelphia Convention to-day to influence, if possible, the deliberations of that body. The author claims that there is no fixed rule defining honorable warfare; what is honorable to-day is dishonorable to-morrow. He cites the case of the use of torpedoes by the South which were characterized by the North as "diabolical, hellish, unchristian, and fiendish infernal machines," but were soon afterward adopted by the North "to save the country from destruction." A number of similar illustrations are made to fortify the argument. After an examination of the usages of war he is "convinced there is no such thing as honorable warfare." He gives numerous cases in modern and ancient warfare of the killing of people at night and by stealthy means, and says: "Murder is to kill a person when you meet him face to face, while assassination is killing from behind. But in both cases there must be previous malice. This is also the definition of the law as given by international writers on the subject, and the nations have accepted it as such. If a person kills another for

---

DYNAMITE.

Professor Mezzeroff Discusses About It and Other Explosive Materials.

There has been a great deal of discussion in the newspapers as to my nativity. I was born in New York. My mother was a Highlander, my father was a Russian, and I am an American citizen. I have diplomas from three colleges, and have devoted my life to the study of medicine. When I was a boy I fought in the Crimean war, and I bear the scars of five wounds. The wholesale massacre disgusted me with autocratic rule. I determined to devote my life to the welfare and elevation of humanity. I have kept my word, and no man or woman or child can to-day say that he or she has been wronged or injured by me. I am going to tell you some secret statistics which I have. I belong to two secret societies and get state secrets from Europe forty-eight hours after they have transpired. Russia has 3,000,000 men under arms to-day, exclusive from the police, the paid

---

CORRESPONDENCIA DE NUEVA-YORK

Septiembre 7 de 1895.

Sr. Director de LA CORRESPONDENCIA.

Con motivo de haber el cabecilla insurrecto Roloff hecho volar algunos puentes y acueductos en la Isla de Cuba con el auxilio de la destructora dinamita, un número reciente del *Herald* recita una curiosa historia. Afirma aquel diario que Roloff es nada menos que Mezzeroff, el terrible dinamitero que estuvo por algún tiempo envuelto en profundo misterio, pero que más tarde se supo era un escocés llamado Rodgers—muy experto en la preparación y uso de materias explosivas—las que empleó en pró del movimiento feniano irlandés y contra Inglaterra.

Dice el "Herald" que Mezzeroff era un hombre de alta estatura y magnífica presencia (como lo es Roloff), y que varios miembros de organizaciones revolucionarias irlandesas dicen que los retratos de este último son muy semejantes en apariencia á los de Mezzeroff ó Rodgers.

Según el mismo "Herald", los mismos amigos de Roloff no aciertan á explicar sus actos ó lugares de residencia antes de decidirse á tomar parte en la revolución de Cuba. "Afirman los cubanos de Nueva-York, (habla el "Herald") que después de la guerra de diez años en la Gran Antilla, Roloff pasó á la América Central y no se oyó siquiera hablar de él hasta el año 1891."

El artículo entero trata de probar que

Figure 7 Three newspaper accounts of Professor Mezzeroff. That in *La Correspondencia de Puerto Rico* (below right) reports that, as late as 1895, the *New York Herald* was confusing other dynamitards with Mezzeroff, said to be 'a man of tall stature and magnificent presence'

Figure 8 Dynamite advocates and dynamite throwers: Johann Most (top left), Jeremiah O'Donovan Rossa (top right), Émile Henry (bottom left) and Sophia Perovskaya (bottom right)

Figure 9 Saint or sinner? Ravachol as man (top), myth (bottom left) and condemned criminal (bottom right)

36ᵉ Année — Nᵒ 2596   1894   24 Décembre 1893

centimes

JOURNAL DU DIMANCHE

Conteur — PASSE-TEMPS — Roman pour tous

Paraissant le Mercredi et le Dimanche

FRANCE . . un an . . . . **8 fr.**   FRANCE . . six mois . . . . **4 fr.**
ÉTRANGER .   — . . . . **10** »   ÉTRANGER .   — . . . . **5** »

Bureaux : 7, rue Montesquieu, 7, Paris

L'ATTENTAT A LA CHAMBRE DES DÉPUTÉS

(SÉANCE DU 9 DÉCEMBRE 1893)

Figure 10 The president of France's Chamber of Deputies, Charles Dupuy, stands firm in the face of Vaillant's nail bomb

LES ANARCHISTES A LONDRES. — ENTERREMENT DE MARTIAL BOURDIN. — Voir notre précédent numéro.

Figure 11 Riot and disorder at Martial Bourdin's funeral

Figure 12 The unremarkable face of terrorism: President McKinley's killer, Leon Czolgosz

Chapter XIV

All towards its end

In the summer of 1902, a Pinkerton spy employed by the German police to monitor anarchists in New York filed his latest in a long line of unexciting reports. Months earlier, he had assumed the persona of a disgruntled factory worker and infiltrated an anarchist reading group, encountering at least one member who was prone to proclaiming that his 'ambition was to go to Europe and become a hero by killing some great ruler'. The monitoring of such sentiments, which, in this and other cases, never moved beyond the blowing of hot air, was only part of the Pinkerton's brief. The other was to unravel more localised plans to avenge Czolgosz, whose life ended in an electric chair in October 1901. Not content with executing McKinley's murderer via this experimental contraption – it took three flicks of the switch to finally kill him – the president's successor, Theodore Roosevelt, delivered a speech to Congress condemning anarchism shortly after the assassin's demise. Pulling no punches, Roosevelt compared Czolgosz and his like to pirates, enslavers and other heinous criminals from history, whose 'evil passions' and 'perverted instincts lead him to prefer confusion and chaos to the most beneficent form of social order'.[1]

This sentiment, issued from the highest office in the United States, dovetailed with the national mood. In Washington State, the other side of the country from where Czolgosz had shot McKinley, a peaceful anarchist commune was set upon by a hastily assembled 'Loyal League' of citizens, whose stated purpose was 'the annihilation of anarchists and anarchism' in revenge for the president's murder. Back in New York, a priest circulated a pamphlet to his congregation calling for America to 'Banish Anarchists!', on the grounds that they were 'worse than rattlesnakes and mad dogs, because these anarchists have brains and minds, possessed of and with, the Devil!' The police responded to McKinley's assassination in the time-honoured tradition, rounding up anarchists and socialists across New York State, many of whom were only tangentially aware of Czolgosz's existence. The prize of this dragnet was Goldman, the 'high priestess of Anarchy', who was reported by some newspapers to have travelled to Buffalo ahead of the shooting, to 'the Michelob saloon in this city and arranged the details of the murder'. Other, less speculative coverage of Goldman focused on the precedent set by the prosecution of Spies and Parsons back in 1886. Like the ill-fated publishers whose words drove events at the Haymarket, her delivery of anarchist theory via lectures Czolgosz attended made Goldman an accessory to his crime. In the end, even this notion faded away when it became clear that Czolgosz was a demented loner who, far from being instructed by Goldman, may have carried out the shooting partly as a means of grabbing her attention – a sad example of the hot-head archetype.[2]

Kropotkin and Malatesta saw him this way. Bluntly, they told the *New York Times* that Czolgosz was 'a common murderer' whose terrorism would bring 'more trouble to the innocent than to the guilty'. Most, for his part, also tried to distance himself from the nationally reviled assassin. However, having decided the day before the shooting to include extracts from Heinzen's *Murder and Liberty* as filler in the latest edition of *Freiheit*, he was again sent to jail for cheerleading a terrorist act. Such a fate seemed inevitable given the connections now established between anarchist thoughts and terrorist deeds. As a pamphlet published shortly after McKinley's murder entitled 'Down with the Anarchists!' explained, the likes of Most and Goldman were ultimately responsible for the arrival in America of this 'mixture of fool and knave', with 'a dagger in one hand, a torch in the other and all his pockets brim-full with dynamite bombs'. This was the threat that Roosevelt warned of in his address to Congress, during which he described anarchists as the world's beastly detritus, their ideology 'a crime against the whole human race'. As such, so the new president declared, 'all mankind should band against the anarchist' to ensure that McKinley would be the last victim of the terrorist storm that had battered the transatlantic world.[3]

And band together much of this world did. Building on the Rome conference, in 1904 a second meeting of statesmen and police took place in St Petersburg, producing a protocol that called for a 'uniform and strict enforcement of the measures that may be adopted against the anarchists', an expansion of the 1898 arrangements for intelligence-sharing and the expulsion of suspected anarchists to their home countries. Roosevelt warmed to this agreement and called for the deportation from America of 'anarchists or persons professing principles hostile to all government' – an updated expression of the fear of the foreigner that had washed over Paris after the Commune's fall. This led to the United States passing the Immigration Act of 1903, a legislative broadside against émigrés whose imported ideologies were now damned as the wellspring of terrorist violence. For all its prior snootiness over such measures, Britain's Parliament similarly passed the Aliens Act in 1905, which, though aimed at the Jews who had arrived from Russia since the pogroms of the 1880s, also opened opportunities to deport anarchists, socialists and other 'undesirable immigrants'. These measures, combined with the policing and intelligence-sharing resolutions of Rome and St Petersburg, created an international framework for fighting both the early-1900s war on terror and the variations of that struggle that have arisen since.[4]

Restrictive immigration policies and enhanced international policing, the censorship of anarchist preaching and the development of new domestic security measures – like the decision made after McKinley's shooting for the Secret Service to keep a tighter vigil over presidents – all played a part in reducing instances of anarchist terrorism in Europe and the United States. The adoption of reformist economic and social policies by governments in Italy, Britain, Germany and France also did much to stifle the grievances that had given anarchism its allure, guiding many of its adherents away from bombs towards suits, ties and politics. There were, of course, exceptions. Barcelona and Madrid were rocked by a series of bombings during the early 1900s, including the attack on King Alfonso and his Queen Victoria, which, though it did not take the monarchs' lives, led to the deaths of twenty-three people and the wounding of over a hundred others. Attempts by anarchists across Spain and its colonies to drag the propaganda of the deed campaign into the twentieth century, however, never gained the same international attention Ravachol enjoyed in the 1890s. The deriding of hot-heads by influential anarchist thinkers and the realisation amongst proponents of violence themselves that blood and fear had not engendered revolution led many of Spain's anarchists to look to collective worker agitation rather than individual acts of violence as a means of furthering their cause.[5]

This ebbing of the anarchist terrorist tide was why, when the Pinkerton began his undercover mission in New York with a mind to foil the schemes of bomb-tossing psychopaths, he came away feeling somewhat underwhelmed. A far cry from the demonic assassins Roosevelt had spoken of, the anarchists wiled away their time picking through the latest issue of *Freiheit*, drinking, arguing and organising fund-raising picnics, for many were habitually cash strapped. They also attended speeches at Irving Hall, a meeting place for German immigrants not far from Union Square, where Orsini had been celebrated as a martyr half a century earlier. Long removed from that moment of radical excitement, the would-be revolutionaries now gathered to hear lectures entitled 'What Should be Done to Interest the American Public in Our Movement?', alongside what another Pinkerton infiltrator described as the 'usual harangues' about the end to global oppression that lay just over the horizon. So tired had this mantra of imminent revolution become, another Pinkerton, codenamed Agent 82, reported how, during one lecture, 'the speaker complained about the lack of interest in our cause and his address was so uninteresting that part of the audience left before he finished'.

This sense of flagging momentum was clear in yet another Pinkerton spy's observations, of anarchist picnics in Chicago and Pittsburgh, which were attended 'mostly by comrades and their families', raising little in the way of fresh funds. Even the fifteenth anniversary of the Haymarket affair was low key, 'with few comrades present'. The greatest disappoint of all to this network of spies was the ageing Most, who seemed to spend more time issuing cantankerous critiques of his revolutionary 'brothers' than mapping out plans to change the world. True, Most still commanded some reverence amongst the radical set, but the crowds he drew increasingly comprised the same 200 people who always came to see him speak. This trend continued until he fell ill and died on the eve of delivering a lecture in Cincinnati in 1906 – and end that coincided with the waning of the hot-head craze he had helped engender. Amidst this state of decline, there were still some anarchists who, crestfallen at the lack of violence within their movement, rued the fading glory of the dynamite age and lamented to their brethren that 'we are sadly in need of another Czolgosz'.[6] As inspiration for renewing revolutionary violence, what these anarchists got was something far more disturbing and uncontrollable than an unbalanced loner with a pistol.

Four years into their undercover operation, the Pinkerton spies of New York and Chicago noted that Russia's shocking defeat in its war against Japan in 1905 and the subsequent outbreak of an anti-tsarist revolution in St Petersburg had injected a sense of hope and excitement into the moribund anarchists they monitored. The arrival of a revolution in which workers took to the streets of the capital in protest and soldiers refused their officers' orders validated the struggle that went back to the early nihilists, whose dreams of breaking Russia's autocracy seemed finally to be coming true. Momentous as this was, what really animated the anarchists was news of how, amidst this revolutionary moment in Russia, a group had emerged called the Socialist Revolutionary Combat Organisation (SR), whose members were taking the lives of tsarist officials using bombs and daggers (in a failed but innovative effort, they also used bullets laced with strychnine). One of the most spectacular of the SR attacks occurred in 1904, when the minister of the interior, Vyacheslav von Plehve – a career servant of tsardom who had been involved in dismantling People's Will decades earlier – was blown apart by a dynamite bomb. This was both an act of defiance against Tsar Nicholas II and the belated delivery of vengeance on the man who had brought his grandfather's infamous killers to heel. The sense that SR was picking up where the nihilists of the 1880s had left off was confirmed by one of the combat organisation's leaders, who recalled with pride how, 'on the question of the terroristic struggle, I inclined to the traditions of Narodnaya Volya'. Likewise, in 1906, an SR publication – suitably entitled *The Past* – published extracts from fifty-year-old letters penned by Nechaev, as a means of proffering the diabolical wisdom of the *Catechism*'s author to Russia's new, resurgent, generation of terrorists.

The teachings of People's Will and Nechaev underpinned SR strategic thinking and organisation. It had an executive committee, clandestine cells that worked independent of each other, and agents tasked with the procurement of weapons and the acquisition of funds through robberies and extortion. Notably, it also had flying squads of dedicated killers, who were given free rein to plan attacks without authorisation from the SR leadership. This was an echo, not of People's Will, but of the leaderless individual violence approved at the London Anarchist Congress – a blending of two terrorist traditions. The goals of the flying squads and other SR terrorists, however, were more tangible than the anarchists' dream of a world without masters. As tsar Nicholas had continued in the autocratic tradition of his predecessors, so the SR found itself violently pursuing the same goal sought by Ishutin, Nechaev and People's Will, to implode the state through terrorism. Better organised and, as the destabilising of the tsar's regime on the road to the 1905 revolution demonstrated, more effective than the anarchists' lonely sentinels, the SR gave, as the *New York Tribune* observed, a 'new impulse to popular agitation' amongst radicals the world over.[7]

This was not journalistic hyperbole. Startled out of the funk of their beige weekly reports, the Pinkertons now took note of the schemes by which America's anarchists intended to support their ideologically divergent terrorist 'brothers' in distant Russia. Suggestions included everything from holding fund-raisers to buy bullets, to sending bombers over to St Petersburg to join in the carnage. There was even a suggestion to ride SR coat-tails and make 'the American anarchistic movement one of the strongest in the world'. This was to involve finding Russian immigrants who would boast of SR successes at workers' meetings and lectures, using stories of terrorist triumph to reinvigorate the violent spirit of America's anarchists – a plan that had more than a whiff of Mezzeroff's old grift about it. Reading as if ripped from the pages of *Hartmann the Anarchist*, these schemes to tie anarchist ambitions in America to nihilist-inspired SR daring in Russia came to nothing. In the end, the most that the anarchists under Agent 82's watch achieved was the raising of 1,000 dollars to purchase ammunition illicitly in Switzerland, and the printing of pamphlets depicting the Japanese emperor whipping Tsar Nicholas.[8]

Materially, it amounted to little. However, the support America's anarchists gave to the SR indicated that the violence Russia's new terrorists practised was of a form that not only aped the conspiratorial methods of People's Will but appealed to anarchists who yearned for a return to the indiscriminate bloodshed of the 1890s. This was because, although ostensibly working within the organisation's structure for the purposes of ending tsarism, many of the SR flying squads were little more than loose gangs of hot-heads who used the excuse of ideology to justify their own violent personal indulgences. The SR bomb-maker Dora Brilliant, for example, was 'not interested in programmatic questions' of socialism or governmental reform and was instead happy with 'terror personifying the revolution'. Terrorism for terrorism's sake was also on the agenda of Boris Moiseenko, whose love of murder bereft of purpose led to him being deemed 'a heretic on many issues' by his more ideologically committed SR brethren.

Even the SR leader Boris Savinkov seemed unsure of the point of the violence he partook in, penning a series of novels in which he mocked terrorists as cynical, idiotic and witless creatures. His protagonist in *Pale Horse* – a character who was likely modelled after himself – has no beliefs and lives only to 'spit at the whole world', killing people and blowing up buildings simply because he can. It is small wonder that the morally devoid and ideologically fluid Savinkov would end up conspiring with British intelligence in the 1920s to try to roll back the Bolshevik Revolution. The presence of such aimless terrorists within the SR spoke to a cruel truth. As inheritors of a legacy that encompassed delusional nihilists trying to obtain an Italian nationalist's bomb, faux Russian conmen colluding with Irish republican dynamiters, and Ravachol murdering pensioners in the belief he was practising revolutionary anarchism, Savinkov, Brilliant and Moiseenko were exemplars of the fact that, despite the Rome conference's assumptions, terrorism did not need an ideology to thrive.[9] By the dawn of twentieth century, the act of killing and inciting fear through violence had become something akin to an ideology of its own – one to which any self-proclaimed revolutionary, criminal or psychopath without purpose could claim allegiance.

This was evident in the various contributors to the sanguinary flood that deluged Russia in the early 1900s, who together created a state of pandemonium greater than anything produced by anarchist propagandists of the deed in the previous decade. As many as 17,000 people perished in terrorist attacks across Russia between 1905 and the outbreak of the First World War. Over a third of the victims were government officials, clerks, civil servants and soldiers, whose service to Nicholas was enough to mark them for death – not that targets needed to be justified. The other victims of the violence were ordinary citizens, blown up by suicide bombers whilst doing their daily shopping, shot at whilst strolling in parks or needlessly slain in the armed robberies of banks and trains. Those who perpetrated the carnage typically justified it by arguing that their supposedly innocent victims were not revolutionary enough to join in 'a violent class struggle for anarchist communes, which will have neither master nor ruler but true equality'. This made their lives forfeit. Such was the excuse for murder printed in a leaflet distributed across Poland in 1903 by a group of terrorists who followed the worst traditions established by Florian, Gallo and other anarchists who had identified ordinary people as their enemies. This group, Chernoe Znamia (Black Banner), took the hot-heads' indiscriminate targeting to its logical extreme, often refusing the pretence that their aim was to change the world for the better. An ideologically incoherent band of Bakunists, Jews seeking vengeance for pogroms, radicalised workers, followers of Friedrich Nietzsche and rage-filled teenagers of the Nechaev school, Black Banner adhered to the most senselessly terrifying concept to have emerged from the previous decades of terrorism's development – the concept of motiveless terrorism.

Nisan Farber was an archetype of the motiveless terrorist. At sixteen years old, this Black Banner recruit stabbed a businessman in Bialystok on the grounds that his ownership of a local mill made him a capitalist oppressor. Farber followed this up a month later by tossing a bomb at a police station. There was no ideology that linked these attacks beyond a vague distaste on Farber's part for people who were not like him. Instead, combining the ethos of Nechaev's doomed revolutionary with the wanton callousness of the hot-head, these violent crimes were committed in the name of slashing and burning Russia to the ground. For Farber and others like him, emancipating peasants, shepherding democracy into the tsarist state and the pursuit of any other reforms were near meaningless. Death and bedlam were all that mattered.[10]

It was not only killers without cause and ideologically ambiguous members of the SR who contributed to this era when Russia was flogged by terrorism. Stirred by the thought that radicalised Jews like Farber were going to bring down tsardom, Russia's anti-Semitic far right joined in the carnage. The main group in this respect was the Black Hundreds, a network of reactionary cut-throats backed by nobility and drawn from the same swamp of conspiratorial anti-Semitism, pan-Slavism and militant monarchism from which the Holy Brotherhood had crawled. In fighting back against the SR and motiveless terrorists, the Black Hundreds published pamphlets calling on patriotic Russians to 'beat the damned traitors' in the streets and build bombs to bring 'death to revolutionaries'. Their gangs of what one contemporary derided as 'mercenary hooligans' also beat Jews with whips and clubs and firebombed their businesses, often with the Okhrana turning a blind eye. With the authorities indifferent, the Black Hundreds also carried out assassinations, such as the gunning down of a suspected SR member in a marketplace. Despairing at the attempts of the Holy Brotherhood alumnus turned Russian prime minister Sergei Witte to police the anti-Semites and establish a Russian parliament in response to the 1905 revolution, Black Hundred bombers also fixed their ire on him and wired his house with dynamite.[11]

With its People's Will-inspired revolutionaries, spiritual successors to the Holy Brotherhood and motiveless hot-heads possessed of callous indifference to human life, early-1900s Russia was a crucible for the decades of terrorist history that preceded it. It was not only the memory of the anarchist propagandists of the deed and the nihilist conspirators of St Petersburg that made this so. By the dawn of the new century, the corpus of terrorist knowledge that Stepniak had first remarked on in the 1880s had grown exponentially. Works of contributors to the first age of terror as diverse as O'Donovan Rossa, Nechaev, Most – whose memoirs came out in 1903 – and Stepniak himself were widely available. This literature on scientific warfare and the art of conspiracy, combined with the myths that had grown to envelop the histories of Orsini, Zasulich and Ravachol, made for a potent terrorist milieu, one that guided not only the motiveless terrorists and SR members in Russia, but radicals of various persuasions from across the world.[12]

As the Pinkerton spies compiled their reports on the now energised anarchists of the United States, on the other side of the Pacific, a young man named Wu Yue was carrying out what a *Times* correspondent in Beijing referred to as 'one of the worst forms of political activity which the East could possibly borrow from the West'. This referred to Wu rushing onto the platform of a Beijing railway station on 26 August 1905 as a party of government officials were embarking on a journey to Japan and Europe to 'study the institutions of foreign countries'. Enraged by the implications of this mission for his country's future, Wu – a member of China's anti-Western underground – armed himself with a bomb and charged screaming into the dignitaries. Before he could collide with his targets, however, the vibrations caused by an arriving train detonated Wu's device, blasting him into pieces, killing four others, injuring over twenty bystanders and leaving the former Chinese ambassador to the United States 'totally deaf' in one ear. Like many a suicidal assassin before him and since, Wu left behind a written justification for his deed, in which he expressed a hope that he would inspire others to launch even deadlier attacks. For, as Wu reasoned, 'killing one frightens a hundred. Killing a hundred frightens a thousand … if we kill them endlessly, the alarm will also be endless'. Given the similarity of this reasoning to widely published sentiments from the likes of Most and Henry, it was unsurprising that the *New York Times* asked its readers 'Are there Chinese anarchists?' whilst musing on whether 'the Russian anarchists have been carrying out proselytising work in Peking'.[13]

There was no official anarchist or nihilist 'mission' to impart Western terrorist wisdom to China's radicals. Rather, the same informal means that had carried the legend of Orsini to the United States and the tale of Zasulich to the foothills of northern Italy were at play in guiding Wu to his self-immolating destiny. Three years before Wu's attack, Li Shizeng, a Chinese student who despised the Qing emperor and the grip his dynasty had held on the Middle Kingdom for centuries, travelled to France. This was meant to be a government-sponsored educational excursion. Instead, already possessed of anti-Qing ideas born of the same underground in which Wu resided, Li met with Reclus, Grave and other anarchists to talk of revolution. He came away from these discussions with a deep understanding of how the printed word had been central to encouraging terrorist violence in Europe. As such, in 1907, Li established a periodical called *Xin Shiji* (New Century) in the same building where Grave's *Les Temps nouveaux* was printed. *Xin Shiji* aired grievances specific to China, such as the corruption of the Qing, the lack of material and economic progress and the plight of the nation's workers, all of which was filtered through anarchist concepts, prominent amongst which was propaganda of the deed.

Excited by the prospect of individual violence as a remedy for China's ills, Li rejected the anti-terrorism stance of the French thinkers with whom he broke bread, and embarked down the same path taken by Most decades earlier, publishing dynamite-lauding pieces in *Xin Shiji*, which Wu and other Chinese hot-heads enthusiastically devoured. This was despite Wu being less consumed with notions of anarchist revolution than he was with racial hatred of the ruling Manchus, who comprised the Qing government. Ironically, he was also driven to anarchist-like terrorism by the fear of Western ideas poisoning China. Like the motiveless terrorists of Russia, Wu eschewed ideological coherence in favour of crafting his own violent agenda, picking what he liked from *Xin Shiji* and connecting it to the extant doctrines of violent resistance within the anti-Qing underground. The outcome was a scene of bomb-blasted horror in Beijing comparable to that which Henry had unleashed in Paris over a decade earlier.[14]

In addition to promoting anarchist terrorism, *Xin Shiji* also ran articles on nihilism, sometimes written by another Chinese dissident who was as ideologically flexible and committed to terrorism as Wu. Years before he became a vehement anti-communist and collaborator with the Japanese during the Second World War, the one-time leftist revolutionary Wang Jingwei wrote in *Xin Shiji* of People's Will, whose shedding of royal blood he praised as an example to be followed. Wang's thoughts dovetailed with those espoused in other radical Chinese magazines and books, in which the history of nihilism from the musings of the *narodniki* to Kibalchich and his dynamite was laid out. In a 1904 pamphlet, 'Anarchism and the Spirit of the Anarchists', a colleague of Wang's spoke in glowing terms not only of the nihilists but also of the anarchists who had terrorised Europe. Breezily ignoring that their goal was to create a world without nations, governments or kings, the pamphlet's author argued that the hot-heads were the brother radicals of China's anti-Qing nationalists, simply because they too 'have openly declared that the end justifies the means'.[15] What worked for anarchists in search of global revolution would, surely, work for the nationalist secret societies of China.

In 1909, Wang and other like-minded souls seized upon this notion and formed an assassination squad, whose purpose was to ape the regicides and hot-heads of Europe and the United States. The myth that these hot-heads' attacks had been coordinated by an Anarchist International had, seemingly, spread across Asia, for Wang decided to plot out his campaign of killing in Tokyo, with the assistance of radical 'brothers' from across the world. Wang's trainee assassins discussed tactics with anti-Western Japanese anarchists – the inheritors of the terrorist tradition begun by the firebrand Yoshida Shōin, whose rise to prominence Bakunin had observed half a century earlier. No less than Wang and his crew, this new generation of Japanese radicals was informed by the terrorist milieu that had seeped into their country from Europe in the years since Shōin's followers carried out their campaign of sword-wielding attacks. Russian nihilists and French anarchists had visited Japan during the 1870s and 1880s and, more recently, the radicals of Tokyo had met with Russian terrorists from Black Banner and the SR. Evidence of this European influence appeared in black and white in 1908, when a Japanese radical magazine placed a picture of Sophia Perovskaya, the 'heroine of Russia's nihilist party', on its cover. This was followed in the next issue by the hauntingly battered visage of the great Bakunin, who might well have cracked a smile from beyond the grave at the coming together of this 'International Brotherhood' of Chinese nationalists, Japanese anarchists and Russian radicals of various persuasions.

Unsurprisingly, when Wang's squad returned to China, they did so with a plan of attack that boasted more than a few echoes of People's Will's legendary campaign. Firstly, they recruited their own Kibalchich – a chemistry student named Yu Peilun – who oversaw the testing of a variety of timed explosive devices in abandoned warehouses in Hong Kong, before the team moved their operation to Beijing. There, just as People's Will had occupied a St Petersburg cheese shop, the assassins established themselves in an innocuous photo studio. In a more unwelcome fit of emulation, Wang's people also encountered a litany of failures, with fuse mishaps, the appearance of unexpected security details and the inability to identify targets on crowded railway platforms disrupting their attempts to kill Qing officials. Likewise, the Chinese assassins' grandest scheme bore the stamp of the plot that Perovskaya and her cohorts had devised to take the tsar's life in St Petersburg. Instead of mining a road, Wang's crew placed a massive, timed device under a bridge that the Qing regent needed to cross to return to his home outside Beijing. So conspicuous were the bombers as they hauled the large wooden box of dynamite and iron shards into place, however, they were reported to the police, who raided the photo studio and arrested Wang and his lieutenants. Plagued by the Confucian notion that through self-sacrifice one might achieve virtue, two years after escaping the raid, the bomb-maker, Yu, charged a line of Qing soldiers with dynamite in hand, gladly destroying himself and his targets.[16]

As the Chinese assassins commenced their doomed plan, a similar turn to European-influenced terrorism was occurring in India, where anti-colonial movements had been festering since the rebellion against British rule in 1857. This was an act of defiance by a garrison of sepoys in Meerut that exploded into a mass insurrection, the British riposte to which involved flaying mutineers alive, the hanging of cooks suspected of poisoning, the razing of villages and the strapping of suspected dissidents to cannons before shouting 'Fire!' As had happened in Poland after the repressions of 1863, these actions did little but grow revolutionary resentments in India, leading to sporadic outbursts of anti-colonial violence during the decades that followed. By the early 1900s, this wave of violence was cresting into a more organised form of nationalist terrorism. Though local traditions of resistance and Hindu resentment at the 1905 partition of Bengal pushed Indian nationalists towards bombings and assassinations, they were also guided by leaders who urged them to study 'the acts of the anarchists', in which 'aristocrats are sought to be removed from the way by dynamite and violent means' as punishment for 'the unrighteous distribution of wealth' – Most could not have said it better. The nationalist revolutionary Bal Gangadhar Tilak did not want his supporters to stop at anarchist wisdom. Aware of the smorgasbord of terrorist influences created in the previous century, in 1906 he called on his brethren to 'look to the examples of Ireland, Japan and Russia and follow their methods'.[17]

Two years after Tilak spoke these words, his comrade Vinayak Damodar Savarkar left for Britain on a terrorism-focused research mission. Armed with a biography of the Italian nationalist Mazzini and empathising with the plight of fellow colonial subjects, Savarkar first reached out to Irish republicans in London. However, such was the richness of the terrorist milieu in what he called the 'den of the British lion', Savarkar also rubbed shoulders with fugitive members of the SR and anarchist émigrés. Whilst he indulged in James Stephens's old dream of creating a 'united anti-British front with a view to rising in revolt simultaneously against the British Empire', Savarkar understood that insurrection alone was no longer the path to this end. Terrorism had consumed the old rebel traditions in France, Ireland and Russia and so too, thought Savarkar, should it do so in India. As such, in addition to organising rifles and ammunition, he also sent an affiliate, Hemchandra Kanungo, to Paris in 1907 to learn terrorist tactics and the art of bomb-making. Kanungo's mission was vital for the Indian nationalists he represented, many of whom had developed a love of dynamite that bordered on the mystical, with some seeing it as a 'magic amulet' capable of breaking the spell of control Britain held over India – a conception of the terrorist superweapon that echoed the reverential nonsense peddled in Most's and Mezzeroff's panegyrics.[18]

Like Khudyakov during his failed mission to Geneva in the 1860s, Kanungo initially feared he would struggle to complete his mission. Much, however, had changed since that nihilist teenager had blundered after the Orsini bomb with little more than rumour and hope as his guide. Now, in a world awash with terrorist expertise, Kanungo was able to quickly find allies willing to impart the dynamite lesson. A French anarchist chemist gave Kanungo and his party 'thrice-a-week practical demonstrations on how to prepare explosives'. This education was complemented by Kanungo's employment of a former Russian artillery officer turned SR member, who first gave instruction to his eager pupils in how to organise a secret society along the lines of People's Will, before moving on to lessons in how to wire fuses, safely assemble explosive material and detonate bombs in such a way that their maximum destructive power could be unleashed. He also gave Kanungo bomb-making manuals, which the latter had translated from their original and impenetrable Cyrillic. Kanungo's education went too far for the Paris police prefecture, who took note of his meeting with a 'Russian anarchist woman' – suspected of being Goldman, who was present in Paris at the time – and notified the British that Europe's terrorists were 'instructing natives of India at Paris in the manufacture of explosives'. With the help of his new allies, however, Kanungo evaded the surveillance placed on him and snuck out of the city, getting the Russian bomb manuals and the knowledge of how anarchists and SR members plied their trade back to the secret societies of India's nationalist movement.[19]

Fresh from carrying out a range of terrorist attacks that included shootings, arson, the derailing of a train and the mutilating of a suspected turncoat, one of these societies – Anushilan Samiti – used Kanungo's dynamite knowledge to immediate effect. In Muzaffarpur in April 1908, a bomb built by Kanungo and based on Russian design was tossed into a carriage that the attackers believed was carrying a British magistrate. The purpose of this assassination was not simply to vent anger at the colonial authorities. Rather, the bombing was an act of retaliation against the magistrate for ordering the flogging of a young boy suspected of working with the revolutionaries. It was also, as Kanungo recalled, conceived of as the first part of a terrorist campaign that, 'if successful, would draw the attention of the public and thereby facilitate the diffusion of revolutionary ideas among them' – propaganda of the deed.

If the goal was to engender a Ravachol-like cycle of repression and radicalisation, then Kanungo had much to cheer. Owing to a case of mistaken carriage, when his bomb exploded it did not kill the offending magistrate but the mother and a daughter of another British official. Outraged at the deaths of the two women, the British authorities rounded up and arrested thirty Indian nationalists, seized radical literature and raided Kanungo's bomb factory outside Kolkata. At the end of the operation, the police were in no doubt that Anushilan Samiti's plan was riven with 'the anarchist tendency' of the 1890s. Unsurprisingly, the fallout followed the patterns of hysteria and retaliation established in Europe. As Kanungo intended, Indian radical magazines responded to the crackdown with what one British observer dubbed 'fanaticism and violence that cannot keep outside the limits of sedition'. The fear that this rage would lead to more violence from Anushilan Samiti led reactionary newspapers to call for a pre-emptive counter-strike. If India now had a hot-head problem, then the only solution was for the magistrate who survived the bombing to carry 'a Mauser pistol, with the nickel filed off the nose of the bullets, or a Colt automatic, which carries a heavy-soft bullet and is a hard-hitting and punishing weapon'. The crescendo of this revenge fantasy was a vision of the magistrate walking the streets of Muzaffarpur, gunning down not only members of Anushilan Samiti, but any 'strange native approaching his house or his person'.[20]

The fears that prompted this bizarre counter-terrorism idea were confirmed in the summer of 1908, when the Dhaka branch of Anushilan Samiti was raided and police uncovered books on Russian nihilism, histories of the French and American Revolutions and Fenian memoirs. Further indications that the dynamite plague was now upon India came through rumours in the press of how a book about Goldman and a totem-like portrait of the high priestess of anarchy were being passed around secret societies in Mumbai as though they were holy relics. Of greater and more tangible concern was the quality of the explosives the Indians now had at their disposal since Kanungo had been 'sent to Paris to study the latest methods of anarchist terrorism'. Three types of bomb were seized by the police in the wake of the botched attack on the magistrate's carriage – throwable grenade-type weapons, timed devices and bridge-blasting heavy explosives, capable of unleashing 'sufficient force to blow everything to atoms within a space with a circumference of 100 yards'. Compounding Anushilan Samiti's 'greater expertise in manufacture' was the fact that India's revolutionaries were not simply replicating the 'anarchist bombs of Europe'. Rather, as Tilak explained, they were following the same path taken by Wang's assassins in China, combining the murderous intent of the anarchists with the conspiratorial organisation and grand strategic designs of Russia's SR and Fenian groups like Clan na Gael. No tool of random malice, the 'Bengal bombs', wrote Tilak, were 'thrown by exasperated patriots with the object of securing a change of administration'.[21] They symbolised Anushilan Samiti's appropriation of selected aspects of the terrorist milieu, for the purposes of addressing a specifically Indian political issue.

In the years since this terrorist milieu formed, radicals from across the world have followed Anushilan Samiti, Wang's assassins, the SR and the Black Hundreds in using their tenets and tactics to violently further their varied ambitions. The cultists from Aum Shinrikyo who attacked the Tokyo subway with the nerve agent sarin in 1995 adhered to Heinzen's idea of using chemicals, just as the 9/11 hijackers answered his call for diabolical innovation when they transformed domestic aircraft into terrorist weapons. Other suicidal jihadists, along with white supremacist spree killers and 'lone wolves' who claim no ideology but murder, are nothing if not beholden to the destructive self-righteousness of Nechaev's 'doomed revolutionary' concept. The Irish Republican Army unleashed a new version of the 1880s dynamite campaign during The Troubles, whilst the Bolsheviks carried the wholesale terror that beset early-1900s Russia into their governance of the Soviet Union. All terrorists since the mid-nineteenth century, irrespective of their ideology and their grievances, understand the importance of the media in promoting the panic and notoriety that sustains their campaigns – a notion that ISIS's online content creators no less than O'Donovan Rossa and Most have exploited to full effect. The terrorists of today, in short, are all the products of the age in which the devils first rose. Few of these terrorists, however, have had as much impact on the world as a diminutive nineteen-year-old who, in the wake of the violence that had blasted through Russia, India and China, walked the streets of Sarajevo in 1914 with murder on his mind.

Epilogue
Ouroboros

Horse-drawn carriages had given way to petrol-driven motorcars, but to glance at the procession that snaked its way through the capital of Bosnia and Herzegovina on the morning of 28 June 1914, one could be forgiven for thinking they were witnessing an episode from the life of Napoleon III or Tsar Alexander II. Six highly polished vehicles comprised the motorcade that ushered Archduke Franz Ferdinand – heir to the throne of Austria-Hungary and nephew of the now eighty-three-year-old Franz Joseph – and his wife Sophie through the city. In response to the assassinations that had recently beset Europe, the royal couple were accompanied by security staff, decked out in finery that complemented the red-and-white-bordered black-eagle flags of Austria-Hungary that fluttered from the bonnet of each vehicle. This visit to Sarajevo by members of the Hapsburg ruling house was to include the inspection of a barracks, a visit to a mosque, the opening of a museum and an official reception at the town hall. Routine in many ways, Franz Ferdinand and Sophie's tour of this multi-ethnic city of Orthodox Christian Serbs and Muslim Bosniaks was poorly timed, scheduled as it was to coincide with the anniversary of the Battle of Kosovo in 1389. This was both an important commemorative event in Serbian nationalist mythos and a battle from which the Ottoman Sultan Murad did not return, on account of being assassinated by a Serbian knight at the conclusion of the fighting.[1]

The importance of this tale of national redemption via an assassin's blade was appreciated by the seven men who deployed across Sarajevo that summer morning, armed with bombs, pistols and poison. Aged between seventeen and twenty-eight, all were members of Young Bosnia, a revolutionary terrorist group that had resolved to murder the archduke as a means of making good on the Kosovo tradition and creating a Slavic state free from Austrian rule. The plot they conceived was not driven solely by this long-standing grievance, which had been inflamed by the annexation of Bosnia and Herzegovina into the Austro-Hungarian Empire in 1908. Both Young Bosnia and the group that sponsored their attack – a conspiracy of Serbian military, political and intelligence figures known as the Black Hand – were, like their terrorist contemporaries in India, China and Russia, influenced by traditions of political violence from the previous century.

Modelled after the Carbonari from which Orsini had sprung, the Black Hand's statutes decreed that it was an 'organization that prefers terrorist actions to cultural activities', as part of its grand aim to 'realize the national ideal … the unification of all Serbs'. It also ran its own periodical, *Pijemont* – a reference to the kingdom of Piedmont that had played a central role in the unification of Italy. In the tradition of the Carbonari, the IRB, People's Will and the Holy Brotherhood, members of the Black Hand had to swear an oath of allegiance, pledging that, 'by the blood of my ancestors, on my honour and on my life, … I will from this moment until my death be faithful to the laws of this organisation, and … I will always be ready to make any sacrifice for it.' As a means of organising itself, the Black Hand also adopted the methods of revolutionary organisation that had been sketched out by Hell, advocated by Nechaev, practised by People's Will and refashioned with hot-head elements by the SR. Its members were divided into cells, some of which handled counter-espionage whilst others trained in bomb-making and shooting. The Black Hand was not governed by a central committee. Instead, members were loosely tied together through coded messages and an iron-clad understanding of their objective to create a greater Serbia – an operational 'system' that borrowed from the principles of collective mission and individual actions outlined by anarchists at the London Congress of 1881.[2]

This ad hoc system suited the assassins of Young Bosnia, for the ghosts of terrorists past haunted and guided them. They accepted that they were 'doomed', each carrying on their person a 'glass tube of cyanide of potas-sium, with which to poison themselves after the accomplishment of the deed'. Most of them had read Bakunin and Stepniak and knew well the concept of propaganda of the deed. One of the archduke's would-be killers, Nedeljko Čabrinović, had a story not dissimilar to Zasulich or Ravachol. The penniless product of a rough childhood, Čabrinović had been kicked out of school for striking a teacher, after which he worked for an illicit anarchist press. An archetypal hot-head, Čabrinović called himself an anarchist and explained at his trial that his intention to kill the archduke was 'driven by a personal motive of revenge', as reprisal for having been deported from Sarajevo for his beliefs. Given such proc-lamations and the fact that Čabrinović and his associates had emerged from the era in which hot-heads took inspiration from terrorist teachers, they were described by Austrian officials as 'characteristic examples of young men who have been poisoned from their school days by the doc-trines of the Narodna Odbrana' – a Serbian nationalist group that had formed after the annexation of Bosnia and Herzegovina. These angry young men were turned to terrorism by thoughts of revenge and the promise of righteous sacrifice in the name of a greater cause.[3]

The terrorists filtered into Sarajevo in the days prior to Franz Ferdinand's arrival, equipping themselves with 'six bombs, four Browning revolvers and a sufficient quantity of ammunition'. So armed, on the day of the royal visit, they took up positions at various points along the motorcade's route. It was the anarchist Čabrinović who was first to act, cracking his grenade against a lamp-post, priming the infer-nal machine before he hurled it at the archduke's car, only for the bomb to roll off the roof and land under the axel of another vehicle. Cursing his failure, Čabrinović ingested the poison in his pocket and threw himself over a bridge. Amazingly, neither the cyanide nor the fall gave Čabrinović the glorious death he craved, leaving him to be swooped on by police, to whom he declared punch-drunk that 'I am a Serb hero'.

With Čabrinović detained and his bomb having exploded without taking the archduke's life, security should have surrounded the motor-cade, the police should have been summoned and the rest of the royal tour called off. The threat should have been ended. However, as Young Bosnia aped their terrorist progenitors, so too did their enemy walk the same hubristic path as those who had perished before him from bombs and bullets. Channelling the stubbornness of Napoleon III and the foolishness of Tsar Alexander II, Franz Ferdinand insisted on continuing to the town hall. There, he and Sophie received a painfully awkward welcoming speech from Sarajevo's shaken mayor – interrupted by an understandably enraged outburst from the archduke demanding why he had been attacked – before they left to visit Čabrinović's victims at the hospital. During their journey, a half-hearted attempt to improve security by rerouting the motorcade along backstreets was thwarted by these instructions not being communicated to the archduke's driver, who made the fatal mistake of turning onto a bridge where Gavrilo Princip was waiting.[4]

Like Čabrinović, Princip was a product of the first age of terror. He had studied the works of Kropotkin and the nihilist-inspiring Chernyshevsky and had voiced admiration for the SR. He was also determined, in the spirit of the suicide bombers of People's Will who persisted even after their plan was foiled, to finish what Čabrinović started. Seizing the moment when the archduke's car halted on the bridge and its driver tried to reverse, Princip stepped forward and shot Franz Ferdinand in the jugular, before discharging a second round into the stomach of his beloved wife, Sophie. In an echo of scenes that had played out decades before at the gates of the Summer Garden in St Petersburg, along the Unter den Linden in Berlin, and in the Temple of Music in Buffalo, the assassin was seized and thrown to the ground before he could take his own life.[5]

Leaving aside the prophetic realisation that his 'shots may destroy the peace of Europe', in its plotting, execution and immediate aftermath there was nothing remarkable about Princip's attack. Coming in the wake of an epoch of assassinations in which the lives of kings, empresses and presidents had been claimed, the shooting of a royal couple from one of Europe's ruling houses seemed to follow a sad yet familiar pattern, the more so once Čabrinović's anarchist connections were seized on by the press. At least one journalist, however, saw through the panic of the subsequent march to war and the fog of mystery that surrounded Young Bosnia to speak the truth of the ties that bound the bloodshed in Sarajevo to the terrorist spectre that had haunted the world for decades. 'Thirty or forty years ago', the *New York Times* reporter claimed, 'there were elaborate conspiracies and reports of secret associations which designated assassins by lot or agreement'. However, more recently, 'the murders of European rulers have been committed by men acting on their own initiative. It is the anarchist way.' Although a streak of the hot-head ran through the terrorists of Sarajevo, they were also 'a reversion to the earlier fashion of crime', for the deaths of Franz Ferdinand and Sophie bore 'all the marks of a carefully planned conspiracy involving many persons'. The assassinations were the apotheosis of terrorism's development since that fateful night in Paris when Orsini threw his bombs.[6] That attack led to the reshaping of Italy and, in the inspiration it gave to radicals across the transatlantic world, forever altered the practice of political violence. The consequences of the Opera House attack paled in comparison, however, to the changes inflicted on the world by the two shots Princip fired. This was not the global revolution that Stieber feared radicals would unleash, but an exercise in annihilation so great that it put any of the hells authored by the nineteenth century's terrorists into the shade. The devils' work had been done.

Notes

Preface

1   I refer to the explosion outside the Liverpool Women's Hospital on 14 November 2021, and the British Crime and Policing Minister's urging for the public to 'remain alert but not alarmed', a phrase first used by a member of the Australian government after the 2002 Bali bombings. See https://www.bbc.co.uk/news/uk-england-merseyside-59308938. See also Anne Aly and Leila Green, 'Fear, anxiety and the state of terror', *Studies in Conflict and Terrorism*, 33:3 (2010), pp. 268–281; Michael Jenkins and John Paul Godges, eds, *The Long Shadow of 9/11: America's Response to Terrorism* (Washington, DC: Rand Corporation, 2011); Kim Walker, 'Alert but not alarmed? The rhetoric of terrorism and life after 9/11', *Contemporary Nurse*, 21:2 (2006), pp. 267–276; Samantha Hauptman, *Criminalization of Immigration: The Post-9/11 Moral Panic* (El Paso: LFB, 2013).

2   'The war on terrorism', *New York Times*, 2 April 1881. See also Silke Zolla, *To Deter and Punish: Global Collaboration Against Terrorism in the 1970s* (New York: Columbia University Press, 2021); Peter C. Messer, 'Feel the terror: Edmund Burke's reflections on the revolution in France', in *Enemies of Humanity: The Nineteenth Century War on Terrorism*, ed. Isaac Land (Basingstoke: Palgrave, 2008), pp. 23–44; Jeffrey D. Simon, 'The forgotten terrorists: lessons from the history of terrorism', *Terrorism and Political Violence*, 20:2 (2008), pp. 195–214; Beverly Gage, *The Day Wall St Exploded: A Story of America in Its First Age of Terror* (New York: Oxford University Press, 2009); Richard Bach Jensen, 'The international anti-anarchist conference of 1898 and the origins of Interpol', *Journal of Contemporary History*, 16:2 (1981), pp. 323–347.

3   Gérard Chaliand and Arnaud Blin, 'Zealots and assassins', in *The History of Terrorism: From Antiquity to Al Qaeda*, ed. Gérard Chaliand and Arnaud

Blin (Berkeley: University of California Press, 2007), pp. 55–78; Paul Wilkinson, *Political Terrorism* (London: Palgrave, 1974), pp. 9–31; Randal D. Law, *Terrorism: A History* (Cambridge: Polity, 2016), pp. 64–70.

4 Lindsay Clutterbuck, 'The progenitors of terrorism: Russian revolutionaries or extreme Irish republicans?', *Terrorism and Political Violence*, 16:4 (2004), pp. 154–181; John Merriman, *The Dynamite Club: How a Bombing in Fin de Siècle Paris Ignited the Age of Modern Terror* (New Haven: Yale University Press, 2013); Carola Dietze, *The Invention of Terrorism in Europe, Russia and the United States* (London: Verso, 2020).

5 Russell F. Farnen, 'Terrorism and mass media: a systematic analysis of a symbiotic process', *Journal of Conflict and Terrorism*, 13:2 (1990), pp. 99–143; Simon J. Potter, 'Webs, networks and systems: globalization and the mass media in the nineteenth and twentieth century British Empire', *Journal of British Studies*, 46:3 (2007), pp. 621–646; Law, *Terrorism*, pp. 69–70.

6 'Fulminating quicksilver', *Scientific American*, 13:36 (1858); Johann Most, 'The case for dynamite', and Karl Heinzen, 'Murder', reprinted in *Voices of Terror: Manifestos, Writings and Manuals of Al-Qaeda, Hamas and Other Terrorists from Around the World and Throughout the Ages*, ed. Walter Laqueur (New York: Reed Press, 2004), p. 341 and p. 64; Lily Hamourtziadou and Jonathan Jackson, '5/11: revisiting the Gunpowder Plot', *Journal of Global Faultlines*, 5:1–2 (2018), pp. 91–95; Max Boot, *War Made New: Weapons, Warriors and the Making of the Modern World* (New York: Gotham, 2006), pp. 109–115; Simon Werrett, 'The science of destruction: terrorism and technology in the nineteenth century', in *Oxford Handbook of the History of Terrorism*, ed. Carola Dietze and Claudia Verhoeven (Oxford: Oxford University Press, 2022), pp. 233–250.

7 See Tim Harper, *Underground Asia: Global Revolutionaries and the Assault on Empire* (London: Penguin, 2020); Priyamvada Gopal, *Insurgent Empire: Anticolonial Resistance and British Dissent* (London: Verso, 2019).

Prologue: The prophet of terror

1 Wilhelm J. C. E. Stieber, *The Chancellor's Spy*, trans. Jan van Heurck (New York: Grove Press, 1980), pp. 24–29; Cyrille Fijnaut, *The Containment of Organized Crime: Thirty-Five Years of Research on Police, Judicial and Administrative Cooperation* (Leiden: Brill, 2006), p. 705; Christine Lattek, *Revolutionary Refugees: German Socialism in Britain, 1840–1860* (London: Routledge, 2006), p. 154; Bernard Porter, *The Refugee Question in Mid-Victorian Politics* (Cambridge: Cambridge University Press, 1979), pp. 52–58.

2 Adam Zamoyski, *Phantom Terror: The Threat of Revolution and the Repression of Liberty, 1789–1848* (London: Harper Collins, 2014), pp. 121–139; Hamil Grant, *Spies and Secret Service: The Story of Espionage, Its Main*

Systems and Chief Exponents (London: Grant Richards, 1915), pp. 168–194; Jonathan Sperber, *The European Revolutions, 1848–1851* (Cambridge: Cambridge University Press, 2005), pp. 56–108.

3   D. M. Bennett, *Sages, Thinkers and Reformers: Being Biographical Sketches of Leading Philosophers, Teachers, Skeptics, Innovators, Founders of New Schools of Thought, Eminent Scientists etc.* (New York: Liberal and Scientific Publishing House, 1876), p. 940; Karl Heinzen, *Murder and Liberty*, trans. H. Lieber (Indianapolis: Lieber, 1881), pp. 20, 23; Carl Wittke, *Refugees of Revolution: The German Forty-Eighters in America* (Philadelphia: University of Pennsylvania Press, 1952).

4   Stieber, *The Chancellor's Spy*, pp. 30–33.

5   Shlomo Avineri, *Karl Marx: Philosophy and Revolution* (New Haven: Yale University Press, 2019), pp. 105–106; *Marx and Engels Collected Works* (New York: International Publishers, 1968), hereafter *MECW*, vol. 39, 5 March 1852, p. 65; *Le Courrier du Gard*, 2 November 1852; Christopher Andrew, *The Secret World: A History of Intelligence* (New Haven: Yale University Press, 2018), pp. 393–394.

6   Cyrille Fijnaut and Gery T. Marx, eds, *Undercover: Police Surveillance in Comparative Perspective* (The Hague: Kluwer, 1995), pp. 6–7; Christine Lattek, 'German socialism in London after 1849', in *Exiles from European Revolutions: Refugees in Mid-Victorian England*, ed. Sabine Freitag and Rudolf Muhs (New York: Berghan, 2003), pp. 187–208, 203–204; the quote on Stieber's appearance is from Friedrich von Holstein,*The Holstein Papers: The Memoirs, Diaries and Correspondence of Friedrich von Holstein*, ed. Norman Rich and M. H. Fisher (Cambridge: Cambridge University Press, 1955), vol. 1, p. 4.

7   Hoover Institution Archives (hereafter HI), HI: 86016 – Hryhorij Nestor Rudenko-Rudolph papers, box 1, 'History of anarchism', appendix II; Kurt Singer, *Spies and Traitors: A Short History of Espionage* (London: W. H. Allen, 1953), pp. 82–85; Richard Evans, *Tales from the German Underworld: Crime and Punishment in the Nineteenth Century* (New Haven: Yale University Press, 1998), pp. 147–148.

8   Quotes: 'There are scandals more fatal to a state', *The Times*, 4 December 1860; 'Prussia', *The Times*, 3 December 1860; 'Foreign intelligence', *Morning Chronicle*, 19 April 1860; Mathieu Deflem, 'International policing in 19th century Europe: the Police Union of German States, 1851–1866', *International Criminal Justice Review*, 6 (1996), pp. 35–57.

9   Stieber, *Chancellor's Spy*, pp. 85–87; Heinzen, *Murder and Liberty*, p. 2; Karl Marx and Friedrich Engels, *The Communist Manifesto*, ed. Ellen Meiksins Wood (New York: Monthly Review Press, 1998), p. 1.

Notes

I. Three bombs in Paris

1 Ernest Alfred Vizetelly, *The Court of the Tuileries, 1852–1870* (London: Chatto and Windus, 1907), pp. 114–115; Charles Mettais, *Histoire Contemporaine: Complète, Détaillée et Authentique* (Paris: Gustav Barba, 1858), pp. 3–10. Quotes are taken from Cour d'Assises de la Seine, *Actes d'accusation des nommés Orsini, de Rudio, Gomez, Pieri et Bernard* (Paris: Valence, 1858), pp. 1–3; 'Latest intelligence', *The Examiner*, 16 January 1858.

2 Imbert de Saint Armand, *The Court of the Second Empire*, trans. Elizabeth Gilbert Martin (New York: Charles Scribner, 1898), pp. 43–44.

3 Howard C. Payne, *The Police State of Louis Napoleon Bonaparte, 1851–1860* (Seattle: University of Washington Press, 1966), pp. 254–269; Fenton Bressler, *Napoleon III: A Life* (London: Harper Collins, 2000), pp. 146–147; Lynn M. Case, *French Opinion on War and Diplomacy During the Second Empire* (Philadelphia: University of Pennsylvania Press, 1954), pp. 3–6.

4 Antonin Bourel, *La Bombe Infernale* (Orléans: Pagnerre, 1858), pp. 1–5; Armand, *Second Empire*, p. 244.

5 Christopher Duggan, *The Force of Destiny: A History of Italy Since 1796* (London: Penguin, 2008), pp. 169–180; Thomas Frost, *The Secret Societies of the European Revolutions* (London: Tinsley Brothers, 1876), vol. 2, pp. 1–6; Zamoyski, *Phantom Terror*, pp. 170–171.

6 Felice Orsini, *Memoirs and Adventures of Felice Orsini* (Edinburgh: Constable, 1857), p. 190; Marco Pinfari, 'Exploring the terrorist nature of political assassinations: a reinterpretation of the Orsini attentat', *Terrorism and Political Violence*, 21 (2010), pp. 580–594; David George, 'Distinguishing classical tyrannicide from modern terrorism', *Review of Politics*, 50:3 (1988), pp. 390–419.

7 Michael Packe, *The Bombs of Orsini* (London: Secker and Warburg, 1957), pp. 251–252, 260–264; Cour d'Assises de la Seine, *Actes d'accusation*, pp. 6–7.

8 Cour d'Assises de la Seine, *Actes d'accusation*, p. 1–2; Porter, *The Refugee Question*, p. 62.

9 Cour d'Assises de la Seine, *Actes d'accusation*, pp. 7–8; James Crossland, 'Radical warfare's first "superweapon": the fears, perceptions and realities of the Orsini bomb, 1858–1896', *Terrorism and Political Violence* (June 2021), DOI: 10.1080/09546553.2021.1924692; James Revil, *Improvised Explosive Devices: The Paradigmatic Weapons of New Wars* (Basingstoke: Palgrave, 2016), p. 7.

10 Alain Plessis, *The Rise and Fall of the Second Empire, 1852–1871*, trans. Jonathan Mandelbaum (Cambridge: Cambridge University Press, 1977), p. 145; Stacey Renee David, 'The memory of opposition: the collective identity of Louis Napoleon's political prisoners', *Western Society for French History*, 32 (2004), pp. 237–255; Christopher Andrew, 'Déchiffrement et diplomatie:

le cabinet noir du Quai d'Orsay sur la Troisième République', *Relations Internationales*, 5 (1976), pp. 37–64; 'France', *Daily News*, 4 March 1858.

11 *Annuaire des Deux Mondes: Histoire Générale des Divers États* (Paris: Bureau de la Revue des Deux Mondes, 1859), pp. 3–5; 'La paix de Villafranca', in *Le Correspondant*, ed. Charles Douniol (Paris: De Simon Raçon, 1859), vol. 47, p. 697.

12 Espinasse to Napoleon, 14 June 1858, in *Papiers secret et correspondance du second Empire*, ed. A. Poulet-Malassis (Paris: Auguste-Ghio, 1877), p. 309; Armand, *Second Empire*, pp. 251–253.

13 Baron D'Ambès, *Intimate Memoirs of Napoleon III: Personal Reminiscences of the Man and the Emperor*, ed. and trans. A. R. Alinson (London: Stanley Paul, 1912), vol. 2, p. 118; Thomas Evans, *Memoirs of Dr Thomas Evans: The Second French Empire* (New York: Appleton and Co., 1905), p. 451; *Le Moniteur Universel*, 10 May 1858; Peter Vantine, 'Censoring/censuring the press under the Second Empire: the Goncourts as journalists and *Charles Demailly*', *Nineteenth Century French Studies*, 43:1–2 (2014), pp. 45–59.

14 'Arrests in Paris', *Daily Telegraph*, 5 April 1858; 'This country', *The Times*, 11 February 1858; 'The right of asylum for exiles and the insolence of the French press', *Huddersfield Chronicle*, 6 February 1858; 'England and the refugees', *Liverpool Mercury*, 5 February 1858; George Jacob Holyoake, *Sixty Years of an Agitator's Life* (London: Fisher and Unwin, 1892), vol. 2, pp. 32–33.

15 Edward Cadogan, *The Life of Cavour* (London: Smith and Elder, 1907), pp. 185–186; *Le Moniteur universel*, 2 April 1858; Armand, *Second Empire*, pp. 254–255.

16 'Orsini's will and his second letter to the Emperor Napoleon', *The Examiner*, 10 April 1858; J. A. Berger, *The Life, Trial and Death of Felice Orsini, with His Letter to the Emperor* (London: Berger, 1858), p. 15.

17 For the motives behind the letter see J. M. Thompson, *Louis Napoleon and the Second Empire* (New York: Noonday Press, 1995), pp. 177–179; Arnold Blumberg, *A Carefully Planned Accident: The Italian War of 1859* (Selinsgrove: Susquehanna University Press, 1990), pp. 71–74; William Blanchard Jerrold, *The Life of Napoleon III* (London: Longman, Greens and Co., 1882), vol. 4, pp. 157–158.

18 Case, *French Opinion*, p. 93. Napoleon's armistice with the Austrians was a betrayal of the idea of emancipating Italy, as it allowed Franz Joseph and the Pope to retain Italian territory.

19 'The Great Battle of Solferino', *Spectator*, 2 July 1859; Case, *French Opinion*, pp. 78–79; 'Telegram Cavriana', *Le Moniteur universel*, 26 June 1859; 'The Battle of Solferino', *Saturday Review*, 2 July 1859; 'Ausland', *Die Presse*, 11 August 1859; 'The emperors on the peace', *New York Times*, 3 August 1859; 'The peace followed upon the heels of the armistice', *The Times*, 14 July 1859.

20 Archives of the Paris police prefecture (hereafter APPP), APPP: BA 510 – Orsini folio.

II. 'The Moloch of radicalism'

1 'Red Republican celebration in New York', *Richmond Daily Dispatch*, 26 April 1858; 'The Orsini and Pierri demonstration', *New York Times*, 23 April 1858; 'News of the day', *Alexandria Gazette*, 10 April 1858; 'Apotheosis of assassins', *Weekly American*, 15 May 1858; 'Orsini meeting in Boston', *Anti-Slavery Bugle*, 15 May 1858.

2 'Orsini worship', *Daily Exchange*, 26 April 1858. For Orsini as 'patient zero' in the global spread of nationalist terrorism see Tom Parker and Nick Sitter, 'The Four Horseman of terrorism: it's not waves, it's strains', *Terrorism and Political Violence*, 28:2 (2016), pp. 197–216. For his impact on pre-bellum America see Mischa Honeck, '"Freeman of all nations bestir yourselves": Felice Orsini's transnational afterlife and the radicalization of America', *Journal of the Early Republic*, 30:4 (2010), pp. 587–615.

3 David M. Potter, *The Impending Crisis: America Before the Civil War, 1848–1861* (New York: Harper and Row, 1977); Stephen Puleo, *The Caning: The Assault That Drove America to Civil War* (Yardley: Westholme, 2012); James A. Rawley, *Bleeding Kansas and the Coming of the Civil War* (Lincoln: University of Nebraska Press, 1979).

4 'The Moloch of radicalism', *New York Times*, 21 April 1858; quotes from the *New York Herald*, *New York Daily Times*, *The Liberator* and *The Black Abolitionist Papers, 1859–1865* appear in Honeck, '"Freeman of all nations bestir yourselves"'. An overview of the connections between German immigrants and abolitionists can be found in Mischa Honeck, *We Are the Revolutionists: German-Speaking Immigrants and American Abolitionists After 1848* (Athens: University of Georgia Press, 2011).

5 David S. Reynolds, *John Brown, Abolitionist: The Man Who Killed Slavery, Sparked the Civil War and Seeded Civil Rights* (New York: Alfred A. Knopf, 2005), pp. 296–308 (Brown quote is from p. 113); Samuel Vanderlip Leech, *The Raid of John Brown at Harper's Ferry as I Saw It* (Washington, DC: Desoto, 1909), pp. 4–7.

6 Osborne P. Anderson, *A Voice from Harper's Ferry: A Narrative of Events* (Boston: printed for the author, 1861), pp. 5–9; J. Hinton, *John Brown and His Men, with Some Account of the Roads They Travelled to Reach Harper's Ferry* (New York: Funk and Wagnalls, 1894), pp. 260, 29; Tony Horwitz, *Midnight Rising: John Brown and the Raid That Sparked the Civil War* (New York: Henry Holt, 2012), ch. 11; Stephen B. Oates, *To Purge This Land with Blood: A Biography of John Brown* (Amherst: University of Massachusetts Press, 1984), ch. 19.

7 'The 9/11 of 1859', *New York Times*, 1 December 2009. For the Brown/terrorist debate see Nicole Etcheson, 'John Brown, terrorist?', *American Nineteenth Century History*, 10:1 (2009), pp. 29–48.

8 'Official report of John Brown's raid upon Harper's Ferry, Virginia, 16–19 October 1859, compiled by Robert E. Lee', *Quarterly of the Oregon History Society*, 10:3 (1909), pp. 314–324; 'Abraham Lincoln's Cooper Union address', *New York Times*, 27 February 1860; John Stauffer and Zoe Trodd, eds, *The Tribunal, Responses to John Brown and the Harper's Ferry Raid* (Boston: Harvard University Press, 2012), introduction; Brian Gabrial, 'A "crisis of Americanism". newspaper coverage of John Brown's raid at Harper's Ferry and the question of loyalty', *Journalism History*, 34:2 (2008), pp. 98–106.

9 Dietze, *The Invention of Terrorism*, pp. 212–216, 264–269; Hinton, *John Brown and His Men*, pp. 146–147; 'The leading abolitionists and Brown's project', *Western Democrat*, 8 November 1859; 'Washington, 4 November', *Holmes County Republican*, 9 November 1859; 'Who is Forbes?', *Nashville Patriot*, 4 November 1859; 'Francis J. Merriam, one of the insurrectionists', *Chicago Tribune*, 3 November 1859; 'Will Brown be executed? – the abolitionists preparing to celebrate the day', *New York Herald*, 5 November 1859; 'Riot at Harper's Ferry', *Daily Intelligencer*, 19 October 1859; 'The leading abolitionists and Brown's project', *Richmond Daily Dispatch*, 29 October 1859; 'The abolition conspiracy of treason – the revelations and their consequences', *Lancaster Ledger*, 9 November 1859; Reynolds, *John Brown*, pp. 240–241.

10 'A plea for Captain John Brown', 30 October 1859, in Henry D. Thoreau, *A Yankee in Canada: With Anti-slavery and Reform Papers* (Boston: Tickner and Fields, 1866), pp. 160–164.

11 'Tages neuigkeiten', *Der Deutsche Correspondent*, 21 April 1858; 'Heinzen's Margen', *Minnesota Staats-Zeitung*, 30 October 1858; 'Infidelity and black republicanism', *Bedford Gazette*, 9 November 1860; Heinzen, *Murder and Liberty*, pp. 16–17.

12 Carl Wittke, *Against the Current: The Life of Karl Heinzen, 1809–1890* (Chicago: University of Chicago Press, 1945), pp. 174–175, 267–268; Daniel Bessner and Michael Stauch, 'Karl Heinzen and the intellectual origins of terrorism', *Terrorism and Political Violence*, 22:2 (2010), pp. 143–176; Honeck, *We Are the Revolutionists*, pp. 147–149.

13 Aaron Mackay, *Allan Pinkerton: The Eye Who Never Slept* (Edinburgh: Mainstream, 1996), pp. 82–86; Rhodri Jeffreys-Jones, *Cloak and Dollar: A History of American Secret Intelligence* (New Haven: Yale University Press, 2002), pp. 28–29.

14 Terry Allford, *Fortune's Fool: The Life of John Wilkes Booth* (New York: Oxford University Press, 2015), pp. 248–249; Allan Pinkerton, *The Spy of the Rebellion: Being a True History of the Spies System of the United States Army* (New York: G. W. Carleton, 1886), pp. 62–65; 'Report on alleged hostile organization against the government within the District of Columbia', 14 February 1861, in *Reports of the Select Committee of Five, 36th Congress, Second Session* (Washington, DC: Government Printing Office, 1861).

15 'Lincoln got scared', *Western Democrat*, 5 March 1861; Harold Holzer, *Lincoln and the Power of the Press: The War for Public Opinion* (New York: Simon and Schuster, 2014), pp. 285–287. Scepticism remains over whether Pinkerton dreamt up the plot to further his career – see Jay Bonansinga, *Pinkerton's War: The Civil War's Greatest Spy and the Birth of the U.S. Secret Service* (Guilford: Lyon's Press, 2012), pp. 34–35; S. Paul O'Hara, *Inventing the Pinkertons, or Spies, Sleuths, Mercenaries and Thugs* (Baltimore: Johns Hopkins University Press, 2016), pp. 18–20.

16 'Report on alleged hostile organization', 5 February 1861, in *Reports of the Select Committee*. On pre-war violence see Joanne Freeman, *The Field of Blood: Violence in Congress on the Road to the Civil War* (New York: Farrar, Strauss and Giroux, 2018).

17 Crossland, 'Radical warfare's first "superweapon"'.

18 'Dans la Principauté', 18/30 November 1858, in *Revue des Races Latines* (Paris: A l'Administration de la revue, 1859), vol. 2, pp. 178–179; Giuseppe Guerzoni, *Garibaldi* (Firenze: G. Barbéra, 1892), vol. 2, p. 515; 'The insurrection in Sicily', *The Times*, 13 June 1860; 'The attack on General Berg', *The Times*, 25 September 1863; 'De Rome', *Le Temps*, 31 July 1861; 'The condition of Rome', *Daily Telegraph*, 2 November 1867.

19 'A terrible engine of destruction', *National Era*, 6 October 1859; *Report of the Board on Behalf of the United States Executives Departments at the International Exhibition, Philadelphia, 1876* (Washington, DC: Government Printing Office, 1884), vol. 1, p. 688; John Rutherford, *The Secret History of the Fenian Conspiracy: Its Origin, Objects and Ramifications* (London: Kegan and Paul, 1877), vol. 2, p. 158. 'Dublin', *Freeman's Journal*, 23 December 1870.

20 'Plots and counter-plots', *New York Herald*, 27 February 1861; 'Mr Lincoln's escapes', *Daily Exchange*, 27 February 1861; John le Barnes' letter to Thomas Wentworth Higginson, 22 November 1859, in Janet Kemper Beck, *Creating the John Brown Legend: Emerson, Thoreau, Child and Higginson in Defense of the Raid on Harper's Ferry* (Jefferson: MacFarland, 2009), p. 128.

III. For those in Hell

1 Ivan Aleksandrovich Khoudiakoff, *Mémoires d'un révolutionnaire* (Paris: Calman Lévy, 1889), pp. 24–40; Alexander Polunov, Thomas C. Owen and Larissa G. Zakharova, eds, trans. Marshall S. Shatz, *Russia in the Nineteenth Century: Autocracy, Reform and Social Change, 1815–1914* (London: Routledge, 2005), pp. 87–108; Samuel D. Kassow, 'The university statute of 1863', in *Russia's Great Reforms, 1855–1881*, ed. Ben Eklof, John Bushnell and Larissa Zakharova (Bloomington: Indiana University Press, 1994), pp. 247–263.

2 Franco Venturi, *A History of the Populist and Socialist Movements in*

Notes

Nineteenth Century Russia, trans. Francis Haskell (London: Weidenfeld and Nicholson, 1952), pp. 337–342.

3 Quote from *Kolokol* taken from Marc Sageman, *Turning to Political Violence: The Emergence of Terrorism* (Philadelphia: University of Pennsylvania Press, 2017), p. 154; Kristian Petrov, '"Strike out, right and left!": a conceptual historical analysis of 1860s Russian nihilism and its notion of negation', *Studies in European Thought*, 71 (2019), pp. 73–97.

4 Khoudiakoff, *Mémoires*, p. 155; Claudia Verhoeven, *The Odd Man Karakozov: Imperial Russia, Modernity and the Birth of Terrorism* (Ithaca: Cornell University Press, 2009), p. 58; Abbott Gleeson, *Young Russia: The Genesis of Russian Radicalism in the 1860s* (New York: Viking, 1980), pp. 303, 309; Dietze, *The Invention of Modern Terrorism*, pp. 396–397; Hinton, *John Brown and His Men*, ch. 14.

5 Paul Avrich, *Anarchist Portraits* (Princeton: Princeton University Press, 1988), pp. 34–35; Christopher Ely, *Underground Petersburg: Radical Populism, Urban Space and the Tactics of Subversion in Reform-Era Russia* (Ithaca: Cornell University Press, 2016), pp. 93–95; Venturi, *Populist and Socialist Movements*, pp. 331–335. On the line of influence from Brown to Chernyshevsky to the Russian nihilists see Dietze, *The Invention of Modern Terrorism*, pp. 416–430.

6 Verhoeven, *The Odd Man Karakozov*, pp. 7–8. 42–43.

7 Adam B. Ulam, *Prophets and Conspirators in Pre-revolutionary Russia* (New York: Routledge, 1998), pp. 144–164; 'Russie', *La Liberté*, 24 September 1866; 'Dimitri Karakozow', *Journal de-Saint Pétersbourg*, 15 September 1866; Khoudiakoff, *Mémoires*, pp. 268–269.

8 Peter Zaichnevsky, *Young Russia* (1862), in James H. Billington, *Fire in the Minds of Men: Origins of the Revolutionary Faith* (New Brunswick: Transaction, 1999), pp. 394–395; quote from 'To My Worker Friends' taken from Verhoeven, *The Odd Man Karakozov*, p. 130; K. C. Tessendorf, *Kill the Tsar! Youth and Terrorism in Old Russia* (New York: Atheneum, 1986), pp. 24–25.

9 A. A. Shilov, *Karakozov i pokushenie 4 aprelîa 1866 goda* (St Petersburg: State Publishing, 1919), pp. 13–14; Khoudiakoff, *Mémoires*, p. 265; 'Russia', *The Times*, 5 May 1866.

10 Documents of Russian Empire, 1860–1869, https://eudocs.lib.byu.edu/index.php/Russia_1796-1917 – Testimony of D. A. Yurasov at Commission of Inquiry into the Assassination Attempt of Tsar Alexander, 31 May 1866. The Russian reportage was reproduced in 'The state of Russia', *The Times*, 23 October 1866; Khoudiakoff, *Mémoires*, p. 265.

11 Ronald Hingley, *The Russian Secret Police* (New York: Dorset, 1970), pp. 54–56; Shilov, *Karakozov i pokushenie*, pp. 15–18; Daniel Balmuth, 'The origins of the Russian press reform of 1865', *Slavonic and East European Review*, 47:109 (1969), pp. 369–388; Claudia Verhoeven, 'The making of Russian

revolutionary terrorism', in *Enemies of Humanity: The Nineteenth Century War on Terrorism*, ed. Isaac Land (Basingstoke: Palgrave, 2008), pp. 99–116, at pp. 102–103.

12 Foreign Relations of the United States (hereafter FRUS) – Clay to Seward, 22 April 1866; *Russky Invalid* is quoted in 'From our correspondent', *The Times*, 23 April 1866; Richard Wortman, *Scenarios of Power: From Alexander II to the Abdication of Nicholas II: Myth and Ceremony in Russian Monarchy* (Princeton: Princeton University Press, 2000), vol. 2, pp. 110–112; Edward Radzinsky, *Alexander II: The Last Great Tsar*, trans. Antonina W. Bouis (New York, Free Press, 2005), pp. 178–180.

13 'Russia, from our correspondent', *The Times*, 5 May 1866; Walter G. Moss, *Russia in the Age of Alexander II, Tolstoy and Dostoevsky* (London: Anthem, 2002), pp. 95–96; Aleksandr Nikitenko, *The Diary of a Russian Censor*, ed. and trans. Helen Saltz Jacobsen (Boston: University of Massachusetts Press, 1975), pp. 312–314; Verhoeven, *The Odd Man Karakozov*, pp. 71–72.

14 Vizetelly, *The Court of the Tuileries*, p. 272; Documents of Russian Empire, 1860–1869, https://eudocs.lib.byu.edu/index.php/Russia_1796-1917 – Telegram no. 117, Paris to St Petersburg, 26 May 1867; 'French affairs', *The Observer*, 21 July 1867.

15 David C. Fisher, 'The rise of the radical intelligentsia', in *Events That Changed Russia Since 1855*, ed. Frank W. Thackeray (Westport: Greenwood Press, 2007), pp. 23–44, at pp. 34–35; Nikitenko, *The Diary of a Russian Censor* – 25 December 1870, p. 343, 9 April 1865, 8 May 1865, pp. 312–314; David Saunders, *Russia in the Age of Reaction and Reform, 1801–1881* (London: Routledge, 2015), pp. 311–321.

16 Peter Kropotkin, *Memoirs of a Revolutionist* (London: Smith and Elder, 1899), vol. 2, pp. 37–38.

IV. Breakers of worlds

1 In keeping with Nechaev's penchant for fantasy, some of the details here are a fabrication on my part. The point that Nechaev had escaped from custody in a daring manner, however, conforms to the narrative he presented to Bakunin – see Anthony Masters, *Bakunin: The Father of Anarchism* (London: Sidgwick and Jackson, 1974), pp. 186–187; Paul Avrich, *Bakunin and Nechaev* (London: Freedom Press, 1974), p. 9; Venturi, *Populist and Socialist Movements*, p. 363.

2 Paul Avrich, 'Bakunin and the United States', *International Review of Social History*, 24:3 (1979), pp. 320–340; Peter Marshall, *Demanding the Impossible: A History of Anarchism* (London: Harper Collins, 1992), pp. 263–308; Phillip Billingsley, 'Bakunin's sojourn in Japan: nailing down an enigma', *Human Sciences Review*, 5 (1993), pp. 35–65; Andrew Silke, 'Honour and expulsion:

terrorism in nineteenth century Japan', *Terrorism and Political Violence*, 9:4 (1997), pp. 58–81.

3 Arthur Lehning, 'Bakunin's conceptions of revolutionary organisations and their role: a study of his "secret societies"', in *Essays in Honour of E. H. Carr*, ed. Chimen Ambramsky and Beryl J. Williams (London: Palgrave, 1974), pp. 57–81; Venturi, *Populist and Socialist Movements*, p. 342.

4 *Bakunin on Anarchy: Selected Works by the Activist Founder of World Anarchism*, ed. and trans. Sam Dolgoff (New York: Vintage, 1971) – *The National Catechism* (1866), p. 98–99, *The Revolution, Catechism* (1866), p. 96, and *The Program of the International Brotherhood* (1869), p. 149.

5 *Daughter of a Revolutionary: Natalie Herzen and the Bakunin-Nechayev Circle*, ed. Michael Confino, trans. Hilary Sternberg and Lydia Bott (LeSalle: Library Press, 1973) – 'Natalie Herzen's reminiscences', pp. 372–373.

6 Arthur P. Mendel, *Mikhail Bakunin: Roots of Apocalypse* (New York: Praeger, 1981), pp. 316–317; Masters, *Bakunin*, p. 190; Bakunin quotes are from *Revolution, Terrorism, Banditry* (1869), in *Voices of Terror*, ed. Laqueur, p. 68, and *Daughter of a Revolutionary*, ed. Confino – Bakunin to James Guillaume, 1 April 1869, p. 149.

7 Philip Pomper, *Sergei Nechaev* (New Jersey: Rutgers University Press, 1979), pp. 45–47; the quote on Nechaev's character is from Avrich, *Anarchist Portraits*, p. 32; Nechaev quotes are from Avrich, *Bakunin and Nechaev*, p. 7, and Sergei Nechaev, *Catechism of a Revolutionary* (London: Anarchist Library, reprint 2009); see also Phillip Pomper, 'Nechaev and tsaricide: the conspiracy within the conspiracy', *Russian Review*, 33:2 (1974), pp. 123–138.

8 *Daughter of a Revolutionary*, ed. Confino – 'Natalie Herzen's diary', no. 80, 28 May 1870, pp. 186–187 and 211.

9 Vera Zasulich, *Memoirs*, in *Five Sisters: Women Against the Tsar*, ed. Barbara A. Engel and Clifford N. Rosenthal (London: Routledge, 1979), pp. 71–72.

10 Jay Bergman, *Vera Zasulich: A Biography* (Palo Alto: Stanford University Press, 1983), pp. 13–16; Woodford McClellan, *Revolutionary Exiles: The Russians in the First International and the Paris Commune* (London: Routledge, 1979), pp. 35–36.

11 Robert Hingley, *Nihilists: Russian Radicals and Revolutionaries in the Reign of Alexander II* (London: Weidenfeld and Nicholson, 1967), p. 57–58; Edward Hallett Carr, *Bakunin* (New York: Vintage, 1961), p. 393.

12 McClellan, *Revolutionary Exiles*, p. 37; Nikitenko, *The Diary of a Russian Censor*, 15 December 1869, p. 337.

13 Bakunin, *The National Catechism*, in *Bakunin on Anarchy*, ed. Dolgoff, p. 100. Historians generally agree that Bakunin took no part in the writing. For a supporting view see Avrich, *Bakunin and Nechaev*, pp. 12–14. For an opposing view see Philip Pomper, 'Bakunin, Nechaev and the "Catechism of a Revolutionary": the case for joint authorship', *Canadian-American Slavic Studies*, 10:4 (1976), pp. 535–551.

14 Nechaev, *Catechism*.

15 Georgios Karakasis, 'The catechism of destruction: Sergei Nechaev and the spirit of nihilism', *Iocana Credintei*, 8:4 (2018), pp. 103–114; Robert Mayer, 'Lenin and the concept of the professional revolutionary', *History of Political Thought*, 14:2 (1993), pp. 249–263; Zeev Ivianski, 'Source of inspiration for revolutionary terrorism – the Bakunin-Nechayev alliance', *Journal of Conflict Studies*, 8:3 (1988), https://journals.lib.unb.ca/index.php/JCS/article/view/14810.

16 Avrich, *Bakunin and Nechaev*, pp. 15–16; Venturi, *Populist and Socialist Movements*, pp. 374–375.

17 Hingley, *Nihilists*, pp. 58–59.

18 *Daughter of a Revolutionary*, ed. Confino – Natalie to Nechaev, 31 May 1870, no. 77, p. 184, Nechaev to Natalie, 18 March 1870, no. 66, p. 172; Natalie to Nechaev, 13 March 1870, no. 62, p. 170; *MECW*, vol. 44 – Engels to Cuno, 24 January 1872, p. 311.

19 *Daughter of a Revolutionary*, ed. Confino – Bakunin to Nechaev, no. 84, 2 June 1870, pp. 238–275.

20 British ambassador (Tempest-Vane) quote from McClellan, *Revolutionary Exiles*, p. 67; George Woodcock, *Anarchism* (New York: Penguin, 1977), pp. 150–151.

V. Insurgents across borders

1 IRB oath in John O'Leary, *Recollections of Fenians and Fenianism* (London: Downey and Co., 1896), vol. 1, p. 120; Christine Kinealy, *Repeal and Revolution: 1848 in Ireland* (Manchester: Manchester University Press, 2009), pp. 60–63, 198–200; Desmond Ryan, *The Fenian Chief: A Biography of James Stephens* (Dublin: Hely Thom, 1967), pp. 229–232; Marta Ramón, *A Provisional Dictator: James Stephens and the Fenian Movement* (Dublin: University College Dublin Press, 2007), p. 218.

2 O'Leary, *Recollections of Fenians*, vol. 2, p. 159; Owen McGee, *The IRB: The Irish Republican Brotherhood from the Land League to Sinn Féin* (Dublin: Four Courts Press, 2005), pp. 30–32; Jonathan Gannt, *Irish Terrorism in the Atlantic Community, 1865–1922* (Basingstoke: Palgrave, 2010), pp. 33–34.

3 Ryan, *The Fenian Chief*, p. 233; Jonathan Sperber, *Karl Marx: A Nineteenth Century Life* (New York: Liveright, 2013), pp. 234–245, 357–358; *MECW*, vol. 42 – Marx to Engels, 15 March 1866, pp. 238–239; Marx, 'From the question of the Ionian Islands', *New York Daily Tribune*, 6 January 1859; Timothy Messer-Kruse, *The Yankee International: Marxism and the American Reform Tradition, 1848–1874* (Chapel Hill: University of North Carolina Press, 1998), pp. 6–9.

4 Quotes on Cluseret are from *Quotes and Letters of Charles Sumner*, ed.

Edward L. Pierce (London: Samson, 1893), p. 128; Holstein, *The Holstein Papers*, vol. 1, p. 86; 'Cluseret's war record', *Marietta Daily Leader*, 1 June 1898; A. Landy, 'A French adventurer and American expansionism after the Civil War', *Science and Society*, 15:4 (1951), pp. 313–333; Cluseret quote is from Gustave Cluseret, 'My connection with Fenianism', *Frazer's Magazine*, July 1872, pp. 31–46.

5 Reginald Whitaker, Gregory S. Kealy and Andrew Parnaby, *Secret Service: Political Policing in Canada from the Fenians to Fortress America* (Toronto: University of Toronto Press, 2012), pp. 23–27, quote on p. 23.

6 *Correspondence Respecting the Recent Fenian Aggression upon Canada* (London: Harrison and Sons, 1867) – Hemans to Monck, 2 and 3 June 1866.

7 Wittke, *Against the Current*, p. 252; William J. Phalen, *The Democratic Soldier: The Life of General Gustave P. Cluseret* (New Delhi: Vij Books, 2015), pp. 48–49; Octave Fariola, 'Amongst the Fenians', *The Irishman*, 1 August 1868.

8 John Newsinger, *Fenianism in Mid-Victorian Britain* (London: Pluto, 1994), pp. 50–51; Patrick Stewart and Brian McGovern, *The Fenians: Irish Rebellion in the North Atlantic World, 1858–1876* (Knoxville: University of Tennessee Press, 2013), pp. 160–161.

9 National Archives of the United Kingdom (hereafter TNA), TNA: HO 45/7799 – British Consulate NY to FO, 16 September 1865, and John Farnworth to Sir George Guy, 16 January 1866.

10 TNA: HO/457799 – 'Statement of Patrick Condon, otherwise called Godfrey Massey'; Shin-Ichi Takagami, 'The Fenian rising in Dublin, March 1867', *Irish Historical Studies*, 29:15 (1995), pp. 340–362; McGee, *The IRB*, pp. 35–36.

11 'A miserable failure', *Irish Times*, 7 March 1867; TNA: HO 45/7799 – 'Statement of Patrick Condon'; Octave Fariola, 'Amongst the Fenians', *The Irishman*, 19 September 1868; Brian Jenkins, *The Fenian Problem: Insurgency and Terrorism in a Liberal State, 1858–1874* (Montreal: McGill University Press, 2008), p. 171; Alban Bargain-Villéger, 'Captain Tin Can: Gustave Cluseret and the socialist leftists, 1848–1900', *Socialist History*, 46 (2016), pp. 13–32; Rutherford, *The Secret History of the Fenian Conspiracy*, pp. 273–282.

12 Steward and McGovern, *The Fenians*, pp. 182–183; 'London, Thursday September 19', *The Times*, 19 September 1867; 'The English panic', *The Spectator*, 5 October 1867; *MECW*, vol. 42 – Marx to Engels, 7 November 1867, p. 464, and *Manchester Examiner* quoted in Michael de Nie, *The Eternal Paddy: Irish Identity and the British Press, 1798–1882* (Madison: University of Wisconsin Press, 2004), p. 163.

13 *Manchester Examiner*, 21 September 1867, p. 443; John Savage, *Fenian Martyrs and Heroes* (Boston: Patrick Donahoe, 1868), pp. 437–443.

14 William Philip Allen and Michael O'Brien speeches, Library Ireland, https://www.libraryireland.com.

15 *MECW*, vol. 42 – Marx to Engels, 24 November 1867.

16   TNA: MEPO 3/1788 – Clerkenwell explosion report; the quote is from *Official Debates of the United Kingdom Parliament, Historic Hansard* (hereafter *Hansard*), 9 March 1868, p. 1217.
17   Bernard Porter, *The Origins of the Vigilant State: The London Metropolitan Police Special Branch Before the First World War* (London: Weidenfeld and Nicholson, 1987), pp. 8–9; Padraic Kennedy, 'The secret service department: a British intelligence bureau in mid-Victorian London, September 1867 to April 1868', *Intelligence and National Security*, 18:3 (2003), pp. 100–127; TNA: HO 103/15 – Home Office memo, 3 February 1868.
18   *Hansard*, 19 March 1868, 1880–1881; TNA: HO 45/7799 – 'Return of special constables', 28 January 1868.
19   'Clerkenwell explosion relief fund', *The Times*, 2 January 1868; 'Anti-Fenian meeting in Bath', *Bath Chronicle*, 2 January 1868; 'Proposed anti-Fenian demonstration', *Daily News*, 15 January 1868; 'At a time when public feeling is excited', *The Times*, 4 January 1868.
20   Robert Anderson, *The Lighter Side of My Official Life* (New York: Hodder and Stoughton, 1910), pp. 27–28.
21   Anderson, *The Lighter Side*, p. 24–25; Nie, *Eternal Paddy*, pp. 166–169; TNA: HO/457799 – Dublin Met Police report, 31 October 1867; 'Breaking up of Fenian headquarters in Paris', *New York Times*, 4 January 1868.
22   The quote from the *Sydney Morning Herald* is from Brian McKinlay, *The First Royal Tour, 1867–1868* (London: Robert Hale, 1971), p. 174; 'The last Fenian plot', *Hertford Mercury*, 2 May 1868; the quote from *The Nation* is from Niall Whelehan, *The Dynamiters: Irish Nationalism and Political Violence in the Wider World, 1867–1900* (Cambridge: Cambridge University Press, 2012), p. 72.
23   Simon Webb, *Dynamite, Treason and Plot: Terrorism in Victorian and Edwardian London* (Stroud: History Press, 2012), pp. 53–54.

VI. Gathering storms

1   Terry Cowdy, *The Enemy Within: A History of Spies, Spymasters and Espionage* (London: Bloomsbury, 2011), p. 180; Jonathan W. Daly, *Autocracy Under Siege: Security Police and Opposition in Russia, 1866–1905* (Ithaca: Cornell University Press, 1998), p. 16; Hingley, *The Russian Secret Police*, pp. 49–50; Martin A. Miller, *The Foundations of Modern Terrorism: State, Society and the Dynamics of Political Violence* (Cambridge: Cambridge University Press, 2013), pp. 62–63.
2   Jonathan Steinberg, *Bismarck: A Life* (Oxford: Oxford University Press, 2011), pp. 465–466; Allan Mitchell, 'Bonapartism as a model for Bismarckian politics', *Journal of Modern History*, 49:2 (1977), pp. 181–199.
3   Frank Lorenz Müller, 'The spectre of a people in arms', *English Historical*

Review, 122:495 (2007), pp. 82–104; Abigail Green, 'Political and diplomatic movements, 1850–1870', in *Germany, 1800–1870*, ed. Jonathan Sperber (Oxford: Oxford University Press, 1987), pp. 69–90.

4   Robert H. Keyserlingk, 'Bismarck and the press: the example of the National Liberals', *Historical Papers*, 2:1 (1967), pp. 198–215; Otto Pflanze, *Bismarck and the Development of Germany: The Period of Unification, 1815–1871* (Princeton: Princeton University Press, 1963), pp. 201–204.

5   Gunter E. Rothenburg, *The Army of Francis Joseph* (West Lafayette: Purdue University Press, 1998), pp. 57–60; International Institute of Social History archives (hereafter IISH), IISH: ARCH 00366, 33 Go.3, Box 4, Report on 'Communism Until the Foundation of the International', 12 April 1872; Dennis Showalter, *The Wars of German Unification* (London: Hodder, 2004), pp. 95–104; Hsi-Huey Liang, *The Rise of Modern Police and the European State System from Metternich to the Second World War* (Cambridge: Cambridge University Press, 1992), pp. 31–33.

6   Woodcock, *Anarchism*, pp. 147–149; Stieber, *The Chancellor's Spy*, pp. 94–95; Deflem, 'International policing', p. 49.

7   John F. Kutolowski, 'English radicals and the Polish insurrection of 1862–1864', *Polish Review*, 11:3 (1966), pp. 3–28; 'Germany', *Daily News*, 8 May 1851; Mikhail Bakunin, *The National Catechism*, in *Bakunin on Anarchy*, ed. Dolgoff; *La Epoca*, 13 October 1868, p. 1; Stieber, *The Chancellor's Spy*, p. 105.

8   Volker Ullrich, *Fünf Schüsse auf Bismarck: Historische Reportagen, 1789–1945* (Munich: C. H. Beck, 2003), pp. 40–46; Boris I. Nicolaevsky, 'Secret societies and the First International', in *The Revolutionary Internationals, 1864–1943*, ed. Milorad M. Drachkovitch (Palo Alto: Stanford University Press, 1966), pp. 36–56, quote at p. 56; 'Ein mordanschlag auf Graf Bismarck', *Provinzial-Correspondenz*, 9 May 1866; 'Fritz Blind', *Le Figaro*, 17 May 1866; 'Prussia', *The Times*, 16 May 1866.

9   'French affairs', *The Observer*, 21 July 1867; 'Attentat contre l'empereur de Russie', *Le Petit Journal*, 9 June 1867; 'Cour d'assises de la Seine', *Journal des débats politiques et littéraires*, 13 July 1867; Stieber, *The Chancellor's Spy*, pp. 124–125; Sageman, *Turning to Political Violence*, pp. 160–162.

10 Oscar Testut, *L'Internationale* (Paris: E. Lachaud, 1871), p. 23; IISH: ARCH 000366, 33 Go.3, Box 4 – Dossier Congrès de L'Internationale, 1868–1874, and Le Congrès de Bâle, 5–11 September 1869.

11 'Congrès de l'Association Internationale des Travailleurs', *Le Temps*, 15 September 1869; 'Le congrès de paix', *Le Temps*, 13 September 1867; 'Ein eigenartiger Friedenskongress', *Provinzial-Correspondenz*, 18 September 1867; 'Genève, le Septembre soir', *Journal des débats politiques et littéraires*, 13 September 1867; Nicolaevsky, 'Secret societies and the First International'.

12 Marxists Internet Archive, 'Proposal to the central committee of the League of Peace and Freedom', 5 September 1867, https://www.marxists.org;

Anthony Campanella, 'Garibaldi and the first Peace Congress in Geneva in 1867', *International Review of Social History*, 5:3 (1960), pp. 456–486.

13 'Conspiracy in France', *Leeds Mercury*, 27 December 1867; 'A French view of Fenianism', *Daily News*, 14 March 1867; 'Congrès de L'association Interntionale des Travailleurs', *Les Etats-Unis d'Europe*, 1 January 1868, pp. 150–151. For the relationship between Fenianism and socialism during this era see Cormac Ó Gráda, 'Fenianism and socialism: the career of Joseph Patrick McDonnell', *Saothar*, 1:1 (1975), pp. 31–41; Newsinger, *Fenianism in Mid-Victorian Britain*, pp. 85–90.

14 Michele Cunningham, *Mexico and the Foreign Policy of Napoleon III* (Basingstoke: Palgrave, 2001), p. 164; Alain Faure, 'The public meeting movements in Paris from 1868 to 1870', in *Voices of the People: The Social Life of 'La Sociale' at the End of the Second Empire*, ed. Adrian Rifkin and Roger Thomas, trans. John Moore (London: Routledge, 1988), pp. 181–234.

15 'Faits divers', *La Rue*, 31 March 1870; *Journal de Commissaires des Police*, no. 16 (1870), pp. 254–256; Joylon Michael Howarth, 'The myth of Blanquism under the Third Republic, 1870–1900', *Journal of Modern History*, 48:3 (1976), pp. 37–68.

16 Charles de Costa, *Les Blanquistes* (Paris: Marcel Rivière, 1912), pp. 10–12; Doug Enaa Greene, *Communist Insurgent: Blanqui's Politics of Revolution* (Chicago: Haymarket Books, 2017), ch. 8; Patrick H. Hutton, *The Cult of the Revolutionary Tradition: The Blanquists in French Politics, 1864–1893* (Berkeley: University of California Press, 1981), pp. 65–67.

17 Louis Auguste Blanqui, *Instructions pour une prise d'armes* (1868); Stewart Neil, *Blanqui* (London: Victor Gollancz, 1939), p. 235–236; Karl Kautsky, *Terrorism and Communism: A Contribution to the Natural History of Revolution*, trans. W. H. Kerridge (New York: Routledge, reissued edition 2011), pp. 76–80; Philippe le Goff, 'The militant politics of Auguste Blanqui', PhD thesis (University of Warwick, 2015).

18 'Les bombes', *Le Courrier du Gard*, 3 May 1870; 'Y-a-t-il Deux Complots?', *Le Figaro*, 22 May 1870; 'Chronique', *Le Temps*, 3 May 1870; 'Service de nuit Angleterre', *Le Constitutionnel*, 5 May 1870; 'On the eve of the plebiscite', *Daily Telegraph*, 2 May 1870; 'The conspirators' banquet', *Penny Illustrated*, 7 May 1870; 'The International Workingman's Association', *Pall Mall Gazette*, 12 May 1870.

19 'If the evidence of the plot…', *Leeds Mercury*, 3 May 1870; 'The conspiracy to assassinate the French emperor', *Manchester Guardian*, 7 May 1870; *MECW*, vol. 21 – 'Concerning the persecution of members', 10 May 1870, p. 127, and vol. 43 – Marx to Vogt, 9 April 1870, pp. 471–476; Richard-Pierre Guiraudou and Michel Rebondy, *Gustave Flourens: Le Chevalier Rouge* (Paris: Le Pré aux Clercs, 1983), pp. 258–262; Neil, *Blanqui*, pp. 242–243.

VII. City of enemies

1   George Hooper, *The Campaign at Sedan, August–September 1870* (London: Hodder and Stoughton, 1914), pp. 289–290; Douglas Fermer, *Sedan, 1870* (Barnsley: Pen and Sword, 2008), pp. 176–179; Venturi, *Populist and Socialist Movements*, p. 381; Stieber, *The Chancellor's Spy*, p. 169.

2   Carr, *Bakunin*, pp. 396–405; J. M. Meijer, *Knowledge and Revolution: The Russian Colony in Zurich, 1870–1873* (Assen: Van Gorcum, 1955), pp. 66–67; Louis Andrieux, *La Commune á Lyon en 1870 et 1871* (Paris: Perrin, 1906), pp. 135–138; declaration reprinted in Marshall, *Demanding the Impossible*, p. 286; 'Le journée du 28 Septembre à Lyon', *Le Courrier du Gard*, 1 October 1870.

3   APPP: BA1015 – Report, 9 July 1871; Phalen, *The Democratic Soldier*, pp. 65–66.

4   George Francis Train, *My Life in Many Foreign Lands* (New York: Appleton, 1902), pp. 303–308; Allen Foster, *Around the World with Citizen Train: The Sensational Adventures of the Real Phileas Fogg* (Decatur: Merlin, 2001); Gustave Paul Cluseret, *Mémoires du Général Cluseret* (Paris: Jules Levy, 1887), vol. 2, pp. 138–139, pp. 180–181.

5   Victor Hugo, *Memoirs of Victor Hugo*, trans. John W. Harding (London: William Heinemann, 1898), p. 336; Alistair Horne, *The Fall of Paris: The Siege and the Commune, 1870–1871* (London: Macmillan, 1965), pp. 61–63; *Letters from Paris: Written by C. de B., a Political Informant to the Head of the London House of Rothschild, 1870–1875*, ed. and trans. Robert Henry (London: J. M. Dent, 1942), 15 September 1870, p. 72.

6   Robert Lowry-Sibbet, *The Siege of Paris by an American Eyewitness* (Harrisburg: Meyers, 1892), pp. 376–377; Louis Auguste Blanqui, *La Patrie en danger compendium* (Paris: Chevalier, 1871), p. 26; Martin Phillip Johnson, *The Paradise of Association: Political Culture and Popular Organizations in the Paris Commune of 1871* (Ann Arbor: University of Michigan Press, 1996), pp. 22–25.

7   Edmond Goncourt and Jules Goncourt, *The Journal of the Goncourts*, ed. Julius West (London: Thomas Nelson, 1908), pp. 127–128; Elihu Washburne, *Recollections of a Minister to France, 1869–1877* (London: Sampson Lowe, 1887), vol. 1, p. 209; *Letters from Paris*, 7 October 1870, p. 82; Alistair Horne, *The Terrible Year: A Paris Commune, 1871* (London: Phoenix, 2004), pp. 29–30.

8   Helmuth von Moltke, *The Franco-German War of 1870–71*, trans. Clara Bell and Henry W. Fischer (London: James R. Osgood, McIlvaine and Co., 1891), vol. 2, p. 283; Lowry-Sibbet, *The Siege of Paris*, pp. 316–318; Goncourt and Goncourt, *The Journal*, pp. 142–143.

9   Edmond Lepelletier, *Histoire de la Commune de 1871* (Paris: Mercure,

1911), vol. 1, p. 402; Louise Michel, *The Red Virgin: The Memoirs of Louise Michel*, ed. and trans. Bullitt Lowry and Elizabeth Ellington Gunter (Alabama: University of Alabama Press, 1981), pp. 58–59; Ernest Vizetelly, *My Adventures in the Commune, 1871* (London: Chatto and Windus), pp. 247–248.

10 Michel, *Red Virgin*, p. 64; Vergès d'Esboeufs, *Le Vérité sur la gouvernement de la Défense nationale La Commune et les Versaillais* (Geneva: Counsel-General's Office, 1871), pp. 232–40; *The Communards of Paris, 1871*, ed. Stewart Edwards (Documents of Revolution series, general editor Heinz Lubasz) (London: Thames and Hudson, 1973), p. 62.

11 Jean Martet, *George Clemenceau: The Events of His Life as Told by Himself to His Former Secretary* (London: Longmans, Green and Co., 1923), pp. 164–167.

12 Robert Tombs, *The Paris Commune, 1871* (London: Routledge, 1999), pp. 80–83; Jonathan Sperber, *Europe, 1850–1914: Progress, Participation and Apprehension* (London: Routledge, 2009), pp. 108–109; Donny Gluckstein, *The Paris Commune: A Revolution in Democracy* (Chicago: Haymarket Books, 2011), pp. 8–16.

13 Maxime Vuillaume, *Mes cahiers rouges au temps de La Commune* (Paris: Librairie Paul Ollendorff, 1900), p. 165; Edward S. Mason, *The Paris Commune: An Episode in the History of the Socialist Movement* (New York: Howard Fertig, 1967), pp. 196–198; Marie Fleming, *The Geography of Freedom: The Odyssey of Élisée Reclus* (St Laurent: Black Rose, 1988), pp. 72–80; Horne, *The Terrible Year*, pp. 85–87.

14 Michel, *Red Virgin*, pp. 47–50, 82–83; Carolyn J. Eichner, *Surmounting the Barricades: Women in the Paris Commune* (Bloomington: Indiana University Press, 2004), pp. 1–16; Dominica Change, '"Un Nouveau '93": Discourses of Mimicry and Terror in the Paris Commune of 1871', *French Historical Studies*, 36:4 (2013), pp. 629–648.

15 Letter to *The Times*, 17 April 1871, in Henry Brackenbury, *Some Memories of My Spare Time* (Edinburgh: William Blackwood, 1909), pp. 204–205; Victor Henri Rochefort, *Les Dernières Causeries du Henri Rochefort*, ed. W. D. Fonvielle (Brussels: Bureau du Petit Journal, 1871), p. 24; 'Deposition of M. Choppin', *Journal des Débats Politiques et Littéraires*, 10 March 1872; 'Letter from Paris', *Pall Mall Gazette*, 24 February 1871; 'Un nouveau complot', *Le Cri du Peuple*, 24 February 1871; 'Bruits', *L'Ami De La France*, 10 January 1871; 'Paris au jour du jour', *Le Figaro*, 24 February 1871; Joanni d'Arsac, *La Guerre Civile et la Commune de Paris en 1871* (Paris: F. Curot, 1871), p. 147.

16 *Letters from Paris*, 20 March 1871, p. 135; IISH: ARCH 00366, 33 Go.3, Box 4 – 'Dossier Congrès De l'Internationale, 1868–1874', 11 April and 1 May 1871; Patrick C. Jamieson, 'Foreign criticisms of the 1871 Paris Commune: the role of British and American newspapers and periodicals', *Intersections*,

11:1 (2010), pp. 100–115; 'The Communists and the Communalists', *The Times*, 29 March 1871.

17 William Gibson, *Paris During the Commune* (London: Methodist Book Room, 1895), pp. 214–215, 235; Philip M. Katz, '"Lessons from Paris": the American clergy responds to the Paris Commune', *Church History*, 63:3 (1994), pp. 393–406; Pope Pius quote from Matthew Beaumont, 'Cacotopianism, the Paris Commune and England's anti-communist imaginary, 1870–1900', *ELH*, 73:2 (2006), pp. 465–487.

18 *Letters from Paris*, p. 146; Carole Witzig, 'Bismarck et la Commune: le reaction des monarchies conservatrices contre les mouvements republicains et socialistes (1870–1872) vue et travers les archives allemandes', *International Review of Social History*, 17:1 (1972), pp. 191–221; Washburne, *Recollections*, vol. 2, p. 126; letter from Louis Rossel in defence of Cluseret, 2 May 1871, in W. Pembroke Fetridge, *The Rise and Fall of the Paris Commune of 1871* (New York: Harper, 1871), pp. 204–205; Cluseret, *Mémoires*, p. 71.

19 Frank Jellinek, *The Paris Commune of 1871* (London: Victor Gollancz, 1965), pp. 319–320; 'Delescluze's proclamation', 21 May 1871, and 'Proclamation by the Committee of the Public Safety', 24 May 1871, in *The Communards*, ed. Edwards, pp. 160–161.

20 Prosper-Oliver Lissagaray, *History of the Commune of 1871*, trans. Eleanor Marx (New York: International Publishing, 1898), pp. 386–387; Jellinek, *The Paris Commune*, pp. 346–350; Fleming, *The Geography of Freedom*, pp. 86–91. For a view of the Bloody Week that estimates a lower death toll see Robert Tombs, 'How bloody was la semaine sanglante of 1871? A revision', *Historical Journal*, 55:3 (2012), pp. 679–704.

21 Washburne, *Recollections*, vol. 2, p. 146; Edith Thomas, *Louise Michel*, trans. Penelope Williams (Montreal: Black Rose, 1980), pp. 89–95; Horne, *The Terrible Year*, pp. 128–138.

22 Thomas, *Louise Michel*, p. 125; Alexander Butterworth, *The World That Never Was: A True Story of Dreamers, Schemers, Anarchists and Secret Agents* (London: Vintage, 2011), pp. 76–80; Alice Bullard, 'Self representation in the arms of defeat: fatal nostalgia and surviving comrades in French New Caledonia, 1871–1880', *Cultural Anthropology*, 12:2 (1997), pp. 179–212.

VIII. Chasing chimeras

1 Samuel Bracebridge Hemyng, *The Commune in London, or, Thirty Years Hence: A Chapter of Anticipated History* (London: Clarke, 1871); George Tomkyns Chesney, *The Battle of Dorking: Reminiscences of a Volunteer* (Edinburgh: Blackwood and Sons, 1871); Beaumont, 'Cacotopianism'.

2 *Enquête Parlementaire sur l'Insurrection du 18 Mars* (Versailles: Imprimeur

de l'Assemblée nationale, 1872), vol. 1, pp. 163–165, Cresson quote vol. 2, p. 18; Andrieux, *La Commune á Lyon*, pp. 123–124.

3   Karl Marx, *The Civil War in France* (New York: International Publishers, 1933), pp. 43, 501–503; Quentin Deluermoz, 'The IWMA and the Commune: a reassessment', trans. Angèle David-Guillou, in *Arise Ye Wretched Earth: The First International in a Global Perspective*, ed. Fabrice Bensimon, Quentin Deluermoz and Jeanne Moisand (Leiden: Brill, 2018), pp. 107–126; Tombs, 'How bloody was la semaine Sanglante?'; A. Nepomniachtchi, 'Elisabeth Dmitrieva sur les barricades de la Commune', *Études Soviétiques*, 204 (1965), pp. 65–67; Monty Johnstone, 'The Paris Commune and Marx's conception of the dictatorship of the proletariat', *Massachusetts Review*, 12:3 (1971), pp. 447–462.

4   *Enquête Parlementaire*, vol. 1, p. 165; Emile Marie Caro, 'La République et les républicains', *Revue des Deux Mondes*, 93 (1871), pp. 516–546, quotes at pp. 521, 531 and 546.

5   *Documents Diplomatiques Français, Ministère des Affaires étrangères* (Paris: Imprimerie Nationale, 1930), vol. 1, 21 April 1872, p. 146; Charles Sowerwine, *France Since 1870: Culture, Society and the Making of the Republic* (Basingstoke: Palgrave, 2009), pp. 25–29; Clive Emsley, *Gendarmes and the State in Nineteenth Century Europe* (Oxford: Oxford University Press, 1999), p. 140.

6   Witzig, 'Bismarck et la Commune'; Otto von Bismarck, *The Man and the Statesman: Being the Reflections and Reminiscences of Otto von Bismarck*, trans. A. J. Butler (Stuttgart: Buchhandlung, 1898), vol. 2, pp. 248–252.

7   August Bebel, *My Life* (Chicago: University of Chicago Press, 1913), pp. 223–233; Robert Justin Goldstein, *Political Repression in Nineteenth Century Europe* (London: Routledge, 2016), pp. 249–251; IISH: ARCH 02927 – Report, 10 April 1875; T. V. Ravindranathan, 'The Paris Commune and the First International in Italy: republicanism versus socialism, 1871–1872', *International History Review*, 3:4 (1981), pp. 482–516; Albert Garcia-Balañà, '1871 in Spain', in *Arise Ye Wretched Earth*, pp. 222–237.

8   IISH: ARCH 00366, Box 3, 33, G0.3 – Baron Whettnall to Vienna minister of foreign affairs, 4 February 1872, and Report on 'Communism until the foundation of the International', 12 April 1872.

9   IISH: ARCH 000366, 33 G0.3, Box 6 – 'Liste supplementaire des étrangers auxquels l'entrée de la Belgique est interdite', May and June 1871; Box 7 – Letters exchanged between Belgian Foreign Ministry and Belgian Consulate in Geneva, 5–6 July 1871; ARCH 02927 – Lists of suspected members of the International, 17 May 1874; APPP: BA 510 – Prefect circular, 24 June 1871.

10   IISH: ARCH 000366, 33 G0.3, Box 7 – Letters exchanged between Belgian Foreign Ministry and Belgian Consulate in Geneva, 5–6 July 1871; TNA: FO 881/2044 – Granville to Lyons, 4 March 1872, Bernal to Granville, 11 March 1872, Hotham to Granville, 6 May 1872; 'The communists of London', *Daily*

Telegraph, 4 June 1872; Laura Forster, 'The Paris Commune in London and the spatial history of ideas, 1871–1900', *Historical Journal*, 62:4 (2019), pp. 1021–1044; Liang, *The Rise of Modern Police*, pp. 86–89.

11 *Hansard*, 2 and 9 June 1871, col. 1776; Michael Pratt, 'A fallen idol: the impact of the Franco-Prussian War on the perception of Germany by British intellectuals', *International History Review*, 7:4 (1985), pp. 545–575; Michèle Martin, 'Conflictual imaginaries: Victorian illustrated periodicals and the Franco-Prussian War (1870–1871)', *Victorian Periodical Review*, 36:1 (2003), pp. 41–58.

12 Samuel Bernstein, 'The First International and the great powers', *Science and Society*, 16:3 (1952), pp. 247–272.

13 P. Martinez, 'A police spy and the exiled Communards, 1871–1873', *English Historical Review*, 97:382 (1982), pp. 99–112.

14 Bernard H. Moss, 'Police spies and labor militants after the Commune', *European and Working-Class History*, 5 (1974), pp. 16–19; Allan Mitchell, 'The xenophobic style: French counterespionage and the emergence of the Dreyfus affair', *Journal of Modern History*, 3 (1980), pp. 414–425.

15 Martin A. Miller, 'Ideological conflicts in Russian populism: the revolutionary manifestoes of the Chaikovsky circles, 1869–1874', *Slavic Review*, 29:1 (1970), pp. 1–21; Sergei Kravchinsky, *Underground Russia: Revolutionary Profiles and Sketches from Life* (New York: Lovell and C., 1883), p. 13.

16 Nikitenko, *The Diary of a Russian Censor*, 5 July 1871, p. 347; *Letters of Fyodor Mikhailovich Dostoyevsky to His Family and Friends*, trans. Ethel Colburn Mayne (London: Chatto and Windus, 1917) – letter to Apollon Nikolayevitch Maikov, 25 March 1870, p. 182; Frederic S. Zuckerman, *The Tsarist Secret Police in Russian Society, 1880–1917* (Basingstoke: Palgrave, 1996), pp. 20–21; Jeffrey Meyers, 'Portraits of a terrorist: Dostoevsky, Conrad and Coetzee', *Antioch Review*, 72:1 (2014), pp. 61–80; McClellan, *Revolutionary Exiles*, pp. 177–181, and the quote on Dmitrieff on p. 157.

17 Fyodor Dostoevsky, *The Possessed*, trans. Constance Garnett (London: William Heinemann, 1914), pp. 9–10; Nikitenko, *The Diary of a Russian Censor*, 22 and 30 July and 28 August 1871, p. 348; McClellan, *Revolutionary Exiles*, pp. 176–180.

18 'Summary of agreement concluded between Count Levachov and the police prefecture of Paris in regard to the arrest of one Nechaev', 9 July 1872, quoted in Liang, *The Rise of Modern Police*, pp. 115–116.

19 Nikitenko, *The Diary of a Russian Censor*, 27 March 1872, p. 351; Meijer, *Knowledge and Revolution*, pp. 85–90, 100–104; McClelland, *Revolutionary Exiles*, pp. 98–200; Pomper, *Sergei Nechaev*, pp. 170–171; *Moscow Gazette* summarised in *Journal de-Saint Pétersbourg*, 17 January 1873.

20 Kravchinsky, *Underground Russia*, p. 31; Peter Kropotkin, *Must We Occupy Ourselves with an Examination of the Ideal of a Future System?* (1872), quoted in Miller, 'Ideological conflicts in Russian populism', pp.

11–12; Anne Peddler, 'Going to the people: the Russian narodniki in 1874–5', *Slavonic Review*, 6:16 (1927), pp. 130–141.

21   Kravchinsky, *Underground Russia*, p. 34; Minister of Justice Count Pahlen's report and Minister of Education Dmitri Tolstoy's circular, in Vera Broido, *Apostles into Terrorists: Women and the Revolutionary Movement in the Russia of Alexander II* (New York: Viking, 1977), pp. 94–95; Daly, *Autocracy Under Siege*, pp. 21–23.

IX. Murder triumphant

1   'Attentat auf den Kaiser', *Berliner Börsen-Zeitung*, 3 June 1878; 'Das zweite attentat', *Berliner Tageblatt*, 3 June 1878.

2   Singer, *Spies and Traitors*, pp. 96–97; Ernest Alfred Vizetelly, *The Anarchists: Their Faith and Their Record* (London: Allen Lane, 1911), pp. 56–57; Andrew R. Carlson, 'Anarchism and terror in the German Empire, 1870–1890', in *Social Protest, Violence and Terror in Nineteenth- and Twentieth-Century Europe*, ed. Wolfgang J. Mommsen and Gerhard Hirschfeld (Basingstoke: Macmillan, 1982), pp. 175–200, at pp. 179–181.

3   APPP: BA 944 – Report from Geneva, 13 April 1872; Stepniak, *Underground Russia*, p. 13; Marx called Bakunin and Cluseret 'asses' following the Lyon uprising – *MECW*, vol. 44, Marx to Beesley, 19 October 1870, p. 88; Alexandre Skirda, *Facing the Enemy: A History of Anarchist Organization from Proudhon to May 1968*, trans. Paul Sharkey (Edinburgh: AK Press, 2002), pp. 23–30.

4   APPP: BA 1015 – Cluseret bio summary (undated), report, 21 January 1872, Report to Lombard, 28 June 1873, and 'Manifeste du General Cluseret', March 1874; 'Spanish horror of the Commune and of Cluseret', *New National Era*, 10 April 1873; Robert Lynn Fuller, *The Origins of the French Nationalist Movement, 1886–1914* (Jefferson: MacFarland, 2012), p. 165.

5   Richard Drake, *Apostles and Agitators: Italy's Marxist Revolutionary Tradition* (Cambridge: Harvard University Press, 2003), pp. 39–41; quote on Malatesta from Kropotkin, *Memoirs*, p. 201; Bakunin quote from Marshall, *Demanding the Impossible*, p. 305.

6   Stepniak, *The Russian Storm Cloud* (London: Swan, 1886), p. 101.

7   Fleming, *The Geography of Freedom*, pp. 112–129, quote on p. 113.

8   Stepniak, *Underground Russia*, pp. 23–38, quotes pp. 27, 37–38; Claudia Verhoeven, 'Time of terror, terror of time: on the impatience of Russian revolutionary terrorism (early 1860s – early 1880s)', *Jahrbücher für Geschichte Osteuropas*, 58 (2010), pp. 254–273.

9   Zasulich, *Memoirs*, in *Five Sisters*, ed. Engel and Rosenthal, pp. 81–84.

10   Stepniak, *Underground Russia*, pp. 44–45; John A. Lynn, *Another Kind of War: The Nature and History of Terrorism* (New Haven: Yale University

Press, 2019), pp. 137–138; Hingley, *The Russian Secret Police*, pp. 59–60; Daly, *Autocracy Under Siege*, pp. 23–24.

11 Sageman, *Turning to Political Violence*, pp. 194–196.

12 Nunzio Pernicone, *Italian Anarchism, 1864–1892* (Princeton: Princeton University Press, 1993), pp. 148–149; James Joll, *The Anarchists* (London: Methuen, 1979), pp. 105–107; 'Attack on a procession', *Daily Telegraph*, 11 February 1878; *Provinzial-Correspondenz*, no. 21, 22 May 1878.

13 George Richard Esenwein, *Anarchist Ideology and the Working-Class Movement in Spain, 1868–1898* (Berkeley: University of California Press, 1989), pp. 64–67; Vernon L. Lidtke, *Outlawed Party: Social Democracy in Germany, 1878–1890* (Princeton: Princeton University Press, 1966), pp. 72–73.

14 Hingley, *The Russian Secret Police*, pp. 60–68.

15 Quotes from *The Terrorist Struggle* and *Terrorism and Routine* are reproduced in Miller, *The Foundations of Modern Terrorism*, pp. 70–74. For Karakozov and Nechaev's influence on People's Will see Verhoeven, 'The making of Russian revolutionary terrorism', pp. 99–116; David Footman, *Red Prelude: A Life of A. I. Zhelyabov* (London: Cresset, 1944), pp. 165–167. For a comparison with Al Qaeda's doctrines, see 'Knights under the Prophet's banner', in Laura Mansfield, trans. and ed., *In His Own Words: A Translation of the Writings of Dr Ayman Al Zawahiri* (Morrisville: Lulu, 2006).

16 Vera Figner, *Memoirs of a Revolutionist* (DeKalb: Northern Illinois University Press, 1991), pp. 75–86, quotes at pp. 75, 80; Lee B. Croft, *Nikolai Ivanovich Kibalchich: Terrorist Rocket Pioneer* (Tempe: Institute for Issues in the History of Science, 2006), pp. 69–72.

17 Hingley, *Nihilists*, pp. 96–115.

18 Richard Bach Jensen, *The Battle Against Anarchist Terrorism: An International History, 1878–1934* (Cambridge: Cambridge University Press, 2014), pp. 68–69; Michael J. Hughes, 'British opinion and Russian terrorism in the 1880s', *European History Quarterly*, 42:2 (2011), pp. 255–277; Liang, *The Rise of Modern Police*, p. 120; Louis Andrieux, *Souvenirs d'un Préfet de Police* (Paris: Rouff, 1885), vol. 2, pp. 124–125; APPP: BA1098 – Interrogation report of Ivan Golovin; 'Russie', *Le Temps*, 19 November 1879; 'Alleged nihilist plots in England', *Daily News*, 8 January 1881.

19 Richard Pipes, *The Degaev Affair: Terror and Treason in Tsarist Russia* (New Haven: Yale University Press, 2003), p. 41; 'The Russian terror', *Pall Mall Gazette*, 1 May 1879; 'Russie', *L'Intransigeant*, 8 October 1880; Nechaev, *Catechism*; FRUS – Hoffman to Evarts, no. 552, 19 February 1880.

20 'The war on terrorism', *New York Times*, 2 April 1881; Sergei Witte, *The Memoirs of Count Witte*, trans. Abraham Yarmolinsky (London: William Heineman, 1921), pp. 22–24.

21 Stepniak, *Underground Russia*, p. 257; 'Ultimatum to Tsar Alexander III', 10

March 1881, Letter from Alexander to Vladimir, 9 May 1881, Grand Duke Vladimir's declaration of Tsar Alexander's Manifesto, 21 May 1881, all in Charles Lowe, *Alexander III of Russia* (New York: Macmillan, 1895), p. 72 and pp. 60–62; Alexander Polunov, 'Konstantin Petrovich Pobedonostsev – man and politician', *Russian Studies in History*, 39:4 (2001), pp. 8–32; Sarah J. Young, ed. and trans., *Writing Resistance: Revolutionary Memoir of Shlissel'burg Prison, 1884–1906* (London: University College London Press, 2021), pp. 5–9.

22 Stephen Lukashevich, 'The Holy Brotherhood, 1881–1883', *American Slavic and East European Review*, 18:4 (1959), pp. 491–509; Andrieux, *Souvenirs*, pp. 119–123; 'To protect the Czar', *Chicago Tribune*, 30 October 1881.

23 'Latest intelligence', *The Times*, 16 April 1881; Kropotkin, *Memoirs*, p. 245; Footman, *Red Prelude*, pp. 205–228.

24 Figner, *Memoirs of a Revolutionist*, p. 123; Derek Offord, *The Russian Revolutionary Movement in the 1880s* (Cambridge: Cambridge University Press, 1986), pp. 39–42.

X. The dynamite lesson

1 'Meeting of revolutionary delegates', *Daily Telegraph*, 19 July 1881; 'Freedom is in danger', *Daily Telegraph*, 27 July 1881; 'Meeting of the revolutionary congress', *Daily News*, 19 July 1881; 'Congrès socialiste universel', *Le Précurseur*, 17 August 1881; *Hansard*, 25 July 1881, vol. 263, col. 1743; Hermia Oliver, *The International Anarchist Movement in Late Victorian London* (New York: St Martin's Press, 1983), pp. 10–16; Jensen, *The Battle Against Anarchist Terrorism*, pp. 16–17.

2 Quotes on Kropotkin are taken from Fleming, *The Geography of Freedom*, p. 133, and Nechaev, *Catechism*; For propaganda of the deed's origins, see Dan Colson, 'Propaganda of the deed: anarchism, violence and the representational impulse', *American Studies*, 56:1 (2017), pp. 163–186.

3 Quotes from the congress are taken from: Butterworth, *The World That Never Was*, pp. 165–167; Joll, *The Anarchists*, p. 109; Woodcock, *Anarchism*, pp. 240–242; Constance Bantman, 'Internationalism without an International? Cross-Channel anarchist networks, 1880–1914', *Revue Belge de Philologie et d'Histoire*, 84:4 (2006), pp. 961–981.

4 'Dynamite: Professor Mezzeroff discusses it and other explosives', *Labor Enquirer*, 23 June 1883; 'Classes in dynamite throwing', *New York Times*, 7 April 1884; Louis Adamic, *Dynamite: A Century of Class Violence in America, 1830–1930* (London: Rebel Press, 1984), pp. 29–31.

5 Joseph A. Daccus, *Annals of the Great Strikes* (Chicago: L. T. Palmer, 1877), p. 235; 'Plain words with strikers', *Chicago Tribune*, 27 July 1877; Eric Foner, *Reconstruction: America's Unfinished Revolution, 1863–1877*

(New York: Harper Perennial, 1988), pp. 512–523; Richard Maxwell Brown, *Historical Studies of American Violence and Vigilantism* (New York: Oxford University Press, 1975), p. 34; O'Hara, *Inventing the Pinkertons*, pp. 56–63.

6   'Anxious for lower rents', *New York Tribune*, 8 May 1883; 'Wanted: a thousand pupils', *New York Sun*, 7 April 1884; 'Dynamitist humbug', *Washington Post*, 16 April 1883; 'More terrible than dynamite', *Eureka Daily Sentinel*, 19 April 1883; 'A dangerous man', *Daily Astorian*, 1 May 1883.

7   *Hansard*, 4 June 1869, vol. 196, cols 1239–1242; R. W. Kostal, 'Rebels in the dock: the prosecution of the Dublin Fenians, 1865–66', *Irish-American Cultural Institute*, 34:4 (1999), pp. 70–96; Shane Kenna, *Jeremiah O'Donovan Rossa: Unrepentant Fenian* (Newbridge: Merrion, 2015), pp. 66–89.

8   Niall Whelehan, '"Cheap as soap and common as sugar": the Fenians, dynamite and scientific warfare', in *The Black Hand of Republicanism: Fenianism in Modern Ireland*, ed. Fearghal McGarry and James McConnell (Dublin: Irish Academic Press, 2009), pp. 105–120; James P. Rodechko, 'An Irish-American journalist and Catholicism: Patrick Ford of the Irish world', *Church History*, 39:4 (1970), pp. 524–540; Shane Kenna, *War in the Shadows: The Irish-American Fenians Who Bombed Victorian Britain* (Newbridge: Merrion, 2014), pp. 6–8; Devoy to Reynolds, 11 April 1881 – *Devoy's Postbag*, ed. William O'Brien and Desmond Ryan (Dublin: Academy Press, 1979), vol. 2, p. 67.

9   'England's fear', *Irish World*, 13 April 1878; 'The Irish revolutionists', *New York Times*, 2 July 1880; 'The United Irishmen', 16 July 1880 and 'O'Donovan Rossa's Skirmishing Fund', 3 July 1880, *New York Sun*; Whelehan, *The Dynamiters*, pp. 75–77.

10   TNA: FO 424/69 – Crump to Thornton, 5 April 1878; England's resources of civilization', *Irish World*, 16 August 1882; Whelehan, *The Dynamiters*, p. 78; Richard Knowles Morris, 'John P. Holland and the Fenians', *Galway Archaeological and Historical Society*, 31:1/2 (1964), pp. 25–38.

11   K. R. M. Short, *The Dynamite War: Irish American Bombers in Victorian Britain* (Atlantic Highlands: Humanities Press, 1979), pp. 50–55.

12   TNA: FO 5/1351 – British Consulate to FO, 22 February 1871; 'London, Friday 14 January', *The Times*, 14 January 1881; 'Attempt to blow up the Mansion House', *Daily Telegraph*, 18 March 1881; *Hansard*, 17 March 1881, vol. 259, cols 1247–1250; 'An atrocious outrage', *Belfast Newsletter*, 18 March 1881; 'Echoes of the weeks', *Newcastle Courant*, 18 March 1881; 'Fenian conspiracy', *Liverpool Mercury*, 17 January 1881; 'Attempt to blow up the Mansion House', *Huddersfield Chronicle*, 19 March 1881; TNA: MEPO 3/3070 – Scotland Yard memo, 15 April 1881, 'A Division posts for the protection of public buildings'.

13   TNA: HO 144/81/A5846 – Campbell Brown to Harcourt, 4 July 1881; Ian Jones, *London: Bombed, Blitzed and Blown Up: The British Capital Under Attack Since 1867* (Barnsley: Frontline, 2016), pp. 20–21.

14   'The revolutionary propaganda of Europe', *Essex Standard*, 2 April 1881; 'Fenian threats', *Portsmouth Evening News*, 13 April 1881; 'Freedom is in danger', *Daily Telegraph*, 27 July 1881; 'Fenianisnim is assuming alarming proportions', *Huddersfield Chronicle*, 13 June 1881; 'France', *The Times*, 9 May 1882; *United Irishman* quoted in 'The United Irishman', *Cheltenham Chronicle*, 9 August 1881; 'The mysterious explosions', *Cheshire Observer*, 18 June 1881.

15   O'Donovan Rossa's disavowal of a Fenian–nihilist connection was made with the broad caveat that the UIA supported 'the righteous and hon-ourable resistance of people inhumanely treated' – 'The revolutionary convention at Chicago', *Manchester Guardian*, 11 August 1881. Quotes are from 'Infernal machines', *Chicago Tribune*, 2 August 1881; William Edwin Adams, *Memoirs of a Social Atom* (London: Hutchinson, 1903), pp. 564–565; 'The United Irishman', *Reynold's Newspaper*, 7 August 1881; Whelehan, *The Dynamiters*, pp. 83–84.

16   'A dynamite circular', 16 September 1883, *Parnell Commission Report with Complete Index and Notes* (London: Irish Loyal and Patriotic Union, 1890), p. 139; Henri Le Caron, *Twenty-Five Years of Secret Service* (London: William Heinemann, 1892), p. 217; Devoy to Ford, 10 April 1881, and Sullivan to Devoy, 2 September 1882, in *Devoy's Postbag*, pp. 62–67, 131–132; Gillian O'Brien, 'Methodology and martyrs: Irish American republicanism in the late nineteenth century', in *Critical Concepts: Terrorism and Literature*, ed. Peter C. Herman (Cambridge: Cambridge University Press, 2018), pp. 70–89.

17   Kenna, *Jeremiah O'Donovan Rossa*, pp. 168–169; 'The people on the crime', *New York Times*, 9 May 1882; 'The assassinations in Dublin', *The Times*, 16 May 1882; 'O'Donovan Rossa and the assassination', *Derby Daily Telegraph*, 13 May 1882.

18   'Irish agitators in New York', *The Times*, 12 April 1884; 'The attempt to damage the Mansion House', *The Standard*, 15 May 1882; 'Latest news', *Freeman's Journal*, 15 May 1882; 'The Dublin murders', *Western Mail*, 15 May 1882; 'Terrible explosions in Glasgow', *Glasgow Herald*, 22 January 1883; Joseph McKenna, *The Irish-American Dynamite Campaign: A History, 1881–1896* (Jefferson: McFarland, 2012), pp. 18–20.

19   Whelehan, *The Dynamiters*, pp. 159–162. For a detailed overview of the cam-paign see Short, *The Dynamite War*, pp. 102–124, 160–163, 178–179, and for the Clan's entry see pp. 125–127; see also Kenna, *War in the Shadows*, ch. 6.

20   'Extraordinary alarm in London', *Freeman's Journal*, 19 December 1883; TNA: MEPO 3/3070 – Jenkinson memo, 31 May 1884, Central Office memo, 17 March 1886; 'Dynamite scare at Cardiff', *Western Mail*, 30 December 1883.

21   'The railway explosions', *Daily Telegraph*, 5 November 1883; 'Meeting of the dynamite faction in New York', *Daily News*, 4 July 1883.

Notes

22 Ray Wilson and Ian Adams, *Special Branch: A History, 1883–2006* (London: Biteback, 2015), pp. 45–54; Rupert Allason, *The Branch: A History of the Metropolitan Police Special Branch, 1883–1983* (London: Secker and Warburg, 1983), pp. 6–12; Porter, *The Origins of the Vigilant State*, pp. 45–49.
23 Le Caron, *Twenty-Five Years*, pp. 246–247; extract from *Irish World* in *Parnell Commission Report*, p. 73; Clutterbuck, 'The progenitors of modern terrorism'.

XI. Thoughts that light fires

1 See Allan Pinkerton, *Strikers, Communists, Tramps and Detectives* (New York: Carleton, 1878), quotes at pp. 67 and 88; 'Progress of the strikes', *Lancaster Intelligencer*, 4 May 1886; James Green, *Death in the Haymarket: A Story of Chicago, the First Labor Movement and the Bombing That Divided Gilded Age America* (New York: Anchor, 2006), pp. 148–168.
2 'Anarchists called to arms', *New York Times*, 5 May 1886; 'The work of the bomb', *New York Times*, 6 May 1886; 'Testimony of Capt. William Ward' – *The People of the State of Illinois vs. August Spies et al.*, 20 July 1886, court transcript consulted via the website of the Chicago Historical Society, http://www.chicagohistoryresources.org/hadc/transcript/trialtoc.htm; 'Speech of Samuel Fielden' – *The Accused, the Accusers: The Famous Speeches of the Eight Chicago Anarchists in Court* (Chicago: Socialistic Publishing Society, 1886), pp. 66–67, also consulted at the website of the Chicago Historical Society.
3 Two of the more polarised accounts are Paul Avrich, *The Haymarket Tragedy* (Princeton: Princeton University Press, 1984) and Timothy Messer-Kruse, *The Haymarket Conspiracy: Transatlantic Anarchist Networks* (Urbana: University of Illinois Press, 2012).
4 'Policemen killed by bombs', *New York Tribune*, 5 May 1886; 'The red flag unseen', *New York Tribune*, 10 May 1886; 'The usual lies', *Labor Enquirer*, 15 May 1886; quotes from *Le Cri du Peuple* and *Le Révolté* are taken from Hubert Perrier, Catherine Collomp, Michel Cordillot and Marianne Debouzy, 'The "Social Revolution" in America? European reactions to the "Great Upheaval" and the Haymarket affair', *International Labor and Working-Class History*, 29 (1986), pp. 38–52.
5 'Nihilist Hartman', *Washington Post*, 6 August 1881; 'Hartman, the nihilist', *New York Times*, 19 August 1881; 'Lev Hartman', *Lancaster Intelligencer*, 2 August 1881; 'Hartman', *New York Tribune*, 5 August 1881; David O. Stowell, *Streets, Railroads and the Great Strike of 1877* (Chicago: Chicago University Press, 1999).
6 FRUS – Sickles to Fish, no. 405, 17 May 1873, Fish to Evarts, no. 458, 2 December 1878; APPP: BA 1015 – Reports, 9 July 1871 and 21 January 1872;

Hiram C. Whitley, *In It* (Cambridge: Riverside Press, 1894), p. 102. For an overview of white supremacist terrorism in the 1870s see Michael Fellman, *In the Name of God and Country: Reconsidering Terrorism in American History* (New Haven: Yale University Press, 2010), pp. 97–142; Elaine Frantz Parsons, *Ku Klux: The Birth of the Klan During Reconstruction* (Chapel Hill: University of North Carolina Press, 2003), pp. 39–53, 144–180; Mitchell Snay, *Fenians, Freedmen and Southern Whites: Race and Nationality in the Era of Reconstruction* (Baton Rouge: Louisiana State University Press, 2007), pp. 10–12. For the Secret Service's battle against the Klan, see Charles Lane, *Freedom's Detective: The Secret Service, the Ku Klux Klan and the Man Who Masterminded America's First War on Terror* (New York: Hanover Square Press, 2019).

7   Robert F. Zeidel, *Robber Barons and Wretched Refuse: Ethnic and Class Dynamics During the Era of American Industrialization* (Ithaca: Cornell University Press, 2020), pp. 61–82; Irving Werstein, *Strangled Voices: The Story of the Haymarket Affair* (New York: Macmillan, 1970), pp. 1–12.

8   Walter Laqueur, *A History of Terrorism* (New Brunswick: Transaction, 2006), pp. 56–57. Quotes are from Johann Most, *The Beast of Property* (1884), *The Science of Revolutionary Warfare* (1885) and *Action as Propaganda* (1894), consulted via the Anarchist Library online, https://www.theanarchistlibrary.org.

9   Most, *Revolutionary Warfare*; IISH: ARCH 30066, Box 7, 33 Go.3 – Report to Baron Solvyne, 18 October 1879; Frederic Trautman, *The Voice of Terror: A Biography of Johann Most* (Westport: Greenwood Press, 1980), pp. 39–41; Elun T. Gabriel, *Assassins and Conspirators: Anarchism, Socialism and Political Culture in Germany* (Ithaca: Cornell University Press, 2014), pp. 27–28.

10 *Freiheit*, 18 December 1880, 8 January 1881 and 19 March 1881. For Hödel and Nobiling see *Freiheit*, 8 November 1884. For Heinzen see *Freiheit*, 18 March 1883. See also John Quail, *The Slow Burning Fuse: The Lost History of the British Anarchists* (London: Freedom Press, 2019), pp. 28–32.

11 'Saturday', *Evening Telegraph*, 2 April 1881; Marx to Sorge, 5 November 1880, 'Unpublished letters of Karl Marx and Friedrich Engels to Americans', ed. and trans. Leonard E. Mins, *Science and Society*, 2:3 (1938), pp. 348–375. See also A. G. Gardiner, *The Life of William Harcourt* (London: Constable, 1923), vol. 1, p. 404; Bernard Porter, 'The *Freiheit* prosecutions, 1881–1882', *Historical Journal*, 23:4 (1980), pp. 833–856; Richard J. Aldrich and Rory Cormac, *The Secret Royals: Spying and the Crown from Victoria to Diana* (London: Atlantic, 2021), ch. 6.

12 TNA: HO 45/9355/29553 – 'Testimony of Detective-Sergeant George Greenham', 24 December 1873; 'The communist refugees in London', *Morning Post*, 16 December 1873; TNA: HO 144/77/A3385 – 'Transcript of the trial of Johann Most', 23 May 1881; *Hansard*, 17 March 1881, vol. 259,

cols 1247–1250, 12 May 1881, vol. 261, col. 265, 25 July 1881, vol. 263, col. 1743; 'Prosecution of the *Freiheit* journal', *Daily News*, 1 April 1881.

13 Trautman, *The Voice of Terror*, p. 69; 'Meeting of the Revolutionary Congress', *Daily News*, 19 July 1881; *Freiheit*, 4 April 1881; Most, *The Beast of Property*.

14 'A bearer of the red flag', 19 December 1882 and 'An anarchist sanctum', 5 December 1885, *New York Sun*; 'Herr Most's ravings', *New York Times*, 9 April 1883; 'Parnell and Lady Dixie', *Indianapolis Journal*, 6 April 1883; 'Chemical and mental dynamite', *San Antonio Light*, 8 June 1883; Trautman, *The Voice of Terror*, p. 87.

15 'Cause and cure of cholera', *New York Tribune*, 14 August 1885; *Freiheit*, 2–23 June 1883; 'A dynamite professor gets a thrashing', *Indianapolis Journal*, 3 February 1885; 'Is this Mezzeroff?', *New York Sun*, 2 February 1885; 'Correspondencia de Nueva-York', *La Correspondencia de Puerto Rico*, 15 September 1895; Messer-Kruse, *The Haymarket Conspiracy*, p. 109.

16 Helene Minkin, *Storm in My Heart: Memories of the Widow of Johann Most*, ed. Tom Goyens, trans. Alisa Braun (Oakland: AK Press, 2015), p. 30; TNA: HO 144/77/A3385 – 'Translations of *Freiheit*', August–December 1882; *Neueste Mittheilungen*, 9 July 1883, p. 2.

17 'Panclastitis', *Sacramento Daily Record Union*, 31 March 1883; 'Not very complimentary', *Seattle Daily Post Intelligencer*, 20 December 1882; 'Herr Most says the coronation of the Czar will not take place', *Indianapolis Journal*, 9 February 1883; 'The Czar in Moscow', *Daily Telegraph*, 4 June 1883; 'Herr Most again heard from', *Los Angeles Herald*, 25 March 1883; 'The anarchists in Switzerland', *Indianapolis Journal*, 23 July 1885; 'Herr Most', *Morning Appeal*, 3 January 1883'; 'King-killers in a riot', *New York Times*, 3 February 1885; IISH: ARCH 00366 – Box 7, Letter to Baron Solvyns, 17 March 1886.

18 'The Pittsburgh Proclamation', 16 October 1883, in Lucy E. Parsons, *The Life of Robert R. Parsons, with a Brief History of the Labor Movement in America* (Chicago: Parsons, 1889), pp. 19–22, pp. 39–40; Chester McDestler, 'Shall Red and Black unite? An American revolutionary document of 1883', *Pacific Historical Review*, 14:4 (1945), pp. 434–451; Tom Goyens, *Beer and Revolution: The German Anarchist Movement in New York City, 1880–1914* (Chicago: University of Illinois Press, 2007), pp. 102–108.

19 'Most advertises his wares', *New York Times*, 24 April 1886; 'Rioting and bloodshed on the streets of Chicago', *New York Times*, 5 May 1886; Spies quote from Green, *Death in the Haymarket*, p. 141; Messer-Kruse, *The Haymarket Conspiracy*, pp. 96–97; Avrich, *The Haymarket Tragedy*, pp. 133–135.

20 'Most in police hands', *New York Times*, 12 May 1886; Francis X. Busch, 'The Haymarket riot and the trial of the anarchists', *Journal of the Illinois State Historical Society*, 48:3 (1955), pp. 247–270, at p. 254.

21 Quotes: 'Dynamite', *The Alarm*, 21 February 1885; 'People's Exhibit 90, *Arbeiter-Zeitung* editorial, 21 April 1886' – *The People of the State of Illinois vs. August Spies et al.*, 20 July 1886, Chicago Historical Society, https://www.chicagohistoryresources.org/hadc/transcript/trialtoc.htm; Busch, 'The Haymarket riot', pp. 261–262; Ann Larabee, *The Wrong Hands: Popular Weapons Manuals and Their Historic Challenges to Democratic Society* (Oxford: Oxford University Press, 2015), pp. 15–16.

22 Hartmut Keil, 'The impact of Haymarket on German-American radicalism', *International Labor and Working-Class History*, 29 (1986), pp. 16–27, quotes at pp. 17–18; 'A preacher of an anarchy', *Argus*, 8 May 1886; 'The unrest of labor', *National Republican*, 10 May 1886.

23 'Inconsistency', *Washington Star*, 10 May 1886; 'A dynamiter's opinion', *Omaha Daily Bee*, 17 May 1886.

24 Molly Amman and J. Reid Meloy, 'Stochastic terrorism: a linguistic and psychological analysis', *Perspectives on Terrorism*, 15:5 (2021), pp. 2–12; IISH: ARCH 01054 – Josef Peukert papers, 61 – Spies to Peukert, 26 October 1886; IISH: ARCH 00366, 33 Go.3, Box 7 – Letter from Van der Velde to Baron Solvyns, 18 March 1886.

XII. No one is safe

1 'Paris au jour du jour', *La Petite Presse*, 24 October 1881; 'Nouvelles diverses', *Journal des débats politiques et littéraires*, 23 October 1881; 'Compagnons anarchiste', *L'Hydre anarchiste*, 9 March 1884; Kropotkin, *Memoirs*, p. 258; Grave quote from Caroline Cahm, *Kropotkin and the Rise of Revolutionary Anarchism, 1872–1886* (Cambridge: Cambridge University Press, 1989), pp. 178–179.

2 FRUS – Sargent to Frelinghuysen, no. 189, 19 March 1883; 'Lettres d'Allemagne', *La Justice*, 4 April 1882; Lukas Keller, 'Beyond the "People's Community": the anarchist movement from the fin de siècle to the First World War in Germany', in *Anarchism, 1914–1918: Internationalism, Anti-Militarism and War*, ed. Matthew S. Adams and Ruth Kina (Manchester: Manchester University Press, 2017), pp. 95–113; Elun Gabriel, 'The left liberal critique of anarchism in Imperial Germany', *German Studies Review*, 33:2 (2010), pp. 331–350.

3 Carlson, 'Anarchism and terror', pp. 188–190; Bantman, 'Internationalism without an International?'; Tom Goyens, 'Johann Most and anarchist violence', Paper presented at the 33rd Annual North American Labor History Conference, Wayne State University, Detroit (October, 2012); Elun Gabriel, 'Anarchism's appeal to German workers, 1878–1914', *Journal for the Study of Radicalism*, 5:1 (2011), pp. 33–65.

4 Joll, *The Anarchists*, p. 112; 'The outrage at the Paris bourse', *The Standard*, 8 March 1886; 'Les procès de demain', *Le Petit Journal*, 26 June 1886.

Notes

5 'Le procès Gallo', *Le Petit Parisien*, 28 June 1886; *Le Figaro*'s description is taken from Gregory Shaya, 'How to make an anarchist-terrorist: an essay on the political imaginary in fin de siècle France', *Journal of Social History*, 44:2 (2010), pp. 521–543. The mental state of terrorists was debated by medical experts and the judiciary – see Edward J. Erickson, 'Punishing the mad bomber: questions of moral responsibility in the trials of French anarchist terrorists, 1886–1897', *French History*, 22:1 (2008), pp. 51–73. For the Anarchist International theory see Richard Bach Jensen, 'Daggers, rifles and dynamite: anarchist terrorism in nineteenth century Europe', *Terrorism and Political Violence*, 16:1 (2010), pp. 116–153.

6 'Meeting of the dynamite faction in New York', *Daily News*, 4 July 1883; FRUS – Sargent to Frelinghuysen, no. 189, 19 March 1883; Whitney Kassel, 'Terrorism and the international anarchist movement of the late nineteenth and early twentieth centuries', *Studies in Conflict and Terrorism*, 32:3 (2009), pp. 237–252; Alexander Sedlmaier, 'The consuming visions of late-nineteenth and early-twentieth century anarchists: actualising political violence transnationally', *European Review of History – Revue européenne d'Histoire*, 14:3 (2007), pp. 283–300.

7 Stepniak, *The Russian Storm Cloud*, pp. 177–178; Crossland, 'Radical warfare's first "superweapon"'; Lynn, *Another Kind of War*, pp. 129–134.

8 Nunzio Pernicone and Fraser M. Ottanelli, *Assassins Against the Old Order: Italian Anarchist Violence in Fin de Siècle Europe* (Urbana: University of Illinois Press, 2018), ch. 3; Julián Casanova, 'Terror and violence: the dark face of Spanish anarchism', *International Labor and Working-Class History*, 67 (2005): 79–99; 'The anarchists', *The Times*, 4 January 1894; 'Bombs thrown in a theatre', *New York Herald: European Edition*, 9 November 1893; 'La dynamite', *Gil Blas*, 12 November 1893; 'L'attentat d'Barcelone', *Le Radical*, 15 November 1893.

9 'Léauthier', *Le Figaro*, 24 February 1894; 'L'anarchiste Léauthier', *Le Petit Parisien*, 24 February 1894; 'Tribunaux', *La Liberty*, 23 February 1894. The Serbian ambassador's assailant, Leon Léauthier, was sentenced to imprisonment on Devil's Island, where he was later involved in an uprising in which he was killed, along with several other anarchists – see Yves Frémion, *Léauthier l'anarchiste: De la propagande par le fait à la Révolte des Bagnards, 1893–1894* (Paris: Echappee, 2019).

10 Edward de Burgh, *Elizabeth: Empress of Austria* (London: Hutchinson, 1899), p. 326; Olivier Hubac-Occhipinti, 'Anarchist terrorists of the nineteenth century', in *A History of Terrorism: From Antiquity to ISIS*, ed. Gérard Chaliand and Arnaud Blin (Berkeley: University of California Press, 2007), pp.113–131, at pp. 117–118. For the attack on the Prince and Princess of Wales see generally TNA: FO 10/74; Scott Miller, *The President and the Assassin: McKinley, Terror and Empire at the Dawn of the American Century* (New York: Random House, 2011) – for Bresci's influence see pp. 262–264.

Notes

11 Minkin, *Storm of My Heart*, p. 69; Alexander Berkman, *Prison Memoirs of an Anarchist* (New York: Mother Earth, 1912), pp. 32–33; 'Prepared a scale', *Wheeling Daily Intelligencer*, 29 July 1892; 'Struck by Emma Goldman', *New York Times*, 20 December 1892; 'Herr Most for the Star', *Evening World*, 6 September 1894; Emma Goldman, *Living My Life* (New York: Meridian, 1977), pp. 105–106.

12 Robert le Texier, *De Ravachol á la bande á Bonnot* (Paris: Éditions France-Empire, 1989), pp. 9–13.

13 'Supplément illustré', *Journal de la Marne*, 10 April 1892; 'Anarchist terrors', *Los Angeles Herald*, 29 March 1892; 'The anarchist Ravachol', *The Times*, 13 March 1892; Woodcock, *Anarchism*, pp. 288–291.

14 Marxists Internet Archive, 'Ravachol's forbidden defence speech' (1892), https://www.marxists.org; 'La dynamite', *Le Courrier du Nord*, 10 April 1892; 'La dynamite', *Le Matin*, 28 March 1892; 'L'arrestation de Ravachol', *Le Petit Journal*, 16 April 1892.

15 'Ravachol's last message', *Auckland Star*, 14 July 1892; 'Ravachol executed', *Tasmanian News*, 12 July 1892; 'Ravachol executed', *Morning Call*, 11 July 1892; Pomper, *Sergei Nechaev*, pp. 214–221.

16 'Paris much frightened', *New York Times*, 18 April 1892; 'La destruction du restaurant Very', *La Petit Journal*, 27 April 1892; Ernest Reynaud, *Souvenirs de police au temps de Ravachol* (Paris: Payot, 1923), pp. 288–289; Julian Bridgestock, 'Resisting with authority? Anarchist laughter and the violence of truth', *Social and Cultural Geography*, 23:2 (2022), pp. 173–191; *Le Père Peinard* quote from Merriman, *The Dynamite Club*, p. 84.

17 See various letters in APPP: BA 510; L'arrestation de Ravachol', *Le Temps*, 1 April 1892.

18 Henri Varennes, *De Ravachol á Caserio – Notes d'Audience* (Paris: Garnier Frères, 1895); 'Assassination of President Carnot', *The Times*, 25 June 1894; James Michael Yeoman, *Print Culture and the Formation of the Anarchist Movement in Spain* (London: Routledge, 2019), pp. 82–84; Merriman, *The Dynamite Club*, pp. 137–201.

19 Max Nomad, 'The anarchist tradition', in *The Revolutionary Internationals, 1864–1943*, ed. Milorad M. Drachkovitch (Palo Alto: Stanford University Press, 1966), pp. 57–92, at p. 77.

20 Alexander Varias, *Paris and the Anarchists: Aesthetes and Subversives During the Fin de Siècle* (New York: St Martin's Press, 1996), pp. 84–89; Howard S. Lay, '"Beau Geste!" On the readability of terrorism', *Yale French Studies*, 101 (2001), pp. 79–100.

21 Errico Malatesta, 'A bit of theory', in *The Method of Freedom: An Errico Malatesta Reader*, ed. Davide Turcato (Oakland: AK Press, 2014), pp. 187–192; *L'En-Dehors*, 1 May 1892.

22 Stepniak, 'The dynamite scare and anarchy', *New Review* (1892), and *The Russian Storm Cloud*, p. 17; Kropotkin and Reclus quotes are from Fleming,

The Geography of Freedom, pp. 160–161; the Michel quotes are from Michel, *The Red Virgin*, pp. 322–324. For Goldman's views see Paul Avrich and Karen Avrich, *Sasha and Emma: The Anarchist Odyssey of Alexander Berkman and Emma Goldman* (Cambridge: Harvard University Press, 2012), pp. 142–143. For Reclus and Kropotkin see Marie Fleming, 'Propaganda by the deed: terrorism and anarchist theory in late nineteenth century Europe', *Studies in Conflict and Terrorism*, 4:1–4 (1980), pp. 1–23.

23   'Émile Henry's defense', April 1894, Anarchist Library online, https://www.theanarchistlibrary.org.

XIII. Of fright and fantasy

1   'Échos la politique', *Le Figaro*, 7 August 1894; 'Les procès des trente', *L'Intransigeant*, 9 August 1894; Jean Grave, *Moribund Society and Anarchy*, trans. Voltairine de Cleyre (San Francisco: A. Isaak, 1899), pp. 117–118; Constance Bantman, 'Jean Grave and French anarchism: a relational approach', *International Review of Social History*, 62:3 (2017), pp. 451–477.

2   'Hunting the anarchists in France', *Daily News*, 3 January 1894; Albert Bataille, *Causes Criminelles et mondaines de 1894: les procès Anarchistes* (Paris: E. Dentu, 1895), p. 13; Richard D. Sonn, *Anarchism* (Woodbridge: Twayne, 1992), pp. 20–26; Constance Bantman, *Jean Grave and the Networks of French Anarchism, 1854–1939* (London: Palgrave, 2021), pp. 98–101.

3   Louis Patsouras, *The Anarchism of Jean Grave* (Montreal: Black Rose Books, 2007), pp. 60–66; Fleming, *The Geography of Freedom*, pp. 173–179; *Le Journal*, 22 September 1897, cited in Thomas, *Louise Michel*, p. 352; Malatesta, *L'Anarchia*, part 1 (1994), Anarchist Library online, https://www.theanarchistlibrary.org; Bataille, *Causes Criminelles*, p. 13; Constance Bantman, 'Louise Michel's London years: a political re-assessment', *Women's History Review*, 26:6 (2017), pp. 994–1012.

4   Félix Dubois, *The Anarchist Peril*, ed. and trans. Ralph Derechef (London: Fisher and Unwin, 1894), pp. 173–176; Camille Mauclair, *Le Soleil des Morts* – in Sonn, *Anarchism*, p. 253; Mary Burgoyne, 'Conrad among the anarchists: documents on Martial Bourdin and the Greenwich bombing', *The Conradian*, 31:1 (2007), pp. 147–185.

5   'The fatal explosion of a bomb at Greenwich', *Liverpool Mercury*, 17 February 1894; TNA: HO 144/257/A55660 – Majendie to Home Office, 27 February 1894; Webb, *Dynamite, Treason and Plot*, pp. 28–29.

6   'Latest intelligence' and 'The Greenwich explosion', *The Times*, 19 and 20 February 1894; 'The terrible death of an anarchist', *Manchester Courier*, 17 February 1894; 'Anarchism at home and abroad', *Pall Mall Gazette*, 16 February 1894; 'Martial Bourdin', *Le Matin*, 7 February 1894; 'Anarchist conspirators in London,' *Freeman's Journal*, 16 February 1894; 'Fate or

providence!', *Hull Daily Mail*, 16 February 1894; 'Anarchy and anarchists', *Reynold's Newspaper*, 4 March 1894; quote from *Liberty* in Burgoyne, 'Conrad among the anarchists', p. 156.

7   'Police raid upon the Autonomie Club', *Daily News*, 17 February 1894; Quail, *The Slow Burning Fuse*, pp. 123–144; Wilson and Adams, *Special Branch*, pp. 65–66; Andrew Cook, *M: MI5's First Spymaster* (Stroud: Tempus, 2006), pp. 132–136; Jonathan Moses, 'The texture of politics: London's anarchist clubs, 1894–1914', *RIBA* (2016), https://www.ribaj.com/intelligence/the-texture-of-politics-london-s-anarchists-clubs-1882-1914.

8   'Anarchists in London', *The Standard*, 17 February 1894; 'Bulletin de jour', *Le Temps*, 17 March 1894; 'Bombe exotique', *L'Intransigeant*, 18 March 1894; Shaya, 'How to make an anarchist-terrorist'.

9   TNA: HO 144/116/A26493G – George Dee to home secretary, 22 October 1895; Abbé Landelin Winterer, *The Social Danger, or Two Years of Socialism in Europe and America*, trans. Joseph P. Roles (Chicago: Belford, Clarke and Co., 1886), pp. 166–168; José Echegaray, 'Los explosivos', *La Lectura* (1894) cited in Jensen, *The Battle Against Anarchist Terrorism*, pp. 39–40; Alfred Nobel to Bertha von Suttner, 7 January 1893, in the World Digital Library, https://www.wdl.org/en/item/11563/.

10 Quotes: Donald McKay, *The Dynamite Ship* (New York: Manhattan Publishing, 1888), p. 155; Norman Sherry, 'The Greenwich bomb outrage and The Secret Agent', *Review of English Studies*, 18:72 (1967), pp. 412–428; Deaglán Ó Donghaile, *Blasted Literature: Victorian Political Fiction and the Shock of Modernism* (Edinburgh: Edinburgh University Press, 2011), Intro and ch.4.

11 Edward Douglas Fawcett, *Hartmann the Anarchist; or, the Doom of the Great City* (London: Edward Arnold, 1893), pp. 46, 8–11, 63, 73, 84, 77, 140, 146–147; Lawrence Freedman, *The Future of War: A History* (London: Penguin, 2018), pp. 11–23; Laqueur, *A History of Terrorism*, p. 59.

12 George Griffith, *The Angel of the Revolution: A Tale of the Coming Terror* (London: Tower, 1894), pp. 32, 183, 279–281; Taylor Stoehr, 'Words and deeds in *The Princess Casamassima*', *ELH*, 37:1 (1970), pp. 95–135; Barbara Arnett Melchiori, *Terrorism in the Late Victorian Novel* (London: Routledge, 1985), pp. 8–10.

13 Cesare Lombroso, 'The physiognomy of the anarchists', *The Monist*, 1 (1891), pp. 346–343; Sarah Cole, *At the Violet Hour: Modernism and Violence in England and Ireland* (New York: Oxford University Press, 2012), pp. 83–87.

14 'The Gladstone bag', *Los Angeles Herald*, 6 February 1892; National Library of Ireland, MS:49 491/2/145 – Vivian Majendie to Charlie Majendie, 25 May 1883; TNA: HO 45/9506/15848 – Majendie memo, 6 July 1877; TNA: WO 94/66/3 – Correspondence concerning the defence of the Tower of London, July 1885–March 1886; TNA: HO 45/9741/A55680 – Majendie to Home Office, 12 April 1894.

15 HI: XX/614 – Viktor Nikolaevich papers, folder 1, 'The work of Okhrana departments in Russia', pp. 1–8; Richard J. Johnson, 'Zagranichnaia Agentura: the tsarist political police in Europe', *Journal of Contemporary History*, 7:1/2 (1972), pp. 221–242; Rita T. Kronenbitter, 'Paris Okhrana, 1885–1905', in *Okhrana: The Paris Operations of the Russian Imperial Police*, ed. Ben B. Fischer (Washington, DC: Central Intelligence Agency, 1997), pp. 19–26; Beatrice de Graaf, 'The Black International conspiracy as security dispositive in the Netherlands, 1880–1900', *Historische Sozialforschung*, 38:1 (2013), pp. 142–165; Patrick Waddington, 'Sleazy digs and coppers' narks: the fate of Russian nihilists in Paris a hundred years ago', *New Zealand Slavonic Journal* (1989–1990), pp. 1–39; Butterworth, *World That Never Was*, pp. 299–300.

16 HI: 26001 – Russia Departament Politsii. Zagranichnaia Agentura (Paris), reel 11, Rachkovsky to prefect of Paris police, undated. For Rachkovsky's alleged involvement in the *Protocols* see Michael Hagemeister, 'The *Protocols of the Elders of Zion*: between history and fiction', *New German Critique*, 103 (2008), pp. 83–95.

17 'Sensational arrests', *Hull Daily Mail*, 8 January 1892; 'Reported anarchist conspiracy', *The Standard*, 8 January 1892; Cook, *M*, pp. 124–129; Michael C. Frank, 'Terrorism for the sake of counterterrorism: undercover policing and the spectre of the agent provocateur in Joseph Conrad's *The Secret Agent*', *Conradiana*, 46:3 (2014), pp. 151–177.

18 'Le soi-disant complot', *Le Figaro*, 15 December 1893; 'Vast anarchist conspiracy', *New York Times*, 16 February 1894; 'Another anarchist plot', *Daily Telegraph*, 5 April 1892; 'Italien', *Neueste Mittheilungen*, 6 July 1894; 'Royalty guarded at Coburg', *New York Times*, 19 April 1894; Mark Shirk, 'The universal eye: anarchist "propaganda of the deed" and the development of the modern surveillance state', *International Studies Quarterly*, 63:2 (2019), pp. 334–345; Jeffreys-Jones, *Cloak and Dollar*, pp. 46–47, 58; Andrew, *The Secret World*, pp. 430–431.

19 Jensen, *The Battle Against Anarchist Terrorism*, pp. 133–136; Butterworth, *The World That Never Was*, p. 370; 'Elizabeth of Austria is slain by an anarchist', *The Call*, 11 September 1898; 'The anti-anarchist conference', *The Times*, 19 December 1898; TNA: FO 881/7179 – 'Propositions submitted by the commission on legislative measures and approved by the conference', 22 December 1898.

20 Vincent to Salisbury, 8 December 1898, in Samuel Henry Jeyes, *The Life of Sir Howard Vincent* (London: George Allen, 1912), pp. 302–303; the Salisbury quote is from TNA/HO 10254/X36450 – Salisbury to HO, 12 October 1898; Vlad Solomon, *State Surveillance, Political Policing and Counterterrorism in Britain, 1880–1914* (London: Boydell and Brewer, 2021), pp. 182–184.

21 Jensen, 'The international anti-anarchist conference'.

XIV. All towards its end

1 HI: XX593 – *Polizeipräsidium* reports, box 1, 1 June 1901–13 July 1902, 'Roosevelt's State of the Union address', 3 December 1901.

2 'Plot to make way with M'Kinley', *Evening World*, 24 September 1901; APPP: BA 1511 – 'Banish anarchists!' and 'Goldman denied bail', 12 September 1901; 'Chicago case a parallel', *Washington Post*, 11 September 1901; Eric Rauchway, *Murdering McKinley: The Making of Theodore Roosevelt's America* (New York: Hill and Wang, 2003), pp. 88–89, 103–105.

3 'Prince Kropotkin's views', *New York Times*, 12 September 1901; Library of Congress, Radical Pamphlets Collection, Box 35 – 'Down with the Anarchists!', p. 2; 'Roosevelt's State of the Union address'; Butterworth, *The World That Never Was*, p. 373.

4 FRUS – Memo from German and Russian ambassadors, 12 December 1901; *Hansard*, 'Alien Bill', cols 768–782, 2 May 1905; Mathieu Defm, 'Wild beasts without nationality: the uncertain origins of Interpol, 1898–1910', in *The Handbook of Transnational Crime and Justice*, ed. Philip Reichel (Thousand Oaks: Sage, 2005), pp. 275–285; Diana Packer, 'Refugee or alien?', *European Judaism: A Journal for the New Europe*, 50:2 (2017), pp. 15–23; Mary S. Barton, 'The global war on anarchism: the United States and international anarchist terrorism, 1898–1904', *Diplomatic History*, 39:2 (2015), pp. 303–330.

5 James A. Baer, *Anarchist Immigrants in Spain and Argentina* (Urbana: University of Illinois Press, 2015), pp. 69–73; Constance Bantman, 'The era of propaganda of the deed', in *The Palgrave Handbook of Anarchism*, ed. Carl Ley and Matthew S. Adams (Basingstoke: Palgrave, 2018), pp. 371–387; Derry Novak, 'Anarchism and individual terrorism', *Canadian Journal of Economics and Political Science*, 20:2 (1954), pp. 176–184; Benedict R. Anderson, *Under Three Flags: Anarchism and the Anti-colonial Imagination* (New York: Verso, 2008), chs 3–4; Jensen, *The Battle Against Anarchist Terrorism*, pp. 341–351.

6 HI: XX593 – *Polizeipräsidium* reports, box 1, 26–29 June 1902, 1 July and 13 July 1902; box 2, 6–7 September 1903, box 7, 21 March 1902, 13 September 1902; Minkin, *Storm of My Heart*, pp. 120–123.

7 Boris Savinkov, *Memoirs of a Terrorist*, trans. Joseph Shaplen (New York: Albert and Charles Boni, 1931), p. 9; 'Sergius killed by a bomb' and 'Shots at Gen. Trepoff', *New York Tribune*, 16 January and 18 February 1905; Anna Geifman, *Thou Shalt Kill: Revolutionary Terrorism in Russia, 1894–1917* (Princeton: Princeton University Press, 1993), pp. 48–58; Robert Henderson, *Vladimir Burtsev and the Struggle for a Free Russia: A Revolutionary in the Time of Tsarism and Bolshevism* (London: Bloomsbury, 2017), pp. 125–126.

8 HI: XX593 – *Polizeipräsidium* reports, box 1, 15 May 1903; box 4, 5 June 1905, 20–23 November 1905 and 4 December 1905.

9   Quotes: Geifman, *Thou Shalt Kill*, p. 49. For Savinkov's novels see pp. 53–54; For his work with the British see Andrew Cook, *Ace of Spies: The True Story of Sidney Reilly* (Stroud: History Press, 2005), pp. 208–248; Law, *Terrorism*, pp. 86–89.

10 Paul Avrich, *The Russian Anarchists* (Princeton: Princeton University Press, 1971), pp. 42–54; Steven G. Marks, *How Russia Shaped the Modern World: From Art to Anti-Semitism, Ballet to Bolshevism* (Princeton: Princeton University Press, 2020), pp. 17–29; Theodore F. Friedgut, 'Jews, violence and the Russian revolutionary movement', in *Jews and Violence: Images, Ideologies, Realities*, ed. Peter Y. Medding (Oxford: Oxford University Press, 2002), pp. 43–58, at pp. 42–43; Anna Geifman, *Death Orders: The Vanguard of Modern Terrorism in Revolutionary Russia* (Santa Barbara: Praeger, 2010), pp. 42–47.

11 Witte, *Memoirs*, p. 364; Jacob Langer, 'Corruption and the counter-revolution: the rise and fall of the Black Hundred', PhD thesis (Duke University, 2007), pp. 81–85, quotes from Black Hundred propaganda pp. 46–47; Charles A. Ruud and Sergei A. Stepanov, *Fontanka 16: The Tsars' Secret Police* (Montreal: McGill University Press, 1999), pp. 106–109.

12 Dietze, *The Invention of Terrorism*, pp. 591–595; Laqueur, *A History of Terrorism*, pp. 38–43.

13 'Things are certainly moving in China', *The Times*, 26 September 1905; 'Bomb deafened Mr. Wu', *New York Times*, 9 November 1905; 'Are there Chinese anarchists?', *New York Times*, 26 September 1905; Pamela Kyle Crossley, *Orphan Warriors: Three Manchu Generations and the End of the Qing World* (Princeton: Princeton University Press, 1990), pp. 189–192.

14 Wu quote in Edward S. Krebs, *Shifu, Soul of Chinese Anarchism* (Lanham: Rowman and Littlefield, 1998), pp. 42–43; Arif Dirlik, 'Vision and revolution: anarchism in Chinese revolutionary thought on the eve of the 1911 revolution', *Modern China*, 12:2 (1986), pp. 123–165; Bantman, *Jean Grave*, pp. 160–161.

15 'Anarchism and the Spirit of the Anarchists' quote in Arif Dirlik, *Anarchism in the Chinese Revolution* (Berkeley: University of California Press, 1991), pp. 65–72; Yin Cao, 'Bombs in Beijing and Delhi: the global spread of bomb-making technology and the revolutionary terrorism in modern China and India', *Journal of World History*, 30:4 (2019), pp. 559–589; Don C. Price, *Russia and the Roots of the Chinese Revolution, 1896–1911* (Cambridge: Harvard University Press, 1974), pp. 121–122; Krebs, *Shifu*, pp. 29–31.

16 Sho Konishi, 'Reopening the "opening of Japan": Russian–Japanese revolutionary encounter and the vision of anarchist progress', *American Historical Review*, 112:1 (2007), pp. 101–130; Vladimir Tikhonov, 'A Russian radical and East Asia in the early twentieth century: Sudzilovsky, China and Japan', *Cross Currents*, 18 (2016), https://cross-currents.berkeley.edu/e-journal/issue-18/tikhonov; Ping-Cheung Lo, 'Confucian views on suicide and

their implications for euthanasia', in *Confucian Bioethics*, ed. Ruiping Fan (Dordrecht: Springer, 1999), pp. 69–101; Cao, 'Bombs in Beijing'.

17 *Bal Gangadhar Tilak: His Speeches and Writings*, ed. Babu Aurobindo Ghose (Madras: Ganesh and Co., 1922), pp. 24–25; Hitendra Patel, *Khudiram Bose: Revolutionary Extraordinaire* (New Delhi: Ministry of Information and Broadcasting, 2008), p. 17; Kim A. Wagner, *Rumours and Rebels: A New History of the Indian Uprising of 1857* (London: Peter Lang, 2017); Michael Silvestri, 'The bomb, Bhadralok, Bhagavad Gita and Dan Breen: terrorism in Bengal and its relation to the European experience', *Terrorism and Political Violence*, 21:1 (2009), pp. 1–27; Peter Heehs, 'Foreign influences on Bengali revolutionary terrorism, 1902–1908', *Modern Asian Studies*, 28:3 (1994), pp. 533–556; Ole Birk Laursen, 'Anti-colonialism, terrorism and the "politics of friendship": Virendranath Chattopadhyaya and the European anarchist movement, 1910–1927', *Anarchist Studies*, 27:1 (2019), pp. 47–62.

18 Michael Silvestri, '"The Sinn Fein of India": Irish nationalism and the policing of revolutionary terrorism in Bengal', *Journal of British Studies*, 39:4 (2000), pp. 454–486; Laqueur, *A History of Terrorism*, p. 45; Amit Kumar Gupta, 'Defying death: nationalist revolutionism in India, 1897–1938', *Social Scientist*, 25:9/10 (1997), pp. 3–27; Dhananjay Keer, *Veer Savarkar* (Bombay: Popular Prakashan, 1950), pp. 28, 41–43.

19 Peter Heehs, *The Bomb in Bengal: The Rise of Revolutionary Terrorism in India, 1900–1910* (New Delhi: Oxford University Press, 1993), pp. 89–91; Hemchandra Kanungo, *An Account of the Revolutionary Movement in Bengal*, ed. Amiya K. Samanta (Kolkata: Setu Prakashani, 2015), pp. 192–195.

20 *The Asian* quoted in Henry Wood Nevinson, *The New Spirit in India* (London: Harper Brothers, 1908), pp. 228–229; 'The Indian bomb outrage', *The Times*, 4 May 1908; 'An account of the Revolutionary organisation in Eastern Bengal with special reference to the Dacca Anushilan Samiti', in *Terrorism in Bengal: A Collection of Documents on Terrorist Activity from 1905–1939* (Kolkata: Government of Western Bengal, 1995), pp. 302–310; Kanungo, *An Account of the Revolutionary Movement*, p. 153.

21 Harper, *Underground Asia*, pp. 103–106; 'Bomb outrage in India' and 'The incitements of the native press', *The Times*, 2 and 4 May 1908; 'School for anarchists', *Nottingham Evening Post*, 9 May 1908; Tilak article in 'Sedition in India', *Aberdeen Journal*, 14 July 1908.

Epilogue: Ouroboros

1 Vladimir Dedijer, *The Road to Sarajevo* (London: Macgibbon and Kee, 1967), pp. 9–12; Dejan Djokić, 'Whose myth? Which nation? The Serbian Kosovo myth revisited', in *Uses and Abuses of the Middle Ages, 19th–21st Century*,

ed. Janos M. Bak, Jörg Jarnut, Pierre Monnet and Bernd Schneidmüller (Munich: Wilhelm Fink, 2009), pp. 215–233.

2 Joachim Remark, *Sarajevo: The Story of a Political Murder* (New York: Criterion, 1959), pp. 42–49, quote from p. 45; Ivor Roberts, 'The Black Hand and the Sarajevo conspiracy'. in *Balkan Legacies of the Great War: The Past Is Never Dead*, ed. Othon Anastasakis, David Madden and Elizabeth Roberts (Basingstoke: Palgrave, 2016), pp. 23–42; Dedijer, *The Road to Sarajevo*, pp. 250–260.

3 'Report on the arch-duke's assassination', in *Source Records of the Great War*, ed. Charles F. Horne (New York: National Alumni, 1923), vol. 1, p. 249; Paul Jackson, '"Union or death!": Gavrilo Princip, Young Bosnia and the role of "sacred time" in the dynamics of nationalist terrorism', *Totalitarian Movements and Political Religions*, 7:1 (2006), pp. 45–65; Christopher Clark, *The Sleepwalkers: How Europe Went to War in 1914* (London: Penguin, 2012), pp. 49–50; Sageman, *Turning to Political Violence*, pp. 340–341.

4 'Report on the arch-duke's assassination', in *Source Records*; Roberta Strauss Feuerlicht, *The Desperate Act: The Assassination of Franz Ferdinand at Sarajevo* (New York: McGraw-Hill, 1968), pp. 95–99.

5 Tim Butcher, *The Trigger: Hunting the Assassin Who Brought the World to War* (London: Chatto and Windus, 2014), pp. 189–194.

6 'Emperor calmly faces tragedies', *Washington Times*, 29 June 1914; 'Fashions in regicide', *New York Times*, 3 July 1914; Dedijer, *The Road to Sarajevo*, pp. 9–17, 172–176.

Bibliography

Archives

Archives of the Paris police prefecture, Paris.
Hoover Institution Archives, Palo Alto.
International Institute of Social History, Amsterdam.
Library of Congress, Washington, DC.
National Archives of the United Kingdom, London.

Published reports and primary source collections

Annuaire des Deux Mondes: Histoire Générale des Divers États (Paris: Bureau de la Revue des Deux Mondes, 1859).

Bakunin on Anarchy: Selected Works by the Activist Founder of World Anarchism, ed. and trans. Sam Dolgoff (New York: Vintage, 1971).

Bal Gangadhar Tilak: His Speeches and Writings, ed. Babu Aurobindo Ghose (Madras: Ganesh and Co., 1922).

Correspondence Respecting the Recent Fenian Aggression upon Canada (London: Harrison and Sons, 1867).

Cour d'Assises de la Seine, Actes d'accusation des nommés Orsini, de Rudio, Gomez, Pieri et Bernard (Paris: Valence, 1858).

Daughter of a Revolutionary: Natalie Herzen and the Bakunin–Nechayev Circle, ed. Michael Confino, trans. Hilary Sternberg and Lydia Bott (LeSalle: Library Press, 1973).

Devoy's Postbag, ed. William O'Brien and Desmond Ryan, 2 vols (Dublin: Academy Press, 1979).

Documents Diplomatiques Français, Ministère des Affaires étrangères (Paris: Imprimerie Nationale, 1930).

Enquête Parlementaire sur l'Insurrection du 18 Mars (Versailles: Imprimeur de l'Assemblée nationale, 1872).

Bibliography

Five Sisters: Women Against the Tsar, ed. Barbara A. Engel and Clifford N. Rosenthal (London: Routledge, 1979).

Le Correspondant, ed. Charles Douniol (Paris: De Simon Raçon, 1859).

Letters from Paris: Written by C. de B., a Political Informant to the Head of the London House of Rothschild, 1870–1875, ed. and trans. Robert Henry (London: J. M. Dent, 1942).

Letters of Fyodor Mikhailovich Dostoyevsky to His Family and Friends, trans. Ethel Colburn Mayne (London: Chatto and Windus, 1917).

Marx and Engels Collected Works (New York: International Publishers, 1968).

Papiers secret et correspondance du second Empire, ed. A. Poulet-Malassis (Paris: Auguste-Ghio, 1877).

Parnell Commission Report with Complete Index and Notes (London: Irish Loyal and Patriotic Union, 1890).

Quotes and Letters of Charles Sumner, ed. Edward L. Pierce (London: Samson, 1893).

'Report of John Brown's raid upon Harper's Ferry, Virginia, 16–19 October 1859, compiled by Robert E. Lee', *Quarterly of the Oregon History Society*, 10:3 (1909), pp. 314–324.

Report of the Board on Behalf of the United States Executives Departments at the International Exhibition, Philadelphia, 1876, vol. 1 (Washington, DC: Government Printing Office, 1884).

Reports of the Select Committee of Five, 36th Congress, Second Session (Washington, DC: Government Printing Office, 1861).

Revue des Races Latines, vol. 2 (Paris: A l'Administration de la revue, 1859).

Source Records of the Great War, vol.1, ed. Charles F. Horne (New York: National Alumni, 1923).

Terrorism in Bengal: A Collection of Documents on Terrorist Activity from 1905–1939 (Kolkata: Government of Western Bengal, 1995).

The Communards of Paris, 1871, ed. Stewart Edwards (Documents of Revolution series, general editor Heinz Lubasz) (London: Thames and Hudson, 1973).

The Method of Freedom: An Errico Malatesta Reader, ed. Davide Turcato (Oakland: AK Press, 2014).

'Unpublished letters of Karl Marx and Friedrich Engels to Americans', ed. And trans. Leonard E. Mins, *Science and Society*, 2:3 (1938), pp. 348–375.

Voices of Terror: Manifestos, Writings and Manuals of Al-Qaeda, Hamas and Other Terrorists from Around the World and Throughout the Ages, ed. Walter Laqueur (New York: Reed Press, 2004).

Online sources

All sources were accessed between 1 February 2018 and 20 September 2021.
Anarchist Library – www.theanarchistlibrary.org
BBC website – www.bbc.co.uk

Bibliography

Chicago Historical Society – www.chicagohistoryresources.org
Documents of Russian Empire, 1860–1869 – www.eurodocs.lib.byu.edu
Foreign Relations of the United States – www.history.state.gov
Library Ireland – www.libraryireland.com
Marxists Internet Archive – www.marxists.org
Official Debates of the United Kingdom Parliament, Historic Hansard – www.hansard.parliament.uk
World Digital Library – https://www.wdl.org

Newspapers and periodicals

Britain

Aberdeen Journal, Bath Chronicle, Belfast Newsletter, Cheltenham Chronicle, Cheshire Observer, Daily Exchange, Daily Mail, Daily News, Daily Telegraph, Derby Daily Telegraph, Essex Standard, Evening Telegraph, The Examiner, Glasgow Herald, Hertford Mercury, Huddersfield Chronicle, Hull Daily Mail, Leeds Mercury, Liverpool Mercury, Manchester Courier, Manchester Examiner, Manchester Guardian, Morning Chronicle, Morning Post, New Review, Newcastle Courant, Nottingham Evening Post, The Observer, Pall Mall Gazette, Penny Illustrated, Portsmouth Evening News, Reynold's Newspaper, Saturday Review, Sheffield Independent, Spectator, The Standard, The Times, Western Mail

France

L'Ami de la France, Le Constitutionnel, Le Courrier du Gard, Le Courrier du Nord, Le Cri du peuple, Les Etats-Unis d'Europe, Gil Blas, L'En-Dehors, Le Figaro, L'Hydre anarchiste, L'Intransigeant, Le Journal, Journal de commissaires des police, Journal des débats politiques et littéraires, Journal de la Marne, La Justice, La Liberté, Le Matin, Le Moniteur universel, Le Petit Journal, Le Petit Parisien, La Petite Presse, Le Précurseur, Le Radical, La Rue, Le Temps

Germany

Berliner Börsen-Zeitung, Berliner Tageblatt, Neueste Mittheilungen, Die Presse, Provinzial-Correspondenz

Bibliography

United States

The Alarm, Alexandria Gazette, Anti-Slavery Bugle, Argus, Bedford Gazette, The Call, Chicago Tribune, La Correspondencia de Puerto Rico, Daily Astorian, Daily Intelligencer, Daily Telegraph, Der Deutsche Correspondent, Eureka Daily Sentinel, Evening World, Freiheit, Holmes County Republican, Indianapolis Journal, Irish World, Labor Enquirer, Lancaster Intelligencer, Lancaster Ledger, Los Angeles Herald, Marietta Daily Leader, Minnesota Staats-Zeitung, Morning Appeal, Morning Call, Nashville Patriot, National Era, National Republican, New National Era, New York Daily Tribune, New York Herald, New York Sun, New York Times, Omaha Daily Bee, Richmond Daily Dispatch, Sacramento Daily Record Union, San Antonio Light, Scientific American, Seattle Daily Post Intelligencer, Washington Post, Washington Star, Washington Times, Weekly American, Western Democrat, Wheeling Daily Intelligencer

Other

Auckland Star, La Epoca, Freeman's Journal, Irish Times, Journal de-Saint Pétersbourg, La Lectura, Tasmanian News

Contemporary histories, diaries, memoirs and treatises

Adams, William Edwin, *Memoirs of a Social Atom* (London: Hutchinson, 1903).

Anderson, Osborne P., *A Voice from Harper's Ferry: A Narrative of Events* (Boston: printed for the author, 1861).

Anderson, Robert, *The Lighter Side of My Official Life* (New York: Hodder and Stoughton, 1910).

Andrieux, Louis, *Souvenirs d'un Préfet de Police*, vol. 2 (Paris: Rouff, 1885).

Andrieux, Louis, *La Commune á Lyon en 1870 et 1871* (Paris: Perrin, 1906).

Anonymous, *The Accused, the Accusers: The Famous Speeches of the Eight Chicago Anarchists in Court* (Chicago: Socialistic Publishing Society, 1886).

Bataille, Albert, *Causes Criminelles et mondaines de 1894: les procès Anarchistes* (Paris: E. Dentu, 1895).

Bebel, August, *My Life* (Chicago: University of Chicago Press, 1913).

Bennett, D. M., *Sages, Thinkers and Reformers: Being Biographical Sketches of Leading Philosophers, Teachers, Skeptics, Innovators, Founders of New Schools of Thought, Eminent Scientists etc.* (New York: Liberal and Scientific Publishing House, 1876).

Berger, J. A. *The Life, Trial and Death of Felice Orsini, with His Letter to the Emperor* (London: Berger, 1858).

Bibliography

Berkman, Alexander, *Prison Memoirs of an Anarchist* (New York: Mother Earth, 1912).

Bismarck, Otto von, *The Man and the Statesman: Being the Reflections and Reminiscences of Otto von Bismarck*, vol. 2, trans. A. J. Butler (Stuttgart: Buchhandlung, 1898).

Blanqui, Auguste, *Instructions pour une prise d'armes* (1868).

Blanqui, Auguste, *La Patrie en danger compendium* (Paris: Chevalier, 1871).

Bourel, Antonin, *La Bombe infernale* (Orléans: Pagnerre, 1858).

Brackenbury, Henry, *Some Memories of My Spare Time* (Edinburgh: William Blackwood, 1909).

Burgh, Edward de, *Elizabeth: Empress of Austria* (London: Hutchinson, 1899).

Cadogan, Edward, *The Life of Cavour* (London: Smith and Elder, 1907).

Caro, Emile Marie, 'La République et les républicains', *Revue des Deux Mondes*, 93 (1871), pp. 516–546.

Chesney, George Tomkyns, *The Battle of Dorking: Reminiscences of a Volunteer* (Edinburgh: Blackwood and Sons, 1871).

Cluseret, Gustave Paul, 'My connection with Fenianism', *Frazer's Magazine* (July 1872), pp. 31–46.

Cluseret, Gustave Paul, *Mémoires du Général Cluseret*, vol. 2 (Paris: Jules Levy, 1887).

Costa, Charles de, *Les Blanquistes* (Paris: Marcel Rivière, 1912).

D'Ambès, Baron, *Intimate Memoirs of Napoleon III: Personal Reminiscences of the Man and the Emperor*, vol. 2, ed. and trans. A. R. Alinson (London: Stanley Paul, 1912).

d'Arsac, Joanni, *La Guerre Civile et la Commune de Paris en 1871* (Paris: F. Curot, 1871).

d'Esboeufs, Vergès, *Le Vérité sur la gouvernement de la Défense nationale la Commune et les Versaillais* (Geneva: Counsel-General's Office, 1871).

Daccus, Joseph A., *Annals of the Great Strikes* (Chicago: L. T. Palmer, 1877).

Dostoevsky, Fyodor, *The Possessed*, trans. Constance Garnett (London: William Heinemann, 1914).

Dubois, Félix, *The Anarchist Peril*, ed. and trans. Ralph Derechef (London: Fisher and Unwin, 1894).

Evans, Thomas, *Memoirs of Dr Thomas Evans: The Second French Empire* (New York: Appleton and Co., 1905).

Fariola, Octave, 'Amongst the Fenians', *The Irishman*, 1 August 1868 and 19 September 1868.

Fawcett, Edward Douglas, *Hartmann the Anarchist; or, the Doom of the Great City* (London: Edward Arnold, 1893).

Fetridge, W. Pembroke, *The Rise and Fall of the Paris Commune of 1871* (New York: Harper, 1871).

Figner, Vera, *Memoirs of a Revolutionist* (DeKalb: Northern Illinois University Press, 1991).

Bibliography

Frost, Thomas, *The Secret Societies of the European Revolutions*, vol. 2 (London: Tinsley Brothers, 1876).

Gardiner, A. G., *The Life of William Harcourt*, vol. 1 (London: Constable, 1923).

Gibson, William, *Paris During the Commune* (London: Methodist Book Room, 1895).

Goldman, Emma, *Living My Life* (New York: Meridian, 1977).

Goncourt, Edmond and Goncourt, Jules, *The Journal of the Goncourts*, ed. Julius West (London: Thomas Nelson, 1908).

Grant, Hamil, *Spies and Secret Service: The Story of Espionage, Its Main Systems and Chief Exponents* (London: Grant Richards, 1915).

Grave, Jean, *Moribund Society and Anarchy*, trans. Voltairine de Cleyre (San Francisco: A. Isaak, 1899).

Griffith, George, *The Angel of the Revolution: A Tale of the Coming Terror* (London: Tower, 1894).

Guerzoni, Giuseppe, *Garibaldi*, vol. 2 (Firenze: G. Barbéra, 1892).

Heinzen, Karl, *Murder and Liberty*, trans. H. Lieber (Indianapolis: Lieber, 1881).

Hemyng, Samuel Bracebridge, *The Commune in London, or, Thirty Years Hence: A Chapter of Anticipated History* (London: Clarke, 1871).

Hinton, Richard J., *John Brown and His Men, with Some Account of the Roads They Travelled to Reach Harper's Ferry* (New York: Funk and Wagnalls, 1894).

Holstein, Friedrich von, *The Holstein Papers: The Memoirs, Diaries and Correspondence of Friedrich von Holstein*, vol. 1, ed. Norman Rich and M. H. Fisher (Cambridge: Cambridge University Press, 1955).

Holyoake, George Jacob, *Sixty Years of an Agitator's Life*, vol. 2 (London: Fisher and Unwin, 1892).

Hooper, George, *The Campaign at Sedan, August–September 1870* (London: Hodder and Stoughton, 1914).

Hugo, Victor, *Memoirs of Victor Hugo*, trans. John W. Harding (London: William Heinemann, 1898).

Imbert de Saint Armand, *The Court of the Second Empire*, trans. Elizabeth Gilbert Martin (New York: Charles Scribner, 1898).

Jerrold, William Blanchard, *The Life of Napoleon III*, vol. 4 (London: Longman, Greens and Co., 1882).

Jeyes, Samuel Henry, *The Life of Sir Howard Vincent* (London: George Allen, 1912).

Kanungo, Hemchandra, *An Account of the Revolutionary Movement in Bengal*, ed. Amiya K. Samanta (Kolkata: Setu Prakashani, 2015).

Khoudiakoff, Ivan Aleksandrovich, *Mémoires d'un révolutionnaire* (Paris: Calman Lévy, 1889).

Kravchinsky, Sergei, 'Stepniak', *Underground Russia: Revolutionary Profiles and Sketches from Life* (New York: Lovell and Co., 1883).

Kravchinsky, Sergei, 'Stepniak', *The Russian Storm Cloud* (London: Swan, 1886).

Kropotkin, Peter, *Memoirs of a Revolutionist*, vol. 2 (London: Smith and Elder, 1899).

Le Caron, Henri, *Twenty-Five Years of Secret Service* (London: William Heinemann, 1892).

Leech, Samuel Vanderlip, *The Raid of John Brown at Harper's Ferry as I Saw It* (Washington, DC: Desoto, 1909).

Lepelletier, Edmond, *Histoire de la Commune de 1871*, vol. 1 (Paris: Mercure, 1911).

Lissagaray, Prosper-Oliver, *History of the Commune of 1871*, trans. Eleanor Marx (New York: International Publishing, 1898).

Lombroso, Cesare, 'The physiognomy of the anarchists', *The Monist*, 1 (1891), pp. 346–343.

Lowe, Charles, *Alexander III of Russia* (New York: Macmillan, 1895).

Lowry-Sibbet, Robert, *The Siege of Paris by an American Eyewitness* (Harrisburg: Meyers, 1892).

Mansfield, Laura, trans and ed., *In His Own Words: A Translation of the Writings of Dr Ayman Al Zawahiri* (Morrisville: Lulu, 2006).

Martet, Jean, *George Clemenceau: The Events of His Life as Told by Himself to His Former Secretary* (London: Longmans, Green and Co., 1923).

Marx, Karl, *The Civil War in France* (New York: International Publishers, 1933).

Marx, Karl and Engels, Friedrich, *The Communist Manifesto*, ed. Ellen Meiksins Wood (New York: Monthly Review Press, 1998).

McKay, Donald, *The Dynamite Ship* (New York: Manhattan Publishing, 1888).

Mettais, Charles, *Histoire Contemporaine: Complète, Détaillée et Authentique* (Paris: Gustav Barba, 1858).

Michel, Louise, *The Red Virgin: The Memoirs of Louise Michel*, ed. and trans. Bullitt Lowry and Elizabeth Ellington Gunter (Alabama: University of Alabama Press, 1981).

Minkin, Helene, *Storm in My Heart: Memories of the Widow of Johann Most*, ed. Tom Goyens, trans. Alisa Braun (Oakland: AK Press, 2015).

Moltke, Helmuth von, *The Franco-German War of 1870–71*, vol. 2, trans. Clara Bell and Henry W. Fischer (London: James R. Osgood, McIlvaine and Co., 1891).

Nechaev, Sergei, *Catechism of a Revolutionary* (London: Anarchist Library, reprint 2009).

Nevinson, Henry Wood, *The New Spirit in India* (London: Harper Brothers, 1908).

Nikitenko, Aleksandr, *The Diary of a Russian Censor*, ed. and trans. Helen Saltz Jacobsen (Boston: University of Massachusetts Press, 1975).

O'Leary, John, *Recollections of Fenians and Fenianism* (London: Downey and Co., 1896).

Orsini, Felice, *Memoirs and Adventures of Felice Orsini* (Edinburgh: Constable, 1857).

Parsons, Lucy E., *The Life of Robert R. Parsons, with a Brief History of the Labor Movement in America* (Chicago: Parsons, 1889).

Pinkerton, Allan, *Strikers, Communists, Tramps and Detectives* (New York: Carleton, 1878).

Pinkerton, Allan, *The Spy of the Rebellion: Being a True History of the Spies System of the United States Army* (New York: G. W. Carleton, 1886).

Reynaud, Ernest, *Souvenirs de police au temps de Ravachol* (Paris: Payot, 1923).

Rochefort, Victor Henri, *Les Dernières Causeries du Henri Rochefort*, ed. W. D. Fonvielle (Brussels: Bureau du Petit Journal, 1871).

Rutherford, John, *The Secret History of the Fenian Conspiracy: Its Origin, Objects and Ramifications*, vol. 2 (London: Kegan and Paul, 1877).

Savage, John, *Fenian Martyrs and Heroes* (Boston: Patrick Donahoe, 1868).

Savinkov, Boris, *Memoirs of a Terrorist*, trans. Joseph Shaplen (New York: Albert and Charles Boni, 1931).

Shilov, A. A., *Karakozov i pokushenie 4 aprelia 1866 goda* (St Petersburg: State Publishing, 1919).

Stieber, Wilhelm J. C. E., *The Chancellor's Spy*, trans. Jan van Heurck (New York: Grove Press, 1980).

Testut, Oscar, *L'Internationale* (Paris: E. Lachaud, 1871).

Thoreau, Henry D., *A Yankee in Canada: With Anti-slavery and Reform Papers* (Boston: Tickner and Fields, 1866).

Train, George Francis, *My Life in Many Foreign Lands* (New York: Appleton, 1902).

Varennes, Henri, *De Ravachol á Caserio – Notes d'Audience* (Paris: Garnier Frères, 1895).

Vizetelly, Ernest Alfred, *The Court of the Tuileries, 1852–1870* (London: Chatto and Windus, 1907).

Vizetelly, Ernest Alfred, *The Anarchists: Their Faith and Their Record* (London: Allen Lane, 1911).

Vizetelly, Ernest Alfred, *My Adventures in the Commune, 1871* (London: Chatto and Windus, 1914).

Vuillaume, Maxime, *Mes cahiers rouges au temps de La Commune* (Paris: Librairie Paul Ollendorff, 1900).

Washburne, Elihu, *Recollections of a Minister to France, 1869–1877* (London: Sampson Lowe, 1887).

Whitley, Hiram C., *In It* (Cambridge: Riverside Press, 1894).

Winterer, Landelin, *The Social Danger, or Two Years of Socialism in Europe and America*, trans. Joseph P. Roles (Chicago: Belford, Clarke and Co., 1886).

Witte, Sergei, *The Memoirs of Count Witte*, trans. Abraham Yarmolinsky (London: William Heineman, 1921).

Bibliography

Secondary sources

Adamic, Louis, *Dynamite: A Century of Class Violence in America, 1830–1930* (London: Rebel Press, 1984).

Aldrich, Richard J. and Cormac, Rory, *The Secret Royals: Spying and the Crown from Victoria to Diana* (London: Atlantic, 2021).

Allason, Rupert, *The Branch: A History of the Metropolitan Police Special Branch, 1883–1983* (London: Secker and Warburg, 1983).

Allford, Terry, *Fortune's Fool: The Life of John Wilkes Booth* (New York: Oxford University Press, 2015).

Aly, Anne and Green, Leila, 'Fear, anxiety and the state of terror', *Studies in Conflict and Terrorism*, 33:3 (2010), pp. 268–281.

Amman, Molly and Meloy, J. Reid, 'Stochastic terrorism: a linguistic and psychological analysis', *Perspectives on Terrorism*, 15:5 (2021), pp. 2–12.

Anderson, Benedict R., *Under Three Flags: Anarchism and the Anti-colonial Imagination* (New York: Verso, 2008).

Andrew, Christopher, 'Déchiffrement et diplomatie: le cabinet noir du Quai d'Orsay sur la Troisième République', *Relations Internationales*, 5 (1976), pp. 37–64.

Andrew, Christopher, *The Secret World: A History of Intelligence* (New Haven: Yale University Press, 2018).

Avineri, Shlomo, *Karl Marx: Philosophy and Revolution* (New Haven: Yale University Press, 2019).

Avrich, Paul, *The Russian Anarchists* (Princeton: Princeton University Press, 1971).

Avrich, Paul, *Bakunin and Nechaev* (London: Freedom Press, 1974).

Avrich, Paul, 'Bakunin and the United States', *International Review of Social History*, 24:3 (1979), pp. 320–340.

Avrich, Paul, *The Haymarket Tragedy* (Princeton: Princeton University Press, 1984).

Avrich, Paul, *Anarchist Portraits* (Princeton: Princeton University Press, 1988).

Avrich, Paul and Avrich, Karen, *Sasha and Emma: The Anarchist Odyssey of Alexander Berkman and Emma Goldman* (Cambridge: Harvard University Press, 2012).

Baer, James A., *Anarchist Immigrants in Spain and Argentina* (Urbana: University of Illinois Press, 2015).

Balmuth, Daniel, 'The origins of the Russian press reform of 1865', *Slavonic and East European Review*, 47:109 (1969), pp. 369–388.

Bantman, Constance, 'Internationalism without an International? Cross-Channel anarchist networks, 1880–1914', *Revue Belge de Philologie et d'Histoire*, 84:4 (2006), pp. 961–981.

Bantman, Constance, 'Jean Grave and French anarchism: a relational approach', *International Review of Social History*, 62:3 (2017), pp. 451–477

Bibliography

Bantman, Constance, 'Louise Michel's London years: a political re-assessment', *Women's History Review*, 26:6 (2017), pp. 994–1012.

Bantman, Constance, 'The era of propaganda of the deed', in *The Palgrave Handbook of Anarchism*, ed. Carl Ley and Matthew S. Adams (Basingstoke: Palgrave, 2018), pp. 371–387.

Bantman, Constance, *Jean Grave and the Networks of French Anarchism, 1854–1939* (London: Palgrave, 2021).

Bargain-Villéger, Alban, 'Captain Tin Can: Gustave Cluseret and the socialist leftists, 1848–1900', *Socialist History*, 46 (2016), pp. 13–32.

Barton, Mary S., 'The global war on anarchism: the United States and international anarchist terrorism, 1898–1904', *Diplomatic History*, 39:2 (2015), pp. 303–330.

Beaumont, Matthew, 'Cacotopianism, the Paris Commune and England's anti-communist imaginary, 1870–1900', *ELH*, 73:2 (2006), pp. 465–487.

Beck, Janet Kemper. *Creating the John Brown Legend: Emerson, Thoreau, Child and Higginson in Defense of the Raid on Harper's Ferry* (Jefferson: MacFarland, 2009).

Bergman, Jay, *Vera Zasulich: A Biography* (Palo Alto: Stanford University Press, 1983).

Bernstein, Samuel, 'The First International and the great powers', *Science and Society*, 16:3 (1952), pp. 247–272.

Bessner, Daniel and Stauch, Michael, 'Karl Heinzen and the intellectual origins of terrorism', *Terrorism and Political Violence*, 22:2 (2010), pp. 143–176.

Billingsley, Phillip, 'Bakunin's sojourn in Japan: nailing down an enigma', *Human Sciences Review*, 5 (1993), pp. 35–65.

Billington, James H., *Fire in the Minds of Men: Origins of the Revolutionary Faith* (New Brunswick: Transaction, 1999).

Blumberg, Arnold, *A Carefully Planned Accident: The Italian War of 1859* (Selinsgrove: Susquehanna University Press, 1990).

Bonansinga, Jay, *Pinkerton's War: The Civil War's Greatest Spy and the Birth of the U.S. Secret Service* (Guilford: Lyon's Press, 2012).

Boot, Max, *War Made New: Weapons, Warriors and the Making of the Modern World* (New York: Gotham, 2006).

Bressler, Fenton, *Napoleon III: A Life* (London: Harper Collins, 2000).

Bridgstocke, Julian, 'Resisting with authority? Anarchist laughter and the violence of truth', *Social and Cultural Geography*, 23:2 (2022), pp. 173–191

Broido, Vera, *Apostles into Terrorists: Women and the Revolutionary Movement in the Russia of Alexander II* (New York: Viking, 1977).

Brown, Richard Maxwell, *Historical Studies of American Violence and Vigilantism* (New York: Oxford University Press, 1975).

Bullard, Alice, 'Self representation in the arms of defeat: fatal nostalgia and surviving comrades in French New Caledonia, 1871–1880', *Cultural Anthropology*, 12:2 (1997), pp. 179–212.

Burgoyne, Mary, 'Conrad among the anarchists: documents on Martial Bourdin and the Greenwich bombing', *The Conradian*, 31:1 (2007), pp. 147–185.

Busch, Francis X., 'The Haymarket riot and the trial of the anarchists', *Journal of the Illinois State Historical Society*, 48:3 (1955), pp. 247–270.

Butcher, Tim, *The Trigger: Hunting the Assassin Who Brought the World to War* (London: Chatto and Windus, 2014).

Butterworth, Alexander, *The World That Never Was: A True Story of Dreamers, Schemers, Anarchists and Secret Agents* (London: Vintage, 2011).

Cahm, Caroline, *Kropotkin and the Rise of Revolutionary Anarchism, 1872–1886* (Cambridge: Cambridge University Press, 1989).

Campanella, Anthony, 'Garibaldi and the first Peace Congress in Geneva in 1867', *International Review of Social History*, 5:3 (1960), pp. 456–486.

Cao, Yin, 'Bombs in Beijing and Delhi: the global spread of bomb-making technology and the revolutionary terrorism in modern China and India', *Journal of World History*, 30:4 (2019), pp. 559–589.

Carlson, Andrew R., 'Anarchism and terror in the German Empire, 1870–1890', in *Social Protest, Violence and Terror in Nineteenth- and Twentieth-Century Europe*, ed. Wolfgang J. Mommsen and Gerhard Hirschfeld (Basingstoke: Macmillan, 1982), pp. 175–200.

Carr, Edward Hallett, *Bakunin* (New York: Vintage, 1961).

Casanova, Julián, 'Terror and violence: the dark face of Spanish anarchism', *International Labor and Working-Class History*, 67 (2005): 79–99.

Case, Lynn M., *French Opinion on War and Diplomacy During the Second Empire* (Philadelphia: University of Pennsylvania Press, 1954).

Chaliand, Gérard and Blin, Arnaud, eds, *The History of Terrorism: From Antiquity to Al Qaeda* (Berkeley: University of California Press, 2007).

Chaliand, Gérard and Blin, Arnaud, 'Zealots and assassins', in *The History of Terrorism: From Antiquity to Al Qaeda*, ed. Gérard Chaliand and Arnaud Blin (Berkeley: University of California Press, 2007), pp. 55–78.

Change, Dominica, '"Un Nouveau '93": discourses of mimicry and terror in the Paris Commune of 1871', *French Historical Studies*, 36:4 (2013), pp. 629–648.

Clark, Christopher, *The Sleepwalkers: How Europe Went to War in 1914* (London: Penguin, 2012).

Clutterbuck, Lindsay, 'The progenitors of terrorism: Russian revolutionaries or extreme Irish republicans?', *Terrorism and Political Violence*, 16:4 (2004), pp. 154–181.

Cole, Sarah, *At the Violet Hour: Modernism and Violence in England and Ireland* (New York: Oxford University Press, 2012).

Colson, Dan, 'Propaganda of the deed: anarchism, violence and the representational impulse', *American Studies*, 56:1 (2017), pp. 163–186.

Cook, Andrew, *Ace of Spies: The True Story of Sidney Reilly* (Stroud: History Press, 2005).

Cook, Andrew, *M: MI5's First Spymaster* (Stroud: Tempus, 2006).

Bibliography

Cowdy, Terry, *The Enemy Within: A History of Spies, Spymasters and Espionage* (London: Bloomsbury, 2011).

Croft, Lee B., *Nikolai Ivanovich Kibalchich: Terrorist Rocket Pioneer* (Tempe: Institute for Issues in the History of Science, 2006).

Crossland, James, 'Radical warfare's first "superweapon": the fears, perceptions and realities of the Orsini bomb, 1858–1896', *Terrorism and Political Violence* (June 2021), DOI: 10.1080/09546553.2021.1924692.

Crossley, Pamela Kyle, *Orphan Warriors: Three Manchu Generations and the End of the Qing World* (Princeton: Princeton University Press, 1990).

Cunningham, Michele, *Mexico and the Foreign Policy of Napoleon III* (Basingstoke: Palgrave, 2001).

Daly, Jonathan W., *Autocracy Under Siege: Security Police and Opposition in Russia, 1866–1905* (Ithaca: Cornell University Press, 1998).

David, Stacey Renee, 'The memory of opposition: the collective identity of Louis Napoleon's political prisoners', *Western Society for French History*, 32 (2004), pp. 237–255.

Dedijer, Vladimir, *The Road to Sarajevo* (London: Macgibbon and Kee, 1967).

Deflem, Mathieu, 'International policing in 19th century Europe: the Police Union of German States, 1851–1866', *International Criminal Justice Review*, 6 (1996), pp. 35–57.

Deflem, Mathieu, 'Wild beasts without nationality: the uncertain origins of Interpol, 1898–1910', in *The Handbook of Transnational Crime and Justice*, ed. Philip Reichel (Thousand Oaks: Sage, 2005), pp. 275–285.

Deluermoz, Quentin, 'The IWMA and the Commune: a reassessment', trans. Angèle David-Guillou, in *Arise Ye Wretched Earth: The First International in a Global Perspective*, ed. Fabrice Bensimon, Quentin Deluermoz and Jeanne Moisand (Leiden: Brill, 2018), pp. 107–126.

Dietze, Carola, *The Invention of Terrorism in Europe, Russia and the United States* (London: Verso, 2020).

Dirlik, Arif, 'Vision and revolution: anarchism in Chinese revolutionary thought on the eve of the 1911 revolution', *Modern China*, 12:2 (1986), pp. 123–165.

Dirlik, Arif, *Anarchism in the Chinese Revolution* (Berkeley: University of California Press, 1991).

Djokić, Dejan, 'Whose myth? Which nation? The Serbian Kosovo myth revisited', in *Uses and Abuses of the Middle Ages, 19th–21st Century*, ed. Janos M. Bak, Jörg Jarnut, Pierre Monnet and Bernd Schneidmüller (Munich: Wilhelm Fink, 2009), pp. 215–233.

Drake, Richard, *Apostles and Agitators: Italy's Marxist Revolutionary Tradition* (Cambridge: Harvard University Press, 2003).

Duggan, Christopher, *The Force of Destiny: A History of Italy Since 1796* (London: Penguin, 2008).

Eichner, Carolyn J., *Surmounting the Barricades: Women in the Paris Commune* (Bloomington: Indiana University Press, 2004).

Bibliography

Ely, Christopher, *Underground Petersburg: Radical Populism, Urban Space and the Tactics of Subversion in Reform-Era Russia* (Ithaca: Cornell University Press, 2016).

Emsley, Clive, *Gendarmes and the State in Nineteenth Century Europe* (Oxford: Oxford University Press, 1999).

Erickson, Edward J., 'Punishing the mad bomber: questions of moral responsibility in the trials of French anarchist terrorists, 1886–1897', *French History*, 22:1 (2008), pp. 51–73.

Esenwein, George Richard, *Anarchist Ideology and the Working-Class Movement in Spain, 1868–1898* (Berkeley: University of California Press, 1989).

Etcheson, Nicole, 'John Brown, terrorist?', *American Nineteenth Century History*, 10:1 (2009), pp. 29–48.

Evans, Richard, *Tales from the German Underworld: Crime and Punishment in the Nineteenth Century* (New Haven: Yale University Press, 1998).

Farnen, Russell F., 'Terrorism and mass media: a systematic analysis of a symbiotic process', *Journal of Conflict and Terrorism*, 13:2 (1990), pp. 99–143.

Faure, Alain, 'The public meeting movements in Paris from 1868 to 1870', in *Voices of the People: The Social Life of 'La Sociale' at the End of the Second Empire*, ed. Adrian Rifkin and Roger Thomas, trans. John Moore (London: Routledge, 1988), pp. 181–234.

Fellman, Michael, *In the Name of God and Country: Reconsidering Terrorism in American History* (New Haven: Yale University Press, 2010).

Fermer, Douglas, *Sedan, 1870* (Barnsley: Pen and Sword, 2008).

Feuerlicht, Roberta Strauss, *The Desperate Act: The Assassination of Franz Ferdinand at Sarajevo* (New York: McGraw Hill, 1968).

Fijnaut, Cyrille, *The Containment of Organized Crime: Thirty-Five Years of Research on Police, Judicial and Administrative Cooperation* (Leiden: Brill, 2006).

Fijnaut, Cyrille and Marx, Gery T., eds, *Undercover: Police Surveillance in Comparative Perspective* (The Hague: Kluwer, 1995).

Fisher, David C., 'The rise of the radical intelligentsia', in *Events That Changed Russia Since 1855*, ed. Frank W. Thackeray (Westport: Greenwood Press, 2007), pp. 23–44.

Fleming, Marie, 'Propaganda by the deed: terrorism and anarchist theory in late nineteenth century Europe', *Studies in Conflict and Terrorism*, 4:1–4 (1980), pp. 1–23.

Fleming, Marie, *The Geography of Freedom: The Odyssey of Élisée Reclus* (St Laurent: Black Rose, 1988).

Foner, Eric, *Reconstruction: America's Unfinished Revolution, 1863–1877* (New York: Harper Perennial, 1988).

Footman, David, *Red Prelude: A Life of A. I. Zhelyabov* (London: Cresset, 1944).

Forster, Laura, 'The Paris Commune in London and the spatial history of ideas, 1871–1900', *Historical Journal*, 62:4 (2019), pp. 1021–1044.

Foster, Allen, *Around the World with Citizen Train: The Sensational Adventures of the Real Phileas Fogg* (Decatur: Merlin, 2001).

Frank, Michael C., 'Terrorism for the sake of counterterrorism: undercover policing and the spectre of the agent provocateur in Joseph Conrad's *The Secret Agent*', *Conradiana*, 46:3 (2014), pp. 151–177.

Freedman, Lawrence, *The Future of War: A History* (London: Penguin, 2018).

Freeman, Joanne, *The Field of Blood: Violence in Congress on the Road to the Civil War* (New York: Farrar, Strauss and Giroux, 2018).

Frémion, Yves, *Léauthier l'anarchiste: De la propagande par le fait à la Révolte des Bagnards, 1893–1894* (Paris: Echappee, 2019).

Friedgut, Theodore F., 'Jews, violence and the Russian revolutionary movement', in *Jews and Violence: Images, Ideologies, Realities*, ed. Peter Y. Medding (Oxford: Oxford University Press, 2002), pp. 43–58.

Fuller, Robert Lynn, *The Origins of the French Nationalist Movement, 1886–1914* (Jefferson: MacFarland, 2012).

Gabrial, Brian, 'A "crisis of Americanism": newspaper coverage of John Brown's raid at Harper's Ferry and the question of loyalty', *Journalism History*, 34:2 (2008), pp. 98–106.

Gabriel, Elun, 'The left liberal critique of anarchism in Imperial Germany', *German Studies Review*, 33:2 (2010), pp. 331–350.

Gabriel, Elun, 'Anarchism's appeal to German workers, 1878–1914', *Journal for the Study of Radicalism*, 5:1 (2011), pp. 33–65.

Gabriel, Elun T., *Assassins and Conspirators: Anarchism, Socialism and Political Culture in Germany* (Ithaca: Cornell University Press, 2014).

Gage, Beverly, *The Day Wall St Exploded: A Story of America in Its First Age of Terror* (New York: Oxford University Press, 2009).

Gannt, Jonathan, *Irish Terrorism in the Atlantic Community, 1865–1922* (Basingstoke: Palgrave, 2010).

Garcia-Balañà, Albert, '1871 in Spain', in *Arise Ye Wretched Earth: The First International in a Global Perspective*, ed. Fabrice Bensimon, Quentin Deluermoz and Jeanne Moisand (Leiden: Brill, 2018), pp. 222–237.

Geifman, Anna, *Thou Shalt Kill: Revolutionary Terrorism in Russia, 1894–1917* (Princeton: Princeton University Press, 1993).

Geifman, Anna, *Death Orders: The Vanguard of Modern Terrorism in Revolutionary Russia* (Santa Barbara: Praeger, 2010).

George, David, 'Distinguishing classical tyrannicide from modern terrorism', *Review of Politics*, 50:3 (1988), pp. 390–419.

Gleeson, Abbott, *Young Russia: The Genesis of Russian Radicalism in the 1860s* (New York: Viking, 1980).

Gluckstein, Donny, *The Paris Commune: A Revolution in Democracy* (Chicago: Haymarket Books, 2011).

Goff, Philippe le, 'The militant politics of Auguste Blanqui', PhD thesis, University of Warwick (2015).

Bibliography

Goldstein, Robert Justin, *Political Repression in Nineteenth Century Europe* (London: Routledge, 2016).

Gopal, Priyamvada, *Insurgent Empire: Anticolonial Resistance and British Dissent* (London: Verso, 2019).

Goyens, Tom, *Beer and Revolution: The German Anarchist Movement in New York City, 1880–1914* (Chicago: University of Illinois Press, 2007).

Goyens, Tom, 'Johann Most and anarchist violence', paper presented at the 33rd Annual North American Labor History Conference, Wayne State University, Detroit (October 2012).

Graaf, Beatrice de, 'The Black International conspiracy as security dispositive in the Netherlands, 1880–1900', *Historische Sozialforschung*, 38:1 (2013), pp. 142–165.

Green, Abigail, 'Political and diplomatic movements, 1850–1870', in *Germany, 1800 1870*, ed. Jonathan Sperber (Oxford: Oxford University Press, 1987), pp. 69–90.

Green, James, *Death in the Haymarket: A Story of Chicago, the First Labor Movement and the Bombing that Divided Gilded Age America* (New York: Anchor, 2006).

Greene, Doug Enaa, *Communist Insurgent: Blanqui's Politics of Revolution* (Chicago: Haymarket Books, 2017).

Guiraudou, Richard-Pierre and Rebondy, Michel, *Gustave Flourens: Le Chevalier Rouge* (Paris: Le Pré aux Clercs, 1983).

Gupta, Amit Kumar, 'Defying death: nationalist revolutionism in India, 1897–1938', *Social Scientist*, 25:9/10 (1997), pp. 3–27.

Hagemeister, Michael, 'The Protocols of the Elders of Zion: between history and fiction', *New German Critique*, 103 (2008), pp. 83–95.

Hamourtziadou, Lily and Jackson, Jonathan, '5/11: revisiting the Gunpowder Plot', *Journal of Global Faultlines*, 5:1–2 (2018), pp. 91–95.

Harper, Tim, *Underground Asia: Global Revolutionaries and the Assault on Empire* (London: Penguin, 2020).

Hauptman, Samantha, *Criminalization of Immigration: The Post-9/11 Moral Panic* (El Paso: LFB, 2013).

Heehs, Peter, *The Bomb in Bengal: The Rise of Revolutionary Terrorism in India, 1900–1910* (New Delhi: Oxford University Press, 1993).

Heehs, Peter, 'Foreign influences on Bengali revolutionary terrorism, 1902–1908', *Modern Asian Studies*, 28:3 (1994), pp. 533–556.

Henderson, Robert, *Vladimir Burtsev and the Struggle for a Free Russia: A Revolutionary in the Time of Tsarism and Bolshevism* (London: Bloomsbury, 2017).

Hingley, Robert, *Nihilists: Russian Radicals and Revolutionaries in the Reign of Alexander II* (London: Weidenfeld and Nicholson, 1967).

Hingley, Robert, *The Russian Secret Police* (New York: Dorset, 1970).

Holzer, Harold, *Lincoln and the Power of the Press: The War for Public Opinion* (New York: Simon and Schuster, 2014).

Honeck, Mischa, '"Freeman of all nations bestir yourselves": Felice Orsini's transnational afterlife and the radicalization of America', *Journal of the Early Republic*, 30:4 (2010), pp. 587–615.

Honeck, Mischa, *We Are the Revolutionists: German-Speaking Immigrants and American Abolitionists After 1848* (Athens: University of Georgia Press, 2011).

Horne, Alistair, *The Fall of Paris: The Siege and the Commune, 1870–1871* (London: Macmillan, 1965).

Horne, Alistair, *The Terrible Year: A Paris Commune, 1871* (London: Phoenix, 2004).

Horwitz, Tony, *Midnight Rising: John Brown and the Raid That Sparked the Civil War* (New York: Henry Holt, 2012).

Howarth, Joylon Michael, 'The myth of Blanquism under the Third Republic, 1870–1900', *Journal of Modern History*, 48:3 (1976), pp. 37–68.

Hubac-Occhipinti, Olivier, 'Anarchist terrorists of the nineteenth century', in *A History of Terrorism: From Antiquity to ISIS*, ed. Gérard Chaliand and Arnaud Blin (Berkeley: University of California Press, 2007), pp. 113–131.

Hughes, Michael J., 'British opinion and Russian terrorism in the 1880s', *European History Quarterly*, 42:2 (2011), pp. 255–277.

Hutton, Patrick H., *The Cult of the Revolutionary Tradition: The Blanquists in French Politics, 1864–1893* (Berkeley: University of California Press, 1981).

Ivianski, Zeev, 'Source of inspiration for revolutionary terrorism – the Bakunin–Nechayev alliance', *Journal of Conflict Studies*, 8:3 (1988), https://journals.lib.unb.ca/index.php/JCS/article/view/14810 (accessed 2 August 2022).

Jackson, Paul, '"Union or death!": Gavrilo Princip, Young Bosnia and the role of "sacred time" in the dynamics of nationalist terrorism', *Totalitarian Movements and Political Religions*, 7:1 (2006), pp. 45–65.

Jamieson, Patrick C., 'Foreign criticisms of the 1871 Paris Commune: the role of British and American newspapers and periodicals', *Intersections*, 11:1 (2010), pp. 100–115.

Jeffreys-Jones, Rhodri, *Cloak and Dollar: A History of American Secret Intelligence* (New Haven: Yale University Press, 2002).

Jellinek, Frank, *The Paris Commune of 1871* (London: Victor Gollancz, 1965).

Jenkins, Brian, *The Fenian Problem: Insurgency and Terrorism in a Liberal State, 1858–1874* (Montreal: McGill University Press, 2008).

Jenkins, Michael and Godges, John Paul, eds, *The Long Shadow of 9/11: America's Response to Terrorism* (Washington, DC: Rand Corporation, 2011).

Jensen, Richard Bach, 'Daggers, rifles and dynamite: anarchist terrorism in nineteenth century Europe', *Terrorism and Political Violence*, 16:1 (2010), pp. 116–153.

Jensen, Richard Bach, 'The international anti-anarchist conference of 1898 and the origins of Interpol', *Journal of Contemporary History*, 16:2 (1981), pp. 323–347.

Jensen, Richard Bach, *The Battle Against Anarchist Terrorism: An International History, 1878–1934* (Cambridge: Cambridge University Press, 2014).

Johnson, Martin Phillip, *The Paradise of Association: Political Culture and Popular Organizations in the Paris Commune of 1871* (Ann Arbor: University of Michigan Press, 1996).

Johnson, Richard J., 'Zagranichnaia Agentura: the tsarist political police in Europe', *Journal of Contemporary History*, 7:1/2 (1972), pp. 221–242.

Johnstone, Monty, 'The Paris Commune and Marx's conception of the dictatorship of the proletariat', *Massachusetts Review*, 12:3 (1971), pp. 447–462.

Joll, James, *The Anarchists* (London: Methuen, 1979).

Jones, Ian, *London: Bombed, Blitzed and Blown Up: The British Capital Under Attack Since 1867* (Barnsley: Frontline, 2016).

Karakasis, Georgios, 'The catechism of destruction: Sergei Nechaev and the spirit of nihilism', *Iocana Credintei*, 8:4 (2018), pp. 103–114.

Kassel, Whitney, 'Terrorism and the international anarchist movement of the late nineteenth and early twentieth centuries', *Studies in Conflict and Terrorism*, 32:3 (2009), pp. 237–252.

Kassow, Samuel D., 'The university statute of 1863', in *Russia's Great Reforms, 1855–1881*, ed. Ben Eklof, John Bushnell and Larissa Zakharova (Bloomington: Indiana University Press, 1994), pp. 247–263.

Katz, Philip M., '"Lessons from Paris": the American clergy responds to the Paris Commune', *Church History*, 63:3 (1994), pp. 393–406.

Kautsky, Karl, *Terrorism and Communism: A Contribution to the Natural History of Revolution*, trans. W. H. Kerridge (New York: Routledge, reissued edition 2011).

Keer, Dhananjay, *Veer Savarkar* (Bombay: Popular Prakashan, 1950).

Keil, Hartmut, 'The impact of Haymarket on German-American radicalism', *International Labor and Working-Class History*, 29 (1986), pp. 16–27.

Keller, Lukas, 'Beyond the "People's Community": the anarchist movement from the fin de siècle to the First World War in Germany', in *Anarchism, 1914–1918: Internationalism, Anti-militarism and War*, ed. Matthew S. Adams and Ruth Kina (Manchester: Manchester University Press, 2017), pp. 95–113.

Kenna, Shane, *Jeremiah O'Donovan Rossa: Unrepentant Fenian* (Kildare: Merrion, 2015).

Kenna, Shane, *War in the Shadows: The Irish-American Fenians Who Bombed Victorian Britain* (Newbridge: Merrion, 2014).

Kennedy, Padraic, 'The secret service department: a British intelligence bureau in mid-Victorian London, September 1867 to April 1868', *Intelligence and National Security*, 18:3 (2003), pp. 100–127.

Keyserlingk, Robert H., 'Bismarck and the press: the example of the National Liberals', *Historical Papers*, 2:1 (1967), pp. 198–215.

Kinealy, Christine, *Repeal and Revolution: 1848 in Ireland* (Manchester: Manchester University Press, 2009).

Konishi, Sho, 'Reopening the "opening of Japan": Russian–Japanese revolutionary encounter and the vision of anarchist progress', *American Historical Review*, 112:1 (2007), pp. 101–130.

Kostal, R. W., 'Rebels in the dock: the prosecution of the Dublin Fenians, 1865–66', *Irish-American Cultural Institute*, 34:4 (1999), pp. 70–96.

Krebs, Edward S., *Shifu, Soul of Chinese Anarchism* (Lanham: Rowman and Littlefield, 1998).

Kronenbitter, Rita T., 'Paris Okhrana, 1885–1905', in *Okhrana: The Paris Operations of the Russian Imperial Police*, ed. Ben B. Fischer (Washington, DC: Central Intelligence Agency,1997), pp. 19–26.

Kutolowski, John F., 'English radicals and the Polish insurrection of 1862–1864', *Polish Review*, 11:3 (1966), pp. 3–28.

Landy, A., 'A French adventurer and American expansionism after the Civil War', *Science and Society*, 15:4 (1951), pp. 313–333.

Lane, Charles, *Freedom's Detective: The Secret Service, the Ku Klux Klan and the Man Who Masterminded America's First War on Terror* (New York: Hanover Square Press, 2019).

Langer, Jacob, 'Corruption and the counter-revolution: the rise and fall of the Black Hundred', PhD thesis, Duke University (2007).

Laqueur, Walter, *A History of Terrorism* (New Brunswick: Transaction, 2006).

Larabee, Ann, *The Wrong Hands: Popular Weapons Manuals and Their Historic Challenges to Democratic Society* (Oxford: Oxford University Press, 2015).

Lattek, Christine, 'German socialism in London after 1849', in *Exiles from European Revolutions: Refugees in Mid-Victorian England*, ed. Sabine Freitag and Rudolf Muhs (New York: Berghan, 2003), pp. 187–208.

Lattek, Christine, *Revolutionary Refugees: German Socialism in Britain, 1840–1860* (London: Routledge, 2006).

Laursen, Ole Birk, 'Anti-colonialism, terrorism and the "politics of friendship": Virendranath Chattopadhyaya and the European anarchist movement, 1910–1927', *Anarchist Studies*, 27:1 (2019), pp. 47–62.

Law, Randal D., *Terrorism: A History* (Cambridge: Polity, 2016).

Lay, Howard S., '"Beau Geste!" On the readability of terrorism', *Yale French Studies*, 101 (2001), pp. 79–100.

Lehning, Arthur, 'Bakunin's conceptions of revolutionary organisations and their role: a study of his "secret societies"', in *Essays in Honour of E. H. Carr*, ed. Chimen Ambramsky and Beryl J. Williams (London: Palgrave, 1974), pp. 57–81.

Liang, Hsi-Huey, *The Rise of Modern Police and the European State System from Metternich to the Second World War* (Cambridge: Cambridge University Press, 1992).

Lidtke, Vernon L., *Outlawed Party: Social Democracy in Germany, 1878–1890* (Princeton: Princeton University Press, 1966).

Lo, Ping-Cheung, 'Confucian views on suicide and their implications for euthanasia', in *Confucian Bioethics*, ed. Ruiping Fan (Dordrecht: Springer, 1999), pp. 69–101.

Lukashevich, Stephen, 'The Holy Brotherhood, 1881–1883', *American Slavic and East European Review*, 18:4 (1959), pp. 491–509.

Lynn, John A., *Another Kind of War: The Nature and History of Terrorism* (New Haven: Yale University Press, 2019).

Mackay, Aaron, *Allan Pinkerton: The Eye Who Never Slept* (Edinburgh: Mainstream, 1996).

Marks, Steven G., *How Russia Shaped the Modern World: From Art to Anti-Semitism, Ballet to Bolshevism* (Princeton: Princeton University Press, 2020).

Marshall, Peter, *Demanding the Impossible: A History of Anarchism* (London: Harper Collins, 1992).

Martin, Michèle, 'Conflictual imaginaries: Victorian illustrated periodicals and the Franco-Prussian War (1870–1871)', *Victorian Periodical Review*, 36:1 (2003), pp. 41–58.

Martinez, P., 'A police spy and the exiled Communards, 1871–1873', *English Historical Review*, 97:382 (1982), pp. 99–112.

Mason, Edward S., *The Paris Commune: An Episode in the History of the Socialist Movement* (New York: Howard Fertig, 1967).

Masters, Anthony, *Bakunin: The Father of Anarchism* (London: Sidgwick and Jackson, 1974).

Mayer, Robert, 'Lenin and the concept of the professional revolutionary', *History of Political Thought*, 14:2 (1993), pp. 249–263.

McClellan, Woodford, *Revolutionary Exiles: The Russians in the First International and the Paris Commune* (London: Routledge, 1979).

McDestler, Chester, 'Shall Red and Black unite? An American revolutionary document of 1883', *Pacific Historical Review*, 14:4 (1945), pp. 434–451.

McGee, Owen, *The IRB: The Irish Republican Brotherhood from the Land League to Sinn Féin* (Dublin: Four Courts Press, 2005).

McKenna, Joseph, *The Irish-American Dynamite Campaign: A History, 1881–1896* (Jefferson: McFarland, 2012).

McKinlay, Brian, *The First Royal Tour, 1867–1868* (London: Robert Hale, 1971).

Meijer, J. M., *Knowledge and Revolution: The Russian Colony in Zurich, 1870–1873* (Assen: Van Gorcum, 1955).

Melchiori, Barbara Arnett, *Terrorism in the Late Victorian Novel* (London: Routledge, 1985).

Mendel, Arthur P., *Mikhail Bakunin: Roots of Apocalypse* (New York: Praeger, 1981).

Merriman, John, *The Dynamite Club: How a Bombing in Fin de Siècle Paris Ignited the Age of Modern Terror* (New Haven: Yale University Press, 2013).

Messer, Peter C., 'Feel the terror: Edmund Burke's reflections on the revolution in France', in *Enemies of Humanity: The Nineteenth Century War on Terrorism*, ed. Isaac Land (Basingstoke: Palgrave, 2008), pp. 23–44.

Messer-Kruse, Timothy, *The Haymarket Conspiracy: Transatlantic Anarchist Networks* (Urbana: University of Illinois Press, 2012).

Messer-Kruse, Timothy, *The Yankee International: Marxism and the American Reform Tradition, 1848–1874* (Chapel Hill: University of North Carolina Press, 1998).

Meyers, Jeffrey, 'Portraits of a terrorist: Dostoevsky, Conrad and Coetzee', *Antioch Review*, 72:1 (2014), pp. 61–80.

Miller, Martin A., 'Ideological conflicts in Russian populism: thehe revolutionary manifestoes of the Chaikovsky circles, 1869–1874', *Slavic Review*, 29:1 (1970), pp. 1–21.

Miller, Martin A., *The Foundations of Modern Terrorism: State, Society and the Dynamics of Political Violence* (Cambridge: Cambridge University Press, 2013).

Miller, Scott, *The President and the Assassin: McKinley, Terror and Empire at the Dawn of the American Century* (New York: Random House, 2011).

Mitchell, Allan, 'Bonapartism as a model for Bismarckian politics', *Journal of Modern History*, 49:2 (1977), pp. 181–199.

Mitchell, Allan, 'The xenophobic style: French counterespionage and the emergence of the Dreyfus affair', *Journal of Modern History*, 3 (1980), pp. 414–425.

Morris, Richard Knowles, 'John P. Holland and the Fenians', *Galway Archaeological and Historical Society*, 31:1/2 (1964), pp. 25–38.

Moses, Jonathan, 'The texture of politics: London's anarchist clubs, 1894–1914', *RIBA* (2016). https://www.ribaj.com/intelligence/the-texture-of-politics-london-s-anarchists-clubs-1882–1914 (accessed 1 August 2022).

Moss, Bernard H., 'Police spies and labor militants after the Commune', *European and Working-Class History*, 5 (1974), pp. 16–19.

Moss, Walter G., *Russia in the Age of Alexander II, Tolstoy and Dostoevsky* (London: Anthem, 2002).

Müller, Frank Lorenz, 'The spectre of a people in arms', *English Historical Review*, 122:495 (2007), pp. 82–104.

Neil, Stewart, *Blanqui* (London: Victor Gollancz, 1939).

Nepomniachtchi, A., 'Elisabeth Dmitrieva sur les barricades de la Commune', *Études Soviétiques*, 204 (1965), pp. 65–67.

Newsinger, John, *Fenianism in Mid-Victorian Britain* (London: Pluto, 1994).

Nicolaevsky, Boris I., 'Secret societies and the First International', in *The Revolutionary Internationals, 1864–1943*, ed. Milorad M. Drachkovitch (Palo Alto: Stanford University Press, 1966), pp. 36–56.

Nie, Michael de, *The Eternal Paddy: Irish Identity and the British Press, 1798–1882* (Madison: University of Wisconsin Press, 2004).

Nomad, Max, 'The anarchist tradition', in *The Revolutionary Internationals,*

1864–1943, ed. Milorad M. Drachkovitch (Palo Alto: Stanford University Press, 1966), pp. 57–92.

Novak, Derry, 'Anarchism and individual terrorism', *Canadian Journal of Economics and Political Science*, 20:2 (1954), pp. 176–184.

O'Brien, Gillian, 'Methodology and martyrs: Irish American republicanism in the late nineteenth century', in *Critical Concepts: Terrorism and Literature*, ed. Peter C. Herman (Cambridge: Cambridge University Press, 2018), pp. 70–89.

Ó Donghaile, Deaglán, *Blasted Literature: Victorian Political Fiction and the Shock of Modernism* (Edinburgh: Edinburgh University Press, 2011).

Ó Gráda, Cormac, 'Fenianism and socialism: the career of Joseph Patrick McDonnell', *Saothar*, 1:1 (1975), pp. 31–41.

O'Hara, S. Paul, *Inventing the Pinkertons, or Spies, Sleuths, Mercenaries and Thugs* (Baltimore: Johns Hopkins University Press, 2016).

Oates, Stephen B., *To Purge This Land with Blood: A Biography of John Brown* (Amherst: University of Massachusetts Press, 1984).

Offord, Derek, *The Russian Revolutionary Movement in the 1880s* (Cambridge: Cambridge University Press, 1986).

Oliver, Hermia, *The International Anarchist Movement in Late Victorian London* (New York: St Martin's Press, 1983).

Packe, Michael, *The Bombs of Orsini* (London: Secker and Warburg, 1957).

Packer, Diana, 'Refugee or alien?', *European Judaism: A Journal for the New Europe*, 50:2 (2017), pp. 15–23.

Parker, Tom and Sitter, Nick, 'The Four Horseman of terrorism: it's not waves, it's strains', *Terrorism and Political Violence*, 28:2 (2016), pp. 197–216.

Parsons, Elaine Frantz, *Ku Klux: The Birth of the Klan During Reconstruction* (Chapel Hill: University of North Carolina Press, 2003).

Patel, Hitendra, *Khudiram Bose: Revolutionary Extraordinaire* (New Delhi: Ministry of Information and Broadcasting, 2008).

Patsouras, Louis, *The Anarchism of Jean Grave* (Montreal: Black Rose Books, 2007).

Payne, Howard C., *The Police State of Louis Napoleon Bonaparte, 1851–1860* (Seattle: University of Washington Press, 1966).

Peddler, Anne, 'Going to the people: the Russian narodniki in 1874–5', *Slavonic Review*, 6:16 (1927), pp. 130–141.

Pernicone, Nunzio, *Italian Anarchism, 1864–1892* (Princeton: Princeton University Press, 1993).

Pernicone, Nunzio and Ottanelli, Fraser M., *Assassins Against the Old Order: Italian Anarchist Violence in Fin de Siècle Europe* (Urbana: University of Illinois Press, 2018).

Perrier, Hubert, Collomp, Catherine, Cordillot, Michel and Debouzy, Marianne, 'The "Social Revolution" in America? European reactions to the "Great

Upheaval" and the Haymarket affair', *International Labor and Working-Class History*, 29 (1986), pp. 38–52.

Petrov, Kristian, '"Strike out, right and left!": a conceptual historical analysis of 1860s Russian nihilism and its notion of negation', *Studies in European Thought*, 71 (2019), pp. 73–97.

Pflanze, Otto, *Bismarck and the Development of Germany: The Period of Unification, 1815–1871* (Princeton: Princeton University Press, 1963).

Phalen, William J., *The Democratic Soldier: The Life of General Gustave P. Cluseret* (New Delhi: Vij Books, 2015).

Pinfari, Marco, 'Exploring the terrorist nature of political assassinations: a reinterpretation of the Orsini attentat', *Terrorism and Political Violence*, 21 (2010), pp. 580–594.

Pipes, Richard, *The Degaev Affair: Terror and Treason in Tsarist Russia* (New Haven: Yale University Press, 2003).

Plessis, Alain, *The Rise and Fall of the Second Empire, 1852–1871*, trans. Jonathan Mandelbaum (Cambridge: Cambridge University Press, 1977).

Polunov, Alexander, 'Konstantin Petrovich Pobedonostsev – man and politician', *Russian Studies in History*, 39:4 (2001), pp. 8–32.

Polunov, Alexander, Owen, Thomas C. and Zakharova, Larissa G., eds, trans. Marshall S. Shatz, *Russia in the Nineteenth Century: Autocracy, Reform and Social Change, 1815–1914* (London: Routledge, 2005).

Pomper, Phillip, 'Nechaev and tsaricide: the conspiracy within the conspiracy', *Russian Review*, 33:2 (1974), pp. 123–138.

Pomper, Phillip, 'Bakunin, Nechaev and the "Catechism of a Revolutionary": the case for joint authorship', *Canadian-American Slavic Studies*, 10:4 (1976), pp. 535–551.

Pomper, Philip, *Sergei Nechaev* (New Jersey: Rutgers University Press, 1979).

Porter, Bernard, *The Refugee Question in Mid-Victorian Politics* (Cambridge: Cambridge University Press, 1979).

Porter, Bernard, 'The *Freiheit* prosecutions, 1881–1882', *Historical Journal*, 23:4 (1980), pp. 833–856.

Porter, Bernard, *The Origins of the Vigilant State: The London Metropolitan Police Special Branch Before the First World War* (London: Weidenfeld and Nicholson, 1987).

Potter, David M., *The Impending Crisis: America Before the Civil War, 1848–1861* (New York: Harper and Row, 1977).

Potter, Simon J., 'Webs, networks and systems: globalization and the mass media in the nineteenth and twentieth century British Empire', *Journal of British Studies*, 46:3 (2007), pp. 621–646.

Pratt, Michael, 'A fallen idol: the impact of the Franco-Prussian War on the perception of Germany by British intellectuals', *International History Review*, 7:4 (1985), pp. 545–575.

Bibliography

Price, Don C., *Russia and the Roots of the Chinese Revolution, 1896–1911* (Cambridge: Harvard University Press, 1974).

Puleo, Stephen, *The Caning: The Assault That Drove America to Civil War* (Yardley: Westholme, 2012).

Quail, John, *The Slow Burning Fuse: The Lost History of the British Anarchists* (London: Freedom Press, 2019).

Radzinsky, Edward, *Alexander II: The Last Great Tsar*, trans. Antonina W. Bouis (New York: Free Press, 2005).

Ramón, Marta, *A Provisional Dictator: James Stephens and the Fenian Movement* (Dublin: University College Dublin Press, 2007).

Rauchway, Eric, *Murdering McKinley: The Making of Theodore Roosevelt's America* (New York: Hill and Wang, 2003).

Ravindranathan, T. V., 'The Paris Commune and the First International in Italy: republicanism versus socialism, 1871–1872', *International History Review*, 3:4 (1981), pp. 482–516.

Rawley, James A., *Bleeding Kansas and the Coming of the Civil War* (Lincoln: University of Nebraska Press, 1979).

Remark, Joachim, *Sarajevo: The Story of a Political Murder* (New York: Criterion, 1959).

Revil, James, *Improvised Explosive Devices: The Paradigmatic Weapons of New Wars* (Basingstoke: Palgrave, 2016).

Reynolds, David S., *John Brown, Abolitionist: The Man Who Killed Slavery, Sparked the Civil War and Seeded Civil Rights* (New York: Alfred A. Knopf, 2005).

Roberts, Ivor, 'The Black Hand and the Sarajevo conspiracy', in *Balkan Legacies of the Great War: The Past Is Never Dead*, ed. Othon Anastasakis, David Madden and Elizabeth Roberts (Basingstoke: Palgrave, 2016), pp. 23–42.

Rodechko, James P., 'An Irish-American journalist and Catholicism: Patrick Ford of the Irish world', *Church History*, 39:4 (1970), pp. 524–540.

Rothenburg, Gunter E., *The Army of Francis Joseph* (West Lafayette: Purdue University Press, 1998).

Ruud, Charles A. and Stepanov, Sergei A., *Fontanka 16: The Tsars' Secret Police* (Montreal: McGill University Press, 1999).

Ryan, Desmond, *The Fenian Chief: A Biography of James Stephens* (Dublin: Hely Thom, 1967).

Sageman, Marc, *Turning to Political Violence: The Emergence of Terrorism* (Philadelphia: University of Pennsylvania Press, 2017).

Saunders, David, *Russia in the Age of Reaction and Reform, 1801–1881* (London: Routledge, 2015).

Sedlmaier, Alexander, 'The consuming visions of late-nineteenth and early-twentieth century anarchists: actualising political violence transnationally', *European Review of History – Revue européenne d'Histoire*, 14:3 (2007), pp. 283–300.

Bibliography

Shaya, Gregory, 'How to make an anarchist-terrorist: an essay on the political imaginary in fin de siècle France', *Journal of Social History*, 44:2 (2010), pp. 521–543.

Shirk, Mark, 'The universal eye: anarchist "propaganda of the deed" and the development of the modern surveillance state', *International Studies Quarterly*, 63:2 (2019), pp. 334–345.

Short, K. R. M., *The Dynamite War: Irish American Bombers in Victorian Britain* (Atlantic Highlands: Humanities Press, 1979).

Showalter, Dennis, *The Wars of German Unification* (London: Hodder, 2004).

Silke, Andrew, 'Honour and expulsion: terrorism in nineteenth century Japan', *Terrorism and Political Violence*, 9:4 (1997), pp. 58–81.

Silvestri, Michael, '"The Sinn Fein of India": Irish nationalism and the policing of revolutionary terrorism in Bengal', *Journal of British Studies*, 39:4 (2000), pp. 454–486.

Silvestri, Michael, 'The bomb, Bhadralok, Bhagavad Gita and Dan Breen: terrorism in Bengal and its relation to the European experience', *Terrorism and Political Violence*, 21:1 (2009), pp. 1–27.

Simon, Jeffrey D., 'The forgotten terrorists: lessons from the history of terrorism', *Terrorism and Political Violence*, 20:2 (2008), pp. 195–214.

Singer, Kurt, *Spies and Traitors: A Short History of Espionage* (London: W. H. Allen, 1953).

Skirda, Alexandre, *Facing the Enemy: A History of Anarchist Organization from Proudhon to May 1968*, trans. Paul Sharkey (Edinburgh: AK Press, 2002).

Snay, Mitchell, *Fenians, Freedmen and Southern Whites: Race and Nationality in the Era of Reconstruction* (Baton Rouge: Louisiana State University Press, 2007).

Solomon, Vlad, *State Surveillance, Political Policing and Counterterrorism in Britain, 1880–1914* (London: Boydell and Brewer, 2021).

Sonn, Richard D., *Anarchism* (Woodbridge: Twayne, 1992)

Sowerwine, Charles, *France Since 1870: Culture, Society and the Making of the Republic* (Basingstoke: Palgrave, 2009).

Sperber, Jonathan, *Europe, 1850–1914: Progress, Participation and Apprehension* (London: Routledge, 2009).

Sperber, Jonathan, *The European Revolutions, 1848–1851* (Cambridge: Cambridge University Press, 2005).

Sperber, Jonathan, *Karl Marx: A Nineteenth Century Life* (New York: Liveright, 2013).

Stauffer, John and Trodd, Zoe, eds, *The Tribunal, Responses to John Brown and the Harper's Ferry Raid* (Boston: Harvard University Press, 2012).

Steinberg, Jonathan, *Bismarck: A Life* (Oxford: Oxford University Press, 2011).

Steward, Patrick and McGovern, Brian, *The Fenians: Irish Rebellion in the North Atlantic World, 1858–1876* (Knoxville: University of Tennessee Press, 2013).

Stoehr, Taylor, 'Words and deeds in *The Princess Casamassima*', *ELH*, 37:1 (1970), pp. 95–135.

Stowell, David O., *Streets, Railroads and the Great Strike of 1877* (Chicago: Chicago University Press, 1999).

Takagami, Shin-Ichi, 'The Fenian rising in Dublin, March 1867', *Irish Historical Studies*, 29:15 (1995), pp. 340–362.

Tessendorf, K. C., *Kill the Tsar! Youth and Terrorism in Old Russia* (New York: Atheneum, 1986).

Texier, Robert le, *De Ravachol á la bande á Bonnot* (Paris: Éditions France-Empire, 1989).

Thomas, Edith, *Louise Michelle*, trans. Penelope Williams (Montreal: Black Rose, 1980).

Thompson, J. M., *Louis Napoleon and the Second Empire* (New York: Noonday Press, 1995).

Tikhonov, Vladimir, 'A Russian radical and East Asia in the early twentieth century: Sudzilovsky, China and Japan', *Cross Currents*, 18 (2016) http://crosscurrents.berkley.edu/e-journal/issue-18 (accessed 2 August 2022).

Tombs, Robert, *The Paris Commune, 1871* (London: Routledge, 1999).

Tombs, Robert, 'How bloody was la semaine sanglante of 1871? A revision', *Historical Journal*, 55:3 (2012), pp. 679–704.

Trautman, Frederic, *The Voice of Terror: A Biography of Johann Most* (Westport: Greenwood Press, 1980).

Ulam, Adam B., *Prophets and Conspirators in Pre-revolutionary Russia* (New York: Routledge, 1998).

Ullrich, Volker, *Fünf Schüsse auf Bismarck: Historische Reportagen, 1789–1945* (Munich: C. H. Beck, 2003).

Vantine, Peter, 'Censoring/censuring the press under the Second Empire: the Goncourts as journalists and *Charles Demailly*', *Nineteenth Century French Studies*, 43:1–2 (2014), pp. 45–59.

Varias, Alexander, *Paris and the Anarchists: Aesthetes and Subversives During the Fin de Siècle* (New York: St Martin's Press, 1996).

Venturi, Franco, *A History of the Populist and Socialist Movements in Nineteenth Century Russia*, trans. Francis Haskell (London: Weidenfeld and Nicholson, 1952).

Verhoeven, Claudia, 'The making of Russian revolutionary terrorism', in *Enemies of Humanity: The Nineteenth Century War on Terrorism*, ed. Isaac Land (Basingstoke: Palgrave, 2008), pp. 99–116.

Verhoeven, Claudia, *The Odd Man Karakozov: Imperial Russia, Modernity and the Birth of Terrorism* (Ithaca: Cornell University Press, 2009).

Verhoeven, Claudia, 'Time of terror, terror of time: on the impatience of Russian revolutionary terrorism (early 1860s – early 1880s)', *Jahrbücher für Geschichte Osteuropas*, 58 (2010), pp. 254–273.

Bibliography

Waddington, Patrick, 'Sleazy digs and coppers' narks: the fate of Russian nihilists in Paris a hundred years ago', *New Zealand Slavonic Journal* (1989–1990), pp. 1–39.

Wagner, Kim A., *Rumours and Rebels: A New History of the Indian Uprising of 1857* (London: Peter Lang, 2017).

Walker, Kim, 'Alert but not alarmed? The rhetoric of terrorism and life after 9/11', *Contemporary Nurse*, 21:2 (2006), pp. 267–276.

Webb, Simon, *Dynamite, Treason and Plot: Terrorism in Victorian and Edwardian London* (Stroud: History Press, 2012).

Werrett, Simon, 'The science of destruction: terrorism and technology in the nineteenth century', *Oxford Handbook of the History of Terrorism*, ed. Carola Dietze and Claudia Verhoeven (Oxford: Oxford University Press, 2014). Online edition: https://www.oxfordhandbooks.com/view/10.1093/oxfordhb/9780199858569.001.0001/oxfordh-9780199858569-e-012.

Werstein, Irving, *Strangled Voices: The Story of the Haymarket Affair* (New York: Macmillan, 1970).

Whelehan, Niall, '"Cheap as soap and common as sugar": the Fenians, dynamite and scientific warfare', in *The Black Hand of Republicanism: Fenianism in Modern Ireland*, ed. Fearghal McGarry and James McConnell (Dublin: Irish Academic Press, 2009), pp. 105–120.

Whelehan, Niall, *The Dynamiters: Irish Nationalism and Political Violence in the Wider World, 1867–1900* (Cambridge: Cambridge University Press, 2012).

Whitaker, Reginald, Kealy, Gregory S. and Parnaby, Andrew, *Secret Service: Political Policing in Canada from the Fenians to Fortress America* (Toronto: University of Toronto Press, 2012).

Wilkinson, Paul, *Political Terrorism* (London: Palgrave, 1974).

Wilson, Ray and Adams, Ian, *Special Branch, A History: 1883–2006* (London: Biteback, 2015).

Wittke, Carl, *Against the Current: The Life of Karl Heinzen, 1809–1890* (Chicago: University of Chicago Press, 1945).

Wittke, Carl, *Refugees of Revolution: The German Forty-Eighters in America* (Philadelphia: University of Pennsylvania Press, 1952)

Witzig, Carole, 'Bismarck et la Commune: le reaction des monarchies conservatrices contre les mouvements republicains et socialistes (1870–1872) vue et travers les archives allemandes', *International Review of Social History*, 17:1 (1972), pp. 191–221.

Woodcock, George, *Anarchism* (New York: Penguin, 1977).

Wortman, Richard, *Scenarios of Power: From Alexander II to the Abdication of Nicholas II: Myth and Ceremony in Russian Monarchy*, vol. 2 (Princeton: Princeton University Press, 2000).

Yeoman, James Michael, *Print Culture and the Formation of the Anarchist Movement in Spain* (London: Routledge, 2019).

Young, Sarah J., ed. and trans., *Writing Resistance: Revolutionary Memoir of Shlissel'burg Prison, 1884–1906* (London: University College London Press, 2021).

Zamoyski, Adam, *Phantom Terror: The Threat of Revolution and the Repression of Liberty, 1789–1848* (London: Harper Collins, 2014).

Zeidel, Robert F., *Robber Barons and Wretched Refuse: Ethnic and Class Dynamics During the Era of American Industrialization* (Ithaca: Cornell University Press, 2020).

Zolla, Silke, *To Deter and Punish: Global Collaboration Against Terrorism in the 1970s* (New York: Columbia University Press, 2021).

Zuckerman, Frederic S., *The Tsarist Secret Police in Russian Society, 1880–1917* (Basingstoke: Palgrave, 1996).

Index

Index

Index

Index

Index